Identity Matters

Supplements

to

Novum Testamentum

VOLUME 118

Identity Matters

John, the Jews and Jewishness

by

Raimo Hakola

BRILL

LEIDEN • BOSTON

2005

This book is printed on acid-free paper.

The Scripture quotations contained herein, unless otherwise noted, are from the New Revised Standard Version Bible, copyright © 1989 by the Division of Christian Education of the National Council of the Churches of Christ in the U.S.A. and are used by permission. All rights reserved.

Library of Congress Cataloging-in-Publication Data

Hakola, Raimo.
    Identity matters : John, the Jews, and Jewishness / by Raimo Hakola.
      p. cm. — (Supplements to Novum Testamentum, ISSN 0167-9732 ; v. 118)
    Includes bibliographical references and index.
    ISBN 90-04-14324-6 (alk. paper)
      1. Bible. N.T. John—Criticism, interpretation, etc. 2. Jews in the New Testament.
  3. Christianity and other religions—Judaism. 4. Judaism—Relations—Christianity.
  5. Christianity and antisemitism. I. Title. II. Series.

BS2615.6.H44H35 2005
226.5'067—dc22
                                                                            2004065979

ISSN 0167–9732
ISBN 90 04 14324 6

CONTENTS

Acknowledgments ix

1. INTRODUCTION 1

   1.1   From the Most Hellenistic Gospel to the Most
        Jewish 5
   1.2   Who Are οἱ Ἰουδαῖοι in John? 10
   1.3   John As a Two-Level Drama 16
   1.4   Early Christians and the Diversity of First Century
        Judaism 22
   1.5   The Outline of the Study 31
   1.6   Methodological Considerations 33

2. FALLACIES IN SCHOLARLY CONSENSUS 41

   2.1   The *birkat ha-minim* and Other Suggested
        Parallels to John 45
   2.2   John and Formative Rabbinic Judaism 55
   2.3   The Pharisees, the Rabbis, and the Synagogue 61
   2.4   Documentary Papyri and post-70 Palestinian Society 65
   2.5   The Pharisees and the Rabbis and the Persecution
        of Early Christians 67
   2.6   Evidence for Jewish Persecution of the Christians 74
   2.7   John in the Context of Jewish-Christians Relations
        in the First Century 79
   2.8   Conclusion: A New Way to Assess John's Jewishness 85

3. JESUS, THE JEWS AND THE WORSHIP OF GOD 87

   3.1   Jesus in the Temple of the Jews (2:13–22) 87
          The Context of the Scene 87
          Jesus' Action in the Temple 88
          Jesus' Ambivalent Attitude to the Temple 92
   3.2   The True Worship of the Father (John 4:20–24) 96
          The Context of the Scene 96
          'The Fathers' and the Worship of the Father 97

Jesus the Jew—a Prophet and the Messiah 100
The Samaritans, the Jews, and the True
Worshipers of the Father 104
3.3 Conclusion: The Johannine Christians, Worship
and Jewishness 109

4. JESUS, THE SABBATH AND CIRCUMCISION 113

4.1 Jesus Breaks the Sabbath and Makes Himself
Equal with God (5:1–18) 113
The Context of the Scene 113
Jesus' Act as an Intentional Provocation 115
The Conflict over the Sabbath 118
Jesus, the Father and the Sabbath 126
4.2 The Jews Do Not Observe the Law Themselves
(7:19–24) 130
The Context of the Scene 131
How Do the Jews Fail to Observe the Law? 135
The Sabbath and Circumcision 136
4.3 Conclusion: The Johannine Christians and Markers
of Jewishness 142

5. JESUS, THE JEWS AND MOSES 146

5.1 The Scriptures and Moses as Jesus' Witnesses
(5:37–47) 146
The Context of Jesus' Speech 146
Jesus and the Revelation at Sinai 149
5.2 The Bread from Heaven and the Manna of
the Jews (6:26–59) 158
The Context of Jesus' Speech 158
The Manna and the True Bread from Heaven
Contrasted 163
The Manna as a Symbol for the Law 166
5.3 Conclusion: Jesus, Moses and the Law in John 170

6. THE BELIEVING JEWS, ABRAHAM AND THE
DEVIL (8:31–59) 177

The Context of the Dialogue 177
The Believing Jews and the Death of Jesus 180

Jesus, the Jews and Abraham 187
The Children of a Murderer: John 8:44 and
    Apocalyptic Polemic 197
John 8:44 and Christian Anti-Judaism 210

7. SYNTHESIS: THE JOHANNINE CHRISTIANS,
THE JEWS AND JEWISHNESS 215

7.1 John's Ambivalent Relationship to Jewishness 215
7.2 John As a Sectarian Jewish Writing? 221
7.3 Who Are the Johannine Jews? 225
7.4 John and the Development of an Autonomous
     Christian Religion 232
7.5 Concluding Remarks 238

BIBLIOGRAPHY 243

Sources, Translations and Reference Works 243
Commentaries on the Fourth Gospel 245
Other Studies 246

INDEX OF MODERN AUTHORS 275
INDEX OF PASSAGES 280

ACKNOWLEDGMENTS

This is a revised version of my dissertation completed in February 2003 at the University of Helsinki. After the approval of the dissertation in April 2003, I have been able to make only slight revisions to it. I have not been able to take account of works which appeared or became available after February 2003.

I have had an opportunity to work with many distinguished scholars whose expertise has been a constant source of inspiration to me. Among my teachers, my greatest debt is to my supervisor Docent Ismo Dunderberg. His critical remarks have sometimes made me desperate, but I can now see clearly how greatly his comments have improved my work. I am fortunate that I have had him as my mentor. I hope that I always have him as my friend.

Prof. Lars Aejmelaeus first introduced me to the historical-critical study of the Bible and thus laid the foundation for all my future studies. Prof. Heikki Räisänen supported my work from its beginnings and made many encouraging and constructive suggestions in its different stages. Prof. Kari Syreeni (Uppsala University, Sweden) has guided me especially on methodological issues and prevented me from losing myself in the jungle of different methodologies which are nowadays applied in the field. As an official reviewer of my work, Prof. Adele Reinhartz (Wilfrid Laurier University, Waterloo, Ontario, Canada) made clear-sighted recommendations which led to the reducing of the manuscript by more than hundred pages. Her advice also helped me to express my thoughts more clearly. Prof. Antti Marjanen helped me put things in the right perspective at critical moments when I was completing the work and was about to lose my faith in myself.

When it comes to literature theory, hermeneutics, the Hebrew Bible, archaeology, the Septuagint, Qumran study, Greek grammar, Hellenistic philosophy, Jewish Christianity, Gnosticism, etc., I have learned more from various discussions with my colleagues at the department of Biblical studies than I have ever learned from books. I am grateful to you all for all those wonderful moments we have shared together.

The major responsibility for editing my English was painstakingly done by Margot Stout Whiting and Robert Whiting. Their careful reading of my manuscript not only improved my language but also helped me to see where I had lost the train of thought in my work. Remaining mistakes in my work, in terms of language or in terms of contents, are due to my own negligence.

I have received financial support from several sources: the Alfred Kordelin foundation, the Finnish Cultural Foundation, the Finnish Graduate School of Theology (funded by the Academy of Finland), the Research Unit on Formation of Early Jewish and Christian Ideology, and the Jenny and Antti Wihuri Foundation. I thank all my supporters. I also wish to express my thanks to professors Margaret M. Mitchell and David P. Moessner, who as managing editors included my study in Supplements to Novum Testamentum.

I am most deeply grateful to my family, my wife Tiina and our sons Leevi, Eelis and Luukas. Their love has always made it clear to me that I cannot find the best things in life in my study. I dedicate this book to my mother Kaisa Hakola. I am especially thankful for any crumbs of her excellent sense of humor and keen interest in good books that I may have inherited from her. Without these two virtues scholarly work—or life for that matter—could perhaps be possible but deadly boring.

Jämsä, September 2004
Raimo Hakola

CHAPTER ONE

INTRODUCTION

Even a cursory comparison of the Fourth Gospel to the synoptic gospels reveals that Jesus' relationship to his Jewish contemporaries is presented in a singular way in this gospel. In the synoptics, Jesus meets a wide variety of groups in Jewish society, including the Pharisees, the Sadducees, the scribes, priests and chief priests, the elders, tax collectors, sinners and the common crowd. Some of these groups also appear in John, but those who speak with Jesus are generally called 'the Jews' (οἱ Ἰουδαῖοι). The difference is striking since this word is used in John seventy-one times but only sixteen times in the synoptics and only five times outside the epithet 'the king of the Jews' that appears in the passion narratives. But the difference is not only statistical. The conflict between Jesus and those called the Jews is more consistent and hostile than the conflict between Jesus and his opponents in the synoptics. The term οἱ Ἰουδαῖοι may sometimes refer to groups that are not openly hostile to Jesus (e.g. 11:19, 31), but the Jews are mostly presented as fierce opponents of Jesus.

In this study I challenge current scholarly consensus concerning John's references to the Jews in two ways. First, I suggest that John's portrayal of the Jews and Jewishness cannot be understood as a response to the violent policy of Jewish leaders in John's environment. While many scholars suggest that John reflects a conflict between the Johannine group and emerging rabbinic Judaism, recent studies on rabbinic Judaism do not support this view. Second, I claim that John's portrayal of Jewishness is much more ambivalent than is often claimed today. Recent views on John reflect the current situation in New Testament studies where early Christian writings are understood more and more as variations of diverse first century Judaism. As to John, it is not exceptional to speak of "the thoroughgoing Jewishness of this first century work."[1] While I do not deny that John originates from a Jewish world, I will argue that it

---

[1] De Boer 2001, 264.

also signals a breaking away from many central Jewish practices and
beliefs that were integral to different forms of Jewish identity.

These two issues are not separate from each other. While many
scholars emphasize John's Jewishness, they have not been able to
shut their eyes to features reflecting an outsider's position in relation to Jewishness. However, they hasten to add that this "is due to
expulsion; it is an outsider position which is not willingly outsider."[2]
It is emphasized time and time again that the Johannine Christians
did not reject the synagogue

> voluntarily nor for theological reasons. They did not assert that the
> faith of the Fathers no longer agreed with the teaching of the revealer
> and that an alternative religious practice would have to be established.[3]

In this work I call into question this position and claim that it was
not external pressure that made the evangelist and his group view
some basics of Jewishness as outsiders. Alternatively, they themselves
saw their faith in Jesus not only in continuity with earlier Jewish tradition but also in contrast with that tradition. I try to show this in
my readings of those passages in John that deal with such central
aspects of Jewish identity as the temple and worship (John 2:13–22;
4:20–24), the Sabbath and circumcision (5:1–18; 7:19–24), the revelation at Sinai, Moses and the law (5:37–47; 6:26–59) and Abraham
(8:31–59).

There are many other issues that are involved in the two main
criticisms that I make in this book. One such issue is the use of the
term οἱ Ἰουδαῖοι in John. Because John is more and more understood
as a Jewish writing, it is denied that the hostile use of this word in
John would refer to Jews in general. Many scholars instead suggest
that the word refers in a distinctive Johannine sense to some particular group, the Judaeans or the Jewish leaders. This is also the
reason why scholars very often put the word *the Jews* in quotation
marks when discussing John. Urban C. von Wahlde has recently
explained this common practice by saying that the quotation marks
indicate that the use of οἱ Ἰουδαῖοι in John is "a literary phenomenon,"
and it is "this usage and the meanings associated with this phenomenon in the gospel that are being discussed and not the Jewish

---

[2] Von Wahlde 2000, 53.
[3] Zumstein 2001, 469–470.

people in their entire historical reality."[4] But when von Wahlde later refers to the exclusion from the synagogue as an explanation for this usage (cf. above), it becomes clear that the Johannine use of this term is not solely a literary phenomenon for him; von Wahlde and many other scholars connect this usage to the alleged conflict between the Johannine Christians and the Jewish leaders. If the evidence for such a conflict is meager, as I claim, this also has important consequences for our understanding of John's references to οἱ Ἰουδαῖοι.

Von Wahlde's discussion of οἱ Ἰουδαῖοι shows that views of John's Jewishness have important theological or hermeneutical implications. Von Wahlde says that

> the discussion of the meaning of the term 'Jews' is not simply academic; it has broad implications for the question whether the gospel is anti-Jewish and, if it is anti-Jewish, for the question of scripture as normative for the believing community.[5]

Von Wahlde argues that "the term was intended to refer to the hostility of authoritative 'Jewish' synagogue officials."[6] Therefore, John's anti-Jewish use in a later "history of hostility" is "the result of the failure to adequately interpret" the rhetoric of the gospel.[7] Von Wahlde here proves correct Adele Reinhartz's suspicion that "the effect of dressing the Johannine Jews in quotation marks is to whitewash this text and absolve it of responsibility for the anti-Jewish emotions and attitudes it conveys."[8] A crucial part of this attempt is the reconstruction of a bitter conflict that is reflected in the gospel. For example, Jean Zumstein admits that John "undoubtedly contributed" to the history of anti-Judaism in the history of the church but excuses John's anti-Judaism by saying that "it is still necessary to recognise that at the time the Fourth Gospel was edited it was the Christians who were victims and the synagogue that was the persecutor."[9]

The views quoted above show how closely historical questions concerning John's attitudes towards the Jews and Jewishness are intertwined with other issues that have far-reaching implications. The discussion of John's Jewishness should not be kept apart from the

---

[4] Von Wahlde 2000, 30 n. 1.
[5] Von Wahlde 2000, 51.
[6] Von Wahlde 2000, 54.
[7] Von Wahlde 2000, 55.
[8] Reinhartz 2001b, 356.
[9] Zumstein 2001, 470.

ongoing discussion concerning first century Judaism. It has become quite common to state that

> there was not one ruling, all-powerful group in Early Judaism; many groups claimed to possess the normative interpretation of the Torah. . . . We should not think in terms of a monolithic first-century Palestinian Judaism.[10]

Thus we can no longer assess John's Jewishness with some pre-fixed ideas of orthodox Judaism in mind. Although we cannot compare the Johannine community with any normative Judaism whatsoever, we can compare this group and its faith to some individual Jewish groups that made up the diverse phenomenon called Judaism at the beginning of the Common Era. I think this comparison enables us to see not only what the Johannine Christians have in common with various Jewish groups of the time, but also how they differ from these groups. Through this kind of comparison, I hope to be able to put John in its proper place among various forms of Judaism and early Christianity as a writing that has deep roots in diverse Jewish traditions but that also anticipates and contributes to the development of an independent early Christian religion.

My approach to the above-mentioned issues emerges from my dissatisfaction with two aspects that are prevailing in many recent Johannine studies: the unfounded assumption of a violent conflict between the Johannine group and a Jewish establishment and the quite unspecified appraisal of John as a completely Jewish writing. But before I proceed to describe more exactly my approach to these questions, I will discuss briefly how John's relationship to the Jews and Jewishness has been understood in the earlier history of scholarship. This survey helps to better understand how contemporary scholarly consensus has emerged.[11]

---

[10] Charlesworth 1990, 37.

[11] The following sketch is not meant as a complete history of the study of John's relationship to Jews and Judaism. I can call on some earlier surveys of the matter. These include the monographs by Schram (1974), Leistner (1974), and Ashton (1991, 3–117). I have also learned much from the articles by Meeks (1975) and von Wahlde (1982 and 2000). For the views on general developments in 20th New Testament scholarship, I am indebted to W. D. Davies 1999, 1–12.

1.1. *From the Most Hellenistic Gospel to the Most Jewish*

The pioneers of the emerging historical-critical study of the Bible clearly recognized how greatly John's portrayal of the conflict between Jesus and his opponents differs from the synoptics. At the beginning of the 19th century, the Johannine portrayal of the Jews and Judaism was understood to show that John is not a reliable source of the teaching of the historical Jesus.[12] By the time of F. C. Baur and the Tübingen school, this position had won wide acceptance. For Baur, John reflects a time when earlier conflicts between Hellenistic Christians and Jewish Christians were left behind and the separation of Christianity from Judaism was complete.[13]

Later scholarship has expressed a variety of views concerning John's relationship to Judaism, but it still has one thing in common with these pioneering views. It is commonly accepted—there are, as always, some exceptions—that the way Jesus' relationship to the Jews is portrayed in John does not correspond to the way in which the historical Jesus related to his Jewish contemporaries. This assumption is also a point of departure for Martyn's influential attempt to locate John in a historical context that would explain John's singular features better than the context of Palestinian society in Jesus' lifetime (see below p. 16).

The view that placed John—and other New Testament writings as well—in the context of Hellenistic ideas dominated the scholarly stage still at the beginning of the twentieth century. The History-of-Religions school sought to understand the New Testament in light of religious parallels, and more often than not these parallels were traced back to Hellenistic mystery religions or to other currents influenced by Hellenistic religious and philosophical thinking. This resulted in

---

[12] One of the first to notice this was Karl Gottlieb Bretschneider in his *Probabilia de evangelii et epistolarum Joannis, apostoli, indole et origine eruditorum judiciis modeste subjecit* (Leipzig, 1820). For Bretschneider, see Kümmel 1972, 85–86; Ashton 1991, 10–11. This view was put forward in detail by a scholar named Fischer in an article "Ueber den Ausdruck: οἱ Ἰουδαῖοι im Evangelium Johannis. Ein Beitrag zur Charakteristik desselben," *Tübinger Zeitschrift für Theologie* (Zweites Heft, 1840), 93–133. This article is cited at length by Schram 1974, 151–155. Schram notes that the article does not contain any initials or any other information on the author. According to Schram, Fischer's view influenced, for example, the views of F. C. Baur and F. Overbeck.

[13] For Baur's views on John, see Kümmel 1972, 137–138; Leistner 1974, 17–18; Schram 1974, 155.

Jesus being platonized and Paul and John being hellenized.[14] Even
though the likes of Johannes Weiss and Albert Schweitzer made bold
attempts to interpret Jesus and early Christianity in the context of
Jewish apocalyptic thinking, the Hellenistic approach to the New
Testament still prevailed in the first decades of the twentieth century. W. D. Davies has provided a personal testimony of the state
of scholarship in the 1930's:

> In short, most biblical scholars looked at the New Testament through
> Greek-colored spectacles and, of course, what they tended to see was
> Greek. Many found parallels to the teaching of Jesus in the Greek
> philosophers; they regarded Paul as a devotee of the Hellenistic Mystery
> religions and viewed the Fourth Gospel (John) and the Epistle to the
> Hebrews as imbued with something like the Hellenistic philosophy of
> Philo of Alexandria. . . . For Greek-trained New Testament scholars, almost
> everything in the New Testament was suffused with a Greek light.[15]

The attempts to interpret early Christianity and also the Fourth Gospel
in relation to first century Judaism never faded away completely, but
these attempts remained in the shadows of the keen interest in the
Hellenistic background of the New Testament. In the field of Johannine
studies, Adolf Schlatter (1903) and Hugo Odeberg (1929) drew heavily on Jewish sources, but in this period their attempts made little
impact on the general course of scholarship.[16]

    The two great names in twentieth century Johannine scholarship,
C. H. Dodd and Rudolf Bultmann, are both linked to the main
scholarly tendency of their time. W. D. Davies describes Dodd's
influential *The Interpretation of the Fourth Gospel* (1953) as "the full
flowering of the emphasis on Hellenism in New Testament study."[17]
Even though Dodd also drew on Jewish sources in his presentation
of John's theology, he believed that John had drifted far from Jewish
concerns. From the point of view of later Johannine studies, it is
amazing how little attention Dodd pays to the problematic use of
the expression οἱ Ἰουδαῖοι in his monumental works on John. In his
Historical Tradition in the Fourth Gospel Dodd dismisses this problem in

---

[14] Cf. W. D. Davies 1999, 5.
[15] W. D. Davies 1999, 4.
[16] See Ashton 1991, 24–26. It is noteworthy that Odeberg's commentary went
through a sort of revival, but not until it was reprinted in the late 60's, in a scholarly atmosphere that was totally changed from that of the 30's.
[17] W. D. Davies 1999, 188.

a footnote, in which he says that "this writer uses the term οἱ Ἰουδαῖοι imprecisely."[18] For Dodd, the use of the term shows that the finished gospel stems from a predominantly non-Jewish environment: "That a Christian writer of the late first century should speak in this way of 'the Jews,' especially if he wrote in a gentile environment, is intelligible enough."

Bultmann was in his earlier days primarily a member of the History-of-Religions school, and he sought to place John in the syncretistic religious world of the Hellenistic era; he traced the origin of John's presentation of Jesus to the gnostic myth that he found in sources that are significantly later than John.[19] This made his proposal an easy target for critics.[20] However, Bultmann never gave up his idea that John stems from a form of Hellenistic syncretism which the evangelist attacks by demythologizing the myth he was using. But in his later writings, including his influential commentary on John, Bultmann turned more and more away from History-of-Religions' interests, moving towards an existential interpretation. Bultmann tried to show how, in John, humanity is presented with an existential challenge to make a decision of faith. In this existential drama, the function of the Jews is to represent the unbelieving world as seen from the point of view of Christian faith.[21] The evangelist uses Judaism as an example of how people have distorted the knowledge of God by making God's demands and promises into possessions.[22] The conflict between Jesus and the Jews is thus elevated above occasional historical circumstances and seen as a timeless expression of humanity confronted by God's revelation.

Erich Gräßer has perhaps taken Bultmann's idea to its most logical conclusion, even though he also acknowledges that the gospel may reflect a real conflict with flesh and blood Jews.[23] Gräßer says that the conflict between the Torah and Christ in John is only "a

---

[18] Dodd 1963, 242 n. 2.
[19] Bultmann's articles dealing with John's gnostic background originally appeared in 1923 and 1925. See now Bultmann 1967, 10–35 and 55–104.
[20] For the problems in Bultmann's proposal, see Ashton 1991, 60–62.
[21] Bultmann's commentary does not have an introduction, and so this view is developed in connection with the exposition of individual passages. See, for example, p. 59 and p. 243. For a more complete presentation, see Bultmann 1984 (1948), 378–385.
[22] Bultmann 1984, 380.
[23] Gräßer's two articles dealing with the Jews in John originally appeared in 1964 and 1967. See Gräßer 1973, 50–83, esp. pp. 59, 67–68.

feature of style" with the help of which John describes a much more
profound crisis. The conflict between Jesus and the Jews becomes a
"paradigm of the revelation as crisis" and the polemics against the
Jews are a part of the Johannine dualism which serves Christianity's
own struggle against secularization.

The opinion that the Jews symbolize the unbelieving world has
some support in the gospel where the connection between the Jews
and the world (ὁ κόσμος) is a close one (cf. 1:9–11; 15:18–25). This
view may also be appealing as a theological actualization of the message of the gospel or as an attempt to circumvent the problems connected with John's polemic against the Jews—this latter purpose is
quite evident in Gräßer's discussion of the matter. However, it is
very unlikely that John's original audience ever understood the references to the Jews and to their religion only as symbolic expressions of the timeless situation of humankind. As John Ashton notes,
this interpretation "is curiously timeless" and "has virtually no social
dimension."[24] In a similar way, Alan Segal, while admitting that the
Jews are often used in a typological way in John, remarks that it is
important to note the obvious fact that

> it is the Jews and not some other group who have been chosen for
> this onerous symbol. The Johannine group is not using symbols arbi-
> trarily. Some social reality must be reflected in the symbolic statement.[25]

The reason that mainstream Johannine scholarship did not follow
Bultmann's lead may not have been some obvious shortcomings in
his approach. The discovery of the Dead Sea Scrolls in the late 40's
changed previous ways of understanding Judaism and Christianity.
The scrolls made evident that there was not just one way of being
a Jew, but that Judaism was divided into many different groups having singular beliefs of their own. The scrolls also contained many
beliefs that had formerly been regarded as alien to Judaism and
characteristic of Hellenistic or gnostic thinking. For example, scholars
soon found some obvious points in common with John's dualism and
the dualism evident in the Community Rule, and there emerged a
lively discussion about these common features.[26] This discussion was

---

[24] Ashton 1991, 101–102.
[25] Segal 1981, 252.
[26] See my discussion in ch. 6 pp. 197–210.

a part of the larger, ongoing process that meant a thorough reversal in the search for the context of early Christianity. Early Christianity
was increasingly placed in the context of diverse first century Judaism,
and early Christians were essentially seen as Jews among other Jews.
This development finally led W. D. Davies—in the footsteps of David
Daube—to speak of "New Testament Judaism."[27] The pendulum of
study also swung, to use Wayne Meeks' words, "from regarding the
Fourth Gospel as the most Hellenistic of the gospels to assessing it
as the most Jewish."[28]

However provocative the term "New Testament Judaism" may
have once sounded, it seems that this approach to early Christianity
has today became all but commonplace. In a popular work, James
A. Sanders writes:

> What has become quite clear is that all early Christians were Jews,
> whether by birth or by conversion. If non-Jews joined 'the Way,' they
> joined a Jewish sect, that is they became Jews even though of a par-
> ticular sort. But all forms of Judaism at the time were of a particular
> sort, no matter the later history of rabbinic Judaism. Jesus and his fol-
> lowers were all Jews. We were all Jews, so to speak. It was not until
> the last third or quarter of the century that Christian Jewish synagogues
> began to break away from any Jewish identity at all.[29]

In this current climate of New Testament study, it would probably
be unwise to use such terms as Christians or Christianity at all
because this is seen as an "anachronistic and misleading" usage.[30] It
is very much this state of New Testament scholarship which also
explains the intense discussion that has emerged about John's use of
the term οἱ Ἰουδαῖοι. This is not to say that the question of who
the Johannine Jews were had not been asked before, but the amount
of attention this question has received in recent Johannine studies
clearly shows how notably the scholarly climate has changed from
the days of C. H. Dodd. Dodd was still able to address the question
in a footnote because he interpreted the gospel mainly as a product

---

[27] W. D. Davies 1999, 78.
[28] Meeks 1975, 163.
[29] J. A. Sanders 1998, 52–53.
[30] Cf. de Boer 2001, 273 n. 46. Though I have not abandoned these terms, I
do not suggest that Judaism and Christianity could be identified as totally independent religions in the first century. But I believe it may be equally anachronistic and misleading to depict all parts of first century Christianity simply as another
variation of Judaism.

of the Hellenistic world and saw the sweeping use of the term οἱ
Ἰουδαῖοι as reflecting this non-Jewish setting of the gospel. But if all
early Christians are set in a Jewish context and regarded as Jews,
as is nowadays so often done, it is clear that the use of this term in
John must be quite unparalleled.

1.2. *Who Are οἱ Ἰουδαῖοι in John?*

C. E. Luthardt already proposed, in his two volume commentary on
John in 1875–76, that the term οἱ Ἰουδαῖοι especially refers to those
who live in Judaea and in Jerusalem, in contrast to the Galileans.
He saw that the Jews in John are often the leaders of the people,
and as such they act as the representatives of the people.[31] Malcolm
Lowe in particular has suggested that the term means 'the Judaeans'
who are separated in the narrative from the Galileans.[32] Lowe is
able to refer to some texts outside the gospel where this geographical meaning of the term is clear, and it is also probable that this
geographical sense was the earliest one in antiquity. But Shaye Cohen
has recently suggested that the term underwent "a semantic shift"
beginning in the Maccabean period when

> the ethnic-geographic self-definition was supplemented by religious (or
> "cultural") and political definitions because it was only in this period
> that the Judaean *ethnos* opened itself to the incorporation of outsiders.[33]

In the Hasmonean period, such nations as the Idumeans and Ituraens
were incorporated into "the Judaean *ethnos*" which meant both a
change in how Jewish identity was understood and in the way the
term οἱ Ἰουδαῖοι was understood. Cohen says that

> even if "Judaean" always retained its ethnic meaning, in the Hasmonean
> period common mode of worship and common way of life became
> very much more important in the new definition of Judaean/Jew.[34]

The change from Judaean to Jew reflects the development in which
Jewishness was increasingly construed in ethnic and religious terms,
not just in an ethnic-geographical sense as earlier. This means, accord-

---

[31] For Luthardt's view, see Schram 1974, 168–169.
[32] Lowe 1976, 101–130.
[33] Cohen 1999c, 70.
[34] Cohen 1999c, 133.

ing to Cohen, that "for most *Ioudaioi* in antiquity, the ethnic definition was supplemented, not replaced, by the religious definition. Jewishness became an ethno-religious identity."[35] But Cohen also insists that "we should not be too consistent in separating 'religion' from 'ethnicity' in antiquity, when the ancients had a much more organic conception of these matters than we do."[36]

Thus the term οἱ Ἰουδαῖοι was primarily used in a religious-ethnic sense in the first century C.E. and it referred to all those who followed the religious practices that were essential to Jewish identity, no matter whether they lived in Judaea or whether they were ethnically from there.[37] Heikki Solin has also emphasized that it is misleading to separate the geographical meaning of the term from its religious meaning because, in the ancient world, the Jews were seen both as an *ethnos* originating from Judaea and as a distinctive religious group. These two aspects overlap to a great extent, both in archaeological material and in written sources where the term appears.[38] There is also no reason to make a clear cultural or religious distinction between the first century Judaeans and the Galileans, which Jonathan Freed has recently shown most convincingly as arguing against those who support the distinction:

> The term *Jewish* is thoroughly appropriate for the inhabitants of Galilee in the first century. . . . Galilean Jews had a different social, economic, and political matrix than Jews living in Judaea or the Diaspora . . . but they were what we should call Jewish.[39]

The narrative of the gospel does not support a neat distinction between Judaeans and Galileans, even though this has often been suggested.[40] The Galileans are also called οἱ Ἰουδαῖοι (ch. 6) and they follow the customs of οἱ Ἰουδαῖοι (2:6). This is quite logical because the meaning of the term was ethnic-religious and not geographical by the time the gospel was written.

---

[35] Cohen 1999c, 137.
[36] Cohen 1999c, 138.
[37] Thus also Reinhartz 2001, 347.
[38] Solin 1983, 647–651, esp. p. 647 n. 150.
[39] Reed 1999b, 104. In a similar vein, Freyne 2000, 126–127: "Thus, to restrict Ἰουδαῖος to a geographical-political meaning, without attending to the very definite associations of the term with worship in the Jerusalem temple and acceptance of the customs, rituals and practices associated with that worship, is to ignore the powerful impetus that religious belief and practice can give in transcending intolerable social and economical factors."
[40] Pace Bassler 1981, 243–257; Meeks 1985, 96–97.

Most scholars today think that the term οἱ Ἰουδαῖοι in John refers to hostile Jewish authorities. In 1922 W. Lütgert already regarded the Johannine Jews as the Pharisees who represented that part of the Jewish nation who most consistently observed the law.[41] In a similar vein, K. Bornhäuser in 1928 defined the Jews in John as "Torah fanatics who are at the same time inquisitors whose job it is to watch over the law and to rectify and punish any infringement."[42] This view is remarkably close to recent understandings of the Johannine Jews, and it is no wonder then that John Ashton approves it with slight modifications.[43] Urban C. von Wahlde is the most well-known supporter of the view that sees the Johannine Jews primarily as Jewish authorities, and he has collected the arguments for this view. The point of departure is the separation of different usages of the term in John: many scholars note that sometimes it refers to the authorities in a hostile way, sometimes to the crowd in a more neutral way, and sometimes to different Jewish customs and festivals.[44] Neutral usage and references to Jewish traditions are in line with the way the term is used elsewhere, and so they are not taken as the typical Johannine usage. Only the negative and overtly hostile use of the term is Johannine in the fullest sense, and it is claimed that, in this sense, the term is used only for the authorities:

> If we speak of the meaning intended by the original author, we are most probably correct to say that he saw them as the religious authorities exclusively.[45]

James Dunn has observed some methodological problems in this reasoning. According to Dunn, the result that the hostile mentions of the Jews refer always to the Jewish authorities "follows directly from the methodological decision to distinguish the hostile references from the rest."[46] But if we ignore the prejudicial distinction between hostile and neutral references,

---

[41] See Schram 1974, 180–182.
[42] As quoted by Ashton 1991, 13.
[43] Ashton 1991, 158.
[44] Already Belser (1902, 168–222) distinguished different ways the term is used in John.
[45] Von Wahlde 1982, 45.
[46] Dunn 1992, 197.

the motif focusing on 'the Jews' is a good deal more complex than some have allowed, and the references to the hostile Jewish authorities have to be seen as only part of a larger plot.[47]

What is singular about the Johannine way of using the term is not that it is used (presumably) for the authorities only in a hostile sense, but the fact that *the very same term* is used both in an extremely hostile sense and in a way familiar from other sources. The combination of both these aspects is what makes the distinctive Johannine usage.[48]

It has been common to argue that the term οἱ Ἰουδαῖοι would refer to some kind of outside point of view from the Jews while some other terms, such as Israel or Israelites, would refer to the self-understanding of the Jews. This suggestion was made especially by Karl Georg Kuhn in 1938 in an often-cited article in the standard reference work *Theologisches Wörterbuch zum Neuen Testament*, and it has been repeated ever since.[49] However, Maurice Casey has recently shown that Kuhn's article reflects an anti-Semitic bias also evident in some other articles in the dictionary that were written in the 1930's. Casey shows that Kuhn's—himself a member of the Nazi party—views reflect the anti-Semitic usage of the German *Jude* more than ancient sources.[50] Most recently, Peter Tomson has suggested in a detailed comparison of John's usage with the Palestinian Talmud, the Synoptics and some New Testament Apocrypha that

> the dual usage typical of Judaism in the Graeco-Roman period involves semantic equivalence but social differentiation of the two names, 'Israel' being the self-appellation Jews use in inner-Jewish situations, and 'Jews' when including non-Jews among the intended audience.[51]

I doubt whether people were so consistent in the way they used different terms that we could make this kind of clear distinction in all ancient literature. Graham Harvey has noted, for example, that, in the writings of the Qumran community, יהודה is used as self-appellation

[47] Dunn 1992, 199.
[48] This is why I think that von Wahlde's reply to Dunn misses the point. Cf. von Wahlde 2000, 43–44 n. 66. Von Wahlde says that "the point of distinguishing a 'Johannine' usage is that one of the ways the term Ἰουδαῖοι is used appears nowhere else in precisely the same way. This usage is 'Johannine' in a way the others are not!"
[49] Kuhn 1938, 360–370.
[50] Casey 1999, 280–291.
[51] Tomson 2001, 301–340.

and sometimes synonymously with 'Israel.'[52] There is no sign of the use of the term οἱ Ἰουδαῖοι in a negative sense in other pre-Christian Jewish sources.[53] Therefore, although a detailed analysis of John would lead us to conclude that this gospel reflects in some respect an outsider's stance on Jewishness, this cannot be deduced on the basis of the use of the term οἱ Ἰουδαῖοι alone.

Those who argue that the term οἱ Ἰουδαῖοι refers exclusively to the Jewish authorities claim that John's use of the term is "distinctive and cannot be understood immediately and simply in terms of its use elsewhere in the ancient world."[54] But if John's use is so distinctive, how could the Johannine writer be sure that his readers understood the term in this distinctive sense and did not confused this distinctive sense with other meanings prevalent in other ancient literature and which also appear in John? Johannes Beutler has recently raised this question when he compares the Johannine usage to other writings in the New Testament. Beutler concludes that "the typical 'Johannine' usage which speaks of the 'Jews' as the Jewish authorities in Jerusalem as opposed to the claims of Jesus seems to be restricted to the Gospel of John."[55] For Beutler, this makes it unlikely that, as John was connected to other New Testament writings, the references to οἱ Ἰουδαῖοι would have been understood in a specific sense as referring to the authorities. But Beutler considers it

> at least thinkable that the first readers of the Gospel of John who read it still as an isolated document of their community were still able to grasp the particular meaning of the expression 'the Jews' as the opponents of Jesus in Jerusalem.

I think, however, that the way the term οἱ Ἰουδαῖοι is used in John gives reasons for believing that not even the Johannine writer had this particular meaning in mind, a meaning modern scholars have found in the gospel.

It is not at all clear that the term οἱ Ἰουδαῖοι always refers in a hostile sense to the authorities. The crux of the interpretation is John

---

[52] Harvey 1996, 21–42 and 99–103.

[53] Cf. Cohen 1999c, 71 n. 5: "It is often stated in the scholarly literature that *Ioudaios* bears a negative valence, but this assertion reflects the valence of *Jew*, *juif*, and *Jude* in modern times, which in turn was influenced by Christianity's assessments of Judaism. A negative valence is nowhere in evidence in any of the texts surveyed here."

[54] Von Wahlde 2002, 30 n. 1.

[55] Beutler 2001, 234.

6:41 and 52 where the term is clearly used for the Galilean crowd in a hostile sense—according to von Wahlde, these are only instances of the seventy-one in the gospel where the term is used in this way.[56] But John 6:41 and 52 may not represent unique usage. At least in John 7:35, it is probable that οἱ Ἰουδαῖοι are some of the crowd and not the leaders who do not seem to be present when the discussion takes place in 7:33–36. In 7:32 the Pharisees and the chief priests send the temple police to arrest Jesus. The return of the police is not mentioned until 7:45. It seems inevitable that the Jews in 7:35 are some of the common crowd; this is suggested by the fact that both the previous discussions in 7:25–31 and the following discussion in 7:37–44 deal with the crowd whereas only in 7:45–52 does the focus of the story change to the Pharisees and the chief priests.[57] The attempts to argue that 7:33–36 deal with the Jewish authorities are based on an *a priori* assumption that the Jews are exclusively the Jewish leaders for the Johannine writer, and this assumption has made it difficult to accept the most natural reading of this passage.[58]

I think we should not fix beforehand what the term οἱ Ἰουδαῖοι means. The meaning of the word should not be assessed only by listing those different passages where it appears and by isolating the distinctive Johannine usage. The basic mistake of earlier attempts to restrict the term to some particular group is that they separate the question of οἱ Ἰουδαῖοι from what John says concerning basic matters related to Jewish identity. We should answer the following questions: What are the characteristic actions and beliefs of those who

---

[56] Von Wahlde 1982, 45 and 2000, 45. I discuss in detail the use of the term οἱ Ἰουδαῖοι in 6:41, 52 in my reading of John 6:26–59, see ch. 5 pp. 160–162.

[57] Pace R. F. Collins (2001, 293 n. 36) who says the Jews in 7:35 are the chief priests and the Pharisees.

[58] Cf. Von Wahlde 1982, 44–45. Von Wahlde argues that the passage in 7:33–36 lacks clear references to time and place and that the sequence in John 7 as a whole is theological rather than historical: "The purpose seems rather to provide a 'typical' response to Jesus and the 'typical' reaction of Jesus rather than specific scenes." Thus the response of the Jews in 7:35–36 is not that of the common people, although the narrative context suggests this. It is problematic, however, that von Wahlde admits that there is confusion concerning the historical settings of some scenes in the gospel, but, at the same time, insists that the writer makes a clear distinction between the Jews as the authorities and the common people. To be sure, von Wahlde admits that the Johannine use of οἱ Ἰουδαῖοι is not "mechanically consistent" (p. 47). I think that the imprecise settings of some scenes in John correspond with how the narrator sometimes refers to Jesus' interlocutors without making a clear distinction between different groups.

are called οἱ Ἰουδαῖοι? Is the term reserved for some particular group
who has its own distinctive features in the narrative? I will return
to these questions as I pull together my own conclusions in the synthesis of this work.

1.3. *John As a Two-Level Drama*

One of the main reasons why it has been so standard in recent
decades to take οἱ Ἰουδαῖοι in John as the Jewish authorities is that
scholars have read John with a quite specific historical context in
mind. It has become an almost undisputed paradigm to maintain that
John reflects a conflict between the Johannine group and the leading
Jewish establishment. Therefore, οἱ Ἰουδαῖοι in John are not only
the Judaean leaders in Jerusalem in Jesus' story, but they symbolize
the opponents of the Johannine community who are quite often
identified with the leaders of emerging rabbinic Judaism. This influential
view was put forward especially by John Louis Martyn in his *History
and Theology in the Fourth Gospel* which first appeared in 1968.[59]

Martyn was not the first to claim that the gospel reflects a conflict
between the Johannine group and its opponents. Many elements in
Martyn's reconstruction were already quite common among New
Testament scholars. Both Rudolf Bultmann and Erich Gräßer, who
understood the Johannine Jews mainly as theological symbols, made
observations pointing to this direction.[60] In fact, the outlines of
Martyn's solution date back to the 19th century.[61] Yet Martyn was
the first to connect this view to a detailed analysis of the gospel's
narrative—or at least of some passages in the gospel. He thus estab-

---

[59] My references are to the revised and enlarged second edition that appeared
in 1979.

[60] Cf. Bultmann's references to the conflict stories in John 5 and 9 in Bultmann
178. See also Gräßer 1973 [1964], 63. Gräßer mentions that Johannine scholars
are quite unanimous that John's anti-Jewish polemic must be explained in reference
to the *Zeitgeschichte* of the evangelist. Gräßer mentions here all the central elements
of Martyn's theory: the expulsion from the synagoge, the *birkat ha-minim*, R. Gamaliel
II as the main force among the Yavnean rabbis. In a note, Gräßer lists scholars
supporting this view: W. Schrage (1960), J. Josz (1953), K. L. Carroll (1957), L. Goppelt
(1954), G. Baum (1963). He mentions even a standard introduction to the NT representing this view (Feine-Behm-Kümmel, 1964). This shows that Martyn's view was
to a great extent already present in previous scholarship, in particular in German-
speaking scholarship.

[61] Cf. Ashton 1991, 11. Ashton mentions an article by M. von Aberle (1861)
who already referred to the *Birkat ha-Minim*.

lished it as a standard way to read the Johannine narrative.[62] Martyn proposes that the gospel of John should be read as a two-level drama that tells not only of Jesus' life, which Martyn calls the *einmalig* level of the story, but also of the contemporary situation of the Johannine Christians. The point of departure for Martyn is John 9 which he actually presents in the form of a drama and then proceeds to reveal what this drama demonstrates of the history of the community.[63] Martyn connects the passages that tell of the exclusion from the synagogue (9:22; 12:42; 16:2) to the *Birkat ha-Minim*, a Jewish prayer against the heretics, and maintains that this prayer played a crucial role in the process that led to the separation of the Johannine Christians from their fellow Jews.[64] The bitterness of this process is reflected in the gospel's portrayal of the Jews as Jesus' enemies. If the gospel is read in this way, it appears that different Jewish groups in the narrative represent real Jewish groups at the time the gospel was written.[65]

Martyn suggested that John belongs not only to a Jewish context in some general sense but to a quite specific Jewish context. Martyn placed the gospel in the context of emerging rabbinic Judaism and claimed that the principal enemies of the Johannine Christians were the early rabbis in Yavneh. For Martyn, the expulsion from the synagogue was not a unique event but part of the larger scene where the rabbinic leaders became the main persecutors of the Johannine Christians, even to the extent that they executed many believers.[66]

Some details in Martyn's reconstruction, such as references to the *Birkat ha-Minim*, have been much discussed and mainly abandoned by most Johannine scholars, but his general picture still dominates the stage in Johannine studies. As D. Moody Smith writes:

> In setting John against a Jewish, rather than a Christian, background, Martyn had predecessors. But he rightly gets credit for a sea-change in Johannine studies for somewhat the same reason that the Wright brothers got credit for the airplane. Others may have gotten off the ground, but Martyn—like the Wright brothers—achieved sustained flight. To extend the metaphor, his vehicle may not have been perfect, but it has proven good enough to maintain itself and stand correction.[67]

---

[62] For Martyn's contribution to Johannine studies, see D. M. Smith 1990, 275–294.
[63] Martyn 1979, 24–36.
[64] Martyn 1979, 50–62.
[65] Martyn 1979, 84–89.
[66] Martyn 1979, 64–81.
[67] D. M. Smith 1990, 279.

These words aptly reflect the influence of Martyn's work on Johannine studies in the last three decades. David Rensberger says that Martyn's work "has become the cornerstone of much current Johannine research."[68] John Ashton even claims that in Martyn's work the question concerning John's audience and situation "has been roughly mapped out. What remains is a matter of adjusting a few details and filling in some gaps."[69] These appraisals were made a decade ago, but Martyn's influence has not waned. Most contributors to the collection *Anti-Judaism and the Fourth Gospel*, which appeared in 2001, refer to Martyn's work, and most do so approvingly.[70] R. Alan Culpepper expresses the attitude of many by saying that

> specific points [in Martyn's model] continue to be debated, [but] it is widely agreed that the Fourth Gospel reflects an intense and apparently violent conflict between Jews and Johannine Christians.[71]

As Adele Reinhartz says: "[The two-level reading] strategy, like the expulsion theory which it supports, has become all but axiomatic in Johannine studies."[72]

Martyn's theory also has been criticized. Most discussions, as Culpepper's words make clear, have dealt with some specific points, while insisting that it is basically correct. I will return to these singular points in my detailed presentation and critique of the theory in the chapter 2. It is surprising, however, that there have not been very many scholars who have had doubts about Martyn's methodological presuppositions. After all, Martyn takes quite a bold leap from the narrative of the gospel to the historical reality behind it. Martyn does not hesitate to take not only the narrative in general but also its minor details as a direct reflection of the social reality of the Johannine Christians.

The venturesome nature of Martyn's proposal has not altogether gone unnoticed by scholars. Marinus de Jonge had some opinions of Martyn and Wayne Meeks especially in mind when he wrote that

> the way from a literary document like the Gospel of John to a reconstruction of the actual situation in which it was written is much longer and much more difficult than some authors seem to realize.[73]

---

[68] Rensberger 1989, 22.
[69] Ashton 1991, 109.
[70] Bieringer et al. 2001a.
[71] Culpepper 2001, 69.
[72] Reinhartz 1998, 117.
[73] De Jonge 1977, 114 n. 70.

This basic methodological problem also caught the eye of Joachim Kügler in an important and—unfortunately—mostly neglected article.[74] Kügler points out that there is no evidence in Jewish sources for the kind of situation Martyn's theory presupposes. This leads him to ask whether everything in a text reflects current problems in the social reality behind it or whether there could also be some features that are only historical reminiscences of the past. Kügler notes that there is not much methodological discussion in current Johannine scholarship about how we can use texts to gain information about social contexts. This gives a reason for Kügler to compare the state of Johannine scholarship to the 19th century *Leben-Jesu-Forschung*, only that now it is the life of a community which scholars think they can trace in its details in the gospel.[75] Kügler ends his article with the plea that historical methods should be subjected to critical evaluation, or Johannine scholarship will turn into a new literary genre, "Isagogic Science Fiction."[76]

Margaret Davies has also noticed the problems in the current consensus view based on Martyn's two-level reading in her *Rhetoric and Reference in the Fourth Gospel*. Davies notes that although many scholars

> recognize that the Gospel's portrait of Judaism is inaccurate for the time of Jesus, they assert that it is accurate for the time when the Gospel was written. But what we know of Judaism during the first two centuries CE from its own sources suggests, on the contrary, that the Fourth Gospel's portrait, taken at face value, is a gross caricature.[77]

For Davies, the gospel is not formed out of real disputes between Jews and Christians. In contrast,

> it suggests that what knowledge of Judaism it contains is derived from Scripture or from traditions about Jesus, not from first-hand evidence. There is no attempt to enter into the world of Jews in order to convince them of Jesus' importance but rather an attempt to convince Christians about the characteristics of their own separate identity.[78]

---

[74] Kügler 1984, 48–61. Kügler's article is especially a response to Klaus Wengst's study (originally in 1981, my references are to the fourth edition, Wengst 1992) but Kügler also mentions Martyn's work. It is revealing of the reception of Kügler's article that it is not mentioned by D. Moody Smith, even though Smith also traces Martyn's influence on German scholarship. Smith mentions only Wengst who is heavily criticized by Kügler. Cf. D. M. Smith 1990, 287–288.
[75] Kügler 1984, 61.
[76] Kügler 1984, 62.
[77] M. Davies 1992, 17.
[78] M. Davies 1992, 303.

It is unfortunate that Margaret Davies chose just to give her "own constructive account" and "eschewed quoting other peoples' writings just to point out prejudices or errors."[79] Therefore, her criticism of the current consensus remains general and unspecified which perhaps explains why it was not able to challenge the course of mainstream Johannine scholarship in the 1990's.

A more detailed and substantial criticism against prevailing consensus is presented in a series of works by Adele Reinhartz.[80] Reinhartz approaches John from a Jewish perspective and acknowledges that her background makes her feel discomfort with current scholarly opinion.[81] Reinhartz provides a resistant reading of the gospel and opposes the way it negates many basics of Jewish identity.[82] Reinhartz does not only engage in an ideological criticism of the Fourth Gospel from a Jewish point of view, but she also challenges the historical presuppositions behind the two-level reading strategy. First, following some earlier critics who have challenged Martyn's references to certain rabbinic passages, Reinhartz notes that this strategy cannot be supported by external evidence.[83] Second, the two-level reading is based one-sidedly on John 9 while there are other models for interaction between Jesus' followers and the Jews in John. If read as a reflection of the social reality behind the gospel, John 11 speaks of ongoing and peaceful communication between Johannine Christians and other Jews.[84] The third point in Reinhartz's criticism is that it is unlikely that the intended audience ever read the gospel as a direct reflection of their own history, but rather as a story of Jesus.[85] On the basis of her criticism, Reinhartz proposes an alternative way of reading John:

> The Gospel reflects the complex social situation of the Johannine community but not the specific historical circumstances which gave rise to

---

[79] M. Davies 1992, 7.

[80] See Reinhartz 1997, 1998, 2001a, 2001b.

[81] See especially Reinhartz 1997, 177–193.

[82] Reinhartz 2001a, 81–98.

[83] Reinhartz 1998, 115–118; 2001a, 37–40.

[84] Reinhartz 1998, 121–130; 2001a, 40–48.

[85] Reinhartz 1998, 137. However, this is a point that Martyn himself seems to admit to some extent. Cf. Martyn 1979, 89: "One may be confident that he [the evangelist] did not intend his readers to analyze the dramatis personae in the way in which we have done it. Indeed, I doubt that he was himself analytically conscious of what I have termed the two-level drama, for his major concern in this regard was to bear witness to the essential integrity of the *einmalig* drama of Jesus' earthly life and the contemporary drama in which the Risen Lord acts through his servants."

that situation. The largely negative portrayal of the Jews and Judaism within the Gospel must therefore be grounded not in a specific experience but in the ongoing process of self-definition and the rhetoric which accompanies it.[86]

Reinhartz here joins Wayne McCready who has read John 9 as a reflection of Johannine self-understanding rather than as a direct history of the community.[87] This notion of self-understanding is important because it suggests that we cannot understand religious texts only as a reflection of historical reality but also and perhaps primarily as a reflection of how writers understand themselves in relation to that reality. It is remarkable how little attention this aspect has received in Johannine scholarship during recent decades although it is quite common in the sociological or anthropological study of religion. For example, Mary Douglas notes in her classic *Natural Symbols* that "small competitive communities tend to believe themselves in a dangerous universe, threatened by sinister powers operated by fellow human beings."[88] Thus, it is hazardous to take what is said of an outside world in a religious writing as direct reflection of that world.[89] When speaking of heresy and apostasy in rabbinic writings, William Scott Green emphasizes how important it is to observe that 'others' are presented in religious literature in light of the self-understanding of a religious community:

> In so constructing 'otherness,' religions do not see the outsiders whole. Rather, a religion mistakes some part of the outsider for outsider and a piece of itself for itself, and it construes each in terms of the other. Each negation of the 'other' is simultaneously an affirmation of self, in terms of some particular trait. This means that 'otherness' is as much about the naming religion as it is about outsiders named. . . . 'Otherness', therefore, is at least as much a reflection of the religious community's self-understanding as it is a response to actual conflicts with the real other.[90]

---

[86] Reinhartz 1998, 137.
[87] McCready 1990, 147–166.
[88] Douglas 1973, 137.
[89] There are some signs that the supporters of the two-level reading strategy are aware of this problem, cf. Rensberger 1989, 110–111. Rensberger discusses what is meant by "oppression" in John's case and concludes that, "at any rate, there is no question that the Johannine group *saw themselves* as oppressed" (italics original). However, in the case of such a religious group as the Johannine community, it is two different things to feel oppressed and to be actually oppressed.
[90] Green 2000b, 366.

I agree with the earlier critics of the two-level reading strategy that it is not just minor details that are wrong in this reading. The careless leap from the narrative of the gospel to the historical reality behind it has resulted in distorted views of the early rabbinic movement, and these views cannot be sustained in light of recent studies. I will argue this in detail in my following criticism of current scholarly consensus in chapter 2. I claim that John's portrayal of the Jews and Jewishness cannot be explained as a response to some external pressure; this portrayal rather reflects the self-understanding of the Johannine Christians who saw their faith in Jesus as the culmination of Jewish tradition but who also saw a clear contrast between the revelation they believed to have in Jesus and God's earlier revelations to such leading figures in Jewish tradition as Moses and Abraham. I think this ambivalence is the main characteristic of John's portrayal of Jewishness even though current New Testament scholarship tends to one-sidedly emphasize the Jewishness of all early Christianity.

1.4. *Early Christians and the Diversity of First Century Judaism*

In some respect, the current climate in New Testament studies seems similar to the state of scholarship in the 1930's described by W. D. Davies in a quotation that I cited above (p. 6). In the 30's "almost everything in the New Testament was suffused with a Greek light," whereas today everything is seen in a Jewish light—with the notable difference that the classics of Greek tradition are many centuries older than early Christian sources whereas a large part of Jewish material used by scholars is quite as many centuries newer than early Christian literature. But is there also a similar danger that the one-sided interest results in superficial readings of some parts of the New Testament? Has the emphasis on the Jewishness of early Christianity gone too far in making scholars blind to the features that already mark a detachment from many basics of Jewish identity in some parts of the New Testament? The development that has led to the current state of scholarship started as a protest against the earlier emphasis on the alleged Hellenistic and non-Jewish character of early Christianity, but maybe what has happened here, so typical of these kinds of protests, is that opinions have moved from one extreme to another.

The more the Jewishness of the New Testament is emphasized, the more imprecise and stereotyped the general descriptions of the

situation of first century Christians have become. As Stephen G.
Wilson notes, the same tendency has made it almost impossible to
use the term Jewish Christianity in a specific sense because all early
Christians are regarded as some sort of Jewish Christians:

> It has recently become commonplace to assign a dramatically more
> important role to Jewish Christianity. The claims may vary, but they
> all point in the same direction (and the more they have been repeated,
> the looser and more sweeping they have become): that all early Christians
> were in some sense Jewish Christians; that they were the dominant
> force throughout the first century; and that they thrived in some areas
> for many centuries, often remaining the dominant form of Christianity
> to be found in any particular locale.[91]

Even some cursory observations suggest that it is quite problematic
to describe all first century Christians as Jewish or even as Jewish
Christians. Paul's letter to the Galatians shows how deeply Paul struggled to defend his view that the Galatians of gentile origin (Gal 4:8)
should not have to be circumcised. Paul's opponents were presumably Jewish Christians who insisted that all those who received Christ
should also be circumcised. It is not evident that these opponents
would have regarded uncircumcised gentiles as Jews. And it is far
from self-evident that those gentiles who remained uncircumcised
ever understood that, by joining an early Christian community, they
joined a Jewish sect. Because Paul elsewhere makes a clear distinction between Jews and gentiles (e.g. 1 Cor 9:20–21), it is not clear
that he regarded the gentile Christians in Galatia as Jews. The very
fact that these questions arise shows that matters connected to early
Christian identity in relation to basic matters of Jewish identity
became already highly problematic and controversial in the 50's and
not just at the end of the first century.[92] It seems that some of Paul's
basic convictions made his view of Jewishness highly ambivalent.[93]

It is not manifest that early Christians were a Jewish group which
remained inseparable from other Jewish groups in the eyes of outsiders the most of the first century. The history of an early Christian

---

[91] Wilson 1995, 144.
[92] Cf. Charlesworth 1990, 48. Although Charlesworth emphasizes Paul's Jewishness,
even he admits that "Paul is often exasperatingly unclear, unrepresentative of many
aspects of Early Judaism, and even selfcontradictory."
[93] For Paul's problematic stance on the Torah in Galatians, see now Kuula 1999.

community in the city of Rome shows this. The emperor Claudius issued an edict in 49 C.E. which

> in effect drove a wedge between [Jews and Christians] by dramatically communicating—especially to non-Christian Jews—that it would be in their best interests to go their separate ways. By reducing interactions between Christians and non-Christians Jews and by altering the context in which those interactions took place, the edict affected the evolution of Christian self-definition in the capital.[94]

Some fifteen years later Nero initiated a persecution against some early Christians in Rome; James Walters has recently emphasized that these events indicate the extent of the break between non-Christians Jews and Christians in this locale:

> The ancient materials are silent how Christians were identified and prosecuted in 64 C.E.; nonetheless, they were identified and prosecuted, and the implications of that datum for the existence of features which distinguished Christians from non-Christian Jews, and Christian communities from Jewish communities, should not be underplayed.[95]

These incidents suggest that early Christians in Rome were a group distinct from other Jews at the *social* level, no matter whether they saw themselves as the true Israel (cf. Rom. 9:24–29), or no matter how greatly they drew on Jewish traditions in their faith. The circumstances in Rome, of course, were quite special and relate to this early Christian community alone. But these events show that it is quite possible to imagine some early Christian groups as distinct from other Jews already before the last quarter of the first century. The early history of Christians in Rome suggests that it is not sufficient to determine the Jewishness of early Christian groups only in relation to their own self-understanding or the traditions they use.

It seems that the seeds for the development that finally led to the break between mainstream Christianity and most Jewish communities were sown, at least to some extent, in the first century C.E. There

---

[94] Walters 1998, 178. In a similar vein Brändle & Stegemann 1998, 126; Lane 1998, 206. It is to some extent unclear whether the edict had to do with a schism between some early Christians and non-Christian Jews. Suetonius says in a famous passage (*Claud.* 25.4) that the Jews were expelled because "they constantly made disturbances at the instigation of Chrestus" (impulsore Chresto). This passage has most often taken as a reference to a conflict evoked by early Christian preaching, but this interpretation is not without problems. See Rutgers 1998, 105–106.

[95] Walters 1998, 179–180.

is no way to return to the thinking that we could pinpoint a specific date in history, 70 c.e. or 135 c.e., when the split between early Christianity and Judaism became complete.[96] But the current emphasis on the Jewishness of all first century Christianity is not able to give a proper answer to the question as to why most forms of Christianity eventually grew apart from most forms of Judaism. This problem is evident in James Dunn's approach to the problem. Dunn shares the view of many when he says that

> as we move into the second century not only certain Christian sects can be described as 'Jewish-Christian,' but Christianity as a whole can still properly be described as 'Jewish Christianity' in a justifiable sense.[97]

However, a little later Dunn notes that

> by the time of Pliny [about 112 c.e.] the issue was clear: Christians are not Jews. By then the perception from outside reinforces the impression that *the partings of the ways had already become effective*, in Asia Minor and in the view from Rome at any rate.[98]

But how can we understand this change, if it was not already going on in the first century? Dunn himself refers to the emerging rabbinic Judaism as "the first real or really effective form of orthodox or normative Judaism" that began "to draw boundaries more tightly round 'Judaism.'"[99] But if this view is no longer tenable, as I argue in detail in the second chapter of this work, then we should not look for some external reasons for Christianity's emergence as a religion of its own. Rather, we should recognize those features in early Christian writings that suggest the ambivalent attitudes some Christian groups had towards some aspects of Jewish tradition. I do not deny in my followings readings that John stems from a Jewish environment, but I claim that due attention should also be paid to those traits that reflect a departure from or even a conflict with central aspects of Jewishness.

The opinion that emphasizes the diversity of first century Judaism and sees Christianity as another variation of Judaism, has led to the

---

[96] Daniel Boyarin has even suggested that we should not speak of Judaism and Christianity as independent religions at all in the context of late Antiquity. See Boyarin 1999, 1–21. I try to assess this view with regard to John's views on Jewishness in my synthesis, ch. 7.4 p. 237.

[97] Dunn 1991, 234.

[98] Dunn 1991, 241 (italics original).

[99] Dunn 1991, 221–222, 238.

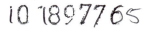

conclusion that we cannot speak of Judaism in the singular but should use the plural Judaisms.[100] But if all groups of Jews—including early Christians or Samaritans—had a Judaism of their own, it is not possible to understand why some groups went their own way and formed what should be regarded in any meaningful sense of the word as a religion of its own.

The notion that we should speak of Judaisms in the first century context is problematic. First, it is based to a great extent on the self-understanding of different texts that make the claim that one group or another is the true Israel.[101] This leads to clear problems in the case of Church Fathers, for example, who also make this claim. But it is problematic not only in case of some early Christian groups to make the self-understanding of a community the point of departure for the assessment of Jewishness in a given writing. Most religious groups, at least sectarian groups, define themselves in sharp contrast to the surrounding society in order to underline their excellence as compared to other groups. Thus they see themselves as unique and isolated from the rest of society. But this self-understanding does not prove that that these groups are in real life that isolated and unique in the eyes of outsiders. Jutta Jokiranta has recently remarked that, while "the model of sectarianism may help us in describing the self-understandings" of such groups as the Qumran community, this model "cannot describe the objective socio-historical situations of the groups."[102] A good case can be made for non-Jews not regarding different Jewish groups as representing different religions, but rather as different Jewish schools, resembling those philosophical schools known in the Hellenistic world.[103] When it comes to other Jews, it is not at all clear that they would have regarded sectarians as representing completely different religious systems. Regarding such groups as the Qumran community, Albert Baumgarten suggests that other Jews

> might have respected the devotion of sectarians, but also resented their exclusivist attitudes somewhat, regarding them with as least some disdain and believing (1) that sectarian ideas were new-fangled inventions of the minds of their devotees, and (2) that if traditional practice had been good enough for generations past there was no need to change it.[104]

---

[100] Chilton & Neusner 1995, 1–18.
[101] For these problems, see Myllykoski & Luomanen 1999, 330–331; Luomanen 2002, 114–119.
[102] Jokiranta 2001, 234.
[103] See Baumgarten 1997, 58–60.
[104] Baumgarten 1997, 62.

The second problem in the notion which considers different Jewish groups as Judaisms of their own is that it presupposes that each ancient writing "speaks of a single, coherent community of Jews" that has a "religious system" of its own.[105] Built into this view is a harmonizing tendency that discards the fact that many ancient writings contain quite conflicting views that do not yield a coherent religious system. The exclusive concentration on independent religious systems tends to detach ancient writings from their social contexts, a point made by John Barclay in his study on the Diaspora Judaism. Barclay traces different forms of Jewish identity in the Diaspora, but although he finds much local diversity, he refuses to speak of many Diaspora Judaisms:

> Such varying Jewish profiles do not necessarily represent different 'Judaisms;' one and the same socio-religious phenomenon can wear many masks. . . . If Judaism is defined—as it should be—as a *social* and not just as an *intellectual* phenomenon, it is hard to see how the plural 'Judaisms' could apply to the Diaspora. In identifying the bonds which held Diaspora Jews together, we will find ourselves most confident at those points where the perceptions of 'outsiders' match those of 'insiders.' If non-Jews repeatedly commented on Jewish characteristics which were also held by Jews to be essential to their way of life, we can be sure that such items were indeed integral to the identity.[106]

Barclay notes that, although Jews in the Diaspora—and I think that the same could be applied to the Palestinian Jews also—held various and divergent beliefs, different groups were united on a social level because they held to distinct convictions and practices that marked the Jews off from other people, even in the eyes of outsiders.[107] In

---

[105] Chilton & Neusner 1995, 7. For the application of this approach on the Qumran study, see Neusner & Avery-Peck & Chilton 2001, vii–xii. The concentration "on a single corpus of evidence, the writings found in the library of Qumran" that speak of "the system as a whole" goes against the prevailing trend in Qumran studies which emphasize the fact that there are many different systems reflected in the scrolls. It is also not at all clear that different systems in the scrolls would always reflect different social contexts and different groups who hold these divergent views. See Metso 1998 and 2000.

[106] Barclay 1996, 401.

[107] The same is emphasized by E. P. Sanders 1999a, 5: "Both Jews and Gentiles regarded the Jews in the Diaspora as intimately linked to the Jews in Palestine. There was, in other words, something that we may call 'common Judaism.' It was based on general acceptance of the Bible, especially the law of Moses, and on a common self-perception: The Jews knew themselves to be Jews and not Gentiles, and to some degree or other they stood apart from other people. We have noted

his detailed discussion of these common denominators of Jewish identity in the Diaspora, Barclay mentions the following things: the ethnic bond, festivals, fasts and Sabbath gatherings in local communities,
links with Jerusalem and the temple (e.g., collections of temple dues),
the law/Jewish scriptures, the figure of Moses, rejection of iconic
cults, food regulations, male circumcision, and Sabbath observance.[108]
Barclay concludes that there is "much diversity in Diaspora interpretations of Judaism, and it appears that hermeneutical unanimity
was unnecessary so long as the web of custom was preserved intact."[109]

In another connection Barclay has studied those examples of individuals or groups who were regarded as apostates in the Diaspora.
The sparse evidence concerning these apostates suggests that the reasons why some Jews became suspect in the eyes of their fellow Jews
had not so much to do with particular beliefs than with withdrawal
from the Jewish community through assimilation; this assimilation
became evident in the abandonment of such practices as food regulations or Sabbath laws and in involvement with gentile religion.[110] For
example, when Philo refers to some 'allegorizers,' he seems to share
their symbolical interpretation of the laws concerning the Sabbath,
festivals and circumcision; he laments that these people have ceased

---

in particular monotheism, abhorrence of idols, circumcision, Sabbath, food laws,
and a few other points." For a discussion of how it was possible to know who was a
Jew in Antiquity, see Cohen 1999c, 25–68. Cohen concludes that it may have been
impossible to tell an individual Jew from those gentiles who observed Jewish rituals and practices. But even Cohen admits—responding to an earlier criticism made
by John Barclay—that he does not "deny that Jewish communities will have been
distinctive, clearly marked off as a group from non-Jewish groups" (p. 67 n. 175).

[108] Barclay 1996, 402–442.
[109] Barclay 1996, 443. A different picture of Diaspora Judaism is given by J. J.
Collins 2000, 273–275. Collins says that 'covenantal nomism,' proposed by E. P.
Sanders as the basic pattern of Judaism both in Palestine and in the Diaspora is
not the only or dominant factor in the religion of Hellenistic Judaism (cf. also pp.
21–24). Collins says that "the Jewish tradition could also be construed as the story
of a glorious past which fostered ethnic pride, with little regard for religious laws
or for anything that could be called nomism" (p. 273). This kind of Judaism would
not place much emphasis on the observance of commandments. For the discussion
of the role of circumcision in the first century Judaism, see also Collins 1985,
164–186. However, Collins may play down the significance of religious practices
for Jewish identity in the Diaspora. Cf. Barclay 1996, 439. Barclay argues against
Collins, that the insignificance of circumcision in the Diaspora cannot be deduced
from the fact that all Diaspora authors do not mention it; circumcision "was not
a topic that naturally arose in the genre in which many of them wrote." The references of many non-Jewish authors to this practice show that it was regarded as
a major characteristic of the Jews. See also Cohen 1999c, 158.
[110] See Barclay 1998, 92.

to observe these laws on the basis of their theology (*Migration* 89–93). Philo is worried because the 'allegorizers' have ceased to observe the practices which mark a Jew off from a gentile, not because they have their own religious system.[111] The presence of the apostates in the Diaspora is a clear sign that, on a *social* level, the borders of Jewishness were not open to every kind of Jewish identity. A deviation from central Jewish practices would not have gone unnoticed but would have resulted in a confrontation between those Jews who continued to observe these practices and those who abandoned them.

Different Jewish groups emerged not because they had their own distinctive religious systems but because they had conflicting views on some basics of Jewish identity. An example of this could be taken from what little we know of the origins of the Qumran community. It seems that the issues related to the calendar and/or to the temple, the cult and priesthood were fundamental in the process that led to the separation of the community from the main body of the Jews.[112] Although the Dead Sea Scrolls contain many theological concepts that may have been rather obscure in the eyes of the rest of the Jews, it is not probable that these ideas played a central role in the formation of the community. The dualistic world view evident in some of the scrolls, for example, may be a result of the alienation of the group rather than its cause.

There may be a difference in the emergence of different deviant groups in Judaism and in Christianity. When discussing the origin of Samaritanism, Ferdinand Dexinger points out that in Christianity sects often "originate from deviating teaching while in Judaism they arise from deviating actions."[113] Dexinger also makes an important observation concerning the rise of Samaritanism. The original process which led to the formation of the recognizable religious community of the Samaritans was probably a long development that was dependent on several factors, religious (e.g., mixed marriages, cult centralization, the priesthood), political and economic (e.g., rivalry between Samaria and Jerusalem, a gentile ruling class in Samaria). Dexinger

---

[111] For this passage in Philo, see Räisänen 1987, 35–36.

[112] For a recent presentation of different theories about the history of the Qumran community, see García Martínez 1998, 194–216. Jokiranta (2001, 234) aptly notes that not all reasons for the emergence of difference groups were religious but included different political, social and cultural factors.

[113] Dexinger 1981, 111. For the discussion of the concepts of Torah and dogma in Judaism and Christianity, cf. also W. D. Davies 1999, 58–78.

notes that "these basic factors which were actually decisive for the separation should be differentiated from later theologizing of the differences."[114] According to Dexinger, theological controversy concerning the question of which side, the Samaritans or the Jews, had the right to be the true Israel was secondary in the process of alienation; this theologizing finally completed the break but was not its original cause.[115]

I believe that if we wish to understand how early Christian writings participated in the development of a growing alienation of many Christian groups from the things that were common to different Jewish groups, we should not be satisfied with unspecified assurances about the Jewishness of all early Christianity. We should also take seriously those features that show tensions and ambiguities in early Christian references to basic matters of Jewishness. Despite the great diversity in first century Judaism, the different groups had a common bond.[116] There was no orthodoxy among the Jews in the first century, but both the Jews in general and the outsiders had similar ideas of what were the things that make a Jew. These things were not written in any credo and their observance was not controlled by any leading body, but these things were connected to Jewishness in the minds of people, as is suggested by Shaye Cohen:

> Most of those in antiquity who identified themselves as *Jews* and were known as *Jews* to their neighbors shared certain important beliefs and practices. For example, they believed in a supreme God who created the world, chose the Israelites/Jews to be his people, revealed his Torah to his servant Moses, and rewards the righteous and punishes the wicked. They also practised the laws of the Torah of Moses, most conspicuously circumcision, Sabbath and abstention from certain foods. Jews interpreted these beliefs and practices in numerous and diverse ways, but it is not for the historian to determine which of these ways is right or 'orthodox.' The appropriate term for this regimen of belief and practice, and the social structures created by its adherents, is not 'orthodox Judaism' but simply 'Judaism.'[117]

---

[114] Dexinger 1981, 113.
[115] Dexinger 1981, 114.
[116] My views on first century Judaism owe much to E. P. Sanders' discussions in various writings, most notably in Sanders 1992. I have avoided quite consciously, however, the use of Sanders' key terms 'common Judaism' and 'covenantal nomism' knowing how controversial they are. For criticism of Sanders, see Chilton & Neusner 1995, 11–18. For a perceptive response to this criticism, see Luomanen 2002, 114–119.
[117] Cohen 1990, 58.

1.5. *The Outline of the Study*

Even though there was much diversity among Jews and there was no group that could control the life of other groups, certain matters connected Jews to each other on a social level. Therefore, it is necessary to evaluate John's Jewishness in light of these basic matters of Jewish identity as they are presented in the gospel.[118] The evangelist does not provide any systematic description of different aspects of Jewish identity and does not mention at all, for example, Jewish food regulations which many Hellenistic writers regarded as distinctive. However, many other aspects of Jewishness are mentioned in the gospel and some of them become main issues in the controversy between Jesus and his Jewish opponents.

Before I analyze the passages dealing with essential matters of Jewishness, I argue in a detailed criticism on scholarly consensus that John's references to these matters do not emerge from the fierce conflict with a Jewish leadership class (ch. 2). After this criticism, I proceed to analyze the narrative of the gospel focusing on some main symbols of Jewish identity. In John 2:13–22 and 4:20–24, Jesus' relationship to the Jerusalem temple and the worship of the Jews is the main topic (ch. 3). In John 5:1–18, Jesus' action on the Sabbath leads him into a controversy with his opponents; this controversy continues in 7:19–24 where the Johannine Jesus refers to the Sabbath and circumcision (ch. 4).[119] In John 5:37–47, the Johannine Jesus refers implicitly to a basic tenet of Jewish identity, the revelation at Sinai. Jesus also here presents Moses and the scriptures as his witnesses, but the discussion in 6:26–59 reveals how ambivalent is the relationship between the Johannine Jesus and Moses (ch. 5). My last close reading of the narrative focuses on John 8:31–59 where Jesus discusses Abraham with the believing Jews; in this chapter is also

---

[118] Also Casey (1991, 23–40) has analyzed John's references to basics of Jewishness. In many cases we come to similar conclusions, but I think that John's portrayal of Jewishness is at times more complex and ambivalent than Casey's reading suggests. Furthermore, I do not share Casey's view of the Johannine Christology as the main expression of the gentile identity reflected in the gospel. See my synthesis, ch. 7.4 p. 233.

[119] I do not offer a detailed discussion of the story in John 9. There are two reasons for this. First, I discuss in detail theories that take this story as their point of departure for the reconstruction of John's historical context in ch. 2. Second, I do not think that a close reading of this story would radically change the conclusions I draw on the basis of my readings of John 5:1–18 and 7:19–24. Cf. the conclusions from these readings, in ch. 4.3 p. 142.

the notorious charge that the Jews are of the devil, a charge which opens up a perspective on the dualistic framework of the narrative. This saying makes it necessary to address the question of John's supposed anti-Judaism (ch. 6). After these readings, I pull together the results of my studies and develop them further in the synthesis (ch. 7). In this synthesis, I try to show how the Fourth Gospel that has its origins so deep in diverse Jewish traditions contributed to the development of a non-Jewish Christian identity.

Following Shaye Cohen's lead in his *The Beginnings Of Jewishness*, I have spoken above of Jewishness and not of Judaism. This corresponds to the way the matters discussed in this work were markers of a certain manner of life or identity rather than any fixed theological dogmas.[120] Judith Lieu aptly notes that words like Judaic or Judaism speak more of a system whereas words like Jewish and Jewishness "more of a people, culture, and set of ideas."[121] As Shaye Cohen says,

> Jewishness, like most—perhaps all—identities, is imagined; it has no empirical, objective, verifiable reality to which we can point and over which we can exclaim, 'This is it!' Jewishness is in the mind.[122]

But even though it is difficult to get a grasp of identities and define them neatly, identities also change. And I believe that this is what is going on in John. I am looking for some traces of this change of identity, but I do not claim to offer a systematic description of all what John says of matters connected to Jewishness.[123] Before I proceed to present my detailed criticism of scholarly consensus and my own readings of John's individual passages, I explain my methodological approach to these passages.

---

[120] Interestingly, the subtitle of Martin de Boer's recent article discusses also "matters of behavior and identity." Cf. de Boer 2001. But in the course of my work and following discussions with de Boer, it comes clear that we mean completely different things. Following his teacher J. Louis Martyn, de Boer concentrates on a group of Jewish authorities who allegedly arbitrated the matters of Jewish identity after 70 C.E. I do not find much evidence of this kind of definition of Jewish identity in rabbinic sources, and so I have turned my attention to how this particular group of early Christians defined their identity in relation to their Jewish background.

[121] Lieu 2001, 129.

[122] Cohen 1999c, 5.

[123] I have not included in my work, for example, detailed readings of some brief references to Jewish rites of purification (2:6; 3:25). It is not at all clear what the role of these rites was in different Jewish groups. Were they a characteristic of a distinct group only (priestly circles, the Pharisees?) or were they commonly practiced among the Jewish people? These rites do not seem to have been such a common mark of Jewishness as some other matters that I discuss in detail.

1.6. *Methodological Considerations*

In the following readings of John's narrative, I rely on the three-world model presented in a number of writings by Kari Syreeni.[124] The three-world model is an attempt to create a holistic context which makes it possible to utilize and combine different methodological approaches that are mostly kept apart in the study of the New Testament. The model is not a new special method among other methods, but more a heuristic reading strategy that aims at understanding different aspects of a literary work in its social and historical context. As Petri Merenlahti notes, the model

> may not necessarily seem to be offering much that is radically new. Rather it systematizes in general terms what has traditionally been the task of modern biblical criticism: to study the text's linguistic form, theology and historical situation.[125]

The three-world model is based on a distinction among a literary work's *text world*, *symbolic world* and the *real world* behind the text. All of these aspects are more or less familiar to everyone working in Biblical scholarship. During recent decades, literary criticism has paid special attention to the New Testament writings as literary artefacts. In gospel studies, this interest has led to the formation of narrative criticism which, especially in its beginnings, challenged the traditional historical-critical way of reading the gospels.[126] This literary dimension is an important part of the three-world model, but this model also challenges the way literary approaches tend to play down the ideological dimension of texts by concentrating exclusively on their aesthetic form.[127] Much of the narrative-critical work done in the past two decades has analyzed the gospels as autonomous narrative worlds, as Petri Merenlahti and I have shown elsewhere.[128] The gospels as narratives thus became detached from their authors' ideological interests and from their historical contexts. In the case of

---

[124] Syreeni 1990, 1994, 1995, 1999. Cf. also Syreeni & Myllykoski *forthcoming*. Petri Luomanen (Luomanen 1998, 32–38) has applied the model to Matthew's view of salvation. For the evaluation of this model, see Merenlahti 2002, 119–124. Merenlahti also compares Syreeni's model to Vernon Robbins' socio-rhetorical theory which, in some respects, resembles Syreeni's model.

[125] Merenlahti 2002, 123.

[126] For narrative criticism, see Merenlahti & Hakola 1999, 13–48; Merenlahti 2002.

[127] Syreeni 1999, 108–112.

[128] See Merenlahti & Hakola 1999, 13–23.

purely fictional texts, this text-centered approach has its merits, even though interest in the author's ideological commitments and socio-cultural context has had a much more prominent role in general literature theory than could be deduced from the manner in which literary theory has been applied to the New Testament. But especially

> in argumentative texts, the text world is very close to the symbolic world, reflecting rather transparently (but never immediately) the author's intentions, judgments, set of values, cultural background, and so on.[129]

This means that the values of the narrator in such non-fictional narratives as the gospels reflect the values of the flesh and blood author.

As a matter fact, this view is not totally foreign to formalistic narrative theory. Narratological theories in the background of narrative criticism have emphasized the need to separate the act of writing from the act of narrating, and this has resulted in the theories that make a distinction between the real author, the implied author, and the narrator. While urging the need to make this distinction, some narratologists note that in 'factual' narratives, to which the gospels undoubtledly belong, this distinction is not at all clear. One of the leading narratologists, Gérard Genette, concludes that "the rigorous identification" of the author with the narrator defines factual narratives; in these narratives "the author assumes a full responsibility for the assertions of his narrative and, consequently, does not grant autonomy to any narrator."[130] In a similar vein, another narrative theorist, Dorrit Cohn, says that "the reader of a non-fictional narrative understands it to have a stable uni-vocal origin, that its narrator is identical to a real person."[131] This means that these narratives are more transparent concerning the aims of the author than purely fictional texts. They thus need to be seen as products of the historical and social context from which they emerged.[132]

The three-world model thus emphasizes that the text world is not all that the reader encounters in a text:

> Entering the deep levels of the text world, the reader approaches the entrance of the text's symbolic world. There is a grey zone where the text ceases to be a text, or where the interpreter lets the text go as

---

[129] Syreeni & Myllykoski *forthcoming*.
[130] Genette 1990, 764.
[131] Cohn 1990, 792.
[132] For the full discussion, see Merenlahti & Hakola 1999, 33–48.

an individual artefact and views it as an exponent of ideological concerns. The structures of the text world are literary; tied with language in general, the particular text type (genre) and the particular text. The symbolic world, as seen from the literary viewpoint, is a textual meta-level, but from a sociology-of-knowledge point of view it is a meta-textual level. The structures of the symbolic world/universe are not (or not only) linguistic but cognitive, emotional, social and behavioural.[133]

As this citation shows, the three-world model draws on the sociology-of-knowledge approach developed by Peter L. Berger and Thomas Luckmann.[134] The fact that the writer's values and convictions are called 'symbolic universe' and not 'theology' underscores the significance of these values in how people and groups construct their social identity. In the field of Johannine studies, Wayne Meeks in particular has helped to understand the christology of the gospel not only in theological terms but also in terms of sociology-of-knowledge. In his classic article, Meeks argued that the faith in Jesus was a crucial part of the Johannine believers' symbolic universe, which gave legitimation for the group's actual isolation from the society at large.[135] In a similar way, it is possible to take what the narrator says of the Jews as a reflection of the symbolic universe of the writer and his community; hence we can ask how the references to Jewishness contribute to the self-understanding of this community.

In the light of post-modern reading strategies 'the interdependence of the three worlds' may be a problem in the three-world model, as Petri Merenlahti notes:

> This interdependence allows none of the three worlds to have an immediate, observable autonomy—which, ultimately, puts the entire model in danger of collapse. For 'reality' can only be spoken of as *a social construct in terms of language*, which means (in Derridean terms) that 'There is nothing outside the text.' Alternatively, to view the same thing the other way round, as material phenomena, textual features are beyond our unlimited access and can only be conceived of as ideological constructs so that 'There are no texts, only readings.'[136]

---

[133] Syreeni & Myllykoski *forthcoming*. For a similar emphasis in the field of literature studies, see Suleiman 1976, 163 and especially 1993 (originally 1983). Suleiman speaks especially of a certain kind of authoritarian fiction, but her discussion could also be applied to the gospels. She considers these narratives from a formalistic point of view, but soon recognizes that formalistic analysis of these narratives involves different ideological aspects too.

[134] Berger & Luckmann 1967.

[135] Meeks 1972, 70.

[136] Merenlahti 2002, 122.

But although Merenlahti is aware of these theoretical problems, he
says that the model is useful in practice because it shows that if a
distinction between textuality, ideology and physical reality is not
made, "confusion is almost certain to follow." Thus

> the real edge of Syreeni's program lies in the critical question whether
> current interpretative practices actually succeed in observing the par-
> adigm that is *already* supposed to be in force. As we have seen, this
> has not been the case either with the traditional historical-critical meth-
> ods (that are insensitive to aspects of textuality and narrativity, and
> have only partially grasped the implications of viewing historical real-
> ity as a social construct), or with the more recent 'literary approaches'
> (that flirt with ahistorical models and fail properly to recognize aspects
> of ideology in texts).[137]

The three-world model, I believe, makes the shortcomings of earlier
approaches to John's views on the Jews and Jewishness clearer. On
the one hand, Bultmann and Gräßer operated on the level of just
two of the three worlds, the text world and the symbolic world,
when they took the Johannine Jews primarily as a theological symbol. They thus ignored the level of the real world reflected in the
text. On the other hand, Martyn's two-level reading strategy presupposes that because certain elements in the text do not match with
what we know of the historical Jesus and his time, they must match
with the historical reality at the time John was written. This position does not take into account that all historical reality in John is
mediated only through the creative imagination of the writer and
his community, i.e. through their symbolic universe. It is telling that
the name of Martyn's book, *History and Theology in the Fourth Gospel*,
suggests that Martyn approaches the presentation of John's Jews both
from the point of view of historical reality and the theology of the
writer. But in his reading of the narrative, Martyn soon forgets the
theological point of view and operates on the levels of the text world
and the real world only.

From the point of view of the three-world model,

> interpretations that are methodologically limited to one or two of these
> worlds are in fact making more or less hidden—thus uncontrolled—
> statements about them all.[138]

---

[137] Merenlahti 2002, 124.
[138] Syreeni & Myllykoski *forthcoming*.

This is especially the case when literary-oriented approaches present what should be seen as an expression of the author's symbolic world as just another part of the rhetoric of a text.[139] In these readings, the level of ideology is replaced with a blind spot. This is the case when the polemics against some Jewish groups in the gospels are seen only as a literary feature that does not have anything to do with any real-life Jewish groups.[140] The three-world model, however, consciously underlines that we should not ignore "the ideological aspect and pay no or insufficient attention to the *mediated* nature of the link between reality and texts, and between texts and their readers."[141]

The emphasis on the ideological aspect of the New Testament narratives calls forth the question concerning our own relationship to the ideology so clearly discernible in these texts. In my opinion, the New Testament gospels as literature come quite close to what Susan Suleiman calls ideological novels, where the author's ideological interests are so penetrating that they, by their very nature, call for a critical response from any reader who does not totally share these interests. In the same way, I suggest in my readings that the way the Johannine writer engages in the negation of Jewishness and urges his readers to share his polemic actually begs for a critical response to this polemic:

> The didactic orientation of the story as a series of events leading to an univocal meaning is here doubled by an interpretative discourse which, through its choice of metaphors or epithets, betrays (or reveals) its prejudices, hoping (or perhaps feigning to assume) that those prejudices will be shared by the reader. This is a risky game, to be sure, for a discourse that is too obviously prejudiced can provoke an actual reader (especially one who does not share the prejudices) into contesting the narrator's right to narrate and into rejecting the story itself as 'unfairly loaded.'[142]

---

[139] Cf. Syreeni 1995, 321–38.
[140] Cf. Merenlahti & Hakola 1999, 40–42. We present some critical remarks against what Mark Allan Powell says of Matthew's presentation of Jewish leaders, cf. Powell 1993, 66 and 88. For Powell's response, see Powell 2001, 119–120 and 219. Powell kindly allowed us to provide a short response to his criticism in his book, see Powell 2001, 237. We still insist in these remarks that Powell has missed the point of our argument, which was based on a heuristic distinction between fictional and non-fictional narratives. Cf. also Petri Merenlahti's response to Powell in Merenlahti 2002, 123 n. 10.
[141] Merenlahti 2002, 124.
[142] Suleiman 1993, 144.

When urging that we should take seriously the ideological aspect of
the New Testament and confront it critically, the three-world model
is again echoing the general state of scholarship. It is hardly a new
invention to combine ideological-critical interests with readings of
even sacred texts. At the level of hermeneutical theory, Paul Ricoeur
has joined critical concerns based on suspicion to a hermeneutical
interest in understanding; he has thus shown that critical attitude
and understanding are both essential parts of the larger hermeneutical
enterprise.[143] In the field of New Testament studies, feminist readings and—as the most recent newcomer—postcolonialistic readings
have combined critical awareness with the interpretation of the New
Testament.[144] But such undertakings should not be regarded as something totally new in the history of the field; rather, they can be seen
to continue the best traditions of historical-*critical* study of the Bible,
as is argued by Heikki Räisänen.[145]

I do not think that we should see an ideological-critical reading
of the New Testament as detrimental to the Christian faith.[146] It is
a great and even a dangerous mistake for Christians to leave the
critical evaluation of their tradition to outsiders. It could always be
argued that we should tone down those features in our readings that
point to the detachment from Jewishness because these features could
be taken out of their critical context and used for some unwarranted

---

[143] Ricoeur 1981, 63–100. For Ricoeur's contribution, see also Jeanrond 1991,
70–77. For ideological criticism as a part of New Testament hermeneutics, see
Schneiders 1999, 120–121 and 174–175. Even though Schneiders admits the relevance of ideological criticism as a part of her interpretational enterprise, she seems
to eschew this critical attitude when it comes to anti-Judaism in the New Testament.
Echoing many she says that the passage in John 8:39–47 and the saying concerning the devil and the Jews in 8:44 is not universal in meaning and thus not anti-
Jewish. Schneiders says that Jesus debates here with some Jewish leaders and speaks
to some particular Jews and "not in terms of their Jewish identity" (p. 164).
Unfortunately, this view does not provide a critical evaluation of the passage, as I
will show in my close analysis of it (pp. 177–214).

[144] For a reading of John 4:1–42 from the perspective of postcolonialism, see
Dube 1996, 37–59.

[145] Räisänen 2000, 9–28.

[146] For a different view, see von Wahlde 2000, 35: "The notion of a resistant reader
necessarily involves the view of those who find fault with the text of the gospel at
face value and who feel that it cannot be accepted as an expression of truth. The
type of resistant reading proposed by Reinhartz is one that a priori a Christian
would not engage in. Because the gospel of John focuses so exclusively on the understanding of Jesus, it has less to say to one who does not share those convictions."

anti-Jewish purposes.[147] But I believe that, in the present state of scholarship, a much more obvious danger is that the presence of these features in our texts is denied and thus their critical—or better *self*-critical—evaluation as well. Thus in the following readings I try to reveal the way in which John negates some basic aspects of Jewish identity so that we might become more aware of this dark side of this writing. I join here Colleen M. Conway, who has John's references to the Jews particularly in mind when she makes a plea for such readings of canonical literature that "implicate the values which are not ours but which can . . . be made to reveal themselves and can become contestable."[148] Conway also notes that, while such readings may challenge John's authority as the source of dogmatic truths, this challenge should be taken "in the interests of keeping the text socially relevant." I hope to be able to suggest this in my readings where I search for signs of a struggle for self-understanding that may not be all that different from our struggles to understand the Christian tradition in new ways in changing contexts.[149]

My following readings depart from many recent narrative-critical readings because I suggest that the close reading of the narrative makes it possible to see some obvious tensions and contradictions in John's portrayal of the Jews and Jewishness. Many recent narrative readings have gone in quite the opposite direction by emphasizing the narrative unity of the gospels, an emphasis that is understandable in light of the history of narrative criticism.[150] The emphasis on unity is not, of course, just a characteristic of many narrative-critical studies. Traditional scholarship has often had a harmonizing tendency when tracing the unified theology of the evangelist. This tendency is clearly evident in the most complete presentation of John's relationship with Judaism, Severino Pancaro's *The Law in the Fourth Gospel* (1975).[151] I try to show this in detail in my analysis where I suggest that some tensions and conflicting views in John's portrayal of Jewishness may be quite interesting because they give us a glimpse of the two worlds

---

[147] This possibility is raised by Bieringer & Pollefeyt & Vandecasteele-Vanneuville 2001b, 16–17.

[148] Conway 2002, 494–495.

[149] See my concluding remarks (pp. 238–242).

[150] For the full discussion, see Merenlahti & Hakola 1999, 23–33.

[151] For criticism of Pancaro, see also Kotila 1988, 5–6. In his work, Kotila presents a source- and redaction-historical analysis of the passages dealing with the law in John, and he succeeds in showing many tensions in John's view on the law.

behind the text.[152] I take the tensions in the narrative as suggestive of a discrepancy between the symbolic universe of the Johannine writer and his community and their situation in the real world. In this way, I try to take seriously the ambivalence in John's portrayal of the Jews and Jewishness.

---

[152] I do not explain the tensions in John's references to Jewishness by referring to the pre-history of the text, as many source- and redaction-critical studies have done. I do not in any way deny in my syncronic reading of the narrative that there are some marks of earlier traditions or later redactions in John, but I share the growing skepticism that we cannot separate with certainty the tradition from the redaction in the present gospel.

CHAPTER TWO

FALLACIES IN SCHOLARLY CONSENSUS

It is usual today to connect the Johannine references to the exclusion from the synagogue with the emergence of rabbinic Judaism after 70 C.E. According to a rabbinic legend, Johanan ben Zakkai managed to escape from the besieged Jerusalem during the first revolt and founded a new rabbinic school in Yavneh (in Greek Ἰαμνία).[1] In previous studies of rabbinic Judaism, this act was often taken as the establishment of a new authoritative body that replaced the priestly leadership which had governed the Jewish people before the destruction of the temple.[2] The new patriarchate and the rabbinic Sanhedrin in Yavneh were understood as leading forces in Jewish society, both in Palestine and in the Diaspora. The early rabbis were seen as the new spiritual leaders who exercized strict halakhic control over other Jews and guarded the unity of the people by dispelling deviant groups from the community.

Many Johannine scholars have become aware of some problems with the earlier view of rabbinic Judaism, but their views on the opponents of the Johannine community are still largely dependent on it.[3] Descriptions of the rabbinic movement are not an insignificant

---

[1] For the critical assessment of various versions of this story, see Schäfer 1979, 43–101.

[2] For the previous political-historical study of rabbinic Judaism, see Hezser 1997, 1–9. Hezser shows that Heinrich Graetz created in his *Geschichte der Juden* (Leipzig, 1863–1876) a paradigmatic history of such major institutions of Jewish self-goverment as the patriarchate and the sanhedrin. Graetz's model has been repeated with minor changes ever since in various studies.

[3] Cf. Martyn 1979, 52 n. 67 and 53 n. 68. These two notes contain discussion that is not found in the first edition of Martyn's book; this discussion shows that Martyn is aware, to a degree, of the criticism leveled against the traditional view of rabbinic Judaism. In spite of this, Martyn still refuses to make any essential change to the view he originally presented. He says that "the idealization [in rabbinic sources] does not materially affect the data" that "would seem reliably to indicate a remarkable growth of Jamnian authority precisely under Gamaliel II." Martyn refers here, for example, to an early work of Jacob Neusner (Neusner 1962, 125). In this work, Neusner's conclusions were much closer to the traditional views of the emergence of rabbinic Judaism than the views he has presented in his later works. Also Klaus Wengst has some hesitations concerning the influence and the authority

detail in the recent consensus but an elementary part of it. The early
rabbinic movement has provided a convenient foil for Johannine
scholars so that they have been able to describe the Johannine community as a Jewish minority group oppressed by the powerful and
hostile majority headed by zealous guardians of the national identity of the Jews. The Yavnean rabbis, especially R. Gamaliel II, have
been interpreted as the main instigators of those acts which made
the life of the Johannine Christians hard and that eventually led to
their traumatic exclusion from the synagogue community and even
to the death of some members of the community.[4] In the following
analysis, I claim that the problems that many scholars have noticed
in the traditional picture of the rabbinic movement should be taken
more seriously in the reconstruction of the situation of the Johannine
community.

Johannine scholars often describe the formation of the rabbinic
movement as the emergence of a kind of orthodoxy that could not
accept those who believed in Jesus as the Messiah and so expelled
them.[5] The circumstances after the destruction of the temple are said
to form the background for the situation described in John. In these
formative years, early rabbis helped the Jewish people through an
identity crisis which was caused by the destruction of the temple and
the cessation of its cult. The need for a new self-definition turned
out to be disastrous for the Johannine group.[6] A new Jewish identity was founded on the idea of the cultic purity of the people and

---

of early rabbis, but these hesitations have not affected his view of the rabbinic
movement in any significant way. Wengst 1992, 98. In his recent commentary
(Wengst I. 21–26), Wengst still repeats his early view.

[4] Schnackenburg I 146–148; Martyn 1979, 52 and *passim*; Pancaro 1975, 245–254;
Barrett 1975, 45–50, 68–69; Brown 1979, 22 and 66; Townsend 1979, 84–88;
Manns 1988, *passim*; Rensberger 1989, 25–26; D. M. Smith 1990b, 83; Ashton
1991, 157–158; Becker 56–58; Lindars 1992, 132–134; Wengst 1992, 71 and *passim*;
Dunn 1991, 158 and 1992, 199–200; J. T. Sanders 1993, 40, 58–67; Painter 1993,
30 and 77; Moloney 1993, 15–16 and 1996, 136; Casey 1996, 98–110; De Boer
1996a, 56; Magrath 2001, 42.

[5] Painter 1993, 30.

[6] Painter 1993, 77. Cf. also Kysar 1993, 121. To be sure, Kysar does not mention explicitly that he is talking about emerging rabbinic Judaism here. Kysar notes
(p. 120 n. 18) that "Martyn's earlier contention that the expulsion should be related
to the 'Twelfth Benediction' (the the *birkat ha-minim*) and the conference of rabbis
at Jamnia was countered vigorously and effectively by historical investigations."
However, the way Kysar describes a synagogue community that expelled Johannine
Christians corresponds to the picture of the Yavnean rabbis as the architects of a
new Jewish identity.

the strict observance of the law.[7] Early rabbinic leaders who affirmed this identity are characterized as vehement defenders of the law who, after gaining power, coerced the people to follow their form of Jewish religion.[8] In doing so, they did not hesitate to take steps that were aimed against such dissident groups as the Johannine community.[9] Scholars are quite explicit that it was the confession of Jesus as the Messiah and not some other reason that provoked the hostility of the new Jewish establishment and the exclusion of believers; this is also what the narrator says in John 9:22.[10] Scholars also often understand the words in John 9:22, "For the Jews *had already agreed* (συνετέθειντο) that anyone who confessed Jesus to be the Messiah would be put out of the synagogue", as an indication of a formal and conscious policy taken up by the early leaders of rabbinic Judaism against the Johannine community.[11]

According to many scholars, the exclusion from the synagogue was not a separate act but reflects the hostile atmosphere surrounding the Johannine Christians. Scholars may speak of "the anger of the Jewish establishment,"[12] or describe the rabbinic leaders in John's environment as "implacably hostile" and "determined that Christianity should not gain a sizable following" in their locale.[13] Many scholars think that the consequences of this hatred for those who believed in Jesus were not restricted to the religious sphere of life. Scholars repeatedly refer to the same rabbinic texts that they take as a direct reflection of the social circumstances of the Johannine community. The story of R. Eliezer's arrest for heresy in *t. Ḥul.* 2:24 is cited as evidence that it was even forbidden to listen to the words spoken by a Christian in John's environment.[14] Commercial interaction with heretics is prohibited in *t. Ḥul.* 2:20–21, and this text is used to show how severe were the social and also economic consequences the exclusion from the synagogue had for John's group.[15] The situation

---

[7] Lindars 1992, 132.
[8] D. M. Smith 1990, 83; Ashton 1991, 158.
[9] Rensberger 1989, 25.
[10] Martyn 1977, 158; Lindars 1992, 133; Wengst 1992, 77; Painter 1993, 72; Moloney 1994, 15–16; Rensberger 1999, 130.
[11] Martyn 1979, 38; Lindars 1992, 133; Horbury 1998, 100.
[12] Ashton 1991, 140.
[13] Rensberger 1989, 43.
[14] Barrett 1975, 69; Martyn 1979, 90. In this connection Martyn also refers to Justin Martyr's Dialogue with Trypho (38.1).
[15] Wengst 1992, 101–102. Wengst is followed by Rensberger 1989, 26–27. Cf.

is seen as threatening not only for those who openly confessed Jesus
as the Messiah but also for those who were connected to them (cf.
John 9:18–23).[16]

Numerous scholars also claim that the Jewish persecution of the
Johannine Christians did not stop after they were excluded from
their Jewish community. The excommunication did not prevent some
synagogue members from converting to the new faith, and therefore
some of those who were proselytizing among their fellow Jews were
arrested and executed by the Jewish authorities.[17] Thus Jesus' words
in John 16:2, "They will put you out of the synagogues. Indeed, an
hour is coming when those who kill you will think that by doing so
they are offering worship to God," are taken as a reflection of the
mortal danger which the Johannine believers faced.[18]

Leaning on recent studies of the emergence and nature of rabbinic Judaism, I call into the question the idea that the Fourth Gospel
reflects a conflict between the Johannine community and the emerging rabbinic Judaism. I have deliberately delayed the discussion about
the alleged connection between John and the *birkat ha-minim*, the twelfth
of the Eighteen Benedictions, in order to emphasize that it is not
only this question that is problematic in recent reconstructions of
John's historical context. It is the whole above-sketched picture that
needs to be reconceived. Many Johannine scholars have admitted that
the *birkat ha-minim* may not have any connection to John, but they
still argue that other elements in the portrayal are correct. It should
be noted, however, that if the connection between the *birkat ha-minim*
and the Fourth Gospel is denied, the Fourth Gospel remains the only
source that suggests that those who confessed Jesus as the Messiah
were expelled from the synagogue by the official decree. It is thus
proper to begin the assessment of current scholarly consensus by
demonstrating why the *birkat ha-minim* should not be linked with John.

---

also J. T. Sanders 1993, 63 and 67. Sanders says that the stories in *t. Hul.* 2:20–24
"make sense only against a background in which Christians lived among other Jews
in something of a pariah status."

[16] Wengst 1992, 123; Rensberger 1989, 48; Cf. also Becker 57.

[17] Martyn 1979, 66, 81; Painter 1993, 425–426; De Boer 1996a, 58–63.

[18] Rensberger 1989, 79 and 128; Lindars 1992, 148; Wengst 1992, 85; Zumstein
2001, 470–471.

2.1. *The* birkat ha-minim *and Other Suggested Parallels to John*

According to *b. Ber.* 28b–29, Samuel the Small composed one of the Eighteen Benedictions (*ʿamidah*) in Yavneh at the request of R. Gamaliel II; this benediction (the *birkat ha-minim*) is often quoted as evidence for the anti-Christian steps taken by the Yavnean rabbis.[19] In the same talmudic passage, it is also stated that Samuel the Small forgot the wording of the benediction in the following year; it is stated that other rabbis did not remove him from his post as a reader of the prayer because he had composed the prayer and was thus not suspected of *minuth*. This was an exception to the rule cited as a saying of Rab Judah in the name of Rab: "If a reader made a mistake in any other benedictions, they do not remove him, but if in the benediction of the *Minim*, he is removed, because we suspect him of being a *Min*" (cf. also *y. Ber.* 5:3). This text is taken to show that the original purpose for the addition of the *birkat ha-minim* to the *ʿamidah* was the detection of those members of the congregation who had heretic beliefs. The reading of the daily prayer in the synagogue is understood as a test for those suspected of being *minim* because it is unlikely that they would have said a prayer in which their destruction was wished for. If a male member of the community faltered when reciting the prayer, the rabbis removed him from the readership and finally excluded him from the synagogue fellowship.[20]

The actual text of the *birkat ha-minim* is not found in rabbinic literature, but the text found in the Cairo Genizah comprises a version that is often regarded as the earliest extant version of the benediction:[21]

---

[19] Cf. Ashton 1991, 11. Ashton refers to M. von Aberle who in 1861 already connected the *birkat ha-minim* to the Johannine situation. For later scholarship, see Horbury 1998, 67–71.

[20] Cf. Martyn 1979, 59–62. Cf. also Alexander 1992, 10. Alexander discusses how the benediction could have served as an instrument of new rabbinic orthodoxy. His discussion is much more nuanced than that of Martyn, but in light of the following arguments, it is unlikely whether the *birkat ha-minim* has ever had a great role in establishing orthodoxy among the Jews. The whole question of 'rabbinic orthodoxy' should be reconsidered, at least in the case of the first centuries C.E.

[21] A medieval fragment containing the *birkat ha-minim* was published by S. Schechter in 1898. For different versions of the benediction, see Schäfer 1975, 57–59. The following translation is taken from Kimelman 1981, 226.

For the apostates let there be no hope. And let the arrogant government be speedily uprooted in our days. Let the *noṣrim* and the *minim*
be destroyed in a moment. And let them be blotted out of the Book
of Life and not be inscribed together with the righteous. Blessed art
thou, O Lord, who humblest the arrogant.

During the recent decades there has been an intense discussion about
the original wording and function of the benediction.[22] It is not certain that the original wording of the *birkat ha-minim* is that found in
the Cairo Genizah fragment. It is almost certain that the term *noṣrim*,
which may refer to Christians or Jewish Christians in certain rabbinic passages, did not belong to the earliest versions of the prayer.[23]
In those versions of the prayer where the term *noṣrim* appears, it
always precedes *minim*. In spite of this, the benediction is always
referred to in rabbinic literature as the *birkat ha-minim*, not as the
birkat ha-noṣrim, which speaks against the wide use of *noṣrim* in the
oldest versions of the prayer. Furthermore, the term *noṣrim* does not
appear in the early rabbinic sources but only in the Babylonian
Talmud.[24] It is likely that it was introduced to the twelfth benediction at a later stage, even though it may be impossible to say when.[25]
Thus the discussion whether *noṣrim* refers to some specific Jewish-
Christian groups or to Christians in general is irrelevant as we try
to assess the alleged significance of the benediction for Jewish-Christian
relations at the end of the first century C.E.[26] It is more important

---

[22] See Schäfer 1975, 55–61; Stemberger 1977, 16–19; Kimelman 1981, 226–244;
Finkel 1981, 231–246; Maier 1982, 136–141; Katz 1984, 63–76; Van der Horst
1994, 363–368; Setzer 1994, 87–91; Wilson 1995, 179–183.

[23] For detailed arguments, see Kimelman 1981, 233–234; Finkel 1981, 236–238;
Katz 1984, 65–69.

[24] Cf. Maier 1978, 64, 110, 234–235, 270 and 1982, 158–168; Kimelman 1981,
233–234; Pritz 1988, 95; Zalcman 1991, 411.

[25] Cf. Urbach 1981, 288. Urbach says that Christians were included among the
minim in the twelfth benediction after the Bar Cochba revolt, and to emphasize
their inclusion, the *noṣrim* were mentioned explicitly. However, a later date for the
inclusion of this term may be more likely. See, for example, Van der Horst 1984,
368. Van der Horst suggests, on the basis of Jerome's references to Nazarenes, that,
"probably not long before Jerome's time, *notsrim*, in the sense of Christians in general, was added to the twelfth benediction."

[26] Pace De Boer 1996b, 199 and 1998, 251. De Boer notes that the *noṣrim* were
mentioned only by the Church Fathers who knew Palestine well, where the *noṣrim*
presented a threat to rabbinic authority and orthodoxy. From this de Boer concludes that "the benediction as reformulated by the rabbis in Jamnia, a town in
Palestine, may well have referred to *Notzrim* from the start" (1998, 251). However,
this conclusion is not supported by Talmudic tradition in which the word *noṣrim*

to find out the meaning of the term *minim* that appears more frequently in rabbinic literature.

In some rabbinic texts, the *minim* seem to be Jewish Christians or Christians in general (e.g. *t. Ḥul.* 2:24). From these kinds of texts, it has sometimes been concluded that in those texts where it is not self-evident who the *minim* are the term must refer to Christians.[27] But in many passages the *minim* are neither Christians in general nor Jewish Christians. Some texts attribute clearly non-Christian beliefs to the *minim*; it is said, for example, that the *minim* deny the resurrection of the dead (*b. Sanh.* 90b), believe only in one world (*m. Ber.* 9:5) or worship idols (*t. Ḥul.* 1,1). Hence the term does not refer exclusively to Christians of any kind or to any other specific heretical group. Rather, the term covers different types of heretics.[28]

It seems that the rabbis were not interested in defining exactly who the *minim* are. Nor did they give any definite list of those beliefs or practices which make a person a *min*. As Richard Kalmin says, rabbinic sources "give us rough stereotypes and sketches drawn in extremely broad strokes rather than finely nuanced portraits or scientifically precise descriptions."[29] Occasionally actions attributed to a *min* in one text appear in another text as actions of an anonymous person who is not called *min*.[30] In some texts, the dialogue

---

appears only in the Babylonian sources but not in the Palestinian ones. Furthermore, de Boer's use of certain rabbinic passages as evidence for the early use of the word is not convincing. A passage in *b. Taʿan.* 27b says that certain temple officials did not fast on Sunday "because of the Nazarenes." But it is highly uncertain whether this saying, attributed to R. Yohanan (third century C.E.), really reflects pre-70 conditions, as de Boer claims. For the problems with this view, see Maier 1982, 164–168. It is noteworthy that there is no reference to *noṣrim* in *m. Taʿan.* 4:3, even though the fast on the first day of the week is mentioned; the reason given for fasting on this day is practical: "They did not fast . . . on Sunday, so as not to go forth from resting and enjoyment to travail and fasting, and so perish" (Neusner's translation). It is not very likely that a Jewish-Christian sect could have had so great an influence in the pre-70 Jewish society that the official practice in the temple would have been adapted according to their beliefs. Furthermore, we do not have any evidence that Sunday replaced the Sabbath as the day of rest and worship among early Jewish Christians in Palestine. For a detailed discussion, see Turner 1982, 124–137. Therefore, if *b. Taʿan.* 27b and some other passages (e.g. *b. ʿAbod. Zar.* 6a) refer to Christians or Jewish Christians at all, they must stem from a later period when Christianity was a notable factor in the society where these passages were formulated. Thus Herford 1903, 172; Kimelman 1981, 241–243.

[27] Herford 1903, 365–381.

[28] Thus Finkel 1981, 238–239; Maier 1982, 137; Katz 1984, 72–73; Miller 1993, 401 and 1999, 151; S. Stern 1994, 110–11; Hayes 1998, 260 n. 29.

[29] Kalmin 1994, 169 and 1999, 72. Cf. also Miller 1993, 401.

[30] See Miller 1993, 396–397.

between the rabbis and the *minim* may reflect discussions within rabbinic Judaism where unacceptable beliefs are externalized and dis-
owned by attributing them to the *minim*.[31] Moreover, those texts that
show that actual contacts took place between the rabbis and the
minim tell mostly of an individual *min* and an individual rabbi, not
well-organized rabbinic reaction to clearly defined heretical groups.[32]

It is thus clear that the way the rabbis dealt with the *minim* is
different from the way the Christian Church Fathers dealt with the
groups they considered heretical.[33] While the conflict with different
heresies was crucial for the self-definition of the early church, the
descriptions of the *minim* in rabbinic literature are far too miscella-
neous and unsystematic to have given them a great role in rabbinic
self-definition.[34] The stories about the *minim* do not suggest in any
way that the rabbis had a large-scale program to purify the people
from deviant beliefs and groups who held those beliefs.[35]

The possibility remains, however, that some Jewish Christians were
included among the *minim* in the prayer. The question whether Jewish
Christians were among those denounced in the prayer at the end of
the first century cannot be solved only by analyzing the use of the
term in the rabbinic writings. Some Church Fathers refer to the custom of the Jews of cursing Christians in their synagogues, which
could lend support to the view that, from the second century C.E.
on, some Christians may have been included by the prayer.[36] But
even this view is not without problems.[37] The question of how promi-

---

[31] This is suggested in the case of *b. Sanh.* 90b–91a by Hayes 1998, 274.
[32] Cf. Miller 1993, 400; 1999, 151.
[33] Cohen 1980, 3; Goodman 1996, 507.
[34] Cf. Goodman 1983, 105 and 1996, 506 n. 23.
[35] Goodman 1996, 508. For a different view, see Alexander 1992, 8–9. Alexander
compares other pejorative terms found in the different versions of the *birkat ha-minim*
to *minim* and concludes: "These terms are general and uncontentious in a way that
minim is not. . . . The term marks a significant attempt to draw a distinction between
orthodoxy and heresy. . . . In condemning the *minim* the Rabbis were in effect condemning all who were not of their party: they were setting themselves up as the
custodians of orthodoxy."
[36] Justin *Dial.* 137; Epiphanius *Pan.* 29.9.2; Jerome *Epist.* 112.13; *Comm. Isa.* 5.18;
49.7; 52.5.
[37] See Thornton 1987, 419–431. According to Thornton, there is no indication
that the imperial authorities regarded Jews as regularly cursing Christians in their
synagogues in the 4th and 5th centuries. Thornton also emphasizes how sparse and
dubious the references of the Church Fathers are. Furthermore, it is difficult to
connect the alleged malediction on Christians in the *birkat ha-minim* to the complaints
of some Church Fathers about the attendance of Christians at the synagogue. For

nent Jewish Christians were among those denounced in the *birkat ha-minim* in the Yavnean era must be assessed in the light of what can be said of the relevance of Jewish Christians and their beliefs to formative Judaism.[38]

It is sometimes understood that formative Judaism defined itself in relation to early Christianity just like Christianity defined itself in relation to Judaism, its mother religion. It is claimed that emerging Christianity posed a threat that compelled early rabbis to define the boundaries of Judaism, a procedure that is reflected, for example, in the *birkat ha-minim*.[39] This view, however, is not supported by early rabbinic literature.[40] We should not retroject later historical circumstances when Christianity became a major political and religious

these complaints, see Kimelman 1981, 239–240. How could the synagogue attract many Christians if they were cursed during worship? And how could the Jews welcome Christians in their synagogues and at the same time denounce them? For an answer to these questions, see Horbury 1998, 101–102. According to him, the malediction was one of those measures that formed "the precondition under which Christian visits to synagogue . . . could be tolerated or even encouraged by the Jewish authorities." Furthermore, "the condemnation of Christianity in the Prayer would attest to Jews and gentile sympathizers the exclusive rights of Judaism in the biblical inheritance, and knowledge of the attitude which this practice expressed might shake the visitor's confidence in the Christian surrogate." As Wilson (1995, 366 n. 47) notes, "this somewhat contorted logic might make some sense from the Jewish point of view, but none at all from the Christian point of view."

[38] Scholars assess differently how high Jewish Christians were on the agenda of the Yavnean rabbis. Kimelman (1981, 232) says that the *birkat ha-minim* "was aimed at Jewish sectarians among whom Jewish Christians figured prominently." Other scholars do not give such a great role to Jewish Christians. Schäfer 1975, 60: "Mit Sicherheit richtete sich die *birkat ha mînîm* jedenfalls nicht ausschliesslich gegen Judenchristen bzw. (später) Christen und war deswegen auch kein 'Mittel zur völligen Scheidung der beiden Religionen.' Eine solche Festlegung . . . überschätzt die Bedeutung der christlichen Religion für das Judentum Palästinas um die Wende des 1. zum 2. nachchristlichen Jahrhundert." Stemberger 1977, 17: "Daß die Formulierung der *birkat ha-minim* durch Schmuel den Kleinen sich primär gegen die Christen gerichtet hat, ist aus historischen Gründen unwahrscheinlich. Die (Juden-)Christen dürften im Einflußbereich Jabne kaum so bedeutend gewesen sein, daß sich die jüdischen Gelehrten speziell damit befassen mußten." Maier 1982, 141: "Es ist möglich daß die rabbinen auch Judenchristen zu den Minim rechneten, doch weisen die meisten *mînîm*-Stellen darauf hin, daß nichtchristliche Personen gemeint waren." Katz 1984, 74: "It was directed against all Jews who after 70 were not in the Pharisaic/rabbinic camp, *not only against Jewish Christians*" (italics original).

[39] Barrett 1975, 68–69.

[40] For the critical study of rabbinic material allegedly referring to Jesus or to Christians, see Maier 1978 and 1982. Maier concludes that there is no tannaitic Jesus-passage in the rabbinic corpus (1978, 268). The passages referring unambiguously to Christians are few (1982, 206–208). Although Maier may push his arguments too far in some cases (cf. Goldenberg 1982), his conclusions are a sound warning against overstating the relevance of early Christianity for rabbinic self-understanding.

factor back to the earliest rabbinic literature that is surprisingly silent about Christians and their beliefs.[41] Christian views may have shaped some rabbinic discussions from the fourth century onwards, but we have no clear references to Christians in the Mishnah, and there are only scattered references in other works that were edited before the fourth century.[42] This should make us cautious about thinking that Jewish Christians were high on the agenda of early rabbis.

The vague use of the term *minim* in the rabbinic sources makes it unlikely that the prayer could have functioned as a test that revealed those who were *minim*. If a male who was appointed to lead the prayer did not consider himself a *min* in advance, he would not have seen himself included in this general and unspecific category and would not have had any problems in reading the prayer. The *birkat ha-minim* could function as a test only if it used definite terms but this was not the case.[43] If, however, it was clear and open who were considered heretics, there would not have been any need for a bizarre probation in front of the community. Why would the Yavnean rabbis, who are described as powerful and resolute leaders of the people, have used such circuitous means for reaching their goals?

Furthermore, even if we took at face value the rabbinic story that tells of the function of the prayer, the prayer does not carry the sense of excommunication. The rabbinic passage cited above (*b. Ber.* 28b–29a) says only that the one who faltered while praying was removed from his post as a reader of the prayer, not from the synagogue or the community. Moreover, this step concerned only the male in question, but it seems that women, slaves and children who believed in Jesus would never have been in danger because they were not asked to

---

[41] See Katz 1984, 47; Wilson 1995, 170. Cf. also Kimelman 1999, 302: "Christian literature is so full of references to Jews and Judaism that the phrase *obsessed with* may be in order. In contrast, the data on Christianity in rabbinic literature is comparably sparse" (italics original).

[42] Cf. Neusner 1987b, 4–7.

[43] Thus Kimelman 1981, 227; Katz 1984, 74–75; Setzer, 1994, 90. For a different view, see Alexander 1992, 9–10. Alexander thinks that the above argument has "some force," but he still says that "anyone opposed to the rabbis would have felt threatened" by the benediction. But this view overestimates the authority of the rabbis over non-rabbinic Jews. To be sure, Alexander seems to be aware of the limitations of the authority and the influence of the rabbis, but this does not prevent him from presenting them as the guardians of new orthodoxy. He admits that "the rabbinic orthodoxy" was not established before the third century (p. 3). De Boer (1998, 251) does not take seriously Alexander's hesitations concerning the establishment of rabbinic authority in his discussion of the matter.

lead the daily *'amidah*.[44] Thus it is clear that the *birkat ha-minim* could never have functioned as an effective tool for excommunicating a *group* of believers from the synagogue.[45]

The dating of rabbinic legends and practices should make us cautious about connecting the *birkat ha-minim* to the first century situation. Even though it has become more and more evident that the attributions of sayings in the rabbinic sources to different rabbis are often suspect historically, most scholars have accepted the stories about Samuel the Small in *b. Ber.* 28b–29a and in *y. Ber.* 5:3 as a historical account of the original purpose of the benediction. But we cannot simply be sure of the accuracy of these stories.[46] In this case, we must be particularly cautious with historical conclusions because the ruling "if a reader made a mistake in any other benedictions, they do not remove him, but if in the benediction of the *Minim*, he is removed, because we suspect him of being a *Min*" is not directly connected to the Yavnean era but is cited in *b. Ber.* 28b–29a as a saying of Rab (third century).[47] In *y. Ber.* 5:3, a different, anonymous, ruling appears which says that anyone who skipped the second ("Who resurrects the dead"), the twelfth ("Who humbles the arrogant") and the fourteenth ("Who builds Jerusalem") is a heretic. This is said to contradict the ruling attributed to R. Joshua b. Levi (first half of the third century) according to which the leader of the *'amidah* was not made to repeat the prayer even though he skipped two or three blessings. These discussions show that the rulings concerning the daily reading of the *'amidah* were not fixed immediately in the Yavnean period but were still debated centuries later.

Moreover, there seems to be no actual story of someone faltering while reciting the benediction and how this *min* was removed from the post (*b. Ber.* 28b–29a states only that Samuel the Small was *not* removed from his post). Hence, the rabbinic rule preserved in *b. Ber.* 28b–29a may have been a theoretical possibility rather than a well-established rabbinic practice. The original function of the *birkat ha-minim* may not have been the detection and expulsion of heretics but rather the establishment of the self-identity of rabbinic circles in the

---

[44] Thus Setzer 1994, 90–91.

[45] Maier 1982, 139.

[46] Only rarely have scholars raised doubts concerning the historical reliability of these stories. This is done by Setzer 1994, 90; Wilson 1995, 362 n. 3.

[47] Maier 1982, 139–140.

face of perceived external threats.[48] It seems that the connection of the *birkat ha-minim* to the Jewish-Christian schism has hindered the proper understanding of the prayer in its rabbinic context.[49]

The historical development of the daily *ʿamidah* is seldom considered, as it is claimed that the *birkat ha-minim* is relevant to Jewish-Christian relations at the end of the first century. It has long been taken for granted that the public daily prayers in the synagogue were already an obligatory and established custom during the Second Temple Period. Yet it has become more and more evident that this view is untenable because the evidence for such prayers in Palestine is scarce.[50] As different sources speak about daily prayers in this period, they most often refer to private prayers at home.[51] We have evidence of daily communal prayers in some sectarian settings, for example, in the Qumran community, but not of wide-spread and regular prayers in synagogues.[52] Even though the content of the *ʿamidah* has many points in common with the pre-70 traditions, we have reasons to believe that the practice of common daily prayers was initiated by the Yavnean rabbis, and especially by R. Gamaliel II.[53] Many discussions about the details of prayers that are connected to R. Gamaliel and his colleagues become intelligible if we assume that the public daily prayer was a rather new development. It is probable that obligatory and public prayers in synagogues only gradually

[48] Thus Finkel 1981, 246; Maier 1982, 140; Wilson 1995, 180.
[49] Thus Wilson 1995, 180.
[50] For the discussion, see L. Levine 1987, 20 and 2000, 151.
[51] The situation may have been different in the Diaspora where many synagogues were called προσευχή. See L. Levine 1987, 20; Flesher 2001, 127. Flesher notes that even in the Diaspora "specific evidence indicating praying in the synagogues is rather scarce." He explains this by saying that "prayer seems to have been so common that it often went unremarked in our sources." But prayer may not have been the main religious activity in Diaspora synagogues either. Cf. Modrzejewski 1995, 95. "The principal form of the synagogue worship, in Egypt as in Judea, was the reading of the Torah, not prayer in the proper sense of the term, but nonetheless a form of veneration."
[52] For the discussion of the relevant sources, see E. P. Sanders 1990, 72–77; 1992, 197; 1999, 10–12; L. Levine 1987, 19–20; 2000 151–158. Cf. also Goodman 1983, 86. Goodman notes that "so far as the evidence goes," public prayer was not connected to synagogues before 70 C.E." See also Cohen 1999b, 323. Contrary to his earlier view, Cohen is no longer persuaded that "the notion of 'statutory prayer' really derives from the Second Temple Period, or that prayer ever established itself as an inherent part of the liturgy of the second temple." For the view that sees prayer as an elementary part of the synagogue liturgy before 70 C.E., see Runesson 2001, 342–350.
[53] Thus L. Levine 1999a, 134–139; 2000, 510–519. Cf. also Reif 1999, 350–351.

evolved into a final form, and that the number and the content of the benedictions in the ʿamidah were still debated in the Yavnean period.[54] The daily reading of the ʿamidah could hardly have functioned as any kind of test for the detection of heretics, if the public daily prayers were not an established practice in synagogues.

The above discussion shows that the birkat ha-minim should not be understood as excommunication from the synagogue. It should also be noted that the Johannine excommunication passages do not suggest in any way that this act was connected to synagogue prayers. Many Johannine scholars today admit that the birkat ha-minim should not be connected to the situation of the Johannine community.[55] But if the connection between the birkat ha-minim and John is denied, John is unique in his claim that those who confessed Jesus as the Messiah were expelled from the synagogue by official decree.[56] The Greek word ἀποσυνάγωγος is unknown in extant sources before John, and it is also difficult to find parallels to the practice of expulsion in earlier or contemporary Jewish sources.

Some biblical passages seem to refer to the exclusion from the holy people (Ezra 10:8), but we do not have any direct evidence before the destruction of the second temple that a member of the Israelite people or a deviant group would have been cut out from the main body of the community. The Jewish community was religiously very heterogeneous, and there was no central authority that could have carried out the expulsion in practice.[57] The development of bans is closely connected to the emergence of sects that tried to draw strict boundaries between themselves and the rest of the

---

[54] Cf. Kimelman 1997, 185; Reif 1999, 350; L. Levine 1999a, 135.

[55] See Meeks 1985, 102–103; Rensberger 1989, 26 and 1999, 129; D. M. Smith 1990, 86; Kysar 1993, 120 n. 18. See, however, de Boer 1998, 249–251. De Boer is aware that "much about this famous benediction is disputed" but still writes that "with this benediction the rabbis effectively sought to exclude Nazoreans (and other minim) from participation in synagogue life." Cf. also Horbury 1998, 100–101. Horbury notes that the benediction "hardly suffices of itself" to bring about exclusion from the synagogue. Following Lindars (1992, 132–134), Horbury suggests that "the Jamnian regulation simply reinforced an earlier, more drastic exclusion of Christians, although the imprecise dating of both the gospel and Gamaliel II's ordinance leaves open the view that the two measures were contemporaneous." This view ignores the lack of any positive evidence for the exclusion of Christians, and it is also based on the wrong presupposition concerning the character and power of the rabbinic movement.

[56] Setzer 1994, 92.

[57] Thus Hare 1967, 50; Forkman 1972, 104; Hunzinger 1980, 161.

society in the late Second Temple Period.[58] The documents of the
Qumran community bear witness to a system of both temporary and
limited exclusion from community life and total and final exclusion
from membership of the community.[59] But scholars have been rightly
hesitant to connect the detailed and complicated discussion in the
documents to the Johannine exclusion passages.[60]

Scholars have also been quite unanimous that the bans discussed
by the rabbis are not real parallels to the excommunication passages
in John.[61] The dating of these bans is not the only problem. Their
nature is also far from the situation described in John. First, bans
were levelled against individuals, not a group of heretics, and mostly
against an individual sage who did not accept the opinion of the
majority.[62] Second, the aim of bans was not to exclude a disobedi-
ent person from the community but, on the contrary, to bring her
or him back under the authority of the rabbinic majority.[63] Third,
the cases that tell of bans show that there was not a central authority that could have enforced bans within the community. Bans were
used by a variety of people, but they were not very effective. They
did not count as a great threat to the banned person unless she or
he acknowledged the authority of the rabbi who issued the ban.[64]

---

[58] Hare 1967, 51; Hunzinger 1980 161–163. According to Horbury (1998, 43–66),
excommunication was not a sectarian practice but a recognized custom among the
Jews in the Second Temple Period. Horbury himself acknowledges that the evidence for this view is "sparse" (p. 59, cf. also p. 66: "not plentiful"). Horbury mentions only two actual examples in support of his view, namely Jos. *Ant.* 11.340,
346f. and 3 Macc 2:33 (pp. 51–53). But these passages hardly prove that general
exclusion was an established practice. For example, in *Ant.* 11.346f. Josephus tells
how the Samaritans accepted apostates from Jerusalem who said that they had been
"unjustly expelled" (ἐκβάλλω, v. l. ἐγκεκλῆσθαι "accused"). Josephus also calls the
inhabitants of Shechem "the apostates from the Jewish nation" (*Ant.* 11.340). But
these mentions are part of Josephus' anti-Samaritan bias and not historically reliable; Josephus' discredits the Samaritans by suggesting that "only those who had
fallen away from the true community and its God-given practices and way of life
could find refuge among the Samaritans." Coggins 1987, 262–263. Horbury seems to
presuppose that there was a "general Jewish body" that regularly excluded apostates
from the people. This gives a very monolithic view of the Jewish community in the
Second Temple Period. For criticism of Horbury, see also Visotzky 2000, 781.

[59] 1QS 6:24–7:25, 8:16–9:2; CD 9:21, 23; 12:4–6; 14:20–21; 20:1–8. Different
copies of manuscripts show that there was great variety in the constitutional rules
of the community, and the question may be raised whether all these rules reflect
the actual practice of the community. See Metso 1998, 186–210.

[60] Schrage 1964, 848–845; Martyn 1979, 44 n. 55.

[61] Strack-Billerbeck IV 329–330; Martyn 1979, 44.

[62] Thus Katz 1984, 49 n. 26. Cf. also Cohen 1984, 42.

[63] Katz 1984, 49; Wilson 1995, 179.

[64] Hezser 1997, 147 and 394.

The Jewish sources discussed above do not help to explain the Johannine references to the final excommunication of Christian believers from the synagogue. John is the only witness to this kind of practice. To be sure, our knowledge of ancient Jewish practices is sparse. Thus the lack of evidence for this practice in other sources does not necessarily mean that excommunication could not have happened somewhere. Many scholars have suggested that John refers to a local and limited phenomenon that is otherwise unattested in our sources.[65] But the little we know about the nature of Jewish society in general and the rabbinic movement in particular after 70 C.E. does not support the view that some Jewish groups could expel other groups from the Jewish community. The lack of explicit evidence for excommunication is only an indication of much more serious problems in recent reconstructions that connect the situation of the Johannine community to the emerging rabbinic Judaism. In the light of recent rabbinic studies, these reconstructions misunderstand the nature and power of the early rabbinic movement.

2.2. *John and Formative Rabbinic Judaism*

During recent years, it has become evident that the traditional view of the emergence and authority of rabbinic Judaism is misleading and based on uncritical readings of rabbinic sources.[66] These sources do not give an unbiased view of the Jewish world but reflect the interests of the rabbis, as William Scott Green has said:

> The documents thus present the restricted discourse of a small number of men who appear primarily engaged in observing, discussing, and analyzing ideas, opinions, and behaviors, sometimes those recounted in Scripture, but most often those promoted within the Rabbinic group itself. Rabbinic writing addresses rabbinic specialists; it is a parochial literature wholly obsessed with itself. . . . It follows that the documents' picture of the world and of the rabbis themselves necessarily is over-determined, manipulated, and incomplete. Rabbinic editors offer no

---

[65] Rensberger 1989, 26; D. M. Smith 1990, 86; Lindars 1991, 133; Setzer 1994, 93; Wilson 1995, 175; Mcgrath 2001, 42.

[66] In the following, I cite several scholars who use different methodologies. I do not claim that they are unanimous on everything. As far as I can see, however, they all think that the rabbis were not the leading group among the Jews, at least in the first two centuries C.E. Opinions differ, however, as to how the situation of the rabbis changed after the compilation of the Mishnah in the third century. For recent studies, see Hezser 1997, 23–36.

comprehensive and nuanced report, no mirror image, of their colleagues and precursors. They produce instead a vision of their world
as they imagined it and described it to themselves.[67]

The stories about the founding of the Yavnean academy are hardly
accurate as such, even though they may contain some historical reminiscences. The story about Vespasian and R. Johanan ben Zakkai
is a foundation legend of the rabbinic movement that may have been
modelled after the scriptural story of Jeremiah and the Babylonian
king Nebuchadnezzar.[68] Some rabbinic traditions see the Yavnean
academy as the replacement of the Jerusalem sanhedrin and R. Johanan
as the successor of the high priest. These traditions follow a stereo-
typical literary structure and are most probably later reflections created
to give the impression that the Yavnean court had the authority to
establish new rules for the people after the destruction of the temple.[69]

The origins of the rabbinic movement have traditionally been traced
to the Pharisaic group in the Second Temple Period. This view is
not without problems, but it is nevertheless probable that at least
some rabbis were also Pharisees, even though other groups in pre-
70 Judaism may also have contributed to the formation of the rabbinic movement.[70] During recent decades there has been an intense
discussion about the nature and influence of the pre-70 Pharisees.[71]
There are still many open questions in this discussion, but the traditional view that the Pharisees were the most dominant group among the
Jewish people has been severely challenged. The traditional picture
of the Pharisees was based on the acceptance of the historical reliability
of the accounts in the gospels, Josephus and early rabbinic literature.
It has become clearer and clearer that these sources do not give an
unbiased portrayal of this group.[72] Therefore, the view that the

---

[67] Green 2000a, 1125.

[68] See Schäfer 1979, 93; Neusner 1988c, 319–328; Hezser 1997, 66–67.

[69] For these traditions, see Hezser 1997, 67–68.

[70] See Cohen 1984; Schäfer 1991, 170; Hezser 1997, 69–77; Stemberger 1999,
91–92.

[71] See M. Smith 1956, 67–81; Neusner 1983a, 61–82; Goodblatt 1989, 12–30;
Schäfer 1991, 125–172; E. P. Sanders 1992, 380–412; Hengel & Deines 1995,
1–70; Mason 1999, 23–56; Grabbe 1999, 35–62 and 2000, 35–47.

[72] The most intense discussion has concerned the role of the Pharisees in Josephus.
The point in dispute has been whether there are differences in Josephus's portrayal
of the Pharisees between his earlier work (*Jewish War*) and later works (*Antiquities*
and *Life*). For a recent contribution to this discussion, see Grabbe 2000, 35–47. Grabbe
maintains that the differences between Josephus's works are real and sometimes

Pharisees were only one party among many Jewish parties in the Second Temple Period has gained wide acceptance.[73] Recent studies on early rabbinic sources support this view because they indicate that the rabbis, the alleged successors of the Pharisees, did not have much influence on other Jews or Jewish society as a whole in the decades or even in the centuries following the destruction of the temple.[74]

Jacob Neusner has shown in his studies on the Mishnaic laws that the earliest laws in the development of the whole Mishnah reflect the needs of a small group focused on matters of ritual purity.[75] The obsession of the Yavnean rabbis with purity laws is wholly reasonable, if we assume that they were somehow successors of a group that already closely observed ritual purity before the destruction of

---

"very great," even though some earlier attempts to explain these differences may have been problematic (pp. 40–41). These differences should caution us not to take Josephus's portrayal as an accurate historical account of the Pharisees. The view that the Pharisees were the leading party in the Second Temple Period is based in particular on Josephus' general statements in *Ant.* 18.15 and 17. For the historical problems with these statements, see E. P. Sanders 1992, 395–399, 468–469 and 488–490.

[73] For a different view, see Deines 1993. Deines connects the chalkstone vessels stemming from Palestine at the beginning of the Common Era with the post-70 rabbinic discussions of ritual purity and concludes that the stone vessels bear witness to the great influence of the Pharisees in pre-70 Jewish society (p. 282). But it is not without problems to connect these archaeological findings with later and highly theoretical rabbinic discussions. It is uncertain whether the stone vessels bear witness to Pharisaic rules of purity. Cf. Reed 1999a. Reed argues quite convincingly that the stone vessels were common to all Jews, and not restricted to a single group, either priests or Pharisees. Reed also notes that the sudden disappearance of the stone vessels after the destruction of the temple may suggest that their use was in some way connected to the Temple. (I kindly thank Professor Reed for sending the manuscript of his unpublished paper to me.)

[74] Pace Deines 1993, 283; Hengel & Deines 1995, 34–35. According to them, the leading position of the early rabbis was based on the authority and influence of the Pharisees in pre-70 Jewish society. But if it took decades or even centuries for the rabbis to gain some authority in the Jewish community, as recent rabbinic studies claim, it is not probable that the Pharisees would have been a leading force in the Second Temple Period.

[75] Neusner has organized the Mishnaic laws chronologically in his multiseries work on the history of the Mishnaic law (43 volumes). Neusner has gathered the results of this monumental work and developed them further in his *Judaism: The Evidence of the Mishnah* (originally 1981; my references are to the second edition, 1988). For Neusner's methodology, see Neusner 1988c, 14–22. Neusner's work has been regarded as a breakthrough in the historical study of the Mishnah, even though his methodology has also been criticized. See Saldarini 1986, 443–445; Cohen 1990, 62–65. Despite these complaints, Neusner's conclusions concerning the preoccupation of the Yavnean rabbis with matters of ritual purity and their lack of interest in civil matters and government are confirmed by the study of early rabbinic cases. Cf. Cohen 1992, 162 and 1999a, 969.

the temple.[76] The Yavnean rabbis do not appear in early legislation as the ones who defined a new Jewish identity and society; at this stage, "no one involved in the formation of the Mishnah evidently imagined that there was need or call for work on civil law and government."[77] Visions that have the whole society in sight belong to a later stage in the development of the Mishnaic law; according to Neusner, the entire framework of the Mishnah was revised after the two wars (70 and 135 C.E.) so that the range of topics discussed dealt with not only the life of a small group but the social and political affairs of the whole nation.[78] In his later writings, Neusner has emphasized the utopian character of the final political and social system of the Mishnah: the rabbis "enjoyed no documented access to power of any kind" and were "unable to coerce many people to do very much." Thus their ideals never "attained realization in the structure of actual institutions and in the system of a working government and . . . never actually dictated how people would do things."[79]

The study of legal case stories in early rabbinic sources confirms Neusner's results concerning the nature of early rabbinic legislation. Especially Shaye Cohen has studied what kinds of cases are connected to rabbis of different periods. Cohen's study shows that the number of cases dealing with purity issues declines as we move from the Yavnean period to the time of R. Judah the Patriarch. As also Catherine Hezser notes, "the spectrum of issues which rabbis dealt with seems to have broadened in amoraic times," but it "still remained limited."[80] The Yavnean rabbis were primarily experts on purity, but they do not seem to have had great influence beyond their own circle in civil matters or in religious matters that are not connected to ritual purity. In such matters as the observance of the Sabbath, people did not need guidance from rabbinic experts.[81]

---

[76] See Neusner 1988c, 101–111. Cf. also Cohen 1999a, 969.
[77] Neusner 1988c, 97.
[78] Neusner 1988c, 76–121.
[79] Neusner 1999, 265–266.
[80] Hezser 1997, 360–368. Cf. Cohen 1992, 160–164 and 1999a, 961–971. See also Neusner 1983b, 196. Neusner concludes on the basis of his analysis of the Jerusalem Talmud, that even in the fourth century Palestine "the rabbi as clerk and bureaucrat dealt with matters of surpassing triviality, a fair portion of them of no interest to anyone but a rabbi."
[81] Cohen 1992, 162 and 1999a, 969. Cf. also Goodman 1983, 101; S. Schwartz, 1999, 212.

Even in those matters where the rabbis were acknowledged experts, their influence on other Jews remained limited. We do not have much evidence of persons who accepted the judgment of a rabbi, if they had not approached him in the first instance and thus acknowledged his authority. Thus the influence of early rabbis was restricted to those who accepted their authority, no matter how they might have tried to impose their views on people.[82] As a matter fact, the rabbinic literature itself is a prime witness to the fact that rabbinic instructions and ideals were most often ignored. Frequent references to non-observance of rabbinic ideals suggest that the great majority of the Jews ignored these ideals and that the rabbis had no means of enforcing their decisions upon negligent people.[83] The Yavnean rabbis were approached mostly on issues of ritual purity, but the purity laws were the most neglected area of rabbinic legislation among Jews who did not belong to rabbinic circles.[84] For most Jews, the issues dealt with by the rabbis were not of great significance.[85]

The nature of such institutions as the sanhedrin and the patriarchate should also be reconsidered. The very existence of the central council or the sanhedrin has become more and more doubtful, both before and after the destruction of the Jerusalem temple. A closer scrutiny of relevant sources suggests that there never was a permanent sanhedrin in the Second Temple Period, and the existence of the Yavnean sanhedrin as the successor of the Jerusalem sanhedrin is also highly questionable.[86] The same is true as regards the office of the patriarch or *nasi*. It is also unlikely that R. Gamaliel II was the first partiarch whose status as a leader of Jewish community was acknowledged by the Romans.[87] In those rare cases where the term *nasi* is used in tannaitic literature, it does not refer to an established institution, but is an honorary title used for *any* important rabbi. In the Greek sources, the words 'etnarch' or 'patriarch' appear only in

---

[82] Goodman 1983, 101; Lapin 1995, 237; Cohen 1999a, 971; Stemberger 1999, 98.

[83] E. P. Sanders 1992, 467–469; Goodman 1983, 102–104; Hezser 1997, 386–394; Cohen 1999a, 967–971.

[84] Cohen 1999a, 971.

[85] Stemberger 1999, 98.

[86] See Efron 1987, 287–338; E. P. Sanders 1992, 472–483; Goodblatt 1994, 77–130; M. Jacobs 1995, 93–99; Hezser 1997, 186–190.

[87] The view that the patriarchate began with R. Gamaliel II is argued by Goodblatt 1994, 176–231. For criticism of Goodblatt's view, see M. Jacobs 1995, 105–114; Hezser 1997, 408–410; S. Schwartz 1999, 209–214. See also Goodman 1983, 111–118.

the third century sources (e.g., Origen).[88] The first rabbi for whom
the title *nasi* is used consistently is R. Judah the Patriarch who
emerges for the first time as some kind of leader among the rabbis;
but even in his case it is debated how great a role he actually had
in the centralization and institutionalization of the rabbinic movement.[89]

R. Gamaliel II is often named as the chief instigator of the actions
against early Christians, but this view overestimates his influence in
Jewish society at the end of the first century. The traditions that
describe R. Gamaliel II as *nasi* stem mostly from later Babylonian
sources and reflect the point of view of later redactors.[90] R. Gamaliel's
prestige among the Yavnean rabbis was not based on an official
political position recognized by the Romans but at least partly on
his wealth which was exceptional among early rabbis. As revealed by
the rabbinic case stories, R. Gamaliel II did not have much influence
over non-rabbinic Jews and was certainly not the leader of the Jewish
people in Palestine.[91] It is also unlikely that Yavneh became the leading center of postwar Judaism; it may even never have been the
only center of rabbinic movement.[92] Some rabbinic traditions suggest that the people acted according to the commonly accepted opinion of the rabbis in Yavneh, but many other texts suggest that people
turned to one particular rabbi and accepted his authority.[93] The rabbinic movement was not centralized, and there was not a single leading academy or school that governed the opinions of different rabbis.[94]

The early rabbinic movement may be characterized as a network
of circles of disciples gathered around different rabbis whose popu-
larity and influence varied.[95] Early rabbis demanded that the whole
nation should study the Torah, but they do not seem to have had
any prepared program or mechanism by which they could reach this

---

[88] See Goodman 1983, 112–113; M. Jacobs 1995, 114.
[89] Cf. Goodman 1983, 114; Cohen 1992, 169 and 1999a 976; M. Jacobs 1995, 350; Hezser 1997, 409–414.
[90] M. Jacobs 1995, 114 and 348–349; Hezser 1997, 410.
[91] Goodman 1983, 113–114; M. Jacobs 1995, 106–111; Hezser 1997, 410.
[92] Cohen 1999a, 967.
[93] Hezser 1997, 383.
[94] Hezser 1997, 383–386; Cohen 1999a, 950–956.
[95] Cf. Hezser 1997, 324–327. Hezser describes the rabbinic network as a "personal alliance system." See also Cohen 1999a, 952. Cohen says that rabbinic schools
in the second century were not academies but circles of disciples. Cohen also says
that the second century rabbinate "resembled a sect, a guild, or a caste, but it was
none of these." Cohen defines it as an "unsalaried profession" (p. 976).

goal. Many traditions suggest that the public was not much interested in the rabbis and their teaching, which speaks against the assumption that they were the teachers of the masses. According to some texts, the study of the Torah is a prerogative of the selected few only, and some passages may even suggest that early rabbis tried to keep their interpretation of the Torah secret from other Jews.[96] The nomenclature of early rabbis shows that rabbinic status was often determined by birth rather than by scholarly achievements, which underlines the exclusiveness of early rabbinic circles. Some passages contain criticism against the view that Torah study belongs only to the sons of rabbis, suggesting that at least some rabbinic circles had these exclusive views.[97]

As Günther Stemberger notes, early rabbis formed "a private movement without notable support among 'normal Jews.'"[98] They were not the architects of a new Jewish society. Although they had some visions of the ideal Israel, they did not have power to fulfil them. The early rabbinic movement is repeatedly described in recent studies as an insular group that produced an insular literature.[99] This view is in sharp contrast to the view that still dominates scholarly discussion about the opponents of the Johannine community. Many Johannine scholars have also taken it for granted that the Pharisees or the rabbis had control over synagogue communities, even though the available evidence points in the opposite direction.

2.3. *The Pharisees, the Rabbis, and the Synagogue*

According to an influential opinion, the synagogue in Palestine was a Pharisaic institution which emerged as a reaction to the temple run by the Sadducees.[100] It is argued that the second temple synagogue

---

[96] Cohen 1992, 168 and 1999a, 954–956; Hezser 1997, 100–104.
[97] Hezser 1997, 96–99; Cohen 1999a, 948–950.
[98] Stemberger 1999, 98.
[99] Cohen 1992, 173 and 1999, 975; Lapin 1998, 23; Green 2000a, 1132. Cf. also S. Stern 1994, 200. Stern speaks of the isolationist worldview of the rabbis which "verges on solipsism." L. Levine (2000, 469) says that the rabbis' way of life "was essentially elitist."
[100] Scholars supporting this view are mentioned by Grabbe 1995, 23 n. 21; Hachlili 1997, 37 and 1998, 16; L. Levine 1999a, 37 n. 67. See also the summary of earlier (German) scholarship in Deines 1997, 525–526. For other theories of the origins of the synagogue, see L. Levine 1987, 8–10 and 2000, 19–26; Urman & Flesher 1995, xx–xxv; Hachlili 1997, 34–37; Runesson 2001, 67–168.

was a central instrument through which the Pharisees exercised their influence among the masses and promoted their own religious program.[101] However, literary or archaeological evidence supporting this view is meager.[102] For example, Josephus does not mention synagogues when he describes the party of the Pharisees (*J.W.* 2.162 and 166, *Ant.* 18.12–15). The famous Theodotus inscription demonstrates that at least this particular synagogue was built and run by a priestly family.[103] The view that the Pharisees had an important role in Palestinian synagogues is mostly based on some passages in the gospels. These passages are tainted by polemic which does not tell much about the relationship of the Pharisees to synagogues. One can hardly take the charge that the Pharisees "love the place of honour at feasts and the best seats in the synagogues" as a valid witness to the important roles of the Pharisees in Palestinian synagogues (Matt 23:6; Luke 11:43; cf. also Mark 12:38–39; Luke 20:46).[104] Because this charge may echo well-established polemical conventions of the time, it is even less credible.[105]

The fragmentary archaeological evidence related to pre-70 synagogues does not support the view that the emergence of synagogues in Palestine was connected to a particular religious movement. This evidence shows the great diversity of both practices connected to

---

[101] Cf. Hengel 1971, 180 and 1974, 79–82; Hengel & Deines 1995, 32.

[102] Thus Saldarini 1988, 52; E. P. Sanders 1990, 77–81 and 1992, 398; Grabbe 1995, 23; L. Levine 2000, 37–38.

[103] See E. P. Sanders 1992, 450–451; L. Levine 2001, 54–56. Sanders notes how Hengel interprets the Theodotus inscription to support his view that synagogue was a Pharisaic institution (for Hengel's view, see above). The inscription says that the synagogue in question was built "for the reading of the law and the study of the commandments." Hengel sees the study of the law as a characteristic of the Pharisees only, and so he takes this evidence to show the Pharisaic nature of this synagogue in particular and Palestinian synagogues in general. In spite of Sanders' criticism, Hengel & Deines (1995, 33–34 n. 86) still claim that "the doubling of the expression" in the inscription ("the reading of the law and the study of the commandments") points to the Pharisaic tradition.

[104] Pace Hengel & Deines 1995, 32–33: "[The synoptic gospels] testify unanimously that the Pharisees and the scribes associated with synagogues played an important role in them." For an analysis of non-rabbinic sources which might indicate Pharisaic or rabbinic leadership of synagogues, see Cohen 1997, 99–114. Cohen emphasizes "the paucity of relevant evidence" that might point explicitly and unambiguously to the authority of the Pharisees/rabbis over synagogues in Palestine.

[105] See Johnson 1989, 430–434, esp. pp. 433–434: "Anyone familiar with the philosophical debates of Hellenism cannot miss the pertinence of the 'chair of Moses' (Matt 23:2), occupied by these rival Jewish teachers, who 'preach but do not practice' (23:3), who love the place of honor at feasts (23:6), and are 'hypocrites' (23:13), outwardly righteous but inwardly full of iniquity (23:28)."

synagogues and their architectual forms.[106] The synagogues of the time seem to have been public and communal places that were used for various religious, judicial, social and political needs of local Jewish communities.[107] We do not have any evidence that the synagogue was seen as a rival or a substitution for the temple at this time. Some early rabbinic traditions describe the synagogue as a holy place, using motifs derived from the temple and its liturgy, but even in these traditions, the holiness of the synagogue is not contrasted with that of the temple.[108] While our sources do not ascribe a great role to the Pharisees in synagogues, some first century sources suggest that priests had special roles in some synagogues, which also shows that the synagogue as an institution was not competing with the temple.[109] Literary evidence suggests that synagogues were used for such religious activities as the reading of the Torah, but synagogues were not yet exclusively religious by their nature. They did not belong to a particular religious group but to a community as a whole.[110] It seems that the role of synagogues as distinctively religious centers developed only gradually after the destruction of the temple. Only after the destruction of the temple does 'holy place' become a standard term for the synagogue in the extant Palestinian inscriptions.[111] A similar enhancement of the religious dimension of the synagogue also took place in the Diaspora.[112]

Both the archaeological and literary evidence suggest that the rabbis were not the leaders of synagogues even after the destruction of the temple. Rabbinic regulations concerning the building of synagogues do not correspond to the extant archaeological evidence but are borrowed from temple traditions.[113] Synagogues from the same period and in the same region may differ from each other notably, which speaks for the diversity of Jewish culture.[114] Most rabbinic stories

---

[106] L. Levine 1987, 10–12.

[107] See Hachlili 1997, 41–43; L. Levine 2000, 48–73.

[108] Fine 1997, 30, 59; Hachlili 1997, 46; Cohen 1999b, 323; L. Levine 2000, 40–41.

[109] E. P. Sanders 1992, 201; L. Levine 2000, 125–126. Also many later sources connect priests with synagogues and show that they had a far more prominent role in them also after the destruction of the temple than has often been assumed. See L. Levine 2000, 491–500. Cf. also Kraabel 1981, 84.

[110] Hachlili 1997, 47; E. P. Sanders 1999a, 12; L. Levine 2000, 70.

[111] M. Williams 1999, 85–86.

[112] Kraabel 1979, 502; White 1990, 64.

[113] See L. Levine 1992, 218 and 2000, 446–447; Bloedhorn & Hüttenmeister 1999, 278–280.

[114] Meyers 1999, 68.

dealing with art reflect opposition to figural representations, but still various symbols appear frequently in synagogue art.[115] In the extant synagogue inscriptions, the title 'rabbi' is used as an honorary designation for a wealthy donor. These individuals cannot be identified with any sage known to us from rabbinic literature.[116] Epigraphic evidence mentions several officials (e.g., *presbyters, archons, archisynagogues*) in Greek speaking synagogues both in Israel and the Diaspora but not rabbis.[117] Together with other archaeological evidence, these inscriptions support the non-rabbinic nature of synagogues in the first centuries C.E.[118]

Many rabbinic passages suggest that the rabbis controlled synagogue life.[119] The critical study of early rabbinic traditions and case stories, however, casts suspicion on these kinds of sweeping generalizations. The early rabbinic traditions connected to the Pharisees do not mention anything special about their roles in synagogues.[120] The synagogue is rarely mentioned in the Mishnah or in the tannaitic midrashim (Mekhilta, Sifra, Sifre), which indicates the limited contact of the rabbis with the synagogue.[121] There is more evidence of rabbinic involvement in synagogue life in later sources, but even in light of these sources, the rabbinic involvement in synagogue affairs remained limited.[122] Many passages show that some rabbis could be very critical towards certain synagogue practices, indicating that many synagogues were run by non-rabbinic Jews.[123]

The institution the rabbis ranked highest in Jewish society was not the synagogue, the *bet ha-knesset*, but the *bet ha-midrash*, the rabbinic study house or academy where the rabbinic Judaism developed and gradually became the leading force in Jewish society.[124] The rabbinic study house should be kept apart from the synagogue, even though

---

[115] L. Levine 1992, 215–216 and 2000, 444. There are stories that may suggest that R. Gamaliel II was more liberal in his attitude to art than most of his colleagues. See Levine 2000, 451–458.

[116] See Cohen, 1981, 10–12; L. Levine 2000, 443–444.

[117] Cohen 1981, 13

[118] Cohen 1981, 15. But see also the cautions mentioned by M. Williams 1999, 80–81 and 87.

[119] See Hezser 1997, 221. R. Joshua b. Levi even says in *y. Meg.* 3:4 that "synagogues and study houses belong to sages and their disciples."

[120] Neusner 1971, 289. Cf. also E. P. Sanders 1992, 398.

[121] Thus L. Levine 1992, 207.

[122] L. Levine 1992, 207. Cf. also Hezser 1997, 223.

[123] L. Levine 1992, 212–214 and 2000, 447–449.

[124] L. Levine 1992, 203–205 and 2000, 449–451; E. P. Sanders 1999a, 13.

these two institutions have sometimes been seen as the one and the same.[125] To be sure, in the *bet ha-midrash* the rabbis also discussed such affairs as synagogue liturgy (see above). But this does not mean that early rabbis fixed the synagogue liturgy immediately; it was one thing to discuss some problems in the academy and another to put these discussions into practice in synagogue life.[126] Various discussions show that rabbinic influence on synagogue life increased only gradually, and perhaps only in early Middle Ages can we speak of synagogue as a rabbinic institution.[127] But we must not retroject this later situation back to the early phases of the rabbinic movement, not to mention overlay modern leadership structures of some synagogues on ancient synagogues.[128]

The studies discussed above suggest that the rabbis controlled neither the post-70 Jewish society in general nor synagogues in particular. Their main interest was not directed towards the reformation of synagogue life, and they could not purify individual synagogues of unwanted elements or groups that did not follow their ideals. This picture is at odds with the views many Johannine scholars have had of early rabbis as synagogue reformers who excluded the Johannine Christians from the synagogue. It seems that post-70 Jewish society was much more diverse than many scholarly descriptions of that period have suggested.

2.4. *Documentary Papyri and post-70 Palestinian Society*

The documentary material stemming from the years before the Bar Kochba war (132–135 C.E.) is an important witness to Palestinian society between the two revolts, the period (70–135 C.E.) we know so little about from other sources.[129] Several legal practices in the

---

[125] For a detailed discussion, see Urman 1995, 232–255.

[126] Cf. Kimelman 1997, 185. When discussing when the *'amidah* became a synagogue norm, Kimelman notes that we do not know "when the Amidah moved from the academy to the synagogue."

[127] Cf. Hezser 1997, 221; Levine 2000, 468–470.

[128] Cf. Hezser 1997, 224; Rajak 2001, 419.

[129] For the relevance of these documentary papyri for the study of Jewish society from 70 to 135 C.E., see Goodman 1991, 169–175; Saldarini 1998, 133–145; Cotton 1998, 167–179; 1999, 221–236 and 2000, 23–30. These papyri have been found in different locales in the Judaean desert: Nahal Hever, Wadi Murabba'at, Nahal Se'elim, Nahal Mishmar, Ketef Jericho, Wadi Sdeir and Wadi Ghuweir.

documents, e.g. marriage contracts, differ notably from rabbinic discussions of the same matters.[130] The documents suggest that the people behind them did not live their lives following rabbinic ideals, if
they knew these ideals at all.[131]

Evidence in this material should not be dismissed by regarding
the people behind it as 'non-Jewish.' Rather, the documents should
be seen as a reflection of Jewish society of the time.[132] The documents
speak not for a marginal group of assimilated Jews in a certain locale,
but the Jews of the documents may well be representative of the
Jews in Judaea between the wars.[133] This material gives us a glimpse
on those Jews who were not influenced by the rabbinic vision of
Jewish society controlled by the halakhic-system. The people of the
documents did not share the tendency of the rabbis to social isolation.[134] It is remarkable that there is no evidence of the use of particular Jewish courts in the documents. There is not the slightest hint
of the authority of rabbinic circles in these documents; these people
felt free to use Roman legal instruments in their affairs.[135] It seems
that it was not the Torah experts who had the legal power or who
set the general cultural atmosphere of the period.[136] The documentary papyri suggest that the rabbinic sources do not depict a real
world governed by Jewish sages but an ideal vision. This material
helps us to see that "readings of the Mishnah and Talmud that picture Jewish life as separate, independent and self-defining . . . need
revision."[137] Showing the extent of contacts between Jews and non-
Jews, this material "throws into doubt the caricature of Jewish social
isolation," a caricature that has its roots in antiquity and that still
pervades many descriptions of that era.[138]

The above picture of post-70 Jewish society fits poorly the picture
Johannine scholars have created of early rabbis as the mighty pro-

---

[130] For differences between marriage contracts and the Rabbinic *ketubah* payment,
see Satlow 1993, 137–141. Cf. also Cotton 1998, 173–179. Cotton also refers to
other areas of legislation where there are clear discrepancies between the legal documents and the Mishnaic law (p. 179).
[131] Stemberger 1999, 98–99.
[132] Goodman 1991, 174; Cotton 1998 172.
[133] For detailed arguments, see Cotton 1998, 172–173 and 1999, 231–233. Cf.
also Saldarini 1998, 144.
[134] Saldarini 1998, 140.
[135] Goodman 1991, 175; Cotton 1998, 177 and 1999, 234; S. Schwartz 1999, 212.
[136] S. Schwartz 1999, 213.
[137] Saldarini 1998, 142–143.
[138] Goodman 1991, 175.

tectors of a new Jewish community. That we do not have any examples of the ultimate excommunication from Jewish communities is not accidental but a reflection of the nature of Jewish communities in this period. The Yavnean rabbis were not leaders of the people who could have enforced their form of Judaism on those who did not share their beliefs. There was not a supreme authority capable of defining the boundaries of Judaism and establishing a new orthodoxy. If this is true in regard to post-70 Palestinian society, it is all the more unlikely that the rabbis could have controlled Jewish communities in the Diaspora.

The portrayal of the Johannine community as a minority persecuted by a powerful Jewish community headed by the Pharisees/the Yavnean rabbis presumes an isolated world where the internal affairs of the Jews belong only to the Jews. How else could we understand the alleged precarious situation of the Johannine Christians, who are said to have suffered from the serious social, political and economic consequences of the policy of the Jewish leaders in their surroundings?[139] The conflict of Jesus and his followers with the hostile world in John takes place in a world dominated by the Jews.[140] While this kind of world found some support in older readings of rabbinic literature, the above discussion has suggested that this world most probably existed only in the visions of rabbinic circles.

2.5. *The Pharisees and the Rabbis and the Persecution of Early Christians*

There is one more reason to doubt whether the Pharisees or the Yavnean rabbis were the ones who persecuted the Johannine community: there is not much evidence indicating that the Pharisees or

---

[139] Cf. Wengst 1992, 155–156. He says that the exclusion from the synagogue could have been a serious problem only for a Jewish-Christian community that lived in a Greek-speaking environment governed by the Jews. For this reason, Ephesus is not a likely candidate for the home of the Johannine community (p. 158). Wengst locates the gospel to the regions of Batanaea and Gaulanitis where Jewish self-government in the time of Agrippa II would have made the Johannine situation understandable (pp. 157–179). Wengst's proposal is accepted, with some reservations, by Ashton 1991, 196–198. This proposal, however, is very problematic historically. See Hengel 1993, 290–291. Wengst's worst mistake is to overestimate the influence of rabbinic Judaism. It is not only problematic to find a *Greek-speaking* world governed by the rabbis, but recent studies suggest that this kind of world never existed even among *Aramaic-speaking* Jewish communities in Palestine.

[140] Cf. Meeks 1985, 101.

the rabbis were the ones who started the actions directed against
early Christians. While the synoptic gospels picture the Pharisees as
Jesus' main opponents in his lifetime and even attribute to them the
willingness to kill Jesus (Mark 3:6 and *par.*), the synoptic passion
accounts show clearly that it was not the Pharisees but the priestly
establishment in Jerusalem that was somehow involved in the death
of Jesus.[141] The same holds true in the case of the persecution of Jesus'
followers after his death. While Paul, a Pharisee, somehow took part
in the actions directed against some early Christians, we do not have
any evidence that the Pharisees as a *group* persecuted early Christians
or that they were the acting force behind early persecution. Luke
reports several times that the priestly circles were active in the oppression of Jesus' early followers (Acts 4:1; 5:17–33; 7:1; 9:1,14,21), but
he also tells how a Pharisee, named Gamaliel, spoke in favor of
Christians (Acts 5:34–40). Luke also presents the Pharisees as favorable to early Christians elsewhere (Acts 23:1–11), which may reflect
his tendency to depict the Pharisees as the Jewish group that was
most like Christians.[142] But Luke would not have chosen the Pharisees
as representatives of favorable Jews if they were regarded generally
as the main persecutors of early Christians. Luke is probably right
in attributing the main role in the opposition to early Christians to
the temple hierarchy.[143]

A similar picture is derived from Josephus' account of how the
high priest Ananus II executed James, the brother of Jesus (*Ant.*
20.199–203). A group of pious Jews, most probably Pharisees, objected
to the execution with the effect that the King Agrippa deposed
Ananus.[144] That some Pharisees were offended by the mistreatment
of a Christian leader suggests that they had at least some sympathy
for James and his group.[145] Their action is hardly understandable if
they thought that James deserved execution.[146]

---

[141] Cf. the discussion in E. P. Sanders 1985, 287–293, esp. p. 290.

[142] Cf. J. T. Sanders 1987, 288–290.

[143] Thus E. P. Sanders 1985, 285.

[144] Josephus says that "those of the inhabitants of the city who were considered
the most fair-minded (ἐπιεικέστατοι) and who were strict (ἀκριβεῖς) in observance
of the law were offended" by James' execution. The use of the word ἀκριβής, which
Josephus often uses to describe the Pharisees, suggests that he also has them in
mind here. Thus Baumgarten 1983, 413–414. Cf. also Hare 1967, 33; E. P. Sanders
1992, 419; J. T. Sanders 1993, 28; Setzer 1994, 108; Bauckham 1999, 222.

[145] See Setzer 1994, 108–109.

[146] Pace Bauckham 1999, 222–229. Bauckham says that Josephus' account indi-

Josephus notes elsewhere that "the Pharisees are naturally lenient (πρὸς τὰς κολάσεις ἐπιεικῶς ἔχουσιν) in the matter of punishments" (*Ant.* 13.294). This remark suggests that the Pharisees were cautious about imposing the death penalty even though it was a prescribed punishment for a number of crimes in the Torah.[147] The rabbis were also unwilling to impose death penalty, as the discussions in the Mishnah tractates *Sanhendrin* and *Makkot* show.[148] These discussions show that the rabbis had an "over-cautious ethos in matters of capital punishments."[149] According to these discussions, a person may be put to death only by a legitimate court that has reliable witnesses, and only after a very complicated and cautious process that makes sure that no error is committed. The procedure described is so laborious and offers so much better chances of acquittal than of conviction that it is difficult to imagine that anyone could be executed according to these court processes.[150]

The discussions about punishments in *Sanhedrin* and *Makkot* are imaginary rather than descriptions of real court practices; it is unlikely that there ever was a central rabbinic council that could have inflicted such punishments.[151] These discussions do not reflect the position of those who had the actual power to execute evildoers, but they may be an attempt by marginal Torah experts to bring into balance scriptural legislation that demanded the execution of various types of sinners and the real world where sinners were not normally executed.

---

cates that a "difference in interpretation of the law between Sadducees and Pharisees must be at stake." According to Bauckham, the Pharisees agreed with Ananus that James' crime merited death; but while Ananus and other Sadducees regarded stoning as the rightful form of capital punishment in this case, the Pharisees would have confined stoning to cases where the Torah explicitly prescribed it. Bauckham says that the discussions of capital punishments in the Mishnah "cannot be presumed to date from the Second Temple Period" (p. 221), but he still takes them as illustrative of "the sort of halakhic differences that could easily have existed at that time" (p. 228). The dating of these discussions is not the only problem, but also their imaginary nature. Furthermore, Hare (1967, 34) rightly notes that the intensity of the Pharisees in Josephus' account suggests that they "were convinced that the executed persons had not been guilty of a capital crime."

[147] Thus Hengel 1989, 168 n. 124.

[148] Cf. *m. Makk.* 1:10 (Neusner's translation): "A sanhedrin which imposes the death penalty once in seven years is called murderous. R. Eleazar b. Azariah says, 'Once in seventy years.' R. Tarfon and R. Aqiba say, 'If we were on a sanhedrin, no one would ever be put to death.' Rabban Simeon b. Gamaliel says, 'So they would multiply the number of murderers in Israel.'"

[149] S. Stern 1994, 168–169.

[150] E. P. Sanders 1992, 420.

[151] Hezser 1997, 462 n. 74.

While ignoring the discussions reflecting the lenient attitude of rabbis, Johannine scholars often refer to a more savage rabbinic tradition
seemingly advocating lynch law. The tradition, connected to a scriptural story that tells of how Phineas slew Zimri, who was guilty of
intermarriage with a Midianite woman (Num 25; *m. Sanh.* 9:6; *Num.
R.* 21.3f.), is said to shed light on John's reference to the killing of
Jesus' followers (John 16:2).[152] This tradition is said to explain the
religious motivation behind these killings.[153] It is true that the deed of
Phineas was taken as an excuse for an immediate execution in certain
cases, but *m. Sanh.* 9:6 is incongruous with other Mishnaic discussions
reflecting more lenient views, and some of its terminology is also unparalleled in the rest of the Mishnah.[154] It is no wonder then that the
deed of Phineas was later said to have taken place without "the approval
of the sages;" it was said that Phineas escaped the excommunication
of the sanhedrin only because of divine intervention (*y. Sanh.* 9:7).
The story of Phineas may have inspired some bloodthirsty legends
in which rabbis may slay those who were found guilty of intercourse
with a non-Jewish woman. These stories may tell how repulsive this
kind of intercourse was seen.[155] It is not appropriate, however, to
use this exceptional tradition to illustrate the basic disposition of early
rabbis because other early evidence suggests that leniency in the matters of capital punishment was one of their characteristics.[156]

---

[152] Strack–Billerbeck II 565; Brown 691–692; Schnackenburg III 139 n. 101;
Lindars 497–498; Wengst 1992, 86 and II, 154:

[153] Especially the saying appearing in *Num. R.* 21.4, "if a man sheds the blood
of the wicked, it is as though he had offered a sacrifice," is often cited to show the
religious motives as behind the persecution of the Johannine believers. It should be
noted, however, that the saying in the midrash is closely connected to the scriptural passage in question. In Num. 25:13 it is said that by slaying Zimri, Pinehas
made atonement (כפר) for the Israelites. The midrash explains in what sense this
was possible: "But did he offer a sacrifice, to justify the expression 'atonement' in
this connection? No, but it serves to teach you that if a man sheds the blood of
the wicked, it is as though he had offered a sacrifice." It is doubtful whether this
exegesis of a particular scriptural story really shows "the lengths to which fanatism
can go" (Lindars 498). It is also quite hazardous to take this passage as an expression of the sentiments of early rabbis: in its final form, Numeri Rabbah dates from
the 12th century, and even though the later part of the work containing this slim
allusion is remarkably older (from the 8th century?), there is still a huge leap from
the early Middle Ages back to the first century situation. For the dating of this
work, see Strack & Stemberger 1982, 285–287.

[154] See S. Stern 1994, 168–169.

[155] S. Stern 1994, 169–170.

[156] Cf. Barrett 484–485: "It would, of course, be a grave error to suppose that
either of these passages [*m. Sanh.* 9:6 and *Num. R.* 21.4] gave general approval to
indiscriminate bloodshed; or indeed was ever taken very seriously."

I do not claim that early rabbis were liberal and tolerant in the modern sense of these words.[157] They could well argue vigorously with each others, condemn the *minim* to gehenna, or develop cruel fantasies of the fate of the godless. But rabbinic polemics do not reflect directly how non-rabbinic Jews were treated in Jewish society; these polemics should be understood as an attempt by a peripheral group to define its boundaries rather than as a well-developed policy towards dissidents.[158] The vagueness of the term *minim* is very telling in regard to the attitude of the rabbis to those outside their own circles. By blending different heresies together, the rabbis could protect themselves against views they considered potentially dangerous. They did not need to take a stand on different heretic groups in detail, but it was sufficient to add these groups to those considered heretics.[159] The rabbis could maintain their view of idyllic Israel who follows their halakha only by regarding as non-existent those groups who did not match their ideals.[160] As Martin Goodman says, "rather than attack heretical Jews, the tannaim preached that heretics should be ignored."[161]

It is probable that the much cited rulings in *t. Ḥul.* 2:20–21, which prohibit contacts with the *minim*, should also be understood as an attempt to ignore the heretics. These same rulings, as a matter of fact, testify that not even the rabbis could avoid contacts with heretics.[162] These rulings do not bear witness to the inferior status of the *minim* in the society because the rabbis had no means of enforcing other Jews to have no dealings with the heretics.[163] Moreover,

---

[157] Pace Cohen 1984, 48–50. Cohen argues that the Yavnean rabbis promoted an "ideology of pluralism" that aimed in "the creation of the society which would tolerate, even foster, disputes and discussions but which could nonetheless maintain order." But Cohen may push his argument too far by making a virtue of the way the Mishnah leaves open many halakhic discussions. Cf. Goodman 1996, 507. Goodman criticizes Cohen and says that the attitudes of the rabbis can not be explained "in terms of the liberal outlook of the tannaim;" what looks like a liberal attitude "may simply reflect the genesis of the Mishna as a compilation of the views of jurists rather than as a law code." For the discussion of Cohen's proposal, see also Hezser 1997, 64 n. 64. Hezser says that the "grand coalition" in Yavneh does not reflect the actual rabbinic society in which different opinions were tolerated; this image was rather "deliberatively created by the editors as a reaction to actual disharmony."

[158] See Green 2000b, 372–373.

[159] Segal 1986, 141.

[160] See especially S. Stern 1994, 132–135.

[161] Goodman 1996, 507.

[162] Cf. Setzer 1994, 161; Kalmin 1999, 72.

[163] Cf. Katz 1984, 53. Katz discusses the rulings in *t. Ḥul.* 2:20–21 and says that

there is no evidence that the reaction of the rabbis to heretics went beyond attempts to avoid contacts with them; for example, there is no passage that would suggest that the *minim* are liable to capital punishment.[164] On the basis of rabbinic evidence, therefore, it is simply misleading to suppose that the rabbis were the instigators of any kind of systematic oppression of the *minim* in general, or early Christians in particular.[165]

I think we should at least clear the reputation of the rabbis as the main oppressors of the early Christians, even though we are not ready to give up the view that the Johannine Christians were faced with actual persecution at the hands of their Jewish opponents—which is what I will suggest below. It is most unlikely that the early Yavnean rabbis were powerful enough to exclude the Johannine Christians from the synagogue and ultimately from Jewish life and to persecute them in other ways.

But might there be some other candidates who could have played such a role in the history of the Johannine community? We cannot rule out the possibility that there was such a Jewish group in the environment of the Johannine group.[166] But the little we know of the government of Jewish synagogue communities speaks against the existence of this kind of leadership class among the Jews. As was argued above, synagogues were local institutions and synagogue authorities did not have any authority other than that given to them by their own community.[167] Furthermore, synagogue officials do not seem to have had great authority in the civil matters of the com-

---

this passage "should be read as forceful social comment recommending the shunning of social intercourse with *minim*," but not as a formal ban. See also Setzer 1994, 161. Setzer notes that *t. Hul.* 2:20–21 "is an attempt to limit contact with people judged to be *minim*. How successful this ruling was is anyone's guess." But Alexander (1992, 16) says that the rulings in *t. Hul.* 2:20–21 are "tantamount to imposing a ban on Jewish Christians." According to Horbury (1998, 100), the excommunication from the synagogue in John is "consistent with the probably second-century Jewish evidence for prohibition of converse with heretics."

[164] Hare 1967, 39 n. 2.
[165] Cohen 1984, 50; Goodman 1996, 506; Setzer 1994, 161.
[166] See Meeks 1985, 102. Unlike most other Johannine scholars, Meeks dismisses the Yavnean rabbis as the opponents of the Johannine community. But Meeks suggests some other Jewish group had sufficient power in synagogues to "expel persons from membership, even to threaten their lives." Meeks locates the Johannine community somewhere in Galilee, Batanaea or "some small *polis*" in a "society dominated by the Jewish community" (p. 103).
[167] L. Levine 1999b, 95 and 2000, 365–366.

munity.[168] For example, as John 12:42 says that some of "the authorities" (ἄρχοντες) did not confess their faith because of fear of the Pharisees, it is as difficult to connect this situation to the post-70 Jewish society as it is to connect it to Jesus' time.[169] In sum, it is not easy to find a group that could have controlled the life of a deviant group in such a thorough manner as is often suggested by Johannine scholars. The basic elements for the portrayal of the enemies of the Johannine community are taken from the earlier readings of rabbinic sources, which have proven very problematic. Consequently, we should abandon altogether the hypothesis of a powerful Jewish establishment rather than go on the endless search for an actual Jewish group that would fit our hypothetical history of the Johannine community.

The recent change in the appraisal of the early rabbinic movement has been coming for some time now, but the traditional picture of the rabbinic takeover still continues to live, especially in the descriptions of the situation of Christians after 70 c.e.[170] I think that scholars may have been unwilling to accept the views on the marginal role of early rabbis partly because the rabbinic movement has been a convenient foil to the development of early Christianity. It has been necessary to describe early rabbis as powerful so that the separation of early Christians from Judaism could be ascribed to

---

[168] Goodman 1983, 124.

[169] Pace Rensberger 1999, 128–129. Rensberger says that the conflict reflected in John took place at a time and in a location where the Pharisees were the most powerful group in the synagogue community. According to Rensberger, ἄρχοντες in John are members of a traditional authority class in John's locale somewhere in the Diaspora. This group could be intimidated by the Pharisees, who held real power. Nicodemus represents secret believers in the local ruling class, whose open confession could have been of real help to the Christian group as a whole. But this reconstruction is highly problematic even in the area of Palestine, not to mention in the Diaspora, where Rensberger locates John.

[170] See Dunn 2001, 52–53. Dunn's way of reacting to recent changes in the study of rabbinic Judaism is typical of many scholars. Dunn is aware that "it took decades and even centuries for the rabbis to establish their interpretation of Judaism as the only authentic form of Judaism, to establish, that is to say, rabbinic Judaism as 'Judaism.'" But still Dunn notes that "the successors to the Pharisees were evidently able to establish themselves as the only effective political force in the land." Furthermore, John appeared at a time "when, with the benefit of hindsight, we can see only two substantive contenders for the heritage of Second Temple Judaism beginning to emerge from the pre-70 factionalism—Christianity and rabbinic Judaism." Dunn still overemphasizes the political power of the rabbis and overestimates the relevance of emerging Christianity for them. Early rabbinic sources do not suggest that there ever was a *contest* between the rabbis and early Christians.

their policy. Thus, the alleged anti-Judaism in some New Testament writings can also be understood as a response to the steps taken by the rabbis. General and recurrent references to some rare rabbinic passages have filled the void in the evidence that would support the assumption that the post-70 Christians were a persecuted Jewish minority. But there is not much that would support this view even in the Christian sources.

2.6. *Evidence for Jewish Persecution of the Christians*

It cannot be denied that some early Christians were faced with Jewish persecution, but we must remember that persecution is a very vague term and can mean many different things. A survey through early Christian sources shows that early Christians soon began to see Jews as their principal enemies. But we must not confuse what early Christians thought of Jews in their symbolic universes with what happened in the real world.

We know that some early Christians were killed in events where some Jews were involved. Luke's tells of Stephen execution in Acts 6–7. According to Acts 6:8–12, some Jews from the Diaspora started the events that led to Stephen's martyrdom, and this detail is hardly Luke's invention.[171] But it may be impossible to say what exactly happened on the basis of Luke's account because Luke has modelled the story on Jesus' trial. The lynchmob aspect is more likely to be original in the story, while Luke has emphasized the parallels between this first Christian martyr and Jesus.[172] The reasons for Stephen's death most probably had to do with the proclamation of the so-called Hellenists who criticized the temple and ceased to circumcise gentiles.[173]

Josephus states that James, the brother of Jesus, was executed by the high priest Ananus II (*Ant.* 20.199–203), and Luke relates how Herod Agrippa I killed James, the brother of John (Acts 12:1–3). We do not know if there were any other early Christians who suffered martyrdom at the hands of the Jews. But as Paul speaks of his earlier persecution of Christians, he does not say that he would have

---

[171] See Räisänen 1992, 166.
[172] Cf. Setzer 1994, 171–173.
[173] See the discussion below in ch. 2.7 pp. 80–81.

been personally responsible for the deaths of some early Christians, even though Luke connects him to the death of Stephen.[174] These early incidents do not speak for a general Jewish persecution of early Christians, but each case has its own distinctive features. It is by no means evident that they were all motivated by religious reasons, but the reasons behind these events may have varied.[175] Early Christian authors saw every single martyrdom as a sign of general persecution and thought that faith in Jesus was the reason for this persecution.[176]

Persecution can also mean something other than death threat. We know that Paul "received forty lashes less one" from some Jews (2 Cor 11:24). This is probably a reference to synagogue discipline, to which some passages in the synoptics also refer (e.g. Mark 13:9; Matt 10:17).[177] But Paul boasts here of his many sufferings which make him unlike the false apostles (2 Cor 11:23). The context suggests that all Christians were not disciplined in this way and that mere faith in Jesus did not result in such a punishment.[178] It is, however, quite understandable that, in the minds of early Christians, the incidents that concerned leading missionaries were soon seen as common to all Christians, which may explain more general references to floggings in the synoptics.

Some passages in the Acts suggest that early Christians were subjected to mob violence where some Jews were involved, but Luke describes the crowd violence in a stereotyped way, and so it is difficult to get a glimpse of the real world.[179] Verbal polemics between Christians and non-Christian Jews was more likely than mob violence. The most likely reaction of the vast majority of non-Christian Jews was not the active pursuit of early Christians in whatever form, but a passive rejection of this new faith. In my earlier discussion of rabbinic evidence, I suggested that the rabbis tried to ignore those they regarded as heretics and ostracized them.[180] If this observation has any general relevance at all, it could be that this was an attitude taken by most non-Christian Jews to early Christians. According

---

[174] Hare 1967, 35.
[175] Hare 1967, 42.
[176] See Hare 1967, 20–43. In a similar vein, E. P. Sanders 1985, 281–287.
[177] See Hare 1967, 43–46; Setzer 1994, 169–170.
[178] Hare 1967, 46.
[179] Cf. Setzer 1994, 59–64.
[180] Cf. ch. 2.5 pp. 71–72.

to Christopher Tuckett, silent ignoring was a typical response to
Christians by the time the saying gospel Q was finished. Tuckett
says also that there is no direct evidence of any systematic persecution
or violent attacks in this source.[181]

The fate of some martyrs and the general atmosphere of rejection
had the result that in the *symbolic universes* of early Christians, Jewish
persecution soon found its fixed place. The tendency to depict the
Jews as the main actors in Jesus' passion and death is clearly seen
in all the gospels, and it was only natural that early Christians saw
their own situation in the light of what they thought had happened
to their Lord. Early Christians did not invent persecutions and martyrs out of thin air, but we must be careful not to confuse how they
perceived the surrounding world in their symbolic universes with
what happened to them in the real world. "How the reality was
perceived, remembered, and manipulated had as profound an effect
on the Christian communities as the reality itself," as Stephen G.
Wilson notes.[182]

As we move to the period after 70 c.e., the references to Jewish
persecution of early Christians become all the more stylized and general.[183] Of course, we could always say that the lack of signs of Jewish
persecution in this period is due to limited source material, but if
there is any discernible tendency in early Christian sources on this
matter, it is to overstate and dramatize the threat of the Jews, not
to play it down. Scholars who imagine Jewish persecution of early
Christians at the end of the first century lean mainly on some scattered references in rabbinic sources (the *birkat ha-minim* and *t. Ḥul.*
2:20–21). But as I have shown in earlier chapters, these references
do not warrant the interpretation that the rabbis ever incited persecution of early Christians.

From the Christian side, the main witness for Jewish persecution
is said to be found in the second century writings of Justin the
Martyr.[184] However, Justin's references to Jewish persecution are

---

[181] Tuckett 1996, 283–323, esp. p. 322.
[182] Wilson 1995, 176.
[183] J. T. Sanders 1993, 60. James Parkes already noted in 1934 that there is no
sign of "any actual persecution of the Christians by the Jews between the death
of James the Just and the outbreak of the Bar Cochba revolt." See Parkes 1961
(1934), 93.
[184] Martyn 1979, 67 n. 89; Lindars 1991, 148; Horbury 1998, 154–160.

vague. He does not refer to any single concrete event (the Bar Cochba revolt notwithstanding) nor mention any martyr by name. He refers many times to the willingness of the Jews to kill Christians but hastens to add that they cannot fulfill their evil intentions. These references, as Claudia Setzer notes, prove, "ironically, that Jews, at the time of his writing, were not personally killing or attacking Christians, however he might have attributed to them a desire to do so."[185]

Judith Lieu has noted that

> persecution and martyrdom become key elements in Christian self-understanding in the second century, providing a context where their distinctive identity could and had to be articulated . . . [It is difficult to] distinguish between the real consequences of actual persecution and the creation of a mental world where persecution and conflict is the norm.[186]

I think that it is safe to assume that the development of this kind of mental world had already begun in the first century C.E. We have a lot of evidence which makes understandable that the Johannine Christians felt themselves to be persecuted in a world governed by the Jews, but we have hardly any evidence of Jewish persecution of Christians at the end of the first century. In addition, the portrayal of persecution in John is general and vague. Jesus' sufferings are a model for the sufferings of his followers in the theology of the gospel (15:18). The only concrete actions against Jesus' followers are the expulsion from the synagogue and murder. Even the death threat in John 16:2 is presented on a very general level and contains traditional topics common to all early Christian descriptions.[187] There is no reference to the most likely form of physical violence, synagogue discipline. The symbolic universe reflected in the text may have developed over the course of a long time and be based on those things that the Johannine Christians learned to know of general early

---

[185] Setzer 1994, 144. In a similar vein with full discussion Lieu 1996, 132–135 and 1998, 279–295; Rajak 2001, 511–533. For a different view, see Horbury 1998, 154–160. Horbury takes all that Justin says of the Jews at face value and speaks of "corporate Jewish rejection of Christianity" (p. 158). Justin shows that "Diaspora contact with the Holy Land continued, and that office-holders and teachers in the communities began to form links with the nascent patriarchate and rabbinic movement." Therefore Justin speaks of "continuity and cohesion in the second-century Jewish community." This all is extremely unlikely, to say the least, in the light of recent developments in the study of early rabbinic Judaism and archaeology in the Diaspora.

[186] Lieu 1996, 282.

[187] Cf. Segal 1981, 408 n. 44; Becker 590; J. T. Sanders 1993, 45; Setzer 1994, 96.

Christian experience and maybe, at least to some extent, also experienced themselves.[188] But we do not, however, need to assume any contemporary real world persecution behind this symbolic universe.

I do not think that John is making "defamatory inventions"[189] or that he is "indulging in paranoid fantasy,"[190] even though I do not accept everything John says about the Jews as a direct reflection of the real world situation behind the text. It should be borne in mind that all religious groups create their distinctive symbolic universes around those things that are most important to them. A part of the Qumran community cherished the traditions of the Jerusalem temple and imagined a world where they are a holy priesthood that goes to the war against the nations at the end of time; the rabbis devoted their lives to the study of the Torah and halakhic discussions and imagined a world where all goes according to their rulings; the Johannine Christians believed they had received God's final revelation in Jesus and imagined a world where Jesus and his followers are in a fierce conflict with the hostile world represented by the Jews. These imagined symbolic worlds are not true in the sense that the nations would have waged war against the Qumran community, the Jewish community would have followed all the rulings of the rabbis, and the Johannine Christians would have been under a constant threat of death from the Jews. But these worlds are not lies either in the sense that they would have been created to deceive. These groups created their distinctive symbolic universes so that they could understand themselves better in relation to the surrounding world, no matter how distorted a picture they may have had of that world.

It is quite conceivable that such evil things as the killing of the righteous take place in the symbolic worlds of religious groups, even though such things have not happened in the real world. According to rabbinic polemical tradition, the Shammaites murdered the Hillelites, which is highly unlikely.[191] Many scholars today are ready to admit

---

[188] Cf. Hengel 1993, 288–289.

[189] Cf. De Boer 2001, 262. De Boer says that if the charges against the Jews in John are not taken as historically plausible actions of certain Jews, they must be "the defamatory inventions of the evangelist." De Boer argues, of course, for the former alternative.

[190] Cf. Rensberger 1999, 127. Rensberger says that it may not be possible to reconcile the expulsion from the synagogue with what is known of Jewish practice from other ancient sources; however, we should not suspect this piece of information because "there is no reason to think that John is indulging in paranoid fantasy."

[191] Cf. *y. Šabb.* 1:4. This charge is a late part of the anti-Shammaite polemic

that the persecutions described in the book of Revelation never took place to the extent described but are "located in the expectations of the author."[192] Even 1 John 3:15 indicates that one Johannine party feared the murderous plans of the other, even though this expectation is most probably exaggerated.[193] It seems that scholars are ready to accept John's vague reference to the Jews killing Christians (16:2) as historically plausible, while they usually dismiss the passages suggesting that Christians killed each other.

I think we should not accept John's portrayal of murderous Jews as a direct reflection of the reality behind the text because other evidence remains meager. We should not try to reconstruct some unique and particular circumstances unattested in other sources to explain John's references to the Jews. Rather, I suggest that John fits quite well with what we know of the development of Jewish-Christian relations from other sources. These sources suggest that the break between early Christians and other Jews resulted from their views on central markers of Jewish identity rather than from their faith in Jesus as such. We do not not need to assume a violent policy by a Jewish establishment to explain this break.

2.7. John in the Context of Jewish-Christians Relations in the First Century

One of the basic assumptions of recent consensus is that the confession of Jesus as the Messiah was the reason why the Johannine Christians were expelled from the synagogue. It is assumed that those who believed in Jesus were otherwise completely observant and kept the whole law. The separation from the Jewish community thus took

---

characteristic of the party of Hillel. See Neusner 1971, 266–268. Cf. also E. P. Sanders 1990, 88. Sanders notes that "the Shammaites and Hillelites did not actually kill one another." Hezser 1997, 243. Hezser says that one should not take the statement in *y. Šabb.* 1:4 too literally, although it "indicates the hostility which went with disagreements."

[192] Räisänen 1997, 40. For the full discussion, see L. L. Thompson 1990.

[193] Cf. Brown 1982, 447: "The reference to murder [in 1 John 3:15] is hyperbole for maltreatment." Rensberger 1997, 99: "Verse 15 then makes explicit the symbolic meaning of the example of Cain: the murderer is anyone who hates a brother or sister. This seems, at first glance, a very sweeping statement . . . [but] it is not necessary to suppose that the opponents posed an actual mortal danger to other Christians."

place against the will of the Johannine Christians: "They did not reject the synagogue (i.e. 'Judaism'); the synagogue rejected them."[194] This view does not take into account the possibility that some decisions of the Johannine group contributed to their alienation from other Jews.[195]

It is not likely that such a theological conviction as faith in Jesus as the Messiah was the main reason for the separation of the Johannine Christians from their parent Jewish community. It is, however, understandable that this faith is presented as the main reason for the conflict with the Jews in John. The obsession of the Jews in John with faith in Jesus reflects the self-understanding of the Johannine community, where this faith had a crucial role. Faith in Jesus is at the heart of John's theological agenda, but it does not follow from this that this faith was originally the most crucial issue in the controversies that led to the separation of the Johannine community. E. P. Sanders has pointed out difficulties in accepting the reasons early Christians give for their sufferings and rejection. Early Christians saw themselves as being persecuted "for the sake of Christ," or "for his name's sake," which shows that they understood their faith in Jesus as the reason for the persecution; nevertheless, as Sanders notes, "the problem is that we cannot be sure just what it was that the *other side* . . . found offensive."[196]

Other early Christian evidence suggests that it was not theological disagreements concerning the role of Jesus as the Messiah that evoked the controversy between some non-Christian Jews and Jesus' early followers. The critical study of early sources suggests that not all those who believed in Jesus were threatened by non-Christian Jews, even though early Christian writers have a tendency not to make any distinctions when they depict the Jewish persecution of early Christians. After telling of the emergence of the so-called Hellenists in the early church, Luke briefly mentions the persecution that followed Stephen's death (Acts 8:1–3).[197] Luke says that the persecution concerned the whole church in Jerusalem, but his picture of the

---

[194] Von Wahlde 2001, 443. See also Martyn 1977, 158.

[195] Cf. Schäfer 1975, 122: "Die Trennung von Juden und Christen erfolgte nicht durch die *birkat ha-mînîm* und die Festlegung des jüdischen Kanons. Sie war überhaupt keine einseitige jüdische 'Willenserklärung', sondern ein sich über einen längeren Zeitraum erstreckender Prozess, auf den *beide* Seiten Einfluss nahmen" (italics original).

[196] E. P. Sanders 1985, 284 (italics original).

[197] For a detailed discussion of the Hellenists, see Räisänen 1992, 149–202.

persecution is highly "schematic and unrealistic."[198] Luke's general-izing picture is in line with his description of Christians as facing a constant threat from the leaders of the Jews. Luke clearly has his own theological and political motives for depicting the Jews as per-secuting all early Christians.[199]

Despite his generalizing tendency, Luke admits that the apostles stayed in Jerusalem although others left the city as a result of the persecution (Acts 8:1). It is not very likely that the leaders of the early Christian movement would have been able to stay in Jerusalem if this persecution concerned *all* those who believed Jesus to be the Messiah and not a more specific group among the early Christians. It is more likely that these events had to do only with the group of Hellenists. The reasons for this early persecution were connected to their criticism of the temple; it may also be that the observance of the Torah and especially the question of circumcision played a promi-nent role in this early controversy.[200]

Paul seems to support the conclusion that it was not faith in Jesus as such but observance of some Jewish practices that was crucial in the early controversy. In Gal 1:13–14, Paul connects his persecution of the church to his great zeal for Judaism and "the traditions of my ancestors." It is likely that

> the zeal for the 'traditions of the fathers' does not refer to theological doctrines. Observance of the law is in focus throughout the passage. . . . Circumcision and the other cherished customs were at stake.[201]

Paul's letter to the Galatians generally shows that, still in the 50's when Paul wrote this letter, circumcision was a major point of dispute between Paul and his opponents. In Gal 5:11 (cf. also 6:12) Paul regards circumcision as a means of avoiding persecution, no matter what kind of persecution he has in mind here.[202] The letter to the Galatians also makes it clear that the apostles, who did not share Paul's liberal stance on circumcision, were in Jerusalem; there is

---

[198] Räisänen 1992, 156.
[199] For Luke's motives, see J. T. Sanders 1987, 304–317; Wilson 1995, 56–71.
[200] See Räisänen 1992, 201–202.
[201] Räisänen 1992, 23. See also Räisänen 2001, 174; Cohen 1999c, 175–195. Cohen notes that just as in Gal 2:14 the term ἰουδαΐζειν means "to follow the cus-toms and manners of the Jews," Ἰουδαϊσμός in Gal 1:14 means "the observance of Jewish traditions."
[202] Räisänen 1992, 186.

nothing to suggest that they were suffering persecution at the time
Paul wrote his letter (Gal 2:1–10).[203]

Paul's reference to the persecution of Christians in 1 Thess 2:14–16
suggests that he has in mind actions that probably concerned only
a certain group of early Christians.[204] Paul uses several traditional
topoi in 1 Thess 2:15, as he describes the persecution in Judaea; he
says that the Jews "killed both the Lord Jesus and the prophets, and
drove us out; they displease God and oppose everyone." In v. 16,
however, Paul clearly differs from traditional polemics against the
Jews as he says that the Jews "hinder us from speaking to the gentiles so that they may be saved."[205] It is noteworthy that when Paul
ceases using traditional motifs and gives an actual example of Jewish
persecution, he has in mind the problems related to the gentile mission. Presumably, circumcision was again one of the most important
of these problems.

It seems that not all early Christians were being persecuted alike.
The reason why some early Christians were harassed by their fellow Jews was not their faith in Jesus as such, but deviation from
religious practices based on the Torah.

It is understandable that faith in Jesus as the Messiah was not the
main cause of early conflict in the light of those beliefs that were
connected to the expectation of a messiah in first century Judaism.
The expectation of a messiah could find support in some scriptural
passages (e.g., Jer 23:5–6; Isa 9:7), and we have evidence that this
expectation was alive at the beginning of the common era (*Pss. Sol.*
17; 1QS 9:9–11 and some other texts of the Qumran community).
However, it seems that many scholars have overstated the role of
messianic expectations among different Jewish groups. As E. P. Sanders
notes, "the expectation of a messiah was not the rule."[206] Furthermore,

---

[203] E. P. Sanders 1985, 283–284.

[204] This passage has often been regarded as an interpolation, especially because
it seems to contradict what Paul says in Rom 11:25ff. But the differences between
these two passages may be explained on the basis of different situations. See Holtz
1986, 97 and 109–110; Räisänen 1987, 263 n. 171.

[205] For the traditional topics in v. 15, see Holtz 1986, 103–106. Holtz says that
v. 16a marks "eine erhebliche Verschiebung" from traditional polemics (p. 106). In
v. 16, Paul may refer to his own difficulties with 'the Jews,' who have tried to hinder his mission to the gentiles. Cf. Räisänen 1987, 263 n. 171.

[206] E. P. Sanders 1992, 295. Cf also W. D. Davies 1999, 32: "There is little in
the Tanak or in later Jewish sources to justify the elevation ascribed to the Messiah
in Christian theology."

there was not a fixed idea of what a messiah would be like. Some texts from the Qumran community show that the expectation of at least two or perhaps even three different messianic figures had an important part in the community's hopes for the future.[207] Although the expectation of multiple messianic figures would have been unusual among other Jews, we have no evidence that these messianic beliefs had any role in the development that led to the separation of the Qumran community from the surrounding society. Messianic beliefs did not lead to an open schism between different groups if they were not connected to the questions concerning the *practice* of religion.[208]

I do not suggest that the question of Jesus' messianity would not have evoked any discussion among non-Christian Jews. It is most probable that the claims that Jesus is the Messiah were debated among non-Christian Jews, and, to the best of our knowledge, these claims were refuted by the majority of the Jews. As Stephen G. Wilson says,

> messianic differences could lead to puzzlement and frustration that the Jews would not believe, but rarely to outright schism—precisely what we would expect since Judaism itself allowed for a considerable range of messianic convictions.[209]

The Christian claims for Jesus' messianity could have become a real stumbling block between Christian and non-Christian Jews in a situation in which similar kinds of claims were made for some other messianic candidate. This may have been one of the reasons why Christians were persecuted during the Bar Cochba revolt because,

---

[207] For different messianic figures at Qumran, see Beall 2001, 125–146.

[208] Thus also W. D. Davies 1999, 60. Cf. also pp. 206–208. Davies says of the Johannine community that "it was not messianism as such that the sages objected to but the Christian variety of it." This leads Davies to conclude that in the period after 70 C.E. "the center of the sages' concentration had shifted to the claims of Jesus of Nazareth, which now that so many Gentiles had so obviously embraced Jesus, was taken with a new seriousness by the sages." Therefore, according to Davies, "until the success of the Gentile mission—a visible fact, not merely a speculation—had emerged, the sages could have regarded early Christianity as a passing phenomenon." I do not accept Davies' views of rabbinic Judaism as the main opponent of the Johannine Christians, but he is probably right as he says that the growing role of gentile Christianity was important to the separation of Christianity from Judaism. Also Schiffman (1985, 75–78) says that the ascendancy of gentile Christianity made the rabbis deal with Christians as members of different religion. This suggests that the faith in Jesus as the Messiah was not *alone* a sufficient reason for the parting of the ways.

[209] Wilson 1995, 7.

at least in some circles, Bar Cochba was regarded as the Messiah.[210]
But the atmosphere and circumstances during the revolt were exceptional, not typical of Jewish-Christian relations in general. The example of Bar Cochba shows, on the one hand, that in some particular
circumstances Christian faith in Jesus as the Messiah could have
become unacceptable in the eyes of other Jews. On the other hand,
however, even some rabbis and part of the masses regarded Bar
Cochba as the Messiah, which shows that it was fully possible to
adopt messianic beliefs and remain a loyal Jew.[211]

The particular circumstances of the Bar Cochba revolt notwithstanding, it seems that the early Christian faith in Jesus as the Messiah
could lead to an open break with non-Christian Jews only in the
case of those who somehow called into question the significance of
some religious practices on the basis of this faith. As Reuven Kimelman
notes, "one who celebrates as a Jew functions as a Jew." However,
Kimelman continues that

> this does not negate the assumption that change in belief can gener-
> ate change in ritual—only that it is change of ritual itself that brings
> about a shift in the boundary markers of religious community.[212]

The faith in Jesus as the Messiah may have had an important role
in the separation of early Christians from other Jews if it led to the
abandonment of some central Jewish religious practices. This is what
happened in the case of the Hellenists and later in the Pauline churches,
and this may have happened in the community of Matthew, although
he emphasizes in his gospel that Jesus has not come to abolish the

---

[210] Wilson 1995, 7. For the question whether Bar Cochba was regarded as the
Messiah or not, see Reinhartz 1989, 171–194. Reinhartz argues that "there was no
single view or perception of Bar Kosiba among the rabbis or indeed among the
populace as a whole" (p. 194). Some circles regarded him as the Messiah, which
evoked criticism when revolt failed. Some other circles were impressed by Bar
Cochba's success and regarded him as a great military leader but not necessarily
as the Messiah. Both these views probably originated already from the period of
the revolt's success.

[211] For a different view, see Wengst 1992, 99. Wengst says that the faith in Jesus
as the Messiah and the messianic claims made for Bar Cochba were different. No
one regarded Bar Cochba as the Messiah after the failure of his revolt, whereas
faith in Jesus as the Messiah emerged only after his death. Wengst says that the
early Christian faith in Jesus as the Messiah was final and eschatological, which
made it look like a sectarian self-understanding and thus was unacceptable for non-
Christian Jews. But Wengst fails to explain why not all who believed Jesus to be
the *resurrected* Messiah were persecuted.

[212] Kimelman 1999, 305.

law and the prophets but to fulfil them (Matt 5:17). After discussing Matthew's view of salvation, Petri Luomanen concludes that

> we can be quite sure that his [i.e., Matthew's] stance has been more liberal than in the communities of his Jewish contemporaries. Most probably, circumcision was not required in connection with the baptism, and food laws and Sabbath observance were not practiced literally.[213]

Craig E. Evans is on the right track when he says that "Christianity's radical view of proselyzation" explains "why Christianity eventually emerged as an essentially non-Jewish religious movement."[214] Evans also notes that "the real cause of the rift was the role of Torah" and not "High Christology," even though this is claimed by some scholars.[215] Questions related to Jesus' person could have been significant if they changed the attitude of the believers to the particular markers of Jewish identity.[216]

2.8. *Conclusion: A New Way to Assess John's Jewishness*

This survey has made it clear that we can no longer regard John's portrayal of the Jews and Jewishness as a response to the hostile policy of the rabbinic establishment. The separation of the Johannine group from the synagogue was not due to the violent policy of the early rabbinic movement. There was not a strong leadership class in post-70 Jewish communities which could have defined a new orthodoxy where there would have been no place for those who believed Jesus to be the Messiah. Early Christian evidence does not yield support for the idea that Christians were facing Jewish persecution

---

[213] Luomanen 1998, 283.

[214] Evans 1993, 12.

[215] Evans 1993, 12 n. 18. Thus also Stemberger 1977, 18; Grabbe 1977, 150–151; Kimelman 1999, 305.

[216] For a different view, see Luz 1999, 64–73. Luz sees that the Christian confession of Jesus played a crucial role in the partings of the ways between Judaism and Christianity. Luz notes that the significance of this issue is in peculiar contrast to the fact that in Judaism the messianic question was not usually a starting point for a schism: "Der Autoritätsanspruch Jesu war so umfassend, dass es zum Konflikt kommen *musste*" (p. 70, italics original). But if Jesus already started the separation of Christianity from Judaism, it is difficult to understand why Jesus' followers were, long after Jesus' death, very much caught up in discussions concerning the central markers of Jewish identity. E. P. Sanders notes (1985, 246) that such controversies are incomprehensible had Jesus already taken a critical attitude towards the law. Thus also Räisänen 1992, 164.

sometime at the end of the first century. It seems also that it was especially those matters connected to basic matters of Jewish identity that caused a break between some early Christians and other Jews, not merely faith in Jesus as the Messiah.

I suggest that things did not go differently in the case of the Johannine community. We do not need an outdated view of early rabbis as the new leaders of the people to explain the break between the Johannine community and its parent body. Instead of speculating what the alleged opponents of the Johannine Christians may have done, I propose that we should ask how these Christians themselves saw their faith in relation to basic markers of Jewish identity. This leads to the question: What is John's relationship to central matters of Jewish identity? I search for an answer to this question in the following chapters, where I analyze what John says about some matters that were essential to Jewishness. I suggest that this analysis shows that the relationship of the Johannine community to their Jewish heritage was highly ambivalent, which speaks for a growing alienation from the community's Jewish roots.

CHAPTER THREE

JESUS, THE JEWS, AND THE WORSHIP OF GOD

3.1. *Jesus in the Temple of the Jews (2:13–22)*

In the Johannine temple episode (John 2:13–22), Jesus seems to know exactly what he is doing when he drives the sellers of the animals and the money changers out of the temple. But the text does not clearly explain why he did so. At first glance, Jesus seems to be upset by the present conditions in the temple and hence wants to *reform* the cult (vv. 14–16). Later on, however, he speaks of *the destruction* and the raising of the temple, but he does not have in his mind the material temple in Jerusalem but his own body (vv. 19–21). Jesus' relationship to one of the basic matters of Jewish identity is thus ambivalent: he is portrayed both as a pious Jew who fights for the sanctity of the material temple and as a replacement for the Jerusalem temple. The story suggests that Jesus' exemplary Jewishness has an important but still limited role in the symbolic world of the Johannine Christians: it serves to show the superiority of their faith to temple-oriented Judaism and thus justifies the displacement of the Jewish cult by faith in Jesus.

The Context of the Scene

Jesus and the group designated as 'the Jews' meet for the first time in John when he goes to the temple in Jerusalem at the time of Passover. Just before this meeting, the narrator relates Jesus' miracle at the wedding in Cana (2:1–11). The juxtaposition of these two incidents at the beginning of Jesus' career suggests that the latter one is meant to both parallel and contrast with the former one.[1] According to the narrator's concluding remark, Jesus performed his first sign (σημεῖον) in Cana and revealed his glory to his disciples, who believed in him (2:11). In the temple episode, the Jews demand that Jesus show them a sign (σημεῖον) that legitimates his action in

---

[1] Thus Fortna 1988, 125. Cf. also Schnackenburg I 359.

the temple (2:18). In his answer to the Jews, Jesus speaks of his coming death and resurrection although the Jews understand that he is
speaking of the destruction and the raising of the temple (2:19–22).
Jesus' coming death and resurrection are thus 'a sign', but the Jews
in the story do not understand this. Jesus' sign to the Jews is contrasted to his earlier sign to the disciples.[2] These two groups are
clearly distinct from each other right at the beginning of the gospel.
The disciples belong to the insiders to whom Jesus reveals his glory,
whereas the Jews are outsiders. Furthermore, the faith of the disciples is contrasted to the misunderstanding of the Jews.[3]

There is a further point of contact between the Cana miracle and
Jesus' action in the temple. The narrator refers to the religious customs of the Jews in a narrative aside, mentioning "six stone water
jars used for the Jewish rites of purification" (2:6). The mention of
the Jewish rites of purification introduces a new symbolic level of
meaning into the story; Jesus' miracle demonstrates that the old religious order of the Jews is replaced by a new one brought by Jesus.
This theme is developed further in the following temple episode
where Jesus' body is presented as the new temple. Both of these stories imply that Jesus substitutes for religious institutions of the Jews.[4]
Thus the temple scene already makes clear to the reader Jesus' attitude towards Jewish traditions at the beginning of the gospel. This
episode foreshadows Jesus' conflict with the Jews described later in
the gospel. This probably explains why the temple episode appears
at the very beginning of Jesus' public career in John while the story
is connected to Jesus' last days in Jerusalem in the synoptics (Mark
11:15–18 and *par*).[5]

Jesus' Action in the Temple

The narrator speaks of the Passover of the Jews at the beginning of
the temple episode (2:13); he emphasizes the Jewishness of different
festivals and customs in a similar way elsewhere in the gospel (2:6;

---

[2] Fortna 1988, 126.
[3] Brown 125.
[4] Dodd 1953, 303; Brown 104; Lindars 133; Derrett 1977, 90; Fortna 1988, 125;
Schnelle 1996, 369–371.
[5] Thus Hoskyns 198; Cullmann 1959–60, 42; Barrett 195; Brown 118; Schnackenburg I 368–370; Lindars 135–137; Derrett 1977, 90–91; Fortna 1988, 125; Söding
1992, 50; E. P. Sanders 1993, 67–68.

4:9; 5:1; 6:4; 7:2; 11:55; 18:20, 39; 19:3, 40). It has been claimed
that these references aim to anchor John's story firmly within a
Jewish context.[6] But why would it have been necessary to insist upon
Jewishness in a narrative where it is self-evident that everything takes
place in a Jewish world? These references suggest rather that the
relationship of the writer and his readers to the matters connected
to Jewish identity was somehow endangered—or even broken—in
the real world. As Robert Kysar writes,

> the effect is to align the reader with the perspective of the narrator,
> who is separated from Judaism. Those who 'own' the festivals are 'Jews,'
> and the narrator is neither a Jew nor leads the reader to Jewishness.[7]

Although the narrator looks at Passover from the point of view of
an outsider, the text does not suggest that Jesus is unlike other Jews
who start a pilgrimage to Jerusalem at the time of Passover.[8] Rather,
Jesus acts like any other pious Jew. His dramatic action in the temple is in accordance with his portrait as a pious Jew. Jesus finds in
the temple those who were selling oxen and sheep and doves, and
the money changers (v. 14). It is said that "making a whip of cords,
he drove them all, with the sheep and oxen, out of the temple."
The Greek text is not quite clear as to whether Jesus drove out the
animals only or the vendors of the animals as well: the word "all"
(πάντας, masc.) can refer to both words.

In its present position, πάντας seems to refer to the sellers, but
then the following phrase τά τε πρόβατα καὶ τοὺς βόας is problematic.
It would be natural to take the expression τε . . . καί (not used elsewhere in John) as an apposition, but in that case one would expect
that the form πάντα would have been used for πάντας ("he drove
them all out, both the sheep and oxen").[9] In the present form of
the text, τά τε πρόβατα καὶ τοὺς βόας is not an apposition but an
advancement on what was said earlier ("he drove out them all, and

---

[6] Thus Moloney 1993, 95; R. F. Collins 2001, 283.

[7] Kysar 1993, 115. In a similar vein, Schnackenburg I 361; D. M. Smith 1984, 202.

[8] Pace Haenchen 198; Becker 146.

[9] Because of these problems, many scholars have taken the words τά τε πρόβατα
καὶ τοὺς βόας as a secondary editorial addition. See Wellhausen 15; Bauer 44;
Bultmann 86 n. 10; Bammel 1970, 16 n. 23; Lindars 138. According to Chilton
(1997, 444–445), this aporia indicates that two different versions of the story—a
synoptic-like version where oxen and sheep were not mentioned and another version that mentioned oxen and sheep—are conflated in John.

also the sheep and oxen").[10] This, however, is not a normal way to use the connective τε . . . καί.[11] But this mention seems to have been so important that the narrator has been ready to break the smooth progression of the story to make clear that Jesus also drove the sheep and the oxen out of the temple. This is understandable when we realize that it is exactly their presence in the temple that would be most scandalous to a pious Jew in John's story.

The synoptic parallel stories do not mention that there were oxen and sheep in the temple (Mark 11:15–18; Matt 21:12–17; Luke 19:45–48). The sale of oxen and sheep is highly unlikely in the temple area, no matter whether the word ἱερόν in John 2:14 refers to the court of the gentiles only or to the temple area as a whole.[12] This kind of trade is unattested in other sources even though some scholars have maintained that there was a flourishing trade in animals for sacrifice in the temple area.[13] Some scholars try to explain the presence of oxen and sheep in the temple by referring to temporary arrangements introduced by Caiaphas in the time of Jesus.[14] But

---

[10] Thus Schnackenburg I (362 n. 1) and most translations.

[11] In this interpretation τε . . . καί comes close in meaning the adverbial meaning of καί (also), but this is not the normal usage of the construction in Greek. See Denniston 1954, 497: "τε, like καί, is used both as a simple collective and as a prepatory particle in corresponsion, τε . . . τε, τε . . . καί. But it hardly, if at all, shares the adverbial function of καί, 'also.'"

[12] Brown (115) says ἱερόν in v. 14 means the court of the gentiles, while ναός in vv. 19–21 refers to the temple proper. Moloney (1993, 96 n. 11) says that ἱερόν usually refers to the temple as a whole, which suggests that this is the meaning intended by the author in v. 14. I believe that Moloney is right.

[13] Jeremias 1958, 55; Schnackenburg I 361 n. 4. For criticism of this view, see E. Stegemann 1990, 508 n. 23; Chilton 1997, 446.

[14] Thus Eppstein 1964, 42–58. Eppstein refers to some late rabbinic texts according to which the Sanhedrin was expelled from its usual meeting place in the temple to the place on the Mount of Olives called Hanuth forty years before the destruction of the temple. Hanuth was known as a place where sacrificial animals were sold. Eppstein says that Caiaphas expelled the Sanhedrin and then for the first time allowed merchants to sell their sacrificial objects within the temple area in order to damage the trade in Hanuth where the expelled Sanhedrin gathered. Eppstein is followed by Brown 119 (but see cautions in Brown 1994, 350); Lindars 138; Chilton 1992, 107–108 and 1997, 447–449. This solution is, to say the least, not convincing. The Mishnah does not mention the expulsion of the Sanhedrin, but rather presupposes that the Sanhedrin met in its ordinary meeting place until the the destruction of the temple. Cf. Schürer 1979, 225. According to Schürer, the tradition concerning the transfer of the meetings of the Sanhedrin is "without serious support." Furthermore, there is no evidence of the connection between the alleged expulsion of the Sanhedrin and the trade in animals within the temple area. For criticism of Eppstein, see Haenchen 199–200; Evans 1997, 429–432. Despite his critical remarks, Evans seems to regard Eppstein's proposal as a possible one (p. 436).

these attempts are not convincing. E. P. Sanders has pointed that a flock and a herd would have caused a great disturbance among the worshipers, and, moreover, the excrement of animals would have profaned the holy area. It is highly unrealistic to think that shepherds daily drove flocks and herds up the steps to the holy mountain through the porticoes of the temple and also brought all the hay and straw needed by ruminants.[15] Furthermore, an individual was not required to sacrifice an ox, and even if the individual could sacrifice an ox as a burnt offering or as a shared offering, only a very few people could have afforded to do so. It would have been of no use to keep a herd of cattle available for purchase.[16] We do not know exactly how the worshipers obtained the sacrificial victims, but it is highly unlikely that the trade of quadrupeds ever took place on the temple mount; pilgrims may have obtained the animals they needed from licensed dealers outside the city.[17]

As many scholars have noticed, John is ignorant of the arrangements in the temple and his description is unrealistic.[18] John's description may not be based on historical facts, but it is clear that Jesus' reaction to the conditions in the temple as presented in the story is reasonable for a pious Jew. If the quadrupeds had been brought *inside* the temple area and been sold there, every devout Jew would have had a reason to protest against the profanation of the temple.[19]

However, it is not clear whether other Jews would have agreed with Jesus' following words to the dove sellers, "Take these things out of here! Stop making my Father's house a market-place!" (v. 16). Unlike the trade in oxen and sheep, the sale of doves was probably an established part of cultic affairs going on in the temple precinct.[20]

---

[15] E. P. Sanders 1992, 87–88. Cf. also M. Davies 1992, 277.

[16] Pace Chilton 1997, 448: "Indeed, *any* (italics original) major feast required the sacrifice of both oxen and sheep (cf. Num 28:11–29:38)." Chilton thinks that Jesus' action in the temple may originally have taken place during the Feast of Booths (Sukkoth) which could explain the great number of oxen in the temple (Num 29:12–38). But the burnt offerings at the beginning of each month (Num 28:11) or during the great festivals (Num 28:19, 27; 29:2, 8, 12–38) were community sacrifices which were supported by the temple tax collected from every adult Jew (Neh 10:33–34). Cf. E. P. Sanders 1992, 104–105. Thus, these offerings do not explain why there should have been a great number of oxen for sale to ordinary people.

[17] Thus E. P. Sanders 1992, 88–89.

[18] Thus Mendner 1956, 104; Derrett 1977, 83; E. Stegemann 1990, 507–508; E. P. Sanders 1992, 87–88; M. Davies 1992, 277; Ådna 1993, 108–109.

[19] Thus also E. Stegemann 1990, 510; E. P. Sanders 1992, 87–88.

[20] Derrett 1977, 84; E. P. Sanders 1992, 88.

Jesus' accusation would have been too sweeping for most Jews because certain amount of trade in sacrificial animals as well as the services of the money changers were absolutely necessary for the cult.[21] But the Johannine Jesus is not interested in these kinds of details, but treats all the trade in the temple as defilement of his Father's house. Thus he reacts against what would have been an apparent profanation of the temple and against what was normal business connected to the sacrificial cult.

The narrator cites the words from Psalm 69:10, "Zeal for your house will consume me" to explain Jesus' action in the temple. This citation "emphasizes Jesus' positive and genuine care for the temple."[22] The term 'zeal' (ὁ ζῆλος) is

> laden with significance in Jewish tradition where zeal often is associated with the temple or with the maintenance of sole fidelity to God alone who is to be acknowledged there.[23]

The narrator thus wants to present Jesus as a keen reformer of the cult who is upset by the present corruption of the temple and wants to restore its sanctity.[24] This picture is somewhat ambiguous, however, because it remains unclear whether Jesus is fighting against the offensive defilement of the temple or normal routines connected with the cult. The following dialogue between Jesus and the Jews makes even clearer how ambivalent Jesus' attitude to the temple is: this dialogue suggests that the point of the story as a whole is not the reform of the cult after all.

Jesus' Ambivalent Attitude to the Temple

After Jesus' demonstration in the temple, the Jews ask Jesus to legitimate his action: "What sign can you show us for doing this? (v. 18)." Jesus does not answer the question directly but begins to speak about the destruction and the raising of the temple: "Destroy this temple, and in three days I will raise it up" (v. 19). Jesus uses expressions that make the following confusion of the Jews understandable and that also make the reader aware of another level of meaning of these words. The verbs 'destroy' (λύω) and 'raise' (ἐγείρω) can refer to a

---

[21] Thus E. P. Sanders 1985, 61–65; Neusner 1989, 22–23.
[22] Seeley 1993, 273.
[23] Lieu 1999, 68.
[24] Cf. Büchsel 47; McKelvey 1969, 77–78; M. Davies 1992, 233; Söding 1992, 47.

building or to the body of Jesus; the verb ἐγείρω and the temporal expression ἐν τρισὶν ἡμέραις[25] in particular direct the thoughts of the reader to the resurrection of Jesus.[26]

Jesus' reply to the Jews does not contain the requested sign. An unbiased reader may consider Jesus' answer both incomprehensible and unfair, but the Johannine narrator does not have a reader of this kind in mind.[27] The point of view of the Jews is restricted to the time of the story, but the narrator helps the reader to understand Jesus' words from a post-resurrection perspective, revealing that Jesus is no longer speaking of the Jerusalem temple but of the temple of his body (vv. 21–22). This information helps the reader to see that Jesus' saying on the destruction and the raising of the temple refers to his death and resurrection. This also makes it understandable why Jesus' saying differs from some parallel passages in other sources in a significant way: in other forms of the temple saying, it is Jesus himself who destroys the temple, but in John it is the Jews who are the destroyers (cf. Matt 26:61; 27:40; Mark 14:58; 15:29; Acts 6:14; Gos. Thom. 71). The Johannine form of the saying already suggests at this point of the gospel narrative that the Jews will eventually destroy Jesus. The reader knows from a retrospective perspective that the Jews will fulfill Jesus' command "Destroy this temple," no matter how these words are understood in detail.[28]

---

[25] Many scholars note that the expression ἐν τρισὶν ἡμέραις is not the same as the expressions used most often in connection with Jesus' resurrection (τῇ ἡμέρᾳ τῇ τρίτῃ: "on the third day" 1 Cor 15:4; Matt 16:21 and others; μετὰ τρεῖς ἡμέρας: Mark 8:31 and others). According to them, Jesus' original saying was not refering to the resurrection, but the temporal expression ἐν τρισὶν ἡμέραις meant only a short but unspecified period of time ("I will build it in a trice"). Thus, for example, Bultmann 88–89 n. 7; Lindars 143. Be that as it may, in John's final narrative ἐν τρισὶν ἡμέραις refers clearly to the resurrection of Jesus.

[26] For a different view, see Moloney 1993, 99: "The use of the future tense 'I will raise it up in three days' can only be a mystery for the reader. There has been nothing in the narrative so far that would give the reader any indication of what 'raising up' might mean. . . . As yet the reader is almost as ignorant as 'the Jews.'" Moloney means by "the reader" an implied reader who reads the gospel for the first time and does not have much knowledge of the story beforehand. It must be asked, however, whether this definition of the implied reader is very useful in the study of the gospels that probably were meant to be read again and again. It is clear that John's reader is supposed to know something of the story beforehand; for example, John 2:22 mentions the resurrection of Jesus as a known fact (cf. Culpepper 1983, 222). Moloney admits that "the intended readers" (i.e., the readers in the Johannine community) may have seen the connection between Jesus' words in v. 19 and his resurrection (p. 99 n. 27).

[27] Mendner 1956, 99–100.

[28] Some have taken the words λύσατε τὸν ναὸν τοῦτον as having an ironic,

The narrator's comment in vv. 21–22 suggests that his interest
has shifted totally from the material temple to the temple of Jesus'
body. But Jesus' words in v. 19 also say something of the fate of
the material temple to the reader who is aware of the destruction
of the Jerusalem temple in 70 c.e. Jesus' play with the words seems
to have

> a double edge: on the one hand drawing an equation between the
> rejection of Jesus and the destruction of temple, and on the other
> replacing that temple with the exalted Christ.[29]

Thus Jesus' temple saying foreshadows the destruction of the temple
and suggests that the Jews were responsible for it.[30] This view is also
expressed in John 11:48 where the Pharisees and the high priests
fear that the Romans will come and take away the temple (τόπος)
and the nation, if they do not punish Jesus; the reader can grasp the
irony of the scene because the very thing the leaders tried to avoid
by deciding to kill Jesus later came true as the temple was destroyed.[31]
Thus, the gospel narrative as a whole is composed with the destruction of the temple in mind, even though this destruction is not explicitly predicted as in the synoptics (Mark 13:2; Matt 24:2; Luke 19:
42–43; 21:6).[32]

We seem to have in John 2:13–22 two different understandings
of Jesus' relationship to the temple. His action implies that he is furious because of the defilement of the temple and that he wants to
reform the cult. His dialogue with the Jews, however, suggests that

---

prophetic imperative meaning, "Go ahead and do this and see what happens." See
Bultmann 88; Brown 115; Wead 1970, 65; Becker 148. Some see here a condi-
tional use of the imperative, "If you destroy." Thus Blass/Debrunner/Rehkopf
1984 § 387.2; Dodd 1953, 302 n. 1; Schnackenburg I 365 n. 1; Porter 1989, 428.
Some others take the words as having a future meaning, "You will destroy." See
Bauer 45; E. Stegemann 1990, 509.

[29] Duke 1985, 50.

[30] Cf. Bultmann 88; McKelvey 1969, 78–79; Wead 1970, 65; Léon-Dufour 1981,
447; Schnelle 1996, 368.

[31] Cf. Schnackenburg II 449; Pancaro 1975, 121–122; Barrett 405; Culpepper
1983, 169–130; Duke 1985, 113; Becker 432; Myllykoski 1991, 75.

[32] Pace Lieu 1999, 66: "At no time in the Johannine ministry does Jesus speak
words of judgment against or anticipate the destruction within the divine dispen-
sation of the Temple—indeed he does not talk *about* the Temple at all." But John's
indirect references to the destruction of the temple are understandable in a context where this event was already taken for granted. It belonged to the past but
was not a matter of urgent and immediate concern, as may have been the case in
some earlier traditions.

the real point of the story is not in the material temple, the destruction of which is already anticipated. Most scholars emphasize the latter part of the story and say that Jesus' body is here presented as the substitute for the temple and the cult.[33] However, it must be asked what the function of the earlier part of the story is. Does it stem from the tradition which was no longer relevant to the evangelist?[34]

The portrayal of a furious Jesus in the temple is not necessarily superfluous to the present narrative, but there is a connection between the two parts of the temple episode. In his zealous defense of the temple and its sanctity, Jesus stands in the best Jewish traditions; as a matter of fact, he is presented as more Jewish than his Jewish contemporaries who profaned the temple. The presence of oxen and sheep in the temple highlights the corrupt conditions in the temple and betrays the degeneration of Jesus' contemporaries.[35] Thus both Jesus' demonstration in the temple and its eventual destruction are made to be seen as justified. From the Johannine point of view, the failure of the Jews to observe the sanctity of the material temple leads to its replacement by the temple of Jesus' body.

The view that the profanation of the cult leads to God's punishment is well attested in the scriptures.[36] According to John, Jesus' contemporaries are thus guilty of the same crime their forefathers have been punished for many times.[37] However, when Jesus visits the temple later in the gospel, there is no reference to Jesus' demonstration. The narrator does not mention the temple episode as one of the reasons that led to Jesus' death, although this is suggested in the episode itself (2:16). Jesus' devout criticism of the temple and the insistence on his exemplary Jewishness have an important but limited role in the gospel; they aim to justify the displacement of the Jewish cult by faith in Jesus.

---

[33] Dodd 1953, 301–302; Schnackenburg I 370; Brown 124–125; Barrett 195; Hartman 1989, 70–79; Schnelle 1996, 371. For a different view, see Lieu 1999, 63–64.

[34] Thus Bultmann 85–86; Becker 147.

[35] Bammel (1970, 16) notes that the introduction of the oxen and sheep to the original temple episode betrays "an anti-cultic tendency." According to Chilton (1997, 448), "the specific reference to oxen and sheep does play into the hands of the anti-cultic tendency of the early Church." However, Chilton thinks that this reference is not an invention of this anti-cultic tendency but is based on true arrangements in the temple in Jesus' time.

[36] 2 Chr 29:6–9; Isa 1:10–20; Jer 7:1–15; Ezek 5:1–11; 8–11; Mal 1:6–2:9; 3:1–3.

[37] Cf. Brown 122.

3.2. *The True Worship of the Father (John 4:20–24)*

After the temple episode, the theme of worship reappears in the
gospel when Jesus meets an unnamed Samaritan woman at a well.
The Jews are not present in the scene but the discussion says a lot
about them. A theme that runs through the whole scene is the breach
between the Jews and the Samaritans. Jesus adopts the point of view
of the Jews as he speaks with the Samaritan woman. He even states
that "we know what we worship, for salvation is from the Jews"
(v. 22b). At first glance, this statement seems to contradict other passages in the gospel where Jesus distances himself from the Jews and
claims that they do not know and have not ever known the Father
(5:37–38; 7:28–29; 8:55). Many scholars have suggested, therefore,
that the saying in 4:22 should not be regarded as an integral part
of the narrative.[38] My suggestion, however, is that the saying is a
crucial part of the narrative which shows how the salvation that
comes from the Jews is now received by the non-Jews, the Samaritans.
An ambivalence that characterizes the gospel as a whole is also evident in this passage: the scene emphasizes the Jewishness of Jesus
and the salvation brought by him, but, at the same time, it contains
features pointing away from Jewish concerns.

The Context of the Scene

In John 3:1–21 it is told how a representative of the Jews, Nicodemus,
failed to understand who Jesus is. At the beginning of John 4, Jesus
leaves the land of the Jews, and starts to Galilee through the land
of the Samaritans, with whom the Jews have no dealings. The episode
in ch. 4 comes to an end as the Samaritans recognize Jesus as the
Savior of the world (v. 42). The way the Samaritans accept Jesus is
contrasted with Nicodemus' previous failure to receive him. The
whole story illustrates, therefore, how Jesus moves away from the
Jews to non-Jews who welcome him. The narrator's remark that the
Jews do not deal with the Samaritans adds irony to the story (v. 9):
a representative of Jesus' own nation failed to receive Jesus, while
those despised by the Jews accept him.

The larger narrative context is important for the interpretation of
the words "salvation is from the Jews" (4:22). The expression εἶναι

---

[38] For the full discussion, see van Belle 2001, 370–400.

ἐκ is a common one in John, and in many cases it means roughly the same as the expression ἔρχεσθαι ἐκ. Both expressions are used to refer to a place or an origin from which a person or a thing comes (for example, 1:44, 46; 7:22, 41, 52; 11:1). In 4:22 the expression is used in the same way: the origin of salvation is from the Jews.[39] Although salvation originates from the Jews, the present context of the saying implies that salvation is now on its way away from them. Salvation is from the Jews to whom Jesus has come (1:11), but in the Johannine narrative it is others, non-Jews, who receive salvation.[40]

'The Fathers' and the Worship of the Father

At first glance, the theme of the right place for worship seems to be loosely connected to the rest of the dialogue in John 4. The discussion between Jesus and the Samaritan woman is full of suprising changes of the subject of conversation. In spite of these twists in the narrative, the different parts are connected to each other, and so each individual theme in the dialogue should be seen in light of the whole conversation. The earlier dialogue concerning the difference between the water drawn from Jacob's well and the living water given by Jesus foreshadows the contrast between the old forms of worship and the worship in spirit and truth. The allusions to the patriarchal traditions are significant for the interpretation of the story. The incident takes place in a field that Jacob gave to his son Joseph, and the well located there is called "Jacob's well" (vv. 5–6).[41] Furthermore, the woman reminds Jesus of the origin of the well and contrasts Jesus and Jacob: "Are you greater than our ancestor Jacob, who gave us the well, and with his sons and his flocks drank from it?" (v. 12). It is important to ask why Jesus and Jacob are contrasted in the story. To answer this question, we must examine the relationship of the Samaritans to the scriptural patriarchs and the different views on the origin of the Samaritans in Jewish tradition.

---

[39] Thus de la Potterie 1983, 90–91. For a different view, see Mussner 1979, 51. According to Mussner, the words "salvation is from the Jews" do not mean "salvation comes from the Jews." In the pre-Johannine tradition, the sentence meant that "the eschatological salvation of the world still remains with Judaism." The evangelist confessed the Jewish roots of the church through the positive reception of this verse. But Mussner's interpretation makes the sentence a general theological statement detached from its context.

[40] Meeks 1967, 41 n. 2; O'Day 1986, 70; Koester 1990, 672.

[41] For attempts to locate Jacob's well, see Zangenberg 1998, 96–106.

The only passage that explicitly mentions "the Samaritans" (שֹׁמְרֹנִים;
LXX: Σαμαρῖται) in the Hebrew Bible is 2 Kgs 17:24–41. In this
context, the name refers to those inhabitants of Samaria who were
brought to Assyria after the downfall of the northern kingdom
(v. 29). It is said that these people feared the Lord but, at the same
time, served their own gods (vv. 32–33; v. 41). In later Jewish tradition, this text was taken as an account of the origin of the Samaritan
people. The earliest evidence of this comes from Josephus, but it is
probable that he already draws upon an existing anti-Samaritan tradition (*Ant.* 9.288–291).[42] But elsewhere in the Hebrew Bible the
inhabitants of Samaria are not necessarily depicted as non-Jews. The
Chronicles does not mention the change in the population after the
downfall of the northern kingdom; rather, the inhabitants of Samaria
are a part of the people of Israel, descendants of Israelite tribes.[43]
This view is not too far removed from the later claims of the
Samaritans themselves—that they are the descendants of Joseph.[44]
Many biblical prophets also continue to refer to the people in Samaria
by the name Ephraim, even after the downfall of the northern kingdom.[45] Samaria included most of the territories that were given to
the two sons of Joseph, Ephraim and Manasseh (Josh 16–17), and
it is thus natural to connect the residents of this area to these two
sons of Joseph.[46] The testimony in the Hebrew Bible concerning the
origin of the Samaritans is thus not uniform, even though from a
later Jewish point of view, they were mostly regarded as non-Jews.[47]

The claim that the Samaritans regarded themselves as descendants
of Joseph's two sons appears for the first time in Josephus (*Ant.* 9.291;
11.341). According to Josephus, the Samaritans claimed that they
were related to the Jews through common ancestors, especially when
they saw the Jews prospering; when the Jews were in trouble, however, the Samaritans denied any kinship with them. This account
reflects, however, Josephus' own anti-Samaritan bias; it does not tell

---

[42] See Coggins 1987, 260.
[43] See Japhet 1989 (1973), 325–334; Williamson 1977, 97–131; Cogan 1988,
289–292.
[44] Cogan 1988, 292.
[45] For example, Jer 31:17–20; 23:5–6; Zech 9:13; 10:6f. Cf. MacDonald 1964,
22–24.
[46] Olsson 1974, 141, n. 18.
[47] Even though rabbinic tradition in its entirety negates the Israelite origin of the
Samaritans, according to some traditions they were true Israelites after their con-
version to Judaism. See Alon, 1977, 354–367.

much about the attitude of the Samaritans towards their own origin.[48] Later rabbinic literature states that the Samaritans claimed to be the descendants of Joseph, and the rabbis take a firm stand against this view.[49] We also meet the same claim in later Samaritan sources where Joseph has a prominent role.[50]

It is not surprising, then, that the Samaritan woman refers to Jacob as "our father." It is noteworthy, however, that the woman refers to Jacob and not to Joseph, who was especially connected to the Samaritans, and held a prominent position among them.[51] It is true, of course, that a claim to have Joseph as an ancestor comes close to a claim to have Jacob as an ancestor.[52] Jacob, however, is not only the father of the Samaritans but the father of all Israel. Thus the woman's question, "Are you greater than our ancestor Jacob?," introduces a new aspect to the story; the issue is no longer the difference between the Jews and the Samaritans but the position of Jesus in comparison to the patriarch of the people of God.[53] The woman's

---

[48] See Hall 1987, 167; Coggins 1987, 257.

[49] Cf. *Gen. Rab.* 94. In *y. 'Abod. Zar.* 3:2 it is said that the Samaritans (the men of Cuth) worshipped Jacob's foot and Joseph's foot. This view probably has to do with the claim of the Samaritans to be descendants of Jacob and Joseph. The rabbis resisted the claims of the Samaritans and mostly used the term "Cutheans" for them. See Alon 1977, 354.

[50] Meeks 1967, 228–231; Kippenberg 1971, 255–275.

[51] According to Olsson (1974, 141), Rabbi Meir calls Jacob the father of the Samaritans in *Pesiqta de Rab Kahana* 10 (in earlier editions number 11). But this is not true. It seems that this mistake goes back to Schlatter (120) according to whom R. Meir says the words "Do you not say that Jacob, your father, is truthful?" to a Samaritan (called a Cuthean) in a story about tithing. In this story, however, it is a Samaritan who asks R. Meir this question; the Samaritan wants to show that Jacob has not fulfilled the law because he has set aside only the tribe of Levi as a tithe although he has more than ten sons (for a parallel story, see *Gen. Rab.* 70). It is doubtful whether rabbis would have called Jacob the father of the Samaritans because other passages show that they denied this claim.

[52] Thus Hall 1987, 231.

[53] Some scholars refer in this connection to late Targumic traditions that would explain why Jesus and Jacob are contrasted in John. See Olsson 1974, 168–173; Neyrey 1979, 421–425; Moloney 1993, 137–138; Zangenberg 1998, 121–123. These traditions tell of Jacob's five miracles; one of these miracles happened when Jacob made a well in Haran to flow for twenty years (*Tg. Neof.* Gen 28:10; *Tg. Ps.-J.* Gen 28:10, cf. also 29:10; *Frg. Tg.* Gen 28:10). These scholars argue that in John's story the question of the Samaritan woman, "Are you greater than our ancestor Jacob?" contains a hidden allusion to this tradition. The problem with this tradition is that we cannot know whether the Targums contain material that goes back to the first century C.E. In this case, we should be especially cautious because the tradition of Jacob's five miracles did not appear in the earliest layers of the Targum tradition. *Tg. Neofiti* is often regarded as the earliest form of the Palestinian Targums, but the

question resembles the question the Jews pose to Jesus later in John
8:53: "Are you greater than our father Abraham, who died?" We
have here a variation of the Johannine theme that asserts Jesus'
superiority to the founding fathers of Jewishness (cf. also 1:17–18;
5:38; 6:32).[54]

It is noteworthy that Jesus does not have any objections when the
woman speaks of Jacob as the father of the Samaritans. From a
mainstream Jewish point of view, the claim of the Samaritans to be
descendants of Joseph was not acceptable.[55] Although Jesus is presented as a Jew when he encounters the Samaritan woman, he is
curiously indifferent to a question that had a prominent role in the
Jewish-Samaritan schism. The later treatment of the controversy concerning the right place for worship also shows the ambivalence of
Jesus' Jewishness in the story: on the one hand, the story attaches
great weight to Jesus' Jewishness, but, on the other hand, Jesus is
indifferent to major Jewish concerns.

The theme of 'the fathers' is continued in the passage dealing with
the right place for worship. The woman appeals to the fathers who
worshiped on Mt. Gerizim just as she earlier appealed to 'Jacob,
our father.'[56] In his answer, Jesus says that 'the Father' will be worshiped in a way that is not limited to any given place (v. 21 and
v. 23). Jesus' mention of 'the Father' undermines the earlier appeals
to many fathers.[57] It also contrasts 'the Father' and many fathers.[58]
From the Johannine point of view, fathers with their cults belong to
the past, whereas the hour has already come when the only Father
is worshiped by the true worshipers.

Jesus the Jew—a Prophet and the Messiah

A section dealing with the personal history of the Samaritan woman
(John 4:16–19) precedes the discussion about the right place for worship (vv. 20–24). These two topics seem to be totally unrelated. In

---

midrashic passages that refer to Jacob's miracles were probably not part of the original *Neofiti*. See Levy 1986, 187–192. The early date of this tradition is supported
only by John's story, but there is no hint in John to any miracle connected with
Jacob's well.

[54] Wead 1970, 63–64; Neyrey 1979, 420; Zangenberg 1998, 129.
[55] Thus Schlatter 120.
[56] Zangenberg 1998, 145.
[57] Thus Duke 1985, 70; O'Day 1986, 68–69; Moloney 1993, 150.
[58] Cf. Koester 1990, 674; Botha 1991, 152.

scholarly literature, there have been different attempts to understand the passage dealing with the woman's five husbands. Some scholars have suggested that the revelation of the woman's past emphasizes her sinful life and moral decline.[59] Jesus does not, however, blame the woman, and moral issues do not have a significant role in the story.[60] Some scholars have interpreted Jesus' words to the woman allegorically: she is seen as a representative of the Samaritan people whose religious past is referred to by Jesus. The woman's husbands correspond to the deities worshiped by different nations who were brought to Samaria (2 Kgs 17:24ff.).[61]

The text is, however, also understandable without an allegorical interpretation.[62] Jesus' words cause the woman to acknowledge him as a prophet, but we could expect that the hidden allusion to idolatry would evoke antagonism.[63] Therefore, Jesus' words to the woman are probably a simple statement of the woman's personal past. It is impossible to determine whether there is an intended secondary allusion to the religious past of the Samaritans in the text; we shall find out below that v. 22 contains an allusion to the syncretism among the Samaritans, and so it would be not far-fetched to already find a reference to this in vv. 16–19.

The Samaritan woman recognizes Jesus as a prophet, after he has revealed her past. Her initial unwillingness is now turned to the confession that Jesus is a prophet (v. 19). There is thus a clear progression in the woman's attitude toward Jesus: first she is suspicious of Jesus and regards him only as "a Jew" (v. 9); now she is ready to accept him as a prophet.[64] It is significant that a non-Jew, who at first was skeptical about Jesus, acknowledges Jesus as a Jewish prophet and deems him as the right person to settle an old controversy concerning the right place for worship. Some scholars think the woman changes the subject for personal reasons because Jesus

---

[59] Hoskyns 242; Bultmann 138; Schnackenburg I 468.

[60] Thus also Odeberg 186; Haenchen 242; Okure 1988, 110; Becker 204–205; Botha 1991, 142–143; Zangenberg 1998, 134–135.

[61] Odeberg 179; Hoskyns 242–243; Dodd 1953, 313; Kippenberg 1971, 115–116; Olsson 1974, 186; Purvis 1975, 193–194; Betz 1987, 424; Botha 1991, 150.

[62] The allegorical interpretation is rejected by Bultmann 138 n. 4; Schnackenburg I 468; Lindars 186–187; Haenchen 242; Okure 1988, 111–112; Becker 205; Moloney 1993, 148–149 n. 69.

[63] Becker 205–206.

[64] Cf. O'Day 1986, 67; Okure 1988, 109; Moloney 1993, 109.

has just revealed her secret past.[65] The woman's question is, however, the most natural one in this context; as she has found out that
she is speaking with a Jewish prophet, she poses a question a prophet
should be able to answer. It is noteworthy that this is the first time
when the woman is the initiator of the topic of conversation.[66] Her
question concerning the right place for worship is tightly connected
to her confession that Jesus is a prophet.[67]

Many scholars have interpreted the woman's confession that Jesus
is a prophet (v. 19) or the Messiah, "who, when he comes shows us
everything" (v. 25) in the light of Samaritan tradition. It is argued
that the woman's words express Samaritan beliefs about the prophet
like Moses or the eschatological figure called Ta'eb.[68] It is unlikely,
however, that the narrator and the readers understand the woman's
confession from a Samaritan point of view.

The earliest sources on Samaritan tradition are from the fourth
century C.E.[69] Except for the Fourth Gospel, there is no evidence
that Samaritan eschatological beliefs found in later sources existed
in the first century C.E.[70] The expectation of a prophet was not only
the property of the Samaritans but part of the common tradition
shared by the Jews and the Samaritans.[71] The beliefs the Samaritan
woman expresses can be explained on the basis of Johannine theology.[72]

---

[65] Cf. Bernard 145; Duke 1985, 103. According to Hoskyns (243), the woman,
whose sins have just been revealed by Jesus, asks the prophet to show the place of
forgiveness.

[66] O'Day 1986, 68.

[67] Cf. Olsson 1974, 187; O'Day 1986, 67–68; Okure 1988, 114–115; Zangenberg
1998, 140.

[68] Montgomery 1968 (1907), 243; Odeberg 181–187; MacDonald 1964, 361, 364;
Brown 171–172, Schnackenburg I 475–476; Freed 1970, 243, 248. It is often noted
that in the woman's words of "the Messiah, who when he comes shows us everything," the term Messiah does not correspond to the early Samaritan eschatology.
Some scholars ponder over the possibility that the term Ta'eb would originally have
been used in the text. Cf. Odeberg 187. According to Meeks (1967, 318 n. 1), the
fact that the title Μεσσίας has been put in the mouth of the Samaritan woman is
"a clear sign of the leveling of different terminologies." Cf. also Kippenberg 1971,
303, 313. According to Kippenberg, the different figures of Ta'eb and the prophet
like Moses should be kept apart in the Samaritan eschatology. Thus the words of
the Samaritan woman in John reflect the Samaritan expectation of the prophet but
have nothing to do with Ta'eb. In a similar vein, Olsson 1974, 190–192.

[69] See Purvis 1975, 162–168.

[70] Hall 1987, 298–299.

[71] Dexinger 1985, 110.

[72] Cf. Hall 1987, 298.

Her faith does not differ from the faith of some other characters in the Johannine narrative (cf. 1:41; 7:41; 9:17).[73] These characters speak of Jesus as 'a prophet' or as 'the Messiah.' The faith of the woman is thus not particularly Samaritan, but she shares her faith with other Johannine characters; her faith is not yet enough but points to the right understanding of Jesus.[74]

There is a clear emphasis on Jesus' Jewishness in the story at this point.[75] The fact that the woman acknowledges Jesus as a Jewish prophet and later begins to wonder whether he is Christ (v. 29), is important for Jesus' teaching of the true worship. The woman realizes that Jesus is the culmination of what has been promised. Because Jesus is presented as the fulfilment of past promises, he can also be presented as the one who surpasses these promises. The Johannine Jesus can reveal that the true worship exceeds previous forms of worship, since the woman recognizes him as a Jewish prophet and later Jesus identifies himself as the expected Messiah (v. 26).[76] The emphasis on Jesus' Jewishness lays a foundation for his teaching according to which neither the Samaritan nor the Jewish way of worship is right.

The words "salvation is from the Jews" are in line with the emphasis on Jesus' Jewishness. In John, salvation is closely connnected to Jesus' person, and, therefore, these words can be interpreted christologically.[77] They imply that Jesus the Jew is the one whom the woman expects.[78] Thus Jesus' words claim implicitly that he is the expected Messiah.[79] Jesus must be a Jew to be the Messiah.[80] The woman, who from a Jewish point of view is an outsider, learns that Jesus the Jew is the bringer of salvation, whereas the Jews themselves have turned away from Jesus. Thus there is an implicit criticism of the

---

[73] Cf. Pamment 1982, 223.
[74] The role of special Samaritan beliefs in ch. 4 is also denied by Pamment 1982, 225; Becker 201–202. Cf. also Meeks 1975, 177–178. In his earlier book (1967), Meeks studied the role of the Samaritan traditions in the shaping of the Johannine christology. Meeks states later that the role of these traditions must not be exaggerated, and that "the author of the gospel shows no sensitivity to specifically Samaritan concerns and terminology" (1975, 178).
[75] Cf. Betz 1987, 424; Okure 1988, 114.
[76] Cf. Leidig 1981, 126.
[77] See Leidig 1981, 125; De la Potterie 1983, 106.
[78] Botha 1991, 146–147.
[79] Cf. Hoskyns 244; Lindars 189; Betz 1987, 433–435; R. F. Collins 2001, 289.
[80] Leidig 1981, 132.

Jews in the story because they have not received Jesus, a prophet and the Messiah, who is one of their own.[81]

The Samaritans, the Jews, and the True Worshipers of the Father

Jesus gets an opportunity to teach the true worship, as the Samaritan woman asks where God should be worshiped: she refers to Mt. Gerizim where the Samaritans had had their own sanctuary until it was destroyed by John Hyrcanus (cf. *Ant.* 12.256). Even after the destruction of the temple, Mt. Gerizim remained as the holy place for the Samaritans.[82] The controversy over the right place for worship was at the heart of the conflict between the Jews and the Samaritans. Josephus twice tells of the Alexandrian Jews quarreling with the Samaritans over which temple is the right place for the worship of God (*Ant.* 12.10; 13.74–79). According to Josephus, these controversies took place in the second century B.C.E., which is, however, problematic. But Josephus' accounts show that in his time, at the latest, the disputes between the Jews and the Samaritans had spread to the Diaspora, and that the quarrel over the true temple was essential to these disputes.[83] Later rabbinic sources also relate this controversy from a Jewish point of view (e.g., *Gen. Rab.* 32 and 81).

The woman asks Jesus a question that was a burning issue in the debates between the Jews and the Samaritans. The discussion about this issue shows that the narrator and his audience had some knowledge of this debate, but they approach it neither from a Jewish nor a Samaritan point of view. The Johannine Jesus is not so much interested in settling the old controversy than in highlighting the difference between the old forms of worship—the Samaritan and the Jewish alike—and the new worship established by him.[84] He refers to a time when God will not be worshiped on Mt. Gerizim or in Jerusalem (v. 21). Although Jesus implies that the new worship transcends the polarity of the earlier forms of worship, he seems to return

---

[81] Okure 1988, 124.
[82] Kippenberg 1971, 98–113.
[83] Cf. Coggins 1975, 97–98.
[84] Cf. Becker 206: "Das Ziel ist es auch nicht, den aktuellen Streit zu entscheiden, sondern der längst christlich entschiedene Streit zu benutzen, um im Kontrast zu ihm das Wesen christlicher Religion zu beschreiben." For a different view, see Betz 1987, 425. According to Betz, the evangelist wants to show how Jesus restores the unity of the people of God and tries to do away with Jewish-Samaritan ignorance and polemics.

to the contrast between the Jews and the Samaritans in the next verse, as he says: "You worship what you do not know but we worship what we know." It must be asked how these words should be understood.

According to some scholars, 'we' in Jesus' mouth refers to Jesus and all the believers who share his teaching of God (cf. John 3:11), not to the Jews.[85] This interpretation, however, detaches the saying from its narrative context where the contrast between the Jews and the Samaritans is essential. Therefore, the difference between the ignorant 'you' and the well-informed 'we' in v. 22 probably refers to the difference between the Samaritans and the Jews.[86] The Johannine Jesus speaks here as one of the Jews and evaluates the religion of the Samaritans from a Jewish point of view.[87] He seems to admit that Jewish worship is superior to that of the Samaritans. Jesus says that the Jews know what they worship although in the rest of the gospel he states that the Jews do not know the Father (5:37–38; 7:28–29; 8:55). To understand Jesus' words, we must see them in the light of their intertextual background.

Jesus' words that the Samaritans do not know what they worship go back to the Jewish anti-Samaritan tradition that is based on the reading of 2 Kgs 17:24–41. It is said in this text that the nations brought to Samaria "do not know the law of the god of the land" (LXX: οὐκ οἴδασιν τὸ κρίμα τοῦ θεοῦ τῆς γῆς). This comes rather close to Jesus' words in John, ὑμεῖς προσκυνεῖτε ὃ οὐκ οἴδατε.[88] Later it is told that the Samaritans indeed began to fear the Lord (2 Kgs 17:32, 34, 41), but still continued to make their own gods and serve them. It is emphatically stated that this is what they and their children do to this day (vv. 34, 41). From a Jewish point of view, the text claims that the Samaritans had not understood in the correct way what it means to worship the only God of Israel. In John, this is expressed by the words "you worship what you do not know." This formulation also recalls those scriptural passages that speak of gentiles who

---

[85] Odeberg 170–171; Olsson 1974, 197; Thyen 1980, 170. Cf. also de la Potterie 1982, 97. According to de la Potterie, the words "we worship what we know" refer only to Jesus, although Jesus uses a plural here. In John, only Jesus has the knowledge of God.

[86] Schackenburg I 470; Lindars 189; Barrett 237; Leidig 1981, 117; O'Day 1986, 69; Betz 1987, 424; Okure 1988, 117; Moloney 1993, 150; Hahn 1996, 108.

[87] Thus Montgomery 1968 (1907); Pamment 1982, 223.

[88] De la Potterie 1982, 96 n. 37; Betz 1987, 423.

do not know the God of Israel.[89] Jesus' words in John, therefore, contain an implicit accusation of idolatry among the Samaritans.[90]

The anti-Samaritan tradition based on 2 Kgs 17 was continued in some sources, according to which the Samaritans were fools, or senseless (Sir 50:26; *T. Levi* 7:2) and liable to syncretism.[91] But it is most probable that the Samaritans in the first centuries C.E. were not syncretists.[92] The implicit reference of the Johannine Jesus to the worship of idols among the Samaritans is thus based more on 2 Kgs 17:24–41 than on first-hand knowledge of Samaritanism. John and his readers share the view of mainstream Judaism that the Samaritans were late-comers as worshipers of the God of Israel; therefore, they lacked the right knowledge of what they worshiped.

Jesus' words that the Jews know what they worship can be understood in the light of what is said about the ignorance of the Samaritans. As late-born servants of God, the Samaritans were ignorant, whereas the Jews worshiped the true God right from the beginning. The Jews had received God's revelation and promises; hence their knowledge of what they worship.[93] According to the Johannine view, Jesus is the fulfilment of this knowledge; the scriptures of the Jews point to him, although the Jews in Jesus' time do not understand this (cf. 5:36–47; 8:37–59). Jesus' words in 4:22 have to do more with the

---

[89] De la Potterie 1982, 96; Koester 1990, 672–673.

[90] Thus Koester 1990, 674.

[91] Josephus states that the Samaritans wanted their temple to be known as the temple of Zeus Hellenios and sees this as unacceptable to any true Jew (*Ant.* 12.257–264). Coggins (1987, 265–266) says, however, that Josephus has emphasized the culpability of the Samaritans on purpose. According to 2 Macc 6:2, the temple on Mt. Gerizim was dedicated to Zeus Xenios. This title meant "the protector of the rights of the strangers" and was probably less offensive than the one mentioned by Josephus. Different hellenistic designations for God were not alien to the Jews of the second century B.C.E., and the naming of the temple would have been inconsequential to most of them. See Goldstein 1976, 137, 142 and 1983, 272. Josephus here implies that there were syncrenistic tendencies among the Samaritans, but he is unable to give any evidence of these tendencies in his own time. The Mishnah does not mention the idolatry among the Samaritans either (Hall 1987, 166, 208). It is not until post-tannaitic rabbinic tradition that we encounter the explicit accusation that the Samaritans practiced idolatry. The rabbis took as their starting point the story that tells how Jacob hid all his families' images of foreign gods under the oak near Shechem (Gen 35:4); according to rabbis, the Samaritans lusted after these images and, therefore, regarded Mt. Gerizim as their holy place. See *Gen. Rab.* 81; *y. ʿAbod. Zar.* 5:4.

[92] Dexinger 1981, 106; Freyne 2000, 122–123.

[93] Cf. Hahn 1996 (1976), 109–116; Leidig 1981, 114–132; Okure 1988, 117; Moloney 1993, 150–151.

Jews as God's own people who have received his law and promises than with the unbelieving and even hostile contemporaries of Jesus.[94] The Jews are thus privileged compared to the Samaritans and other non-Jews, but they can lose their privilege if they do not accept Jesus. Indeed, this is what the story in John 4 illustrates: the Jews who had knowledge, and from whom salvation comes, have lost their privileged position to those who have received the Savior of the world.[95] Especially because the Jews were the ones who had knowledge, they can also be accused of the neglect of what they had been given.[96]

It has become clear that the words "we know what we worship, for salvation is from the Jews" do not refer to the continuing priority of the Jews over the non-Jews in John. The division between two different eras reflected in Jesus' words confirms this.[97] The use of the adversative conjunction ἀλλά in the beginning of v. 23 denotes a clear division of time into an era before Jesus' coming and into that which has begun with his coming: the situation described in v. 22 has changed and now belongs to the past.[98] There is no clear continuity between the old and the new era but

> false or incomplete cultic actions presently give way to 'true worshipers' and the old mode of worship is supplanted by 'worshiping in spirit and truth.' Indeed nothing of the old tradition remains; it is totally supplanted.[99]

Jesus calls the worshipers of the new era 'the true worshipers' (οἱ ἀληθινοὶ προσκυνηταί) and twice says that they worship the Father 'in spirit and truth' (ἐν πνεύματι καὶ ἀληθείᾳ). The adjective ἀληθινός in John "implies exclusivity in the sense of 'the only real,' as compared with the putative or would-be."[100] The true worshipers in the

---

[94] Cf. de la Potterie 1982, 92.
[95] See Leidig 1981, 119.
[96] Cf. Hahn 1996, 115.
[97] See de la Potterie 1982, 88–93.
[98] Cf. Schnackenburg I 471. However, see Thyen 1980, 177. According to Thyen, the saying "salvation is from the Jews" does not refer only to the past phase of salvation history and to the Jewish origin of Christianity. Thyen says that the saying has a more fundamental and actual meaning connected to the violent expulsion from the synagogue. John 4:22 shows that the Johannine community cannot deny its roots, even though it has experienced the expulsion as a misfortune and as an injustice. But there is nothing in the immeadite context of the saying that would connect it to the alleged expulsion from the synagogue. The saying is connected to the Jewish-Samaritan schism but not to the expulsion from the synagogue.
[99] Neyrey 1979, 433.
[100] Brown 500. Cf. also Barrett 160 and 473.

new era are thus contrasted with the previous worshipers who did not worship God in the right way. It is not difficult to connect the implicit criticism of Jewish worship in this verse to the explicit criticism of the corrupted worship in John 2:13–22. From the Johannine point of view, both the Samaritan and the Jewish worshipers are untrue worshipers of God, and their worship is supplanted by the worship of the true worshipers. Jesus promises the Samaritan woman that "the hour is coming when you will worship the Father neither on this mountain nor in Jerusalem" (v. 21). This implies that also the old worshipers may take part in the true worship of the Father, if they are ready to abandon their former modes of worship. The text is already distanced from traditional Samaritan or Jewish concerns, and presents the new worshipers as a new group distinct from both the Samaritans and the Jews.[101]

Just as both truth and spirit are closely connected to Jesus in John, so the worship in spirit and truth is also. The new worship in the Johannine sense does not mean spiritual worship as contrasted to external forms of worship.[102] The contrast is rather between the worship apart from Jesus and the worship established by Jesus.[103] Although the new worship is not bound to any given place or local traditions, it is bound to the person of Jesus.[104] The true worship in spirit and truth is thus a response to Jesus' revelation of the Father.[105]

The way Jesus speaks of the true worship and true worshipers is not without parallels in the Hebrew Bible or in subsequent Jewish tradition. In many scriptural passages God or his representatives criticize the old forms of worship and demand their replacement by obedience to God (e.g., 1 Sam 15:22–23; Isa 1:10–20; Mic 6:6–8; Hos 6:6).[106] The idea that the worship of God is not limited to any given place is also attested in the Hebrew Bible (1 Kgs 8:27; Isa 66:1). The closest parallel to 'the worship in spirit and truth' can be found in the writings of Qumran where both 'truth' and 'spirit' are connected to the worship of the community.[107] After the destruction

---

[101] Cf. Zangenberg 1998, 153.
[102] This is now universally agreed, see Brown 180–181; Lindars 189; Schnackenburg I 471. For an earlier view, see Odeberg 170 and 172.
[103] Lindars 189; Haenchen 245.
[104] Betz 1987, 432.
[105] Becker 210.
[106] Cf. Freed 1969, 40; Haenchen 244.
[107] See Schnackenburg 1959, 88–94; Freed 1969, 38–48; Betz 1987, 429–432.

of the temple, the emerging rabbinic Judaism also redefined its relationship to the temple and to the worship of God.[108] The Johannine
view of the true worship can be seen as a part of this development.
The Johannine Jesus, however, does not present the true worship of
the Father as something that grows naturally out of earlier traditions
but as something totally new.[109] According to the Johannine Jesus,
the earlier forms of worship, the Samaritan and the Jewish alike,
were bound to certain places which shows that they were not the
true worship of God. There is no sign in the text of those forms of
Judaism that established the worship of God in a way that was not
restricted to certain places. The Judaism to which the new worship
of the Father is contrasted here is thus the Judaism of the Second
Temple Period rather than the Judaism that emerged after the destruction of the temple in 70 C.E. Thus the image of temple-orientated
Judaism was still the prevailing form of Judaism in the minds of the
Johannine Christians although they probably lived at a time when
the material temple no longer existed.[110]

3.3. *Conclusion: The Johannine Christians, Worship and Jewishness*

Both in John 2:13–22 and in 4:20–24, Jesus' attitude to a central
feature of Jewishness, worship in the Jerusalem temple, is ambivalent.
We can clarify this ambivalent attitude with the help of the three-
world model introduced in the introduction to this study. In John
2:13–22, the conflicting ways of understanding Jesus both as a reformer
of the Jerusalem temple and as its substitute may reflect discrepancy
between the symbolic universe of the Johannine Christians and their
real world situation. In their symbolic universe, the Johannine Christians
pictured Jesus as a loyal cherisher of the best Jewish traditions. It is

---

[108] See Neusner 1975, 46–49.
[109] Pace Freed 1969, 47: "And it was not 'the expected Messiah' who brought
'the true worship of God in spirit and truth.' Such worship was already present in
Judaism. According to John, Jesus only confirmed it."
[110] Cf. Zangenberg 1998, 228. Zangenberg says that the formulation in John
4:20, "you say that the place where people must worship is in Jerusalem," suggests
that John could have been written before 70 C.E. But I do not see this as a reason to rethink the traditional view that dates John to the end of the first century.
The reference to the worship in Jerusalem in John 4:20–24 suggests only that, for
the Johannine Christians, Judaism was still very much bound to the Jerusalem temple and its cult even after the destruction of the temple.

likely that this is how they also understood themselves in relation to
Jewish tradition. They saw themselves as a part of that tradition and
their faith in Jesus as its culmination. The statement in John 4:22
can be taken as an acknowledgment of this heritage. The Johannine
Christians saw the Jews as the bearers of God's past promises who
know what they worship and from whom salvation comes.

But both John 2:13–22 and 4:20–22 also suggest that the Johannine
Christians had become alienated from their Jewish heritage in real
life. The narrator views a major Jewish festival, the Passover, as an
outsider. The description of the conditions in the temple is unrealistic, and Jesus' attack remains unspecified and does not lead to anything in the gospel as a whole. The interest in the reformation of
the cult soon disappears and all that counts is faith in Jesus. It seems
that the Johannine Christians know the temple cult only as something from the past, and they take for granted its abolition.[111] Also
in John 4, Jesus the Jew is indifferent to central Jewish concerns,
the patriarchs and worship in the Jerusalem temple. Jesus is presented as a Jew and the Messiah in this story, but the story also
refers to the breaking away of the writer and his audience from
other Jews in the real world. They have already formed a defined
group of their own, they identify themselves neither with the Jews
nor with the Samaritans but regard themselves as true worshipers
who have been able put behind earlier—and from their point of
view—untrue ways of worshiping God.[112] The text speaks, therefore,
for the emergence of a new Christian identity distinct from Judaism.

The Johannine view of Jesus' body as the new temple that has
superseded the material temple and its worship can be taken as one
of many Jewish and early Christian ways of coping with the situation where the material temple and its cult no longer existed.[113] It
is by no means clear that "circumstances dictated that [the significance

---

[111] Haenchen 206.

[112] Cf. Zangenberg 1998, 165–166. According to Zangenberg, John does not
argue either for the Samaritan or for the Jewish forms of worship, but wants to
establish a new, third way to worship God.

[113] See Dunderberg 1998, 58. Dunderberg analyzes Jesus' temple saying in John
2:19 in relation to a parallel saying in *Gos. Thom.* 71. Dunderberg argues convincingly that there is not a direct relatioship between these two sayings, but they both
may "reflect vanishing eschatological hopes in connection with the destruction of
the temple."

of the temple] was going to be undermined in one way or another anyway," even though John and some other early Christian sources would suggest this.[114] Both rabbinic literature and the remnants of Diaspora synagogues show that "centuries after the destruction of Jerusalem, the image and meaning of the temple and its cult are never something wholly of the past."[115] However, the Johannine Christians went a different way in their relation to the temple, a central Jewish symbol. They could imagine Jesus as a reformer of the corrupted cult, which confirmed that they were right in abandoning the temple, but their faith was not nurtured by the traditions connected to the temple, and the temple and its cult did not have a lasting symbolic value for them.

The above analyses show how John understands Jesus' Jewishness. In John 2, Jesus' exemplary Jewishness justifies the displacement of the material temple by faith in Jesus. In John 4, Jesus' Jewishness lays the ground for the conviction that he is a prophet and the expected Messiah who redefines the way God should be worshiped. This is also how the saying, "salvation is from the Jews," should be understood. The Johannine Jesus is not alone in deriving the origins of the Christian faith from the people of God and their Scriptures; this was the prevailing view among early Christians.[116] But it seems that the Jewishness of Jesus and salvation is a self-evident historical fact for John rather than a far-reaching theological confession.

Many scholars, however, regard the saying "salvation is from the Jews" as a potential corrective to some other passages in John that are more open to anti-Jewish interpretations. According to them, by means of this saying John admits the lasting value and importance of Judaism to the Christian faith.[117] The above reading, unfortunately, does not support this conclusion. It seems that many scholars are not equally critical of this passage as they are of John's more overtly anti-Jewish passages.[118] The very fact that the saying appears in a

---

[114] Pace Dunn 1991, 96.
[115] Meyers & Kraabel 1986, 195. Cf. also Kraabel 1981, 86; Cohen 1987, 219. Cohen notes that "more than half of the Mishnah is devoted to one aspect or another of the temple and its cult."
[116] Moloney 1993, 151.
[117] Cf. Mussner 1979, 51; Thyen 1980, 169; Söding 2000, 21–41; Van Belle 2001, 400.
[118] Bieringer & Pollefeyt & Vandecasteele-Vanneuville 2001b, 36.

story dealing with non-Jews who receive Jesus shows that it functions
against the Jews rather than for them. The saying underlines the
culpability of the Jews who have failed to receive the Messiah who
comes from their midst.[119] This belief may be acceptable in a first
century context but perilous if taken as a model for Christianity's
relationship with Judaism in today.

---

[119] Thus also Bieringer & Pollefeyt & Vandecasteele-Vanneuville 2001b, 36.

CHAPTER FOUR

JESUS, THE SABBATH AND CIRCUMCISION

4.1. *Jesus Breaks the Sabbath and Makes Himself*
Equal with God (5:1–18)

The story in John 5:1–18 gives us the opportunity to evaluate what
kind of stand Jesus the Jew takes towards a central symbol of
Jewishness, the Sabbath. The story tells how Jesus falls into conflict
with the Jews after he has healed a lame man at the pool of Bethzatha.
The Jews accuse him of breaking the Sabbath and later of making
himself equal to God. It is important to ask how the Johannine narrator understands these charges that throw suspicion on the Jewishness
of his hero. I suggest that the way the story is told in John 5:1–18
as well as contemporary Jewish Sabbath legislation show that the
Jews in the story do not misunderstand Jesus' action. The narrator
presents Jesus as deliberately provoking a clash over the Sabbath.
The story as a whole and the narrator's remarks in 5:16 and 18 in
particular are revealing because they imply that the narrator and his
audience already take for granted Jesus' liberal attitude to the Sabbath.
Furthermore, the Jewish persecution of Jesus has already become a
fixed and predetermined part of their view of the world. Just like
earlier stories in John 2 and 4, this story contains traces of the departure of the Johannine Christians from the Jewish way of life: Jesus'
action on the Sabbath shows them that he is equal to God, but the
Sabbath is no longer a legal question for them, and they are likely
to have given up its literal observance.

The Context of the Scene

The incident at the pool of Bethzatha is Jesus' third sign which is
described in detail in John. It differs to a great extent from the earlier signs. The narrator has previously related how Jesus transformed
water into wine in Cana (2:1–11), and how he healed the son of a
official after returning to Galilee from Judaea (4:46–54). There are
many points of contact between these two stories.[1] In both stories it

---

[1] See Culpepper 1993, 198–99.

is not Jesus who takes the initiative in performing the sign, but both
incidents begin with a supplicant presenting Jesus with a request (2:3;
4:47). In both cases, Jesus first rebuffs the request (2:4; 4:48), but
when the supplicant persists, he grants the request (2:5,7; 4:49–50).
At the end of both stories, the sign is verified by a third party (2:10;
4:51–53) and a response of faith is recorded (2:11; 4:53).

The third sign story in John, the healing of a lame man, is "a
deliberate variation on the form of a sign," when compared to the
two previous sign stories.[2] At the pool of Bethzatha, Jesus himself,
not the supplicant, takes the initiative. At first, the narrator describes
a multitude of invalids, blind, lame, and paralyzed who lie in the
porticoes at the pool (v. 3). Then he focuses on a man who has been
ill for thirty-eight years (v. 4).[3] After that, the narrator tells how Jesus
saw the man and reveals also that Jesus knew that the man had
been ill for a long time. The dialogue between the man and Jesus
begins as Jesus asks the lame man, "Do you want to be made well?"
(v. 6). It is clear this time that Jesus controls the action and initiates the sign.[4] There is no indication of his being hesitant to perform the miracle, as in the previous stories. The one who is hesitant
is the lame man when he answers Jesus' question (v. 7).

Jesus' question "Do you want to be made well?" is quite surprising
in the context of a healing story; there is no parallel to it in other
miracle stories in John or in the rest of the New Testament.[5] It has
been suggested that Jesus' question and the lame man's answer make
it clear that the man did not have the will to be healed. This will
would mean the same as πίστις in some synoptic healing narratives.[6]
This explanation is not satisfactory, however, because the man gives
in his answer a reason why the healing he has longed for has not
yet taken place.[7] The man's answer is not in line with Jesus' question, but not because he lacks the will to be healed but because he
does not understand who Jesus is. The man sees in Jesus a potential helper who could put him into the pool at the right moment.[8]

---

[2] Culpepper 1993, 199.
[3] Culpepper 1993, 201; Becker 278.
[4] Haenchen 268.
[5] Witkamp 1985, 40 n. 39 and 40.
[6] Thus Dodd 1963, 176; Brown 209; Beasley-Murray 74; Culpepper 1993, 204.
[7] Thus Haenchen 269; Lindars 215; Witkamp 1985, 23; Fortna 1988, 114.
[8] Schnackenburg II 121; Haenchen 269; Asiedu-Peprah 2001, 64.

Like many other characters in the gospel, the lame man misunderstands Jesus' words because he fails to see who Jesus really is. We have here a typical Johannine misunderstanding.[9] The reader is already prepared to witness another sign of Jesus and understands Jesus' question as the promise of a miracle. Therefore, the reader cannot but notice the irony of the scene, as the man does not recognize Jesus who offers him what he has been awaiting.[10]

The miracle in 5:1–9 is told in a surprising way, but it has not become clear thus far why Jesus takes the initiative and heals the lame man. The man's misunderstanding underlines Jesus' determined action and raises the question as to why Jesus initiates the sign this time and heals the lame man. The change of the miracle story into a controversy between Jesus and the Jews explains the unusual features of the miracle story.

Jesus' Act as an Intentional Provocation

There is a surprising twist in the story that has begun as a simple healing story (v. 9). The narrator states that the lame man was healed at once as Jesus spoke to him, and that the man took up his mat and walked. Instead of telling of the possible response to the miracle, the narrator says, in a narrative aside, that the miracle took place on the Sabbath. This mention is rather belated, and many scholars have argued that the Sabbath question has been secondarily joined to the original miracle story.[11] But even in this case, the mention of the Sabbath is by no means random. The narrator withholds this information until this point in the story and "forces the reader to review the healing from a new perspective which catches the reader by surprise."[12] The reader may now guess why Jesus himself took the initiative to perform a miracle this time. Jesus' action appears as a deliberate transgression of Sabbath laws when it is reconsidered in the light of the narrator's belated mention of the Sabbath.[13] This

---

[9] Witkamp 1985, 23–25; Dunderberg 1994, 105.

[10] Cf. Asiedu-Peprah 2001, 64.

[11] For the literature, see Witkamp 1985, 19–21; Kotila 1988, 12 n. 2; Dunderberg 1994, 101 n. 5.

[12] Culpepper 1993, 205–6. Cf. also Staley 1991, 59–60; Welck 1994, 151; Asiedu-Peprah 2001, 66–67.

[13] Cf. Welck 1994, 151.

becomes evident as we take a closer look at how Jesus' action violates Jewish Sabbath laws.

According to a rabbinic rule, healing is allowed on the Sabbath
if there is possibility that life is in danger. This view most likely represents a common Jewish understanding already in the first century
C.E.[14] But the situation described in John was not a case of emergency
that would justify work. It is noteworthy, however, that Jesus heals
the lame man by telling him to rise up—not by doing anything
which could be regarded as work (cf. Mk 3:1–6 and *par.*) It is not
at all clear that Jesus' healing *as such* violates the Sabbath because
Jesus heals by his word, and speaking was not regarded as work in
any Jewish tradition.[15]

Jesus' command to the man, "Stand up, take your mat and walk,"
is a totally different matter, however. It surely goes against the
Sabbath laws that were shared by many different Jewish groups.[16]
Most Sabbath passages in the Pentateuch simply state a general pro-

---

[14] There appears the following rule in *m. Yoma* 8:6: "And any matter of doubt
as to danger of life overrides the prohibitions of the Sabbath" (Neusner's translation). This axiom is attributed to R. Mattiah b. Harash (early second century) but
it was probably known earlier. The same rule also appears in *Mek. Šabb.* 1 where
it is derived from the principle that bloodshed in self-defense overrides the Sabbath.
The opinion that allows bloodshed in self-defense already appears in 1 Macc 2:41
and later in several passages in Josephus (*Ant.* 13.12–13; 18.318–324; J.W. 1.146).
See Rowland 1982, 50. Just as the view which allows bloodshed in self-defense on
the Sabbath is an early one, it is probable that the view which allows danger to
life to override the Sabbath is a pre-rabbinic one. The discussions of minor cures
recorded in rabbinic literature (*m. Šabb.* 14:3–4; *t. Šabb.* 12:8–14) imply that work
was allowed in case of serious danger or illness. Therefore, E. P. Sanders (1990,
13) is probably right when he concludes that the rule in *m. Yoma* 8:6 was a common understanding since the days of the Hasmonean wars.

[15] Thus M. Davies 1992, 298–99. For a different view, see Back 1995, 46–49.
Back argues that the healing of a person suffering from a non-mortal illness did
not in any case override the Sabbath according to the Pharisaic halakhic tradition.
Jesus' healings described in the gospels were thus transgressions of Pharisaic halakhah,
even though Jesus did not engage in anything which was regarded as work. Back
cites *m. Šabb* 14:2–3 and 22:6, but both these passages suggest that healings achieved
without using special remedies or cures were allowed, whereas one should avoid
everything which could be understood as practicing medicine on the Sabbath. In
light of these passages, it is not at all clear whether the healings which Jesus performed by his word would have been regarded as practising medicine and thus illegal. We should remember that Sabbath laws were not created for such exceptional
cases as miracles. The conflict stories in the gospels do not necessarily describe the
responses of any real Jewish group to Jesus. They may well reflect the need of the
early church to create stories in which Jesus criticizes Jewish law and is in turn
criticized by the Jews. Thus E. P. Sanders 1993, 212–218.

[16] For surveys of Jewish Sabbath laws, see Hasel 1992, 849–856; Back 1995, 20–51.

hibition of all work on the Sabbath (e.g., Exod 20:8–11; 23:12; 31:12–17; Lev 23:3; Deut 5:12–15). Some passages prohibit explicitly some forms of work (Exod 16; 34:21; 35:2–3), but there is no specific definition of what work is or an extensive list of different forms of work prohibited on the Sabbath in the Pentateuch.

In subsequent writings the Sabbath laws become more specified. Neh 13:15–22 prohibits trade on the Sabbath. In Jer 17:19–27, God commissions the prophet to forbid carrying a burden in or out of a city, and in or out of a house on the Sabbath. The influence of this passage on later Sabbath observance was great. The prohibition against carrying a burden out of a house appears among other forms of work prohibited on the Sabbath in the *Jubilees* (2:30; 50:8), in the *Damascus Document* (11:7–8), in Philo (*Migration* 91) and in the Mishnah (*m. Šabb.* 7:3–9:7; cf. also *m. Šabb.* 10:5). The significance of this prohibition is also evident in the practice of 'fusion' or 'interweaving' (*'êrûb*) of houses which made possible to carry things from one part of the fused house to another and thus eased the observance of impractical Sabbath regulations. This practice was probably already developed by the Pharisees, whereas the Sadducees were stricter in their Sabbath observance and rejected it (cf. *m. 'Erub.* 6:2).[17] But both parties agreed that it is not allowed to transport anything from one domain to another on the Sabbath.

It seems clear that most Jews would have agreed, as the Jews in John say to the cured man, "It is the Sabbath, it is not lawful for you to carry your mat" (v. 10). This charge does not presuppose any exceptionally strict Sabbath halakha, but represents a common Jewish understanding.[18] It is most unlikely that the narrator and the readers would have been unaware how clear a transgression the carrying of the mat on the Sabbath is. Jesus' command is "a public violation of the Sabbath and consequently a challenge to the Jews."[19] The reader already knows that the man is doing what Jesus told him to do and, therefore, may expect that the incident will finally result in a conflict between Jesus and the Jews. The reader also

---

[17] Thus E. P. Sanders 1990, 8–9 and 106–7.

[18] Pace Bacchiocchi (1981, 18) who says that "healing a paralyzed man and returning him to his dwelling carrying his bed did not fall under the prohibition of the Mosaic law, rightly understood." According to Bacchiocchi, Jesus only clarifies the meaning of the Sabbath law of the Hebrew Bible but does not negate the Sabbath.

[19] Lohse 1971, 26.

knows that Jesus' healing on the Sabbath did not take place by accident, but Jesus himself initiated it. The whole story is told in such
way that it calls forth the question as to "whether or not John expects
his readers to believe that Jesus performed this miracle to provoke
a confrontation."[20] The answer to this question is yes; Jesus' surprising
and determined action appears as an intentional violation of the
Sabbath commandment as soon as the reader learns that it took
place on the Sabbath.[21] At this point of the story, it is not quite
clear why Jesus deliberately violates the Sabbath. The end of the
story gives an answer to this question: the Johannine Jesus provokes
a clash over the Sabbath because his action reveals that he is equal
to God who does not rest on the Sabbath. The narrator also makes
it clear that Jesus' action and the controversy caused by it were not
isolated incidents.

The Conflict over the Sabbath

The narrator uses vague expressions when speaking about the response
of the Jews to Jesus' action at the end of the story. The narrator
remarks that the Jews persecuted Jesus because he did this ($\tau\alpha\hat{\upsilon}\tau\alpha$)
on the Sabbath (v. 16). The preceding verse, where the narrator
recounts that the man told the Jews that it was Jesus who had healed
him, suggests that the pronoun $\tau\alpha\hat{\upsilon}\tau\alpha$ refers to the healing of the
man. In this case, the Jews persecute Jesus because he healed the
lame man on the Sabbath. Jesus' answer to the Jews also points in
this direction. Jesus defends himself by saying that "my Father is
working still, and I also am working" (v. 17). This saying is close to
Jesus' words to his disciples in connection with another healing on
the Sabbath: "We must work the works of him who sent me while
it is day" (9:4). In both cases, Jesus' words about 'working' and 'work'

---

[20] Carson 1982, 81. Carson clearly sees that this question arises, but he denies that
Jesus' action is a deliberate provocation. According to him, the command to carry the
pallet on the Sabbath contravenes no clear proscription in Torah. He says that it
is "remotely possible that Jesus is here presented as provoking a clash over rabbinical
legalism about the Sabbath" but there is no reason to suppose that "Jesus is pre-
cipitating a crisis over Torah." But many different Jewish sources make it clear that
the carrying of the mat would have been interpreted as a violation of the Sabbath
commandment. Carson (p. 96 n. 146) says that the prohibition against carrying
things in Jer 17:19–27 was originally written with commerce in mind, but it is clear
that this passage was interpreted much more literally in later Jewish tradition.
[21] Thus also Strathmann 101; Haenchen 269–70.

are connected to his healing activity. Thus Jesus' words in 5:17 seem to be an answer to the accusation that the healing he performed on the Sabbath was illegal.

Jesus also defends his action on the Sabbath in John 7: he refers to the healing of the lame man by speaking of one deed he has done (7:21: ἕν ἔργον ἐποίησα) and asks whether the Jews are angry because he made the man's whole body well (7:23).[22] Jesus' argumentation here presupposes that it is the healing on the Sabbath which is unlawful, not his command that the man should go and take up his mat.[23]

It is noteworthy, however, that the story in 5:1–15 suggests that it is the carrying of the mat which is regarded as unlawful by the Jews. The carrying of the mat is also self-evidently against Jewish Sabbath practices, whereas it is uncertain whether Jesus' healing as such would have been regarded as breaking the Sabbath. The Jews of the story note what would have been an apparent violation of the Sabbath, whereas the man, the narrator, and Jesus are interested in the healing only. For the man, Jesus is "the one who healed me" (v. 11, 15), the narrator speaks about the man as "the one who had been healed" (v. 10, 13) and Jesus addresses the man by saying "See, you have been made well" (v. 14). There are thus two different points of view towards the incident in the story.[24] At the end of the story, however, different points of view seem to intermingle when the narrator comments on the reasons for Jesus' persecution. It is thus unclear whether the reason for the persecution is Jesus' healing on the Sabbath or Jesus' command to the man.[25]

---

[22] For a detailed analysis of this passage, see the next chapter.

[23] Haenchen 284.

[24] Staley 1991, 60.

[25] Thus Lindars 217–218. Also Kotila (1988, 22) notes that it is unclear whether the words ταῦτα ἐποίει ἐν σαββάτῳ refer to Jesus' healing or to Jesus' command. Kotila says that the writer is thinking here of Jesus' action in this episode as a whole. He sees that the episode stems from the sign source, the writer of which tries to justify the liberal Sabbath practice of his community (p. 45). In a similar vein, Weiss 1991, 311–314. But the general and vague expressions in v. 16 are likely to have been formulated by a writer whose main interest is not the Sabbath question. This writer is probably the evangelist who—as Kotila also notes (p. 43)— is interested in the Sabbath for the sake of his own christological argumentation only. The Sabbath theme is also ascribed to the signs source by Bultmann 177; Becker 279. Most scholars, however, ascribe it to the evangelist. See Dodd 1963, 178; Lindars 215; Schnackenburg II 117; Witkamp 1985, 30–31; Fortna 1988, 115; Neyrey 1988, 10.

It is not likely that the story in John 5:1–16 was formulated in order to jusfify a certain kind of Sabbath practice. Had the writer of 5:1–16 thought of an actual discussion concerning Sabbath practice, he would have stated more clearly what in Jesus' action evoked the anger of the Jews.[26] The very fact that the reason for the controversy is given so imprecisely suggests that the main issue in the controversy between Jesus and the Jews is, from the narrator's point of view, not the Sabbath.[27] Jesus' Sabbath healing leads him to the dispute with the Jews, but the Sabbath theme soon makes way for Jesus' claim to be equal to God, a theme that is treated in detail in 5:19–30. The Sabbath question is not treated as a legal issue here, but it serves as a means to assert Jesus' close relationship to his Father.[28]

The narrator not only leaves the reason for the persecution unspecified but also does not reveal the exact nature of this persecution. In his remark in 5:16, the narrator uses the verb διώκω, which may mean "pursue," "chase," "drive away," "prosecute," or "persecute." The narrator says later in v. 18 that "the Jews were seeking *all the more* to kill him," which suggests that the verb διώκω in v. 16 already refers to the efforts of the Jews to kill Jesus.[29] The narrator uses verbs in the imperfect to describe both the response of the Jews and Jesus' action on the Sabbath (v. 16: ἐδίωκον οἱ Ἰουδαῖοι τὸν

---

[26] Cf. Labahn 1999, 258. Labahn supports the idea that the evangelist has used a traditional conflict story in vv. 9–16. But Labahn thinks that the Sabbath question already had a minor role in this traditional story which was primarily interested in Jesus' person and not in Sabbath practices. The evangelist followed this tendency and made it more explicit in vv. 17–18.

[27] Pace Asiedu-Peprah 2001, 24–34 and 52–75. Asiedu-Peprah analyzes the Johannine Sabbath stories (John 5 and 9) as a two-party juridical controversy on the Sabbath question. The charge the Jews level against the lame man in John 5:10 ("It is the Sabbath; it is not lawful for you to carry your mat.") is "a formal accusation in a declarative form" that signals "the beginning of the controversy and at the same time indicates to the other party the reason for the dispute" (pp. 25–26; cf. also p. 68). In 5:16, this original accusation is automatically shifted to Jesus, which "sets up a juridical controversy between Jesus and the Jews on the issue of the Sabbath law" (p. 74). However, it is a substantial weakness in this proposal that the very accusation which should give a reason for the following juridical dispute is formulated so imprecisely in John 5:16.

[28] Thus Freyne, 1985, 123; Ashton 1991, 139; Becker 280.

[29] Many manuscripts (for example, A, Θ, Ψ, and the majority text) make this clear by adding the words ἐζήτουν αὐτὸν ἀποκτεῖναι to v. 16. According to some scholars, the difference between v. 16 and v. 18 shows that these verses belong to different redactional layers. See Kotila 1988, 13; Dunderberg 1994, 103; Labahn 1999, 248.

Ἰησοῦν; ταῦτα ἐποίει[30] ἐν σαββάτῳ; v. 18: ἐζήτουν αὐτὸν . . . ἀποκτεῖναι; ἔλυεν τὸ σάββατον). The imperfects are best interpreted as iterative imperfects: the narrator is not thinking of an individual incident but speaks of Jesus' action on the Sabbath and the persecution of the Jews as repeated events.[31] Jesus habitually broke the Sabbath, and the Jews responded to this by persecuting him.[32] This shows that the conflict between the Johannine Jesus and the Jews was a continuous one and not limited to this single event.

It is striking how abruptly the narrator begins to speak about Jesus' habit of breaking the Sabbath and about the intense hostility of the Jews. For the first time in the gospel, Jesus is presented as acting against the law of the Jews.[33] The narrator has not, until this point, explicitly mentioned the hostile attitude of the Jews either. As D. M. Smith notes,

> the Jews' persecution of Jesus is suddenly presented as already in progress, already attaining its full intensity, without its development having been described fully in narrative form.[34]

The narrator's brief remarks are quite revealing because they tell more about his stance on the Sabbath and on the Jews than a detailed report; they suggest that the narrator has in his mind a reader who is not surprised at Jesus' breaking of the Sabbath or at the persecution that followed this apparent transgression.

---

[30] Some manuscripts ($\mathfrak{P}^{75}$, 579) read the aorist ἐποίησεν instead of the imperfect ἐποίει; the aorist would refer to this single event and not to recurrent events as the imperfect would.

[31] Some alternative interpretations for the imperfects have been suggested. Bernard (235) and Back (1995, 150 n. 16) read the imperfect ἐδίωκον (v. 16) as an inchoative imperfect that may be translated "began to persecute." According to Sanders & Mastin (163), ἐδίωκον has a conative force and may be translated "tried to persecute." The form ἔλυεν (v. 18) may also be taken either as a conative imperfect ("he tried or was seeking to abrogate the Sabbath") or as an iterative imperfect ("he used to break the Sabbath"). These different shades of meaning are not necessarily mutually exclusive. In any case, the imperfects show that the narrator "generalizes beyond the present incident" (Barrett 256).

[32] Thus Bauer 78; Hoskyns 266; Bultmann 182; Strathmann 102; Schnackenburg II 126, 128; Haenchen 273; Witkamp 1985, 31; Meeks 1990, 310–311; M. Davies 1992, 52, 307; Welck 1994, 153; Asiedu-Peprah 2001, 71.

[33] The cleansing of the temple (2:13–22) is clearly a provocation, but no explicit breaking of the law is involved.

[34] D. M. Smith 1984, 203. In a similar vein Hahn 1970, 73; Fortna 1988, 278; Ashton 1991, 137; Becker 280.

The narrator uses the verb λύω in v. 18: "For this reason the
Jews were seeking all the more to kill him, because he was not only
breaking (ἔλυεν) the Sabbath, but was also calling God his own
Father, thereby making himself equal to God." The verb λύω means
either 'to break' a law or 'to annul' (abrogate, repeal, destroy) a
law.[35] In John, the verb is used twice in legal connections in the
passive voice (7:23; 10:35). These passages do not, however, show
how the verb should be translated in 5:18; in 7:23 the verb λύω
means "to break the law," while in 10:35 it means "to annul the
scriptures." The verb also appears in a similar context in Matthew,
but it can mean either "to break" or "to abrogate" a commandment (Matt 5:19).[36] In addition to John 5:18, the verb is used at
least once in connection with Sabbath legislation. Philo uses the verb
when speaking of a group that has allegorized the commandments
of the Torah and given up their literal observance. In this connection, the verb refers to the abrogation of the Sabbath laws (*Migration*
91).[37] Thus, it is possible that also in John 5:18 λύω means that Jesus
abrogated the Sabbath, not that he broke it.[38] However, this view
cannot be substantiated on the basis of linguistic evidence alone. In
any case, the meaning of the narrator's comment (v. 18) does not
change much, even if we understand λύω to mean that Jesus broke
the Sabbath. In that case, the iterative imperfect ἔλυεν means that
Jesus habitually broke the Sabbath, and this is not far from saying
that Jesus abrogated the Sabbath.

The narrator's comment in v. 18 explains why the Jews persecuted
Jesus, but there is no hint that the Jews of the story misunderstood
Jesus. Rather, the Jews correctly see Jesus' action as a deliberate
provocation and understand immediately the theological implications

---

[35] According to Bauer/Aland/Aland (1988, 982), the verb λύω in John 5:18
means that Jesus is not accused of breaking the Sabbath, but of doing away with
it. But as Luz (1978, 415 n. 82 and 83) shows, λύω may mean either 'to repeal
or annul laws', or 'to break a legal agreement or obligation.'

[36] Thus Luz 1989, 239.

[37] Philo admits that the Sabbath indeed has a symbolic meaning as the allegorizers say, but still tells his readers not to abrogate the laws laid down for its observance (*Migration* 91: μὴ ... τα ἐπ᾽ αὐτῇ νομοθετηθέντα λύωμεν). Further on Philo
speaks in a similar manner about the law of circumcision. In this connection he
uses the verb ἀναιρέω that without any reservations means "to repeal" (*Migration*
92: μηδ᾽ ... ἀνέλωμεν τὸν ἐπὶ τῇ περιτομῇ τεθέντα νόμον). This parallel expression
suggests that λύω also means "to repeal."

[38] Thus Lohse 1971, 27; Schnackenburg II 128; Pancaro 1975, 160; Haenchen
286, Becker 275.

of his words in v. 17.[39] Had the narrator wanted to make sure that the reader realizes that Jesus actually did not act against the Sabbath or that Jesus was not equal to God, he would have selected his words more carefully.

The way the narrator hints in a passing remark that Jesus abrogated the Sabbath or that he habitually broke it suggests that the reader has some prior information about Jesus' attitude toward the Sabbath. V. 18 suggests that it is nothing new for the reader that Jesus broke the Sabbath; the new information in this verse is that the Jews also persecuted Jesus because he called God his Father, not only because he broke the Sabbath. This generalizing comment on Jesus' action on the Sabbath is surprising unless the reader is already in advance familiar with Jesus' liberal attitude toward the Sabbath. We seem to have here an example of how the narrator presupposes that the reader knows the main of points of the gospel story beforehand.[40]

The narrator also uses imprecise expressions when speaking of the conflict that followed Jesus' Sabbath action. It is likely that the narrator may refer in a vague way to the Jewish persecution of Jesus because the reader already knows that Jesus' Sabbath activity aroused hostility and even murderous plans among the Jews. Persecution and the death threat is combined with Jesus' Sabbath activity in some synoptic passages (Matt 12:14; Mark 3:6; Luke 6:11). We do not need to assume, however, that John is dependent directly on these passages at this point; the reader may know about Jesus' action on the Sabbath on the basis of the synoptic gospels or on the basis of some synoptic traditions.[41]

---

[39] Many scholars think, however, that the Jews mistake Jesus' action as a breaking of the law. See Weiss 1991, 317; Lee 1994, 111–112; Asiedu-Peprah 2001, 83. Meeks (1990, 310) notes that the Jews are wrong in 5:18 only when they say that Jesus *made himself* equal to God, while John claims that Jesus *was* equal to God from the beginning. But it is uncertain whether v. 18 is formulated with this fine theological distinction in mind.

[40] Cf. Culpepper 1983, 211–223. Culpepper analyzes what kind of prior information John's narrator presupposes from his readers; Culpepper concludes that "the reader has prior knowledge of many of the key elements of the gospel story" (p. 223).

[41] John 5:1–18 also has other affinities, especially with the Markan controversy stories (Mark 2:1–3:6). Jesus' command to the lame man (ἔγειρε ἆρον τὸν κράβαττόν σου καὶ περιπάτει) has a close parallel in Mark (Mark 2:9–11; cf. also Matt 9:5–6; Luke 5:24–5). For a detailed discussion of these common points, see Dunderberg 1994, 108–124. According to Dunderberg, Markan influence on John is possible, but it cannot be proved. The death threat in Mark 3:6 could explain the sudden appearance of this theme in John 5:18, but the ending of John's story could also be explained without supposing that John is dependent on Mark at this point (p. 121).

The willingness to persecute Jesus is a pre-fixed character trait of the Jews for the narrator and his readers, which explains why the theme of conflict appears in the story without warning. And this is the reason why the references to Jewish persecution are sporadic and vague in the gospel, and the Jews remain surprisingly ineffective in their efforts to kill Jesus (7:1,19,25; 8:59; 10:31; 11:8). As Robert T. Fortna says, "we have here not historical causality but a portrayal of a cosmic struggle between good and evil necessarily taking place in the events of Jesus' life."[42] For the narrator and his readers, the Jewish persecution of Jesus has already become a fixed and inevitable part of the role of the Jews as the enemies of God's eternal word, as is already implied in the prologue of the gospel (1:11).

It is important to notice that the way the Jews in John respond to Jesus' Sabbath breaking is not the most likely response to Sabbath breakings in a first century context. The response of the Jews echoes scriptural Sabbath legislation rather than any first century practice. The law demands that those who break the Sabbath should be executed (Exod 31:14–15), which practice is also exemplified by a story in the book of Numbers (Num 15:32–36). It is doubtful, however, to what extent the letter of the law was ever put into practice; such passages as Neh 13:15–22 and Jer 17:19–27 suggest, at least, that "the prohibition was not then enforced through the public authorities."[43] Some later sources also prescribe death as punishment for Sabbath transgressions (*Jub.* 50:13). However, other sources show that more lenient and more realistic punishments were allowed.[44] The *Damascus Document* represents very strict and literal observance of the Sabbath, but still it is stated explicitly that the one who defiles the Sabbath shall not be put to death (*CD* 12:3–6). Many Mishnaic discussions also show that punishments others than capital punishments were allowed (*m. Šabb.* 7:1; *m. Sanh.* 7:8). These discussions may not have been enforced anywhere, but they still show what kinds of punishments early rabbis had in mind when they discussed Sabbath transgressions. E. P. Sanders concludes, on the basis of these discussions, that

---

[42] Fortna 1988, 279.
[43] Thus Westbrook 1992, 549.
[44] Cf. E. P. Sanders 1990, 16–19.

intentional transgression of the sort that would incur the death penalty was impossible; and that the most unlikely excuses by an offender would be accepted as showing that he or she was 'unwitting.'[45]

The Jews in John, however, respond to Jesus' Sabbath transgression with a fierceness typical of scriptural Sabbath regulations rather than the more lenient practices reflected in the *Damascus Document* or in the Mishnah. Nothing in the story suggests that it was important for John's Jews to make sure that the alleged Sabbath breaking had not happened unwittingly. The response of the Johannine Jews reflects some fixed stereotypes concerning the Jews and their Sabbath practices rather than the actual practices of some Jewish groups.[46] The synoptic Sabbath passages show that these kinds of stereotypes were common among early Christians.[47]

The vague and brief references to Jesus' Sabbath breakings suggest that the main interest of the Johannine narrator is not the Sabbath question. The Sabbath issue prepares the way for the presentation of John's central theological claim that Jesus is equal to God. A closer scrutiny of John's arguments reaffirms my earlier conclusion that John and his readers already take for granted Jesus' liberal attitude to the Sabbath.

---

[45] E. P. Sanders 1990, 19. For the leniency of the rabbis concerning the Sabbath transgressions, see also Rowland 1982, 51.

[46] For a different view, see Asiedu-Peprah 2001, 79. Asiedu-Peprah says that the death threat in John 5:18 "does not constitute a sentence, but an intended action whose implementation depends essentially on the response of the accused to the accusation being levelled against him. In other words, the intended sanction, in a juridical controversy, is still subject to the defence of the accused after which it may either be confirmed or refuted." But I think that the plain comment of the Johannine narrator, "they sought all the more to kill him," does not fit well with this scheme of a juridical controversy.

[47] It is methodologically unacceptable to take this kind of stereotyped presentation as a direct reflection of the real world situation of the Johannine Christians. This is done, however, by Ashton 1991, 140: "The explanation, then, for the abruptness of the death threat is that it reflects the anger of the Jewish establishment at the effrontery of the Johannine group within its ranks. John's earliest readers will have readily detected the reference to a hatred whose effects they had recently endured themselves, but the nature of the gospel form is such that this experience can only be alluded to obliquely by the evangelist." The story is also taken as a valid witness of the policy of John's opponents by Bultmann 178; Martyn 1979, 70; Witkamp 1985, 33.

Jesus, the Father and the Sabbath

Jesus compares his action to God's action in v. 17: "My Father is working still, and I also am working." Jesus' action on the Sabbath serves to show here that Jesus does the same work as the Father. The main issue for John is Jesus' close relationship to his Father, but the Sabbath theme has a crucial role in the argumentation developed here. Jesus' healing on the Sabbath shows that the legislation aiming to protect the Sabbath observance does not bind him, just as it does not bind God. In the background of Jesus' words is Jewish exegesis which states that God did not rest completely on the Sabbath, although God's rest on the seventh day serves as a model for the Sabbath laws of the Pentateuch (Exod 20:11). The tradition that denies God's Sabbath rest appears in Philo (*Alleg. Interp.* I, 5–6; *Cherubim* 88) and in some later rabbinic passages (*Gen. Rab.* 11; *Exod. Rabb.* 30). The opinion that God works continually also appears in the *Let. Aris.* 210 but without a specific reference to God's work on the Sabbath.

The Johannine Jesus takes up this idea but in a very singular way. As a justification of his Sabbath activity, Jesus' words make sense only if it is acknowledged that Jesus acts on behalf of God. For the reader, this is already clear on the basis of the prologue. The reader can understand, therefore, that Jesus' words in 5:17 show that Jesus' activity on the Sabbath is a crucial part of his mission in the world. Jesus' action on the Sabbath reveals his heavenly origin, which explains why he deliberately acts against the Sabbath legislation.

The Jews of the story, of course, cannot know anything about these basic claims of the gospel at this point. Jesus' words indicate to them that he made himself equal to God. This accusation is in line with scriptural traditions according to which no being is like God or equal to God.[48] The will to be like God is presented as the the very reason for the fall of Adam and Eve (Gen 3:5, 22), and some other passages connect this sin to different earthly rulers (Isa 14:14; Ezek 28:2). This same tradition continues in later writings.[49] The tenet that no one is equal to God is especially prominent in Philo's writ-

---

[48] E.g., Exod 15:11; Deut 3:24; 1 Kgs 8:23 and 2 Chr 6:14; 1 Chr 17:20; Ps 35:10; 40:6; 71:19; 86:8; 89:7; Isa 40:25; 44:7; 46:5; Jer 10:6.

[49] 2 Macc 9:12 has Antiochus Epiphanes admit on his deathbed that "it is right to be subject to God; mortals should not think that they are equal to God/not think what is arrogant." The manuscript tradition of the LXX is divided in this

ings.[50] In several places, Philo uses expressions that come close to John 5:18. Philo notes that "there is nothing equal to Him (*Sacrifices* 92: οὐδὲ ἴσον), or that "God is equal to Himself and like Himself" (*Eternity* 43: ἴσος γὰρ αὐτὸς ἑαυτῷ καὶ ὅμοιος ὁ θεός), or that "there is nothing equal or superior to God" (*Alleg. Interp.* II, 3: οὔτε δὲ ἴσον οὔτε κρεῖσσον ἐστι θεοῦ). According to Philo, "the mind is self-loving and without God, when it thinks to be equal to God (οἰόμενος ἴσος εἶναι θεῷ) and when it regards itself as an agent although it is found to be passive" (*Alleg. Interp.* I, 49). Philo's words in *Cherubim* 77 almost sound like a denial of the claim made for Jesus in John: "What a more hostile enemy to the soul can there be than he who in his arrogance attributes to himself what belongs to God? For it belongs to God to act, and this may not be ascribed to any created being; but it belongs to the created to suffer."[51]

There is, of course, no reason to suppose any direct connection between Philo and John. They are both influenced by the same scriptural tradition that explains the affinities between them. The same kind of language shows that it was an ordinary Jewish concept that no human being has the right to claim to be equal to God. Therefore, the claim made in John 5:17 would have been unacceptable to most Jews.[52] The response of the Jews in John is thus typical in the light of Jewish traditions based on the scriptures.[53] Because of this, it may be impossible to tell whether this response reflects the opinion of some actual Jews in John's surroundings or just John's expectations of what the response to the claims made for Jesus would be like.[54]

---

verse: some manuscripts or translations read μὴ θνητὸν ὄντα ἰσόθεα φρονεῖν (e.g., V and La), and some others μὴ θνητὸν ὄντα ὑπερήφανα φρονεῖν (A). One manuscript has combined these variant readings: ἰσόθεα φρονεῖν ὑπερηφάνως (L). Josephus relates in *Ant.* XIX 4 how Caius Caligula "would have deified himself and demanded from his subjects honours that were no longer such as may be rendered to a man."

[50] In some passages Philo is ready to present Moses as divine or even calls him θεός. But in some other passages Philo says that Moses is called "god" in Exod 7:1 only in a figurative sense. For Philo's view, see Meeks 1967, 103–106.

[51] Cf. also *Embassy* 75 where Philo says of Caius that "sooner could God change into a human being than a human being into God."

[52] Thus Meeks 1990, 315. Meeks notes, referring to 2 Macc 9:12 and to Philo's *Alleg. Interp.* 1:49, that other Jews were bound to see Jesus' words in John 5:17 as blasphemy.

[53] Cf. Becker 280: "Die Juden reagieren prompt und typisch."

[54] See, however, Segal 1977, 215–219. Segal says the response of the Jews in John 5:18, 8:58–59 and 10:33 echoes the rabbinic polemic against the heretics who believed in "two powers in heaven." For Segal, these Johannine passages demonstrate that the traditions which on the basis of rabbinic sources could be dated only

The Johannine Jesus develops here an argumentation that has its roots in Jewish scriptural exegesis but in a way that is unique in Jewish tradition. As James F. McGrath has noted, the idea that some-one may work on the Sabbath because of God's Sabbath work is not claimed for "any other figure in Israel's history anywhere in the extant literature."[55] The argument made for Jesus in John is not only excessive but also circular, because it is based on the acceptance of Jesus as God's agent on earth. Only those who accept this can take Jesus' Sabbath action as a sign of his close relationship to God, whereas others are bound to see this action as a transgression of the Sabbath. This suggests that the whole argumentation is meant to reinforce the faith of the believers in Jesus and not to convince those who falsely blame Jesus for transgressing the Sabbath.[56] In John, Jesus' well-known habit of breaking the Sabbath is connected to a Jewish view that God does not rest on the Sabbath. In light of this view, Jesus' liberal attitude towards the Sabbath regulations is taken as a demonstration of his heavenly origin. This line of argumenta-tion shows what relevance the Sabbath has for the narrator and his readers: for them, the Sabbath question is relevant but only because

---

to the second century C.E. actually date to the first century (pp. 217–218). But I think John cannot be taken as a witness for the early date of these traditions. My earlier discussion has shown that the early rabbis were not interested in the detailed content of the heresies they opposed but rather lumped different heretical views together (cf. ch. 2 pp. 47–48, 71). It is thus unlikely that they were well informed on the beliefs of a particular peripheral Christian group. It is more probable that the Christian faith in Jesus became heretical in the eyes of the rabbis only when mainstream Christianity began to regard Jesus as a divine figure, and this faith became more well known. This development took place in the second century C.E., and at this stage the rabbis may have included some Christians among those who believed in two powers. Segal admits that there is "no uniquely anti-Christian theme in the rabbinic attack" (p. 218). This suggests that Christians were not the only offending group and that the polemic was not originally directed against them. The response of the Jews in John is in line with scriptural traditions and does not pre-suppose a response of a particular Jewish group.

[55] McGrath 2001, 91. McGrath notes that the evangelist appeals to traditional images here but accentuates these images in a new way. McGrath suggests that even some non-Christian Jews may have found the argument in John persuasive, or at least concluded that there was nothing blasphemous or scandalous in Jesus' claims because they are based on general categories of agency or sonship. But I doubt whether any Jew, who was not *already* convinced that Jesus is God's agent on earth, would have accepted Jesus' words as a justification for the breaking of the Sabbath.

[56] For a different view, see Asiedu-peprah 2001, 231. Asiedu-Peprah says that the Johannine Sabbath stories would have functioned as "a means of persuasion and an appeal to the opponents of the Johannine Christians" to acknowledge the christological claims made in these stories.

it reveals Jesus' true identity. Jesus' liberal stance on the Sabbath is no longer a disputed matter, but the narrator takes this stance for granted when making his basic christological claim.

When compared to many different Jewish groups, the Johannine Christians seem to have undergone a significant change in their attitude to the Sabbath. We have evidence that such Jews as Philo sometimes approached the Sabbath as a theological question, but still the Sabbath was, even for Philo and also for many other Jews, primarily a matter of religious practice. Lists of activities prohibited on the Sabbath in different writings suggest that Jewish groups were keen on observing the Sabbath commandment of the Pentateuch, even though opinions may have varied on what exactly was allowed on the Sabbath and what not.[57] Various references to the Jews in Hellenistic and Roman authors also show that the literal Sabbath observance was main sign of Jewish identity in the eyes of outsiders.[58] But the Johannine Christians were no longer interested in the Sabbath as a legal question. The Sabbath was not a matter of practice and identity for them, but a means to support their views on Jesus.

Those scholars who want to argue that John does not present Jesus breaking the law here tend to theologize the Sabbath and overlook questions concerning its observance in practice. For example, Dorothy A. Lee says that "on the literal level" Jesus' sign in John 5:1–18

> signifies that Jesus has broken the Law, on a symbolic level it means that Jesus is engaged in doing the ἔργον of God. That he should break the Law is, in Johannine terms, absurd.[59]

Severino Pancaro says that Jesus' attitude toward the Sabbath is paradoxical because "as the Son of God, Jesus does not violate the Sabbath, he abolishes it." John 5:17 shows "that, although the Sabbath is abolished, the law is fulfilled, not violated."[60] Pancaro also notes that John "avoids having even the Pharisees say that Jesus violates or abrogates the Law; what he (apparently) violates and abrogates

---

[57] For such lists, see *Jub.* 2:25–33; 50:1–13; *CD* 10:14–11:18; Philo's *Migration 91; m. Šabb.* 7:2.

[58] Cf. E. P. Sanders 1999a, 2–5. Sanders mentions, for example, a passage where Seneca ridicules the Jewish Sabbath and refers to the practice of the Jews of not lighting lamps on the Sabbath (*Ep.* 95.47). This shows that outsiders were aware of some details of Jewish Sabbath practices. For other Graeco-Roman writers who referred to the Jewish Sabbath, see Feldman & Reinhold 1996, 366–373.

[59] Lee 1994, 112.

[60] Pancaro 1975, 30.

is the Sabbath."[61] These kinds of explanations spiritualize the Sabbath in a way that was foreign to most Jews.[62] It is not likely that any Jew would have understood how one can fulfil the purpose of the law by acting deliberately against one of its principal commandments. The obedience to the law created a foundation for the Jewish way of life, and most Jews would have recognised clearly what the deliberate breaking of some part of the law meant, as is stated by E. P. Sanders:

> The principle on which the law rests is perfectly clear: God gave the Torah to Israel by the hand of Moses; obedience to the Torah is the condition for retaining the covenant promises; intentional and unrepenting disobedience implies rejection of the law, rejection of the covenant for which it is the condition, and rejection of the God who gave the law and the covenant. This is an understanding which is so uniform in the literature which survives from the approximate period that Jesus and his followers could not possibly have been ignorant of it.[63]

It is highly unlikely that the Johannine Christians would have been unaware of the consequences of the action described in John 5:1–18. But it seems that it was not a problem for them to imagine their Lord breaking the Sabbath, a central feature of the law. But before drawing further conclusions concerning the relevance of major Jewish religious practices for the Johannine Christians, we must turn to another passage where the Johannine Jesus refers to these practices.

4.2. *The Jews Do Not Observe the Law Themselves (7:19–24)*

In John 7, Jesus returns to the discussion that began in John 5 where he healed the lame man and was accused of the breaking of the Sabbath. In this passage, the Johannine Jesus refers to the practice of circumcising a male child also on the Sabbath. This reference to two principal pillars of Jewish identity, the Sabbath and circumcision, could be taken at first glance as an attempt to show that Jesus' Sabbath action was not against the law if understood correctly. But closer scrutiny of the argumentation suggests that the Johannine Jesus is more interested in showing that the Jews habitually broke the law

---

[61] Pancaro 1975, 522.
[62] For other attempts to find sophisticated Sabbath theology in John, see Cullmann 1966, 189; Bacchiocchi 1981, 19; Weiss 1991, 319.
[63] E. P. Sanders 1985, 56–57.

rather than defending his own action. The passage reaffirms my earlier conclusion that the narrator and his readers already take an outsider's stance on the central markers of Jewish identity.

The Context of the Scene

There appear several links between Jesus' discussions with the Jews
in John 5 and in 7:15–24, and many scholars have proposed that
these two discussions originally belonged together.[64] At first glance,
the introduction of Moses into the discussion in 7:19 is abrupt, and
the Sabbath theme (7:19–24) seems to be loosely connected to its
present narrative context. Despite these sudden twists in the narrative, there are also links between the seemingly unrelated themes in
John 7, which makes it possible to analyze the chapter as a thematic whole closely related to John 8.[65]

One recurring theme in John 7 and 8 is that Jesus is in mortal
danger because the Jews seek to kill him.[66] The presence of this danger is already mentioned in 7:1, and it is referred to several times
in the course of the narrative (7:13,19,25,30,44; 8:37,40,59). These
mentions form a background for the dialogues between Jesus and
the Jews, and underline the severity of the conflict between them.

Jesus' question, "Why are you looking for an opportunity to kill
me?" seems to come without warning in its immediate context, but
it is well in line with the general narrative atmosphere in John 7–8.
It is not the Jews, who were last mentioned in 7:15, who answer
this question. It is the crowd (ὁ ὄχλος) that seizes Jesus' question and
turns it back to Jesus: "You have a demon! Who is trying to kill
you?" (v. 20). This counterquestion is usually interpreted as meaning
that the crowd is ignorant of the intentions to kill Jesus and should
be separated from the leaders of the people who are called 'the
Jews' and who chase after Jesus.[67] To be sure, there is a distinction

---

[64] For the discussion, see Schnackenburg II 183–184; Attridge 1980, 164–170;
Kotila 1988, 35–39.

[65] See Dodd 1953, 345–354; Schneider 1954, 108–119; Lindars 277–280; Attridge
1980, 160–164; Schenke 1990, 173–188; Rochais 1993, 357–370; Neyrey 1996,
108–116.

[66] Cf. Dodd 1953, 347; Schenke 1990, 178–179; Rochais 1993, 363–364.

[67] This interpretation is represented by the majority of scholars. For example,
see Bultmann 208–209; Schnackenburg II 187; von Wahlde 1982, 44; Beasley-
Murray 109; Carson 314; Moloney 1996, 78; Wilckens 126. Thus also Lindars (290)
and Barrett (20) with some cautions.

between the common people and the Jewish leaders in some passages of the gospel and even in John 7 (cf. 7:12–13). But I think
this is not the case in 7:20.[68]

John 7 as a whole shows that the plans of the Jews to kill Jesus
were by no means hidden from the common people (cf. 7:13,25).
|It is not probable that the crowd in v. 20 would consist of some
pilgrims who are not aware of the intentions to kill Jesus.[69] Jesus'
answer to the crowd in vv. 21–24 makes it clear that he is speaking to those who know of his earlier 'work' on the Sabbath and who
are angry with him because of this work (v. 23). Jesus' words in vv.
21–24 are intelligible only if they are addressed to those who made
the allegation that he has broken the Sabbath.[70] It seems, therefore,
that the crowd in 7:20 should not to be separated from the Jews
mentioned earlier in 5:10–18 or in 7:15.[71] The allegation of the
crowd, that Jesus has a demon, appears elsewhere in the gospel, and
always on the lips of some of the Jews (8:48, 52; 10:20), which also
supports this conclusion.[72] Furthermore, it is not only the leaders
who seek to arrest Jesus, but also some of the crowd want to do so
(7:44). We will see elsewhere that it is not unusual in the gospel for
the words 'the crowd' and 'the Jews' to be used interchangeably.[73]
Also in John 7:35, it seems that οἱ Ἰουδαῖοι are some of the crowd
and not the leaders, who are not present when the discussion in
question takes place.[74]

It is thus not probable that ὁ ὄχλος in 7:20 refers to an ignorant
crowd that does not know anything about the intentions of the Jews.
The question "Who is trying to kill you?" is not a sign of ignorance
but an attempt to deny that anyone seeks Jesus' life. The crowd
accuse Jesus of paranoia, and, at the same time, hide their real inten-

---

[68] Cf. also Duke 1985, 73–74.
[69] This possibility is referred to by Brown 317. According to Brown, it is also
possible that Jesus is speaking to the Jews here.
[70] Thus Schram 1974, 95. According to Schram, the crowd interrupts Jesus at
v. 20, and in v. 21 Jesus resumes his address to the same audience as in vv. 16–19.
But Jesus' words in v. 21 are presented as an answer to the previous question of
the crowd in vv. 20–21.
[71] Thus Becker 309. Also D. M. Smith (1965, 132 n. 53) thinks that οἱ Ἰουδαῖοι
in v. 15 and ὄχλος in v. 20 are the same. However, Smith thinks that Jesus' interlocutors in 7:15–24 are the same as τινες ἐκ τῶν Ἰεροσολυμιτῶν (7:25) who are
divided in judgment on Jesus and unlike the hostile Jews in ch. 5 (p. 134).
[72] Thus Duke 1985, 74.
[73] See the analysis in ch. 5. 2 pp. 160–162.
[74] See my discussion in the introduction, ch. 1. 2 pp. 14–15.

tions and lie to Jesus.[75] The narrative function of the crowd's question becomes clearer if it is taken as an intentional lie and not as a
sign of ignorance.

The lie is to be seen in light of what Jesus has said of himself
earlier. In 7:18 Jesus has stated that "he who seeks the glory of the
one who sent him is truthful (ἀληθής), and there is no falsehood
(ἀδικία) in him." The word ἀδικία is used in John only here. In the
LXX, this term often translates the Hebrew word שֶׁקֶר, meaning
"lie," "falsehood," or "deception."[76] It is possible that ἀδικία contains the connotation of a lie also here.[77] Unlike Jesus, the Jews, who
are called the crowd this time, lie as they say that no one is seeking to kill Jesus. The contrast with them and Jesus is evident.[78] In
the following discussion, Jesus does not answer the crowd's question
directly but refers to his earlier work on the Sabbath (v. 21). Scholars
have often been at pains to explain this question that seems to be
of no significance for the following discussion.[79] The point is, however, that there is no need to answer the question because its narrative function has already been fulfilled. The reader knows that
those who ask "Who is trying to kill you?" are the very ones who
chase after Jesus; thus "the intent here is to convict 'the Jews' of lies
and hypocrisy."[80]

It is interesting that the Jews are presented as both liars and murderers in this scene. These two cardinal vices are attached to the
Jews later in the narrative by Jesus, who accuses them of being the
children of the devil, the murderer and the father of lies (8:44).
There appears in this passage the same contrast between Jesus and
the Jews as in 7:18–20: Jesus is presented as the one who speaks
the truth and who cannot be convicted of sin, whereas the Jews are
like their father, the devil, whose nature it is to lie (8:45–46). The
scene in 7:19–24, therefore, foreshadows the explicit charges Jesus
makes in 8:44.[81]

---

[75] The question of the crowd is interpreted as a lie by Hoskyns 315; Sandmel
1978, 378; Neyrey 1996, 112.
[76] See Schrenk 1933, 154; Bultmann 207 n. 7; Günther 1971, 1193.
[77] Thus Brown 312; Günther 1971, 1194.
[78] Cf. Haenchen 254; Dunderberg 1994, 105. Both Haenchen and Dunderberg
note that the Jews and Jesus are deliberately put in contrast here although they do
not discuss the deceptive attempt of the crowd to deny that they seek Jesus' life.
[79] Bultmann (208) notes that the question of the crowd does not have any
significance for the following argumentation.
[80] Sandmel 1978, 378.
[81] Cf. Neyrey 1996, 111–112.

The previous debate in John 7:14–18 explains the seemingly abrupt reference to Moses in v. 19. In v. 15 the Jews marvel at Jesus' teaching and ask: "How does this man have such learning, when he has never been taught?" The Jews thus call into question the authority of Jesus' teaching, which makes Jesus to mention Moses and his law, the ultimate authority of all the teaching of the Jews.[82] Jesus turns the accusation of the Jews back to them by saying that no one of them keeps the law. This shows that they persecute him without reason, and their judgment is not correct but they judge by appearances (7:24). In the course of this dialogue, there is an occurrence characteristic of many Johannine scenes: Jesus is first judged by his opponents, but in the end he turns the tables on them and becomes their judge.[83] In this context, the example of the Jews circumcising on the Sabbath "actually provides the warrant for the true accusation against these judges: namely, that they judge unjustly."[84]

The reference to circumsion on the Sabbath is thus not primarily a justification of Jesus' Sabbath work. This is even more evident if we compare John 7:19–24 to John 5:17. In 5:17 Jesus answers the accusations levelled at him by saying, "My Father is working still, and I also am working." As I showed in the previous chapter, the idea here is that Jesus' Sabbath action reveals his close relationship to his Father because, as the Son of God, he must work on the Sabbath as his Father does. This sovereign claim makes Jesus' reference to the Sabbath and circumcision superfluous if this reference is taken as an apology for his Sabbath work.[85] This reinforces the view that Jesus' point in 7:19–24 is not to defend his own action but to show that the charges against him are weak and that his opponents persecute him unjustly.[86] This becomes clearer as I move on to analyze Jesus' arguments in more detail.

---

[82] Cf. Brown 316; Lindars 289.

[83] Cf. Neyrey 1996, 110–116; Scholtissek 1998, 251–252; Malina & Rohrbaugh 147–148.

[84] Neyrey 1996, 112.

[85] Cf. Pancaro 1975, 164: "Jesus, as Son of God, must work on the Sabbath also; he does not need to have recourse to an exception established by Moses to justify his activity on the Sabbath." According to Pancaro, this shows that John does not refer to circumcision on the Sabbath because this practice gives a precedent for how the Sabbath may be broken in some cases. I think, however, that this is the function of this reference. Pancaro fails to notice that the reference to the Sabbath and circumcision is not so much a justification of Jesus' own action but a part of the claim that the Jews do not keep the law themselves.

[86] Thus also Räisänen 1987, 90; Back 1995, 154–155.

How do the Jews Fail to Observe the Law?

In 7:19 Jesus accuses his opponents: "Did not Moses give you the law? Yet none of you keeps the law. Why are you looking for an opportunity to kill me?" The claim that the Jews do not keep the law is not a Johannine peculiarity; this charge is a common theme in early Christian polemic (cf. Matt 23:23; Acts 7:53; Rom 2:17–29; Justin's *Dial.* 12.2, 20.4, 27.4).[87] It is not clear, however, what this charge exactly means here.[88] According to the most common interpretation, the willingness of the Jews to kill Jesus shows that they do not keep the law because murder was prohibited by the law (Exod 20:13).[89] But there are reasons which speak against this interpretation.

If there is a reference to the fifth commandment in the text, it should be taken in light of Jesus' teaching recorded in Matthew's Sermon on the Mount, where even the desire to kill is a sign of a breach of this commandment (Matt 5:21–22).[90] Jesus' sweeping charge "*no one* of you keeps the law" suggests, however, that he is not speaking only of those who try to kill him but points to a more central and persistent problem in Jewish observance of the law.[91] In the text, the question "Why are you looking for an opportunity to kill me?" does not give reasons for the previous statement "no one of you keeps the law," but rather the statement serves as an introduction that motivates the question.[92] The text could be paraphrased, "If you yourself do not keep the law why do you want to kill me if I do not keep it?"[93] That the Jews do not keep the law and that they seek Jesus' life are two different things; the point is to show that the reasons why the Jews wish to kill Jesus are baseless because they

---

[87] See Schnackenburg II 187 n. 3; Räisänen 1987, 120.

[88] For different views, see Pancaro 1975, 136–137; Kotila 1988, 39–40.

[89] Thus Brown 316; Lindars 289; Barrett 319; Brooke 1988, 105; Carson 314. If there is an allusion to the fifth commandment here, it could be asked why the verb is ἀποκτείνω and not φονεύω as used in the LXX. According to Brooke (1988, 105–106), the author has deliberately used ἀποκτείνω instead of φονεύω, but this is very unlikely.

[90] Thus Lindars 289.

[91] Carson (314) seems to be aware of this problem as he writes: "The only evidence that Jesus adduces to support this contention [no one of you keeps the law] is the hatred that stands behind the desire to kill him: *Why are you trying to kill me?* He does not mean that every Jew breaks the law *at this point*, but any large crowd in the temple precincts inevitably includes some of the authorities who are guilty at this very point" (italics original).

[92] Thus Bultmann 208; Kotila 1988, 39.

[93] Thus Haenchen 354. Cf. also Becker 309.

themselves do not keep the law. The statement "no one of you keeps the law" is a general thesis, which is shown to be correct by the following reference to circumcision on the Sabbath (vv. 22–23).[94] This practice shows that, for the Johannine Jesus, the Jews themselves fail to observe all the commandments in the Torah. A detailed analysis of vv. 22–23 confirms this interpretation.

The Sabbath and Circumcision

There is a disagreement among scholars concerning the punctuation of the text in the beginning of v. 22. Some take the words διὰ τοῦτο as the end of the previous sentence: "I performed one work, and all of you are astonished *by this*."[95] This does not, however, correspond to how θαυμάζειν or διὰ τοῦτο are used elsewhere in John.[96] Therefore, many scholars and most versions read διὰ τοῦτο as an introduction to v. 22: "I performed one work, and all of you are astonished. Because of this Moses gave you circumcision . . .).[97] Sentences beginning with διὰ τοῦτο are usually followed by a ὅτι-clause (the reason why . . . is that . . .), but this time the ὅτι-clause is missing. This makes the interpretation somewhat complicated, but still the meaning is clear enough. It is said that the reason why Moses gave circumcision is connected to what Jesus did on the Sabbath. There are two different ways of understanding how circumcision on the Sabbath and Jesus' healing on the Sabbath are connected to each other.

According to the first interpretation, circumcision foreshadows the gift of life that Jesus gives by healing the lame man.[98] Scholars cite

---

[94] Thus Bernard 261; Kotila 1988, 40. According to Barrett (319), this was perhaps the meaning of the passage in the source used by the evangelist who, however, connects the transgression of the law with the attempt to kill Jesus. See also Neyrey 1996, 111. According to Neyrey, Jesus is "presumably" speaking of circumcision on the Sabbath, as he accuses the Jews of failing to keep the law, but "this may cryptically refer to other aspects of Moses' law, such as just judgment . . . or the prohibition against murder and lying."

[95] Bernard 263; Bultmann 208 n. 10; Brown 310; Lindars 290.

[96] For example, see Pancaro 1975, 163 n. 20. θαυμάζειν is used in John with a direct object (5:28), with a ὅτι-clause (3:7; 4:27), absolutely (5:20; 7:15) but never with διὰ (this construction appears in the NT only in Mark 6:6; Rev 17:7). διὰ τοῦτο is frequently used to introduce a sentence (1:31; 5:16, 18; 6:65; 8:47; 9:23; 10:17; 12:18, 39; 13:11; 15:19; 16:15; 19:11), but it is never found at the end of a sentence in John.

[97] Thus Hoskyns 315; Barrett 319; Pancaro 1975, 163; Becker 297.

[98] See Hoskyns 315–316; Barrett 319; Pancaro 1975, 164; Beasley-Murray 110; Brooke 1988, 104; Derrett 1991, 214–217, 223–224; Moloney 1996, 78–79; Labahn 1999, 253–254.

a rabbinic passage which states that the purpose of circumcision was to make a male complete.[99] Jesus' words that he made a *whole* man well (ὅλον ἄνθρωπον ὑγιῆ ἐποίησα) on the Sabbath are seen to reflect this view; by healing the lame man, Jesus has accomplished the purpose of circumcision. He has thus fulfilled the intention of the law and not broken it.

I think this interpretation is problematic. First, we do not know how wellknown or early was the view that the purpose of circumcision is to make a person complete; as far as I know, scholars have been able to trace this view only to a single passage in the Mishnah. Second, circumcision is not the main point in Jesus' argumentation and should not be overemphasized. Jesus does not mention circumcision for its own sake but because the practice of the Jews is to circumcise even on the Sabbath. What is being compared to Jesus' healing on the Sabbath is not circumcision *per se*, but circumcision performed on the Sabbath. It is doubtful whether Jesus' brief allusion to circumcision contains a hidden reference to the original intention of this practice.

According to the second, more likely, interpretation, Jesus refers to circumcision on the Sabbath, because circumcision gives a precedent for how the Sabbath can be broken in certain cases.[100] According to the law, every male infant should be circumcised when he is eight days old (Gen 17:12; Lev 12:3). There was a difference in opinion among some rabbis concerning what kinds of things could be done if the day of circumcision fell on the Sabbath; but different parties agreed on the general rule that a male child should be circumcised even on the Sabbath, because "circumcision overrides the Sabbath." This rule had already become generally accepted by the time of these discussions and was most probably wellknown at the end of the first century.[101] The Johannine Jesus refers to this view in order

---

[99] *m. Ned.* 3:11 (Neusner's translation): "Great is circumcision, for, despite all commandments which Abraham our father carried out, he was called complete and whole only when he had circumcised himself as it is said, *Walk before me and be perfect*" (Gen 17:1).

[100] Thus Bultmann 208; Schneider 1954, 115; Lindars 291; Sandmel 1978, 378; Luz 1981, 120; Kotila 1988, 40; Becker 310; Neyrey 1996, 112.

[101] Cf. *m. Šabb.* 18:3; 19:1–3. For this discussion, see Neusner 1973b, 179 and 1981, 169–173. R. Eliezer was for the most liberal view according to which one may do anything at all in connection with circumcision on the Sabbath. According to R. ʿAqiba, however, only those things which cannot be prepared in advance on the eve of the Sabbath can be done on the Sabbath. The point of departure for both of these conflicting views is the axiom that circumcision overrides the Sabbath

to show that the Jews themselves put aside strict Sabbath regulations when it comes to circumcision on the Sabbath. There is a clear
contrast in Jesus' words between the Jews who habitually break the
Sabbath when they circumcise on the Sabbath and Jesus who did
only one 'work' on the Sabbath (ἕν ἔργον ἐποίησα).[102]

This interpretation has caused objections because the clause ἵνα
μὴ λυθῇ ὁ νόμος Μωϋσέως in v. 23 implies that circumcision on the
Sabbath is performed in order that the law of Moses would *not* be
broken. This would not match with the view that sees circumcision
on the Sabbath as a precedent for breaking the law.[103] The ἵνα-
clause is taken to mean that the Jews circumcise on the Sabbath in
order to fulfil the law as did Jesus when he healed the lame man.[104]
But this explanation misses the implied irony of the ἵνα-clause; the
purpose of the Jews may indeed be the fulfilment of the law, but
the Johannine Jesus claims that this practice actually shows their failure to keep the Sabbath. Jesus here accuses the Jews of acting in
an inconsistent way: they regard his work on the Sabbath as a transgression of the law although they do not regard circumcision on the
Sabbath as such. They apply to their own action different standards
than to his action, which means that their judgment is not correct
(v. 24).

The way the Johannine Jesus uses the law against the Jews reveals
that his stance on the law is ambiguous. He refers to an example
of how the law is applied in a certain problematic situation. He does
not pick up this example to show that what he once did is not a
breach of the law but to show that what his opponents do regularly
is also against the law. The aim here is not a more profound understanding of the law which would show that Jesus did not act against
the law. Instead, Jesus refers to a contradiction between the Sabbath
laws and circumcision on the Sabbath and uses this contradiction to
show that even the Jews are not consistent in their observance. The
law of the Jews is viewed from the point of view of an outsider
which is in accordance with Jesus' use of second person plurals here:
"Did not Moses give *you* the law; Moses gave *you* circumcision . . . and

---

which suggests that the practice of circumcising on the Sabbath was earlier. Cf.
also Thomas 1991, 173–174.
[102] Bultmann 208.
[103] Thus Pancaro 1975, 164.
[104] Pancaro 1975, 164.

you circumcise a man on the Sabbath." Jesus also uses pronouns in the second person plural elsewhere in the gospel when referring to the law of the Jews (8:17; 10:34; cf. also 15:25: "their law"; 8:56: "Abraham, your father"). As many scholars have noted, this kind of language reflects an outsider's relation to the law.[105] This is also true in John 7:22–23, even though the Johannine Jesus uses here the so-called *qal* (or *qol*) *wā-ḥômer* argument known from rabbinic sources.

Jesus deduces from the fact that the Jews circumcise a man on the Sabbath that it is unfair for the Jews to be angry with him if he has made a whole man well on the Sabbath. Jesus' reasoning here resembles the *qal wā-ḥômer* principle which was the first of the exegetical principles (*middôt*) connected to Hillel and Ishmael. According to the rabbis, this hermeneutical rule was already used in the scriptures. This reasoning also has parallels in Hellenistic rhetoric.[106] The *qal wā-ḥômer* argument was used to make an inference from something less important or less problematic ('the lesser') to a case that was more important or more problematic ('the greater').[107] This

---

[105] Bultmann 59 n. 2; Dodd 1953, 82; Brown 312; Barrett 319 and 1975, 70; Räisänen 1987, 217; Dunderberg 1994, 106. However, see Augenstein 1997, 311–313. According to Augenstein, the use of the second person plurals does not show distance from the law. Augenstein compares this usage to Deuteronomy and to the Book of Joshua where Moses and Joshua speak to the people using such expressions as "your God," "your father," "the land that is given to you." The references in these scriptural books are not, however, strictly comparable to the Johannine references to "your law." Moses and Joshua often blame the people for forgetting the Lord, but there is no hostile conflict between them and the people that characterizes the relationship between Jesus and the Jews in John. The use of the second person plurals is not the only sign of detachment from the law in John; for example, Jesus and the law are contrasted with each other in John 6 (see the next chapter). The detachment of the Johannine Jesus from basic matters of Jewish identity is evident also in other passages, and so it is natural to take the second person plural forms as an expression of this detachment.

[106] For the *middôt* of Hillel and Ishmael and the *qal wā-ḥômer* see Starfelt 1959, 68–92; L. Jacobs 1961, 3–8; Zeitlin 1963, 161–173; Strack & Stemberger 1982, 26–32; Derrett 1991, 220–221. According to *Gen. Rab.* 92, there are ten examples of the *qal wā-ḥômer* in the Torah (e.g., Gen 44:8; Exod 6:12; Deut 31:27). The exact relationship of this argument to the more general *a minore ad maius* principle used in Hellenistic rhetoric is debated. Alexander (1983, 242–244) points to many open problems in the study of the *middôt* and concludes that "the *middôt* are hardly in a fit state for use in New Testament study." In case of the *qal wā-ḥômer*, however, these problems are perhaps not so crucial. The *qal wā-ḥômer* is one of the best attested of the *middôt* and it is always mentioned first on different lists. The examples in the scriptures and the use of *a minore ad maius* argument in the Hellenistic world also show that this kind of reasoning was probably widely known, no matter when the exact hermeneutical rule was formulated.

[107] Derrett 1991, 220.

argumentation was also applied to circumcision on the Sabbath in a manner that is formally quite close to Jesus' reasoning in John.

In *t. Šabb 15:16* the following saying is attributed to R. Eliezer b. Hyrcanus: "Why do they override the Sabbath on account of circumcision? Because they are liable for cutting off on account of doing it after its time. And lo, a *qal wā-ḥômer* argument: If on account of one limb from him they set aside the Sabbath, is not logical that he should set aside the Sabbath on account of his whole body! [Thus proving that they set aside the Sabbath in order to save a life.]"[108] Elsewhere the same kind of reasoning is attributed to R. Eleazar b. 'Azariah.[109] Although Jesus' reasoning in John formally follows these rabbinic passages, there is a notable difference between John and these texts. The rabbinic passages deal with the question of whether it is permitted to save life on the Sabbath or not. The argument based on circumcision is one of many arguments that are used in order to show that one may save life on the Sabbath. But even in this connection, this argument is met with some objections.[110] The situation, however, is quite different in John where the man healed by Jesus had been ill for 38 years.[111] In order for Jesus' argumentation to be persuasive, circumcision and the miraculous healing of the lame man should somehow be comparable acts.[112] But this is not the case, because

> circumcision, though it enables a Jew to live by other commandments is neither more important than, nor less important than miraculous healing of paralysis, for the two are not comparable.[113]

---

[108] Translation taken from Neusner 1973a, 94.

[109] See *Mek. Šabbeta* 1; *b. Yoma* 85b.

[110] In both *t. Šabb 15:16* and in *Mek. Šabbeta* 1, the argument that circumcision on the Sabbath justifies the saving of the whole man is followed by a counter-argument; it is said that one may save a life on the Sabbath only if it is certain that someone will die if one does not take action on the Sabbath.

[111] Cf. Brown 313; Barrett 320; Pancaro 1975, 163; Haenchen 355; Schulz 116; Kotila 1988, 41; Derrett 1991, 219.

[112] It is stated in *Mek. Neziqin* 1 that "it suffices for that which is derived by inference to be like that from which it is derived." Cf. Patte 1975, 112 n. 102.

[113] Derrett 1991, 220–221. Derrett argues quite convincingly that in the present case "*qal wā-ḥômer* is inapplicable, either as a technical aid to interpretation of texts, or as a feature of popular reasoning." Derrett suggests that another rabbinic canon of interpretation, the so called *p̄ʿraṭ û-kʿlāl* ("particular and general"), may be applicable to Jesus' reasoning here. Derrett is eager to show that Jesus' argumentation somehow followed the accepted rules of interpretation, even though he rules out the *qal wā-ḥômer* argument. But Jesus' original argumentation can be taken as a sign that we do not have a genuine halakhic discussion here, even though a halakhic-

It is likely that Jesus' argumentation "would . . . have convinced no Jew."[114] The close analysis of this argument reinforces that these verses reflect detachment from two basic matters of Jewish identity, the Sabbath and circumcision. The *Sitz im Leben* of Jesus' argumentation is not an inner-Jewish debate on what is and what is not permissible on the Sabbath.[115] The Sabbath and circumcision are rather considered from the standpoint of an outsider in order to show that Jesus' opponents also act against the law because this law is not consistent.[116] The Sabbath and circumcision are referred to in a similar way by Justin Martyr in his *Dialogue with Trypho*.[117] For Justin, the contradiction between the Sabbath and the commandment to circumcise on the eighth day after birth provides a rationale for the abandonment of both circumcision and the Sabbath. For the Johannine Jesus, circumcision on the Sabbath shows that the Jews themselves do not keep the law in all circumstances. What is common to both Jesus in John and Justin is that they see a contrast between Sabbath observance and circumcision on the eighth day, and they use this contrast to undermine the claims of their opponents. The way two principal pillars of Jewish identity are contrasted with each other

---

like argument is used to show that Jesus' opponents are wrong. Derrett concludes (p. 222): "John 7:23 certainly goes back to an apologist for Christ's behaviour who felt no need to squeeze the feet of Christ into rabbinical shoes. An original argument was called for, for miracles do not form any chapter of halakha, which is human behaviour subject to juristic theory. Christ's advocate here has at his disposal genuine Jewish biblical learning, and he uses it as originally as such circumstances could suggest."

[114] M. Davies 1991, 308. Cf. also Pancaro 1975, 163: "The weakness of such reasoning is obvious." Also p. 167: "At 7:23, the words of Jesus would be, at best, a specious argument, at worst, an argument with only a semblance of reason, were we simply in the presence of a 'humanitarian' motive." This is the reason why Pancaro seeks for a more profound interpretation of the passage (cf. above p. 136 n. 98).

[115] Pace Kotila 1988, 42; Weiss 1991, 314; Labahn 1999, 254.

[116] Thus Dunderberg 1994, 107.

[117] Justin *Dial.* 27.5: "Or did He [God] wish that they who received or performed circumcision on that day [on the Sabbath] be guilty of sin, since it is His command that circumcision be given on the eighth day after birth, even though that day may fall on the Sabbath? If He knew it would be sinful to perform that act on a Sabbath, could He not have decreed that infants be circumcised either a day before or a day after the Sabbath? And why did He not instruct those persons who lived before the time of Moses and Abraham to observe these same precepts; men, who are called just and were pleasing to God, even though they were not circumcised in the flesh, and did not keep the Sabbath?" (Translated by Thomas B. Falls in *The Fathers of the Church* 6.) Justin's argumentation is referred to by Bauer 107; Bultmann 208 n. 3; Haenchen 355; Dunderberg 1994, 107. According to Barrett (321), Justin's passage is "a similar but by no means identical treatment" of this theme.

betrays the detachment of both the Johannine Jesus and Justin from these institutions.

The arguments of the Johannine Jesus in John 7:19–24 suggest that he looks at the Sabbath and circumcision as an outsider. The Jews of the story are presented as zealous to convict Jesus for breaking the law, although they do not notice that they themselves do not always keep the law. The Jews do not have, therefore, any excuses for their hatred of Jesus.

4.3. Conclusion: The Johannine Christians and Markers of Jewishness

The passages in John 5:1–18 and 7:19–24 make it possible to say something about the relevance of basic Jewish identity matters for the Johannine Christians.[118] First, it is remarkable how little is actually said about such things as the Sabbath or circumcision in the gospel as a whole; this is in line with the fact that nothing at all is said, for example, about Jewish dietary regulations which were essential to Jewish identity and an important topic also in other early Christian sources (e.g., Gal 2:11–14; Acts 10–11; 15:1–21; Mark 7:1–23 *par.*). But it is not just the paucity of the material related to central Jewish practices, but also the way this material is developed that is noteworthy in John. In John 5 the Sabbath is not a main issue, but the controversy soon focuses solely on Jesus' person. As John Ashton notes,

> questions of halakah that still occupy the Synoptics, worry Paul, and absorb the rabbis, are totally remote from his [John's] concern. For him the Sabbath healing is just a stepping-stone to the affirmation of Jesus' divinity.[119]

---

[118] The Sabbath theme is dealt with also in John 9 where Jesus heals the man born blind. But I think this passage adds little to the conclusions I have made on the basis of John 5:1–18 regarding the observance of the Sabbath regulations in the Johannine community. In John 9 Jesus heals the blind man by making clay, and there is no question that he breaks the law by doing so. Cf. Moloney 1996, 123. The following discussion between the once blind man and the Pharisees concerns the question of whether a person who does not keep the Sabbath can be from God or not. But it is never denied that Jesus' healing contravened the Sabbath. Thus, just like John 5:1–18, the story in John 9 shows that the Johannine Christians were quite ready to imagine their Lord acting against Sabbath laws. It is most probable that both stories were formulated by a group that had given up literal observance of the Sabbath.

[119] Ashton 1991, 139.

It is noteworthy that a passage that could be understood as an apology for Jesus' Sabbath action, John 7:19–24, does not appear in a context where Jesus is originally accused of breaking the Sabbath. As I have shown, this passage does not function as an apology for Jesus in its present context, but it serves to show that even the Jews habitually break the Sabbath.

Lloyd Gaston has suggested that the lack of detailed discussion of basic Jewish identity markers in John shows that the community behind the gospel was still observing the Sabbath and practicing circumcision. Gaston remarks rightly that

> for a group of Jews to renounce in principle some or all of the commandments of Torah is not a matter to be passed over in silence as if it were trivial.[120]

Gaston thinks that, because "we find no discussion at all in John of specific commandments for Christian Jews," it is likely that these issues had not yet arisen. He rejects here "the older (Protestant) assumption" that John reflects a situation where

> the 'battle' over the Law was fought and successfully won by Paul, that knight of faith who slew the dragon Law once for all for the universal church.[121]

But we do not need to share this caricatured view of the relationship between Paul and John, if we believe that the Johannine Christians had already dropped the observance of the law. It is fully possible that Paul and John shared some of the same early Christian traditions that took a liberal stance towards observance of some principal markers of Jewish identity and that thus gave an impetus to their final abandonment.[122] Be that as it may, both John 5:1–18 and 7:19–24 suggest that the gospel already reflects a situation where non-observance was taken as self-evident and did not need any justification. John 5:1–18 does not aim at justifying a liberal attitude to the Sabbath but rather takes this attitude for granted and develops

---

[120] Gaston 1993, 117.

[121] Gaston 1993, 118. Gaston here argues especially against Brown 1979, 55–59. To be sure, Gaston finds "a very strange distancing" of the Johannine Christians from the law and notes that "no thought seems to have been given to the Law as such." But he concludes that "presumably people [Johannine Christians] continued to keep the commandments."

[122] It has been argued that Johannine Christianity may have had some contacts at an early phase with the Hellenists in the early church in Jerusalem. See Cullmann 1975, 44–56; Becker 1997, 26.

it further. The story may not tell explicitly about Sabbath observance among the Johannine Christians, but it is not very likely that
the Johannine Christians would have continued to keep the Sabbath
themselves while accepting without further ado that their Lord habitually broke it or even abrogated it. Their faith in Jesus as God's
agent on earth had become the centre of their symbolic universe
and made literal Sabbath observance irrevelant. The way the Sabbath
theme is subordinated to the christological argumentation in John
suggests that whatever discussions and controversies were connected
to the original decision to drop the observance of the Sabbath, the
period of these discussions was already over for the Johannine
Christians.[123] It is not accidental, therefore, that the narrator speaks
of "the Jewish day of preparation" in John 19:42 and thus betrays
his alienation from this custom.

In a similar way, John 7:19–24 suggests that the Johannine Christians did not regard circumcision as a central marker of their identity, even though the story does not explicitly address the question
of whether one should continue the practice of circumcision. But it
is unlikely that people for whom circumcision was a crucial part of
their Jewishness would have referred to the contradiction between
circumcision and the Sabbath laws in the way the Johannine Jesus
does. Only from an outsider's point of view does circumcision on

---

[123] Pace Martyn 1977, 158. Martyn says that the traditions of the early period of
the Johannine community "give not the slightest indication that this inner-synagogue
group engaged in debates about the validity of Torah; form critical analysis clearly
shows that the references to breach of Sabbath in 5,9.10.16.18 and in 9,14.16
belong to the later strata." For Martyn's attempt to combine source criticism and
the history of the community, see also Martyn 1986, 99–121. But Martyn's argument is methodologically dubious: the connection between the Sabbath theme and
the original healing story may be secondary on form critical grounds, but it does
not follow that the references to the breach of the Sabbath would reflect a later
stage in the history of the community. The Sabbath theme was probably already
combined with Jesus' healing activity in some early pre-synoptic traditions (cf. Mark
3:1–6 and *par.*). For the detailed discussion of Mark 3:1–6, see Kiilunen 1985,
222–248. Kiilunen argues that it is not possible to separate an independent healing story from the present story in Mark 3:1–6; the Sabbath conflict was already
combined to the healing story before Mark. When it comes to John, the Sabbath
theme serves as material for the christological claim, which suggests that the Sabbath
conflict as such in some form or another is earlier than the present gospel. A
detailed source and redaction critical analysis of the Sabbath stories in John 5:1–18
and in John 9 suggests that the Sabbath theme does not belong to the latest stage
in the development of these stories. See Kotila 1988, 11–23 and 61–83; Dunderberg
1994, 100–107 and 177–180.

the Sabbath mean a violation of the Sabbath laws and thus shows that the law is not always kept. The Johannine Christians may have referred to the Sabbath and circumcision to support their views on Jesus, but it seems that neither of these principal matters of Jewishness was of practical importance for them.

CHAPTER FIVE

JESUS, THE JEWS AND MOSES

5.1. *The Scriptures and Moses as Jesus' Witnesses (5:37–47)*

In the previous chapter it was suggested that the Johannine Christians had already ceased to observe two basic matters of Jewish identity, the Sabbath and circumcision. Now I turn to passages dealing with the relationship of the Johannine Jesus to the revelation at Sinai and the law given by Moses. I claim that these passages show that the decision of the Johannine Christians to drop the practical observance of some commandments of the law is not accidental but reflects their growing alienation from what created the basis of Jewishness in the minds of many Jews. In the first of these passages, John 5:37–47, the Johannine Jesus makes some harsh statements that hit at the heart of Jewish identity. This discussion shows that Moses and the revelation at Sinai have only a limited role for John, even though he claims that Moses and his scriptures bear witness to Jesus.

The Context of Jesus' Speech

Jesus' references to the testimony of the scriptures and Moses in John 5:37–47 are a part of Jesus' lengthy speech where he defends himself against the claim that he has broken the Sabbath and made himself equal to God (5:18). The Jews are not mentioned in this speech after v. 18, but the latter part of the speech makes clear that Jesus still has his Jewish opponents in mind.

In John 5:30, Jesus returns to the assertion he originally made in 5:19, as he answered the claim of his opponents: as the Son of God he does not do anything on his own accord, but does what he sees his Father do. After this there seems to be a change of topic in Jesus' speech, as he begins to speak about those things that bear witness to him (v. 31ff.). Jesus adopts here the point of view of his opponents by speaking on their behalf and expressing a likely objection against his previous words: "If I testify about myself, my testimony is not true."[1] The theme of testimony is thus logically connected

---

[1] Strathmann 107; Brown 227; Beutler 1972, 179; Asiedu-Peprah 2001, 97.

to Jesus' previous claims about his close relationship to his Father.

A typical Johannine role reversal takes place in John 5:37–47, when Jesus who at first was the accused becomes the one who attacks his accusers.[2] This role reversal connects the end of Jesus' speech to its original narrative setting. At the end of his speech, Jesus refers to Moses who will accuse the Jews because they do not believe him and his writings (vv. 45–47). The introduction of Moses, the ultimate authority of the Jews, brings the story back to the conflict in which Jesus was accused of breaking the law.[3] The Johannine Jesus knocks the bottom out of the accusations of his opponents by saying that Moses is on his side and against them.

There is another connection between the end of Jesus' speech and the previous story about the Sabbath conflict. While attacking his opponents, Jesus declares that they do not seek the glory that comes from the only God but receive glory from one another (5:44). The designation "the only God" (ὁ μόνος θεός) appears in John here and in a slightly different form in 17:3 (ὁ μόνος ἀληθινὸς θεός).[4] The use of this expression is understandable in this context. Jesus' opponents have earlier in the story accused him of challenging the belief in one God by claiming that he has made himself equal to God. Jesus now turns this accusation back on the Jews by claiming that they do not seek the glory that comes from the only God.[5] Jesus' speech as a whole aims to show that his opponents have no case against him: they cannot appeal to the law of Moses, because Moses bears witness to Jesus and they cannot appeal to their faith in one God, because they themselves are not serving the only God in the right way.

Jesus' words about the scriptures and Moses are closely connected to his earlier words about different witnesses that speak for him. In his speech Jesus refers to a well known legal principle: a person may not testify in his or her own behalf, and so Jesus' testimony is not true if he bears witness to himself (5:31). This principle was known

---

[2] Cf. Scholtissek 1998, 251–252.

[3] Cf. Lee 1994, 120 and 124.

[4] Many early and important witnesses (e. g. $\mathfrak{P}^{66,\ 75}$, B, W, Origen, Eusebius) omit the word θεοῦ in 5:44 and read "the glory that comes from the only one." If this were the original reading, this would be the only case that the word ὁ μόνος alone is used for God in John. The reading with θεοῦ is supported by ℵ, A, D, K. L, $f^{1.13}$ and many other witnesses. The omission of θεοῦ may be explained as a scribal error: some manuscripts have accidentally omitted the letters ΘΥ that are a contraction for θεοῦ from the text. Thus Bernard 256; Brown 225; Barrett 269; Metzger 1994, 180.

[5] Cf. Whitacre 1982, 78; Klappert 1990, 630; Wilckens 125.

both in Graeco-Roman and in Jewish legal praxis.[6] After mentioning this principle Jesus makes a cryptic allusion to "another who
testifies on my behalf" (v. 32). What follows this allusion is a passage
dealing with the testimony of John the Baptist. But it is not probable that Jesus has the Baptist in mind in v. 32, because he states
that he does not receive the testimony of a human being; he refers only
to the testimony of the Baptist that the Jews may be saved (v. 34).
It is more likely that the testimony of God is in Jesus' mind already
in v. 32.[7] In this verse Jesus states the basic thesis for the following
discussion in which this thesis is developed further.[8] Because Jesus
does not reveal at once who 'another' is, his speech develops gradually towards the explicit disclosure of the identity of 'another' in
v. 37.[9]

The same pattern characterizes the response of the Jews to different
witnesses of Jesus: Jesus claims that they accept these witnesses at a
superficial and irrelevant level, but do not understand the real function
of these witnesses. The Jews were willing to rejoice for a while in
the light of John the Baptist, but they did not accept his testimony to
the truth (5:33–35). The Jews search the Scriptures, but do not realize that they bear witness to Jesus (5:39). The role of the scriptures
as a witness to Jesus is thus similar to that of the Baptist.[10] This is
true also with the works of Jesus (5:36). It is repeatedly said in the
gospel that at least some of the Jews believed in Jesus because of
his signs (2:23; 3:2; 7:31; 11:45), but this faith does not, however,
lead to a real understanding of Jesus (cf. 2:23; 12:37–43). From the
Johannine point of view, the Baptist, the scriptures and Jesus' works
should point away from themselves to Jesus, but the Jews of the
story fail to understand this.

Different witnesses have another common feature. Jesus' witnesses
may turn into the accusers of those who do not believe in the testimony of these witnesses.[11] The Jews have not accepted the witness
of the scriptures, and therefore, Moses, who has written of Jesus,
accuses them (5:45). The same is true in the case of Jesus' works,

---

[6] For Graeco-Roman parallels, see Bauer 84; Schnelle 111. Jewish parallels
include Philo's *Alleg. Interp.* III 205 and *m. Ketub.* 2:7.
[7] John Chrysostom took Jesus' mention of "another" as a reference to John the
Baptist, but this interpretation is today quite commonly disputed. Cf. Brown 224.
[8] Thus Pancaro 1975, 211; Becker 301.
[9] Pancaro 1975, 211; Asiedu-Peprah 2001, 98–99.
[10] Barrett 265.
[11] Cf. von Wahlde 1981, 404.

as he says in his farewell speech: "If I had not done among them the works that no one else did, they would not have sin. But now they have seen and hated both me and my Father" (15:24). The testimony of the Baptist is also a potential witness against the Jews. The purpose of John's mission is that Jesus might be revealed to Israel (John 1:31).[12] John's witness is accepted by the few (1:47), whereas the narrative of the gospel as a whole suggests that it is rejected by the majority of God's people. The Johannine Jesus claims that he does not receive a testimony from people but acknowledges the value of John's witness to the Jews as he says, "I say this so that you may be saved" (5:34). Jesus does not say it directly, but his words imply that the Baptist becomes a witness against the Jews if they fail to receive his testimony.[13]

Jesus and the Revelation at Sinai

After dealing with the witness of the Baptist and the witness of the works Jesus mentions the witness of the Father: "And the Father who sent me has himself borne witness to me" (v. 37). Jesus does not describe the testimony of the Father any further, and scholars have understood this testimony in different ways. Some scholars interpret this passage in light of 1 John 5:9–10 affirming that Jesus is speaking of the Father's direct, internal testimony within the hearts of the believers.[14] The problem with this interpretation is that Jesus is speaking in this context to his opponents, and all the other witnesses he is talking about are external, perceptible witnesses that his opponents should also have recognised.

---

[12] According to Pancaro (1974–75, 396–405 and 1975, 294ff.), the terms Ἰσραήλ and Ἰσραηλίτης always have a positive sense in John and should be separated from the term Ἰουδαῖος. The 'Jews' in John refers to the Jewish nation as a religious-national body, whereas 'Israel' refers to a new people of God that is dissociated from the Jews as a nation; thus an 'Israelite' in John is the one who accepts Jesus and becomes a member of this new people (1:47). Pancaro says that the witness of the Baptist in John 1:31 was not intended for the 'Jews' but for 'Israel' (1974–75, 399; 1975, 297). But there is not a clear-cut distinction between the terms Ἰσραήλ/Ἰσραηλίτης and Ἰουδαῖος in John. For example, Nicodemus is called both a ruler of the Jews (ἄρχων τῶν Ἰουδαίων) and a teacher of Israel (ὁ διδάσκαλος τοῦ Ἰσραήλ). For criticism of Pancaro, see Painter 1979, 107–111. As Painter notes, manifesting Jesus to Israel does not imply that all Israel will believe as a consequence (p. 108).

[13] Blank 1964, 203: "Johannes wird zum Belastungszeugen gegen die Juden."

[14] Bernard 250–251; Dodd 1953, 330; Brown 227; Barrett 266–267. For criticism of this view, see Kotila 1988, 32.

According to an alternative interpretation, Jesus means by the testimony of his Father in 5:37 the testimony of works mentioned just
before in v. 36. Jesus' reference to his works is sometimes understood to refer to his mission as a whole.[15] But this solution does not
take into account the great role of Jesus' individual signs in the
gospel. Therefore, it has been suggested that the witness of the Father
coincides rather with Jesus' individual signs. These signs are taken
as "the events through which the Father has already borne witness to
Jesus."[16] But this explanation is not very well in line with the basic
idea of the section mentioned in 5:32: Jesus says that he has another
who bears witness for him, which suggests that this witness is clearly
separate from Jesus himself.[17] The use of the connective καί in the
beginning of 5:37 also suggests that the witness of the Father is not
the same as the witness of the works mentioned in 5:36.[18]

Most scholars understand that the testimony of the Father in v. 37
is closely connected to the testimony of the scriptures mentioned
in v. 39.[19] The use of the perfect μεμαρτύρηκεν fits well with this
interpretation: it refers to the past testimony of the Father that still

---

[15] Becker 305. Becker does not attach great importance to distinct, concrete witnesses to Jesus; what matters is the mission of Jesus as a whole. Becker also devalues the scriptures as a real witness to Jesus; like the Baptist, they have only a
subsidiary function when they point to Jesus (p. 307). This does not, however,
explain why Jesus deals with the witness of the scriptures and Moses so extensively
in 5:39–47. According to Becker, there can be no external witnesses to Jesus, but
this is the very theme in 5:31–47.

[16] Asiedu-Peprah 2001, 106.

[17] This also makes unlikely the solution proposed by von Wahlde 1981, 390. Von
Wahlde claims that the testimony of the Father is identical to the word which the
Father has given to Jesus and which Jesus gives to the world. But it is difficult to
see how a witness to Jesus (περὶ ἐμοῦ) could be identical with the words spoken by
Jesus. Thus Kotila 1988, 32.

[18] Thus Kotila 1988, 31. Kotila argues convincingly against Schnackenburg (II, 174)
who takes καί in 5:37 as epexegetical. Asiedu-Peprah (2001, 105) understands καί as
consecutive, which makes it possible to connect the testimony of the Father to the
testimony of the works. But it is noteworthy that both v. 36 and v. 37 begin with
a connective: v. 36 begins with the words "But I have" (ἐγὼ δὲ ἔχω) and v. 37 with
the words "And the Father who sent me" (καὶ ὁ πέμψας με πατήρ). The clause in
v. 39, however, begins without a connective ("You search the scriptures"). This
suggests that this verse belongs together with vv. 37–38. Vv. 37–39 all speak of the
testimony of the Father that coincides with the testimony of the scriptures. This
testimony should be separated from the testimony of the works mentioned in v. 36.

[19] Bauer 85; Bultmann 200; Hoskyns 273; Strathmann 108; Blank 1964, 205;
Meeks 1967, 300; Beutler 1972, 260–261; Lindars 229; Pancaro 1975, 218; Dahl
1986, 130; Beasley-Murray 78; Schnelle 112.

is valid today.[20] The terminology used in this connection is the most decisive argument for this interpretation. After mentioning the testimony of the Father, Jesus says in 5:37: "You have never heard his voice or seen his form." In a Jewish context, this language brings to mind traditions according to which God appeared to his people at Sinai and made a lasting covenant with them.[21] It is most likely that the Johannine Jesus refers here to these scriptural traditions already before explicitly mentioning the witness of the scriptures. The Johannine Jesus is thus speaking of a founding act of distinct Jewish identity, but close reading of his arguments shows a clear departure from how the role of the Sinai event was understood in Jewish tradition.

Different passages in the book of Exodus are ambiguous as to whether the Israelites really saw God on Mount Sinai or not.[22] God says in Exod 20:22 to the people that "you have seen for yourselves that I have spoke with you from heaven." Exod 24:9–11 tells how Moses and the elders of Israel saw the God of Israel and even ate with him. Some other, and probably later, passages deny that the people see God. Exod 19:21–22 tells how God descended on Mount Sinai and warned the people lest they "break through to the Lord to look; otherwise many of them will perish." Exod 33:20 explicitly says that a human being cannot see God and stay alive. This same tendency is seen also in the Book of Deuteronomy: it is stated explicitly that the people heard only God's voice but did not see his form (Deut 4:12,15). According to Deut 4:36, God spoke to the people from heaven, and on earth he let the people see his great fire, and out of the midst of this fire the people heard his voice.[23] In this connection it is said also that the revelation at Sinai made the people of Israel distinct from all other nations (Deut 4:32–35).

The tenet that God revealed himself to his people at Sinai was kept alive in many different forms of Judaism. According to Ben

---

[20] Thus Bultmann 200. Asiedu-Peprah (2001, 105–106) takes the perfect μεμαρτύρηκεν as an "internal analepsis" that refers to Jesus' signs related earlier in the gospel.

[21] See Schlatter 157; Dahl 1986 (1962), 130; Borgen 1965, 151; Brown 225; Meeks 1967, 299–300 and 1976, 57–58; Beutler 1972, 261 (with some reservations); Pancaro 1975, 220; Richter 1977a, 226; Beasley-Murray 78; Menken 2001, 446.

[22] For relevant scriptural material, see Pancaro 1975, 220–224.

[23] By combining the speaking from heaven with the fire on the mountain the deuteronomistic writer advances his abstract concept of revelation. See Weinfeld 1991, 212–213.

Sira, the Israelites saw at Sinai "his glorious majesty and their ears heard the glory of his voice" (Sir 17:13). It is said here that the revelation of God and the law given at Sinai is the special privilege of Israel (17:17). According to some early rabbinic midrashim, the people at Sinai "saw what Isaiah and Ezekiel never saw."[24] Again this revelation is taken to mean that Israel is unique among the nations.[25] Philo also takes it as a special privilege of Israel to have seen God, although he does not always connect this view to the revelation at Sinai. For Philo the very word "Israel" means "the one who sees God," even though this is hardly a correct etymological explanation of the word.[26] Philo uses this etymology to show "that which is specific of the Jewish religion in a siglum that points to the special relationship between the one God and the Jewish people."[27]

Jesus' words about the testimony of his Father in John 5:37 are best understood as an implicit reference to the theophany at Sinai. His claim that, "You have never heard his voice or seen his form," is a "cavalier denial of a central Jewish belief."[28] Also, the following words "and you do not have his word abiding in you" (v. 38) should be interpreted in light of the scriptures. According to many passages in the Book of Deuteronomy, God urges the people to keep the words he has spoken in their hearts so that they will always remember them (Deut 6:6–7; 11:18–19). Moses demands that the people take to heart his words and obey all the words of the law (Deut 32:46–47). In Deut 30:11–14, God promises the people that "the word (LXX: ῥῆμα) is very near to you; it is in your mouth and in your heart for you to observe" (v. 14). When the Johannine Jesus says, "you do not have his word abiding in you," he denies what is promised to

---

[24] *Mek. Baḥodeš* 3. Cf. also *Mek. Širata* 3.

[25] *Mek. Baḥodeš* 9.

[26] For this etymology in Philo, see Borgen 1965, 115–118; Delling 1984, 27–41; Harvey 1996, 219–224. The etymology is based on Hebrew, although the only Hebrew example of its use is attested only in a late source (*S. Eli. Rab.* 25 [138]). The etymology appears, however, in a fragmentary Jewish source (*The Prayer of Joseph*) cited by Origen (*Comm. Jo.* 2.25) as well as in a Nag Hammadi writing (*Orig. World* 105.24–25).

[27] Delling 1984, 41.

[28] Meeks 1976, 58. For a different view, see von Wahlde 1981, 394. Von Wahlde says that it is not necessary to determine what kind of experience is referred to by "seeing" and "hearing" in v. 37, since the point of the verse is that only Jesus has had direct experience of God. But Jesus is not talking in abstract terms here; other taunts he makes here are also closely connected basic matters of Jewish identity.

the Israelite people in these texts.[29] The following ὅτι-clause in v. 38 explains why Jesus denies here these basic Jewish convictions.

The ὅτι-clause in v. 38 can be interpreted in two ways. First, it can be taken as a cause for what is stated earlier: "You have never heard . . . and have not seen . . .; and you do not have . . ., because you do not believe him whom he has sent."[30] Second, the ὅτι-clause can be taken as a sign of what is said earlier: "You have never heard . . . and have not seen . . .; and you do not have . . ., which is shown by the fact that you do not believe him whom he has sent."[31] The context of the verse gives more support for the latter interpretation that takes the ὅτι-clause as a sign of the unbelief of the Jews.

The Johannine Jesus says in 5:39: "You search the scriptures, because you think that in them you have eternal life; and it is they that testify on my behalf."[32] The belief that the study of the scriptures brings life is wide-spread in Jewish sources.[33] But according to John, only faith in Jesus guarantees the right understanding of the scriptures. The same idea is expressed in other words when Jesus later speaks of Moses: "If you believed Moses, you would believe me" (v. 46: εἰ γὰρ ἐπιστεύετε Μωϋσεῖ, ἐπιστεύετε ἂν ἐμοί). The contrary-to-fact conditional sentence makes clear that by rejecting Jesus the Jews show that they have not believed what Moses has written. This is the basic idea of the whole passage in vv. 36–47. That the Jews do not receive Jesus shows that they have not shared in the earlier revelation of God either.[34] The meaning of the words "you have never heard . . . and have not seen . . ." is not that God did not reveal himself at Sinai, or that the Jews met only with a representative of God.[35] The idea is that the Jews have never heard

---

[29] The words "you do not have his word abiding in you" are connected to Deut 30:11–14 also by Meeks 1967, 300 and 1976, 57–58.

[30] Thus Bernard 252; Von Wahlde 1981, 394. Von Wahlde mentions more scholars supporting this interpretation (p. 389, n. 17).

[31] Thus Bultmann 201; Blank 1964, 206; Beutler 1972, 262; Pancaro 1975, 226; Beasley-Murray 78; Schnelle 112. According to Barrett (267), both interpretations of ὅτι are correct.

[32] The verb ἐραυνάω used in this connection is a Greek equivalent to the Hebrew verb שׁרד, a *terminus technicus* for the study of the scriptures in the writings of Qumran community and in rabbinic literature. Cf. Schnackenburg II 175.

[33] For example, Lev 18:5; Deut 32:46–47; Bar 4:1; *Pss. Sol.* 14:1. For more material, see Strack-Billerbeck III 129–132.

[34] Cf. Blank 1964, 205; Meeks 1967, 300; Richter 1977a, 226.

[35] According to Schlatter (157), Jesus refers here to a view that ascribed the voice at Sinai to an angelic agency. Also Lindars (229) refers to this view and says that

God's voice or seen his form in a real way.[36] From the Johannine perspective, God has indeed given his revelation at Sinai and borne witness to Jesus, but the Jews have never understood this, as their failure to receive Jesus shows.

Jesus' attack against the unbelief of the Jews continues in vv. 41–47. Jesus states in v. 42 that his opponents do not have the love of God within them. This charge can be interpreted in two ways. First, the genitive ἡ ἀγάπη τοῦ θεοῦ can be taken as a subjective genitive in which case the meaning is that the Jews are not those whom God loves.[37] Second, the genitive may be read as an objective genitive, which means that the Jews do not have love for God in them.[38] The context speaks for the latter interpretation.[39]

Jesus charges his audience that they will receive another who comes in his own name but do not receive him who has come in the name of the Father (v. 43). He says also that they receive glory from one another but do not seek the glory that comes from the only God (v. 44). These charges have to do with the failures of the Jews, and this is also likely with the charge in v. 42. Jesus here accuses his opponents of the neglect of the first commandment of the law, the love for God (Deut 6:4–5).[40] The belief in one God and the love for him had a fundamental role in different forms of Judaism.[41] Therefore, this charge is especially harsh.[42] It is, however, well in line with the previous statements that denied the sharings of the Jews in God's revelation. These claims revoke all the privileges Jesus' Jewish opponents may claim for themselves on the basis of God's revelation and the law given to them.

According to the Johannine Jesus, the Jews fail to keep the first commandment because they receive glory from one another and do

---

the Johannine Jesus denies here that there could be direct sight or hearing of God. According to other passages in the gospel, however, the figures in the Hebrew Bible could have shared in Jesus' revelation (cf. 8:56; 12:41). The unbelief of the Jews, however, shows that they have never understood this revelation in the right way.

[36] Thus Bultmann 200 n. 6.

[37] Beutler (1986, 226 n. 7) mentions scholars such as Hoskyns, Mollat, Wikenhauser and Painter as supporters of this interpretation.

[38] Thus Bauer 86; Bultmann 202; Dodd 1953, 330; Schnackenburg II 178; Lindars 231; Barrett 269; Beutler 1986, 227–228; Becker 308; Schnelle 112.

[39] Cf. Beutler 1986, 227.

[40] Thus especially Beutler 1986, 228. Cf. also Schnackenburg II 180; Becker 308; Schnelle 112.

[41] For example, see E. P. Sanders 1992, 195–196.

[42] Thus Schnackenburg II 180; Becker 308.

not seek the glory that comes from God. This charge reappers in John 12:43, and it has parallels in contemporary polemical writings. In *Psalms of Solomon* there appears a polemical passage directed against those who try to please their fellow human beings (οἱ ἀνθρωπάρεσκοι) although their hearts are far from the Lord (*Pss. Sol.* 4:1–12). Some Christian writings speak in a positive way of those who have not sought human glory but have tried to please God only (1 Thess 2:3–6), while some others attack those who do all their works to be seen by others (Matt 23:5–7). Paul contrasts those who are Jews only outwardly to those who are Jews inwardly and who receive their praise not from human beings but from God (Rom 2:28–29). Rabbinic tradition warns of seeking one's own glory and makes a distinction between human glory and the glory of God.[43] In Hellenistic rhetoric, the charge that someone is a lover of glory was an established *topos*.[44] It was conventional to say that someone exercises philosophy only for the sake of glory and not for the sake of love for philosophy.[45] The charge the Johannine Jesus directs against his opponents here echoes this wide-spread tradition; the love of glory was a typical vice attached to anyone who was regarded as an opponent. Therefore, this charge that does not reflect necessarily a characteristic of any particular Jewish group.[46]

Jesus makes a conventional slur theologically significant by connecting it to the first commandment of the law. In a manner typical of all polemics the Johannine Jesus maintains that the wrong ideas the Jews have about him and God are based ultimately on their immoral behavior. The Jews in question both act in a dubious way and lack the right theology.

Jesus' attack reaches its culmination when he states that he himself will not accuse them to the Father; it is Moses, on whom they set their hope, who accuses them (v. 45). Like Jesus' earlier claims,

---

[43] Warnings against the searching of glory: *m. 'Abot* 4:5, 21. The distinction between the human glory and the glory of God: *b. Qidd.* 32b = *Sipre Deut* 38; *b. Yoma* 38a; *Seder Eliyahu Rabba* 14 (65).

[44] Johnson 1989, 432.

[45] For examples, see Johnson 1989, 432 n. 47.

[46] Pace Lindars 232. According to Lindars, Jesus' words refer to "a group of teachers who are a sort of 'mutual admiration society,' and have a vested interest in maintaining their own traditions." Pancaro (1975, 241–253) connects the charge to the situation of the Johannine Christians after they were expelled from the synagogue. As Kotila (1988, 25 n. 30) notes, Pancaro reads too much into the text here.

this one also has a scriptural basis. In the end of the Book of Deuteronomy, Moses says that both his words (Deut 31:19,21) and the book of the law (Deut 31:25–27) will function as a witness for the rebellious and stubborn people. The Johannine Jesus refers to these ideas when he claims that Moses accuses the Jews because they refuse to believe that Moses has written about him.[47] The statement that Moses is the accuser (ὁ κατηγορῶν) of the Jews turns upside down a common Jewish view that held Moses to be the defender (συνήγορος, παράκλητος) of Israel before God.[48] Moses' function is similar to that of the scriptures discussed earlier by Jesus: both Moses and his scriptures bear witness to Jesus, but the Jews of the story fail to understand this and, accordingly, these witnesses turn into their accusers.[49]

Jesus' words about Moses continue to strip his opponents of basics of Jewishness. According to the Johannine Jesus, his opponents have never received God's revelation; they do not have the word of God abiding in them; their study of the scriptures is misguided; they do not keep the main commandment of the law, the love for God; and they set in vain their hope on the founder of their religion, Moses. The reason for these failures is that they do not receive Jesus. This means that the significance of the Sinai event and Moses is reduced to a witness for Jesus and an accuser of the Jews. This conviction does not grant any independent role to these pillars of Jewishness. For John, the faith in Jesus is in the center of his symbolic universe, and this faith determines the significance of previous scriptural history. John may claim that Moses bears witness to Jesus, but the passage in John 5:37–47 also implies the actual negation of some basic matters of Jewishness, as is detailed by Adele Reinhartz:

> At the same time as the Gospel describes the principal pillars of Jewish identity, however, it also engages in their negation. From the perspective of Jewish covenantal theology, these pillars support a self-understanding as God's elect people in loving relationship to God. The role of the Jewish individual and the Jewish community as a whole is to love God. This love is demonstrated through the attempt to live

---

[47] See especially Meeks 1967, 306–307. Cf. also Brown 226; Kotila 1988, 27.

[48] This view appears in Philo, Josephus, *As. Mos.*, Pseudo-Philo, Qumran, and rabbinic midrashim. For the material, see Meeks 1967, 118, 137, 159–161, 174, 200–204. Cf. also Bultmann 205; Dahl 1986 (1962), 130; Schnackenburg II 181; Pancaro 1975, 256–257.

[49] Pancaro (1975, 255–259) sees a difference here between the role of the scriptures and the role of Moses, but there are no reasons for this in the text.

according to God's will as revealed in the Written and Oral Torah
and further described in the prophetic and other canonical litarature.
As the Gospel narrative progresses, each of these pillars, and the Jewish
understanding thereof, is undermined, contradicted, and exposed as
misguided, misused, and even deliberately perverted.[50]

In the course of his speech, Jesus does not identify his opponents any
more precisely, which makes it possible to say that he has in mind
here a particular group of the Jews, not Jews in some more general
sense.[51] But the very fact that Jesus here connects the Jews who
accuse him of breaking the Sabbath and making himself equal to
God with the past Sinai generation shows that οἱ Ἰουδαῖοι in John
5:1–18 are not just a particular authoritative group among the Jews.
For John, Jesus' Jewish opponents are also representatives of the past
people of God, not just an identifiable group of the Jews in their
surroundings. Therefore, it is understandable that Jesus' attack against
his opponents in 5:37–47 deals with basic matters of Jewishness. The
things discussed were not characteristics of a particular Jewish group
but were fundamental to many different groups of the Jews. From
the Johannine point of view, all those who do not receive Jesus do
not share in God's revelation either. What is actually at stake here
is not loyalty to Moses but loyalty to Jesus. The passage suggest that
John and his readers no longer base their identity on the Sinai event,
but rather evaluate this event from the point of view of their faith
in Jesus. This means that the charges that may originally have been
a part of inner-Jewish polemic are now made from the standpoint
of those who no longer share common Jewish identity.[52] In this passage the negation of basic matters of Jewishness may be only implicit,
but this negation is expressed more clearly in the discussion about
the bread of life following in John 6.

---

[50] Reinhartz 1997, 185. Reinhartz refers in this connection to such texts as John
5:39–47 and 8:39–44.
[51] Thus Asiedu-Peprah 2001, 106 n. 216. Asiedu-Peprah says that Jesus' words
here cannot refer to the revelation at Sinai, because this view "mistakenly assumes
that οἱ Ἰουδαῖοι who are Jesus' interlocutors in the present context are the Jewish
people, past and present."
[52] Pace van Belle 2001, 388. For van Belle, John 5:31–37 has to do with intra-
Jewish polemic; Jesus' claim that the Jews have never heard God's voice nor seen
his face does not mean that he is no longer able to identify himself with his people. Van Belle admits, however, that "in an extra-Jewish situation this might well
have been the case."

5.2. *The Bread from Heaven and the Manna of the Jews (6:26–59)*

The relationship between Jesus, Moses, and the Jews is elaborated
further in John 6 where Jesus feeds five thousand men and speaks
about the bread from heaven. It is the crowd—later called the Jews
(vv. 41, 52)—that introduces Moses into the discussion by demand-
ing that Jesus perform a miracle similar to the manna miracle experienced by the wilderness generation (vv. 30–31). This challenge gives
Jesus a reason to specify his relationship to scriptural manna traditions. Jesus identifies himself as the bread of life that comes from
heaven and contrasts this bread to the manna given by Moses. Jesus
makes clear here that the revelation given by him is far superior to
the manna. According to this text, there is a clear contrast between
Jesus and Moses. This passage illustrates that the relationship of the
Johannine Christians to Moses and the scriptures is ambiguous: on
the one hand, Moses and his scriptures bear witness to Jesus, but,
on the other hand, they are contrasted to the revelation of Jesus.

The Context of Jesus' Speech

There has been much scholarly discussion about the proper place
of John 6 in the narrative outline of the gospel because the transition from John 5 to John 6 is not without problems.[53] In spite of
these problems, these two chapters have a thematic connection. At
the end of his speech in John 5, Jesus deals with the testimony of
the scriptures on a general level. Moses and his scriptures have an
important role to play also in John 6. The crowd cites the scriptures
and makes a reference to the manna miracle experienced by the
Israelite people in the wilderness (6:31). This scriptural background
is crucial for the whole speech in John 6. This speech can be seen
as an elaboration of the theme introduced in John 5. Jesus states
generally in John 5:37–47 that the scriptures bear witness to him,
and the speech about the bread of life is used as an illustration of
this general statement.[54]

Jesus' speech about the bread from heaven is preceded by two
miracle stories: first, the narrator tells how Jesus feeds five thousand
men (6:1–15) and then how Jesus walks on the sea (6:16–21). The
speech is connected especially to the first of these stories. At the end

---

[53] See Becker 191.
[54] Borgen 1965, 152 and 1997, 112; Lindars 234; Von Wahlde 1981, 397–398.

of the feeding story, the people regarded Jesus as the prophet, because they saw the sign he had done. The narrator tells, however, that Jesus knew that they were going to make him king, and so he withdrew again to the mountain by himself (vv. 14–15). It is surprising that later the crowd asks Jesus to perform such a sign as the manna miracle so that they may see and believe in him (vv. 30–31). They seem to have forgotten completely that they had witnessed such a sign just the day before. The function of the crowd's request in the story is important for the characterization of Jesus' interlocutors.[55]

According to many interpreters, the crowd asks Jesus to perform a greater miracle than the one they witnessed a day before. The feeding miracle was only an individual event, whereas what they demand now is a continuous feeding such as the manna in the wilderness that rained from heaven every day (Exod 16).[56] Many scholars refer to views that connected the descending of manna and the coming age of salvation: by repeating the manna miracle Jesus would show that the time of salvation had come.[57] According to a slightly different interpretation, the people ask for a further miracle to show that Jesus is the heavenly Son of Man; the feeding miracle demonstrated only that Jesus was the Moses-like prophet.[58] These interpretations do not recognize, however, the irony implied in the crowd's request; the irony here "is very heavy, for precisely the 'sign' which they request—one analogous to the manna which Moses gave— has already been provided."[59] So the awkward request can be taken as "a literary device intended by the evangelist to emphasize the blindness of the Jews."[60] This becomes more evident as we interpret the demand of the crowd in light of its narrative context.

---

[55] The difficulties between the crowd's request for a sign and the feeding story were recognised early. For source critical attempts to solve this difficulty, see E. Schwartz 1907–08, 500–501; Brown 258.

[56] Strathmann 120; Becker 246; Theobald 1997, 348; Wilckens 101.

[57] Cf. Rev 2:17; 2 *Bar.* 29:8; *Sib. Or.* 7:148–149 and fragm. 3:46–49. These views date back to at least the end of the first century C.E., as is shown by Menken 1988a, 47. In a late rabbinic source (*Eccl. Rab.* 1.9) the descending of manna is connected to the appearance of the final redeemer.

[58] Thus Borgen 1997, 103–104.

[59] Meeks 1972, 58. Cf. also Martyn 1979, 125–126; Culpepper 1983, 172 and 177; Duke 1985, 112; Malina & Rohrbaugh 130.

[60] Von Wahlde 1984, 578. Von Wahlde compares this passage to the two passages where the Jews ask about the identity of Jesus (8:25, 10:24). What is common to all three cases is that the Jews (or the crowd in 6:30) have had "clear evidence in the immediate context that should have made their questions unnecessary."

After revealing that he is the bread of life (v. 35) Jesus blames the crowd for unbelief: "But I said you that you have seen and yet do not believe" (v. 36).[61] The problem with this saying is that Jesus has not said these words earlier to the crowd or to anyone else in the gospel. It is not, however, unusual that Jesus quotes his own words that are not found in the gospel. In John 10:25 Jesus says to the Jews, "I have told you and you do not believe," after they have demanded himself to reveal whether he is the Christ.[62] Again, there is no clear reference for Jesus' words. In both cases Jesus' opponents ask for proof that would show who Jesus is, and in both cases Jesus answers by saying that they have already received the needed evidence although they have not believed it. Jesus blames in 6:36 the crowd for not realizing his sign after they saw it. This may seem to contradict John 6:14 according to which the people saw the sign and said that Jesus is the prophet who is to come into the world. But Jesus' withdrawal in John 6:15 shows that the people misunderstood the true nature of Jesus' sign. This misunderstanding paves the way for the request of the sign in 6:30–31 which finally reveals "the inadequate nature of the crowd's understanding."[63]

In the first part of John 6, those who contend with Jesus are identified as the crowd (ὁ ὄχλος; v. 2, 5, 22, 24). Later, however, the narrator calls them the Jews (οἱ Ἰουδαῖοι; v. 41, 52). It has been proposed that the Jews here are a distinct group from the Galilean crowd that appeared in the earlier part of the story. Some scholars interpret the scene in light of some synoptic passages and regard the Jews as representatives of the establishment who had come down

---

[61] A few witnesses (ℵ, A, a, b, e, syr^{c, s}) lack the word με after ἑωράκατε, whereas the majority of witnesses (for example, 𝔓^{66}, and probably also 𝔓^{75}) read the text with με (you have seen *me*). Although the reading with με is better attested, it is perhaps not the original one. The context may have given a reason for the interpolation of the personal pronoun: in v. 35 Jesus speaks emphatically of himself using first person (I am the bread of life . . . everyone who comes to *me* . . ., everyone who believes in *me*); the reading with με also corresponds v. 40 where Jesus says, "everyone who sees the Son." The reading without me is taken as the original one by Bauer 93; Bultmann 173 n. 3; Lindars 260; Barrett 293; Metzger 1994, 182 (with some reservations). If the text is read without με the connection of v. 36 to v. 26 and to the previous sign of Jesus is clearer. Cf. Brown 270. Brown reads the text with the personal pronoun and explains its omission by "the scribal desire to leave vs. 36 more vague so that its antecedent might be found in vs. 26." Brown is followed by Anderson 1996, 205.
[62] Von Wahlde 1984, 580.
[63] Lee 1994, 142. Cf. also Anderson 1996, 201.

from Jerusalem to Galilee (cf. Mark 3:22; 7:1).[64] It is, however, problematic to connect what is said in the synoptics to the Johannine
text. Nor is there any indication in the text that the Jews are 'experts
on law' who are a separate group from the common crowd.[65] It is
the common people who make the reference to the manna miracle
and appeal to the law in (6:30). Furthermore, other passages in John
do not support the distinction between the common crowd and the
Jews as the experts on law. In the course of the gospel narrative,
Jesus is in a debate with the crowd on the interpretation of the
Sabbath and circumcision (7:20, in 7:15 the narrator has mentioned
the Jews), and some of the crowd refer to the scriptures when they
are wondering who Jesus is (7:42) or appeal to the law as they argue
against Jesus (12:34). So not only do 'experts on law' refer to the
law in John, but the common people do so too.

Both the Galilean crowd and the Jews are described as unbelievers in the text, which also suggests that there is not a clear-cut distinction between them.[66] By murmuring (γογγύζω) against Jesus the
Jews of the story show that they repeat the unbelief of the wilderness
generation, who were stubborn and rebelled against God.[67] The earlier misunderstanding of the crowd has set up this accusation of clear
unbelief. In John 6:31, the crowd refers to the wilderness generation
as "our fathers," and in the following discussion with the Jews, Jesus
continues this theme by referring to "your fathers" (v. 49) or to "the
fathers" (v. 58). This suggests that Jesus' entire speech is addressed
to those who appealed to the manna miracle in the first place, and

---

[64] Leistner 1974, 143–144; Robinson 1985, 85.

[65] Pace Painter 1997, 86; Borgen 1997, 108.

[66] Painter (1997, 78) regards the unbelief of the crowd in 6:36 "as a shocking
announcement." Painter takes the first part of this chapter (6:1–40) as a quest story
that presents an honest quest of the crowd; the original ending of this story has
been replaced in the present text by vv. 36–40 that emphasize the unbelief of the
crowd and form a transition to the rejection stories in 6:40–71 (p. 83). According
to Painter, the crowd do not reject Jesus or his words in any way while the Jews
"do nothing but raise objections to what Jesus has said" (p. 87). See also Kysar
1997, 169. Kysar regards the crowd as "genuine seekers" whereas the Jews from
v. 41 onward are clearly hostile. I cannot see this kind difference between the crowd
and the Jews here.

[67] Exod 15:24; 16:2–12; Num 14:2, 26–36; 16:11, 41; 17:5, 10; Ps 78:11, 17–19,
40–43, 56–57; Ps 106:13–14, 24–25. See Painter 1997, 86; M. M. Thompson 1997,
235–236. As Painter notes, Ashton (1991, 200) makes an "extraordinary" comment
as he says that the murmuring of the Jews "is prompted more by bewilderment
than by a real antagonism."

Jesus' discussion partners do not change in the course of the dialogue.[68]

Jesus' speech about the bread of life is thus not separated from its context but is a part of narrative dialogue between Jesus and those who appeal to past manna traditions. It is not a midrashic homily explaining a given text of the scriptures, even though Peder Borgen and some others have claimed so.[69] Borgen has claimed that the scriptural citation in John 6:31 is the starting point for the following speech, which is an exposition of it. The scriptural citation has an important function in the dialogue, but the discussion of the bread of life already starts in John 6:25–27 where the crowd finally finds Jesus who addresses them and refers to two different kinds of food.[70] The scriptural citation is referred to by the crowd whose unbelief becomes evident in the course of the dialogue, and this is a further sign that the citation is not the cornerstone of Jesus' speech.[71] The questions and comments made by the misunderstanding crowd or by the Jews represent beliefs that the Johannine Jesus undermines and repudiates in the course of the dialogue.[72] The core of Jesus' speech

---

[68] Thus Schram 1974, 89; Schnackenburg 75; Theobald 1997, 336.

[69] Borgen 1965, 28–58. According to Borgen, John 6:31–58 is an independent homily, the first part of which (6:32–48) discusses the first part of the scriptural quotation in 6:31 ("He gave them bread from heaven"), and the second part (6:49–58) interprets the last word of the quotation ("to eat"). Cf. also Brown 277–278; Malina 1968, 102; Lindars 250–253; Schnackenburg II 42; Barrett 284–285; Von Wahlde 1981, 398; Moloney 1997, 131–132. Meeks (1972, 58 n. 48) says that Borgen has demonstrated the midrashic character of the discourse, although many details in his reconstruction are unconvincing. For justified criticism of Borgen, see Anderson 1996, 52–61; Obermann 1996, 141–143; Painter 1997, 79–80; Theobald 1997, 332–340. I refer in more detail in the following to some points in this criticism.

[70] Thus Richter 1977, 235; Anderson 1996, 61; Obermann 1996, 142. In his interpretation, Borgen detaches the supposed homily from its natural textual context, and he seems to do this also as he analyses the manna motif in other writings. Anderson (1996, 58–61 and 272–273) says that Borgen has misidentified the homiletic form of the manna tradition in Philo, John, Exodus Mekilta and Midrash Rabbah. In these texts the manna motif and Exod 16:4 are not a primary text, but rather the writers are dealing with some other points that are illustrated by references to the manna motif.

[71] Becker 239.

[72] Borgen (1997, 100) does not pay enough attention to the irony that the two levels of understanding create in the story. Borgen takes the crowd's questions and Jesus' answers as an example of problem-solving exegesis found in rabbinic midrashim and in Philo. But the examples Borgen gives from Philo (for example, *QG* II 28) are not real parallels to the *narrative* dialogue in John where questions and possible objections to the main argument are not raised by the author himself but by a misundersanding crowd in the story. In his argumentation, Borgen ignores the difference between narrative literature and non-narrative literary forms (e.g., speeches, homilies, religious or philosophical treatises).

is 6:35 where he discloses that he is the bread of life; it is this statement that is explicated and elaborated in the course of the following
dialogue and not the scriptural text.[73] Jesus does not appear here in
the role of an expert who reveals the true meaning of the scriptures,
but his words portray a clear contrast between his own revelation
and the revelation told in the scriptures.

The Manna and the True Bread from Heaven Contrasted

The crowd makes their request for a sign more effective by referring to the scriptures: "Our ancestors ate the manna in the wilderness; as it is written, 'He gave them bread from heaven to eat'"
(6:31). Since the words the crowd cites from the scriptures are not
in full accordance with any known scriptural passage, the source of
the citation is debated. Such texts as Exod 16:4 and 15, Ps 78 (LXX
77):24, and Neh 9:15 are mentioned as the possible source of the
citation; sometimes the citation is said to be a combination of some
or all of these passages.[74] The wording of the citation is closest to
the LXX form of Ps 78 (77):24, that is most likely the source of the
citation.[75] The differences between John's citation and the Psalm text
are easy to explain on the basis of Johannine redaction.[76] The crowd
cites here the psalm that paraphrases the events related in Exod 16
and understands these events as a part of God's saving deeds in the
past. The crowd thus refers to basic traditions of the Israelite people.

---

[73] Cf. Painter 1997, 80; Theobald 1997, 340.

[74] For different interpretations, see Richter 1977, 202–211; Schuchard 1992, 35–36.

[75] For detailed arguments, see Menken 1988a, 41–46; Schuchard 1992, 34–38;
Obermann 1996, 132–135; Theobald 1996, 328–331; Anderson 1996, 202–204.
Geiger (1984, 449–464) goes too far when explaining the whole structure of John
6 to be dependent on Ps 78. The reason for arguing that John's citation is based
on the LXX form of the Psalm is that this is the only case in the LXX where
ἄρτος appears as a rendering for the Hebrew word דגן (normally translated as σῖτος).

[76] Ps 78:24 is an example of synonymous parallelism, and John's citation follows
quite closely the latter part of the parallelism (καὶ ἄρτον οὐρανοῦ ἔδωκεν αὐτοῖς) but
adds the infinitive φαγεῖν at the end of the citation. This addition is taken probably from the first part of the parallelism (καὶ ἔβρεξεν αὐτοῖς μαννα φαγεῖν). The use
of the expression ἄρτος ἐκ τοῦ οὐρανοῦ instead of ἄρτος οὐρανοῦ is in line with
John's basic claim that Jesus comes from heaven; the expression ἀπῆρεν νότον ἐξ
οὐρανοῦ in v. 26 of the cited Psalm may also have influenced the choice of the
wording here. According to Borgen (1965, 41), John must be dependent on Exod
16, since the murmuring in John 6:41 and 51 seems to be a paraphrase of Exod
16:2. This is, however, not a decisive argument: the theme of murmuring (without
using the verb γογγύζω or related terms) is found in other traditions about the
manna (cf. Num 11:4–6; Ps 78:17–22, 32–43; Neh 9:16–19).

In his answer, Jesus makes the contrast between these traditions and the true bread from heaven a basic theme of his speech.

Jesus corrects the understanding of the crowd: "Very truly I tell you, it was not Moses who gave you the bread from heaven, but my Father gives you the true bread from heaven." These words can be understood basically in two different ways: (1) it was not Moses who gave you bread from heaven but God; (2) what Moses gave you was not the (true) bread from heaven.[77] The words of the Johannine Jesus show that the latter interpretation is right: it is especially the contrast between the manna and the true bread from heaven that is at stake here.

Jesus does not say that it was not Moses but God who has given the (past) bread from heaven. What he says is that it was not Moses who has given the bread from heaven but God who *gives* you the true bread from heaven. The change from the perfect δέδωκεν to the present δίδωσιν is significant, for it shows that the manna was given in the past whereas Jesus' Father gives the true bread in the present time.[78] The use of the adjective ἀληθινός emphasizes the contrast between these two gifts: the use of this word in John implies a difference between what is real and what is not real (cf. 1:9; 4:23; 15:1).[79] Jesus implies that the Father only now gives the true bread from heaven whereas the manna given previously lacked this quality. The manna is not the true bread from heaven, but is connected to the perishable food that does not lead to eternal life (v. 27).[80] The main function of Jesus' words is, therefore, to proclaim Jesus as the only true bread from heaven and to deny that the manna was the bread from heaven; Jesus is not interested in showing that the manna in the wilderness was given by God and not by Moses.[81]

It is clear, therefore, that in his reply Jesus *contrasts* the true bread from heaven with the manna. This becomes even clearer when Jesus

---

[77] For different views, see Pancaro 1975, 462; Barrett 288; Kotila 1988, 168.

[78] Some manuscripts (B, D, L and some others) read the aorist ἔδωκεν instead of the perfect δέδωκεν in v. 32. Jesus' words are thus adapted to the previous citation in v. 31 where the aorist is used. On the other hand, some manuscripts (e.g. א, W, and Θ) have changed the original aorist in v. 31 to the perfect so that the citation would correspond to the following words of Jesus.

[79] See ch. 3. 2 p. 107.

[80] Thus Theobald 1997, 351

[81] Thus especially Richter 1977, 222. Cf. also Dodd 1953, 335–336; Sandelin 1986, 183; Kotila 1988, 169; Becker 246–247; Lee 1994, 144; Dietzfelbringer 1996, 205; Theobald 1997, 351.

later says that the fathers who ate the manna died whereas those who eat the true bread that descends from heaven will not die (vv. 49–51, 58). Jesus alone is capable of producing life, whereas the manna of Moses is associated with death. It is not clear whether Jesus is referring here to the traditions that tell how the wilderness generation died as a result of obduracy before entering the promised land (Num 14:20–24, 28–35; 26:63–65; 32:11; Deut 1:35). In these traditions and in later Jewish exegesis, it is especially the unbelief of the wilderness generation that occasioned their death.[82] This motif does not, however, appear in John. The death of the fathers is not due to their obduracy, but they died because the manna they ate was not the true bread from heaven, the bread of life.[83] It is denied that the manna of the past has any relevance for salvation and life in the Johannine sense, and the wilderness generation is excluded from the salvation and life manifested only in Jesus.[84] From the Johannine point of view, the same is true also in the case of those who appeal to these fathers and to the manna given in the past.

The way the Johannine Jesus uses the manna motif seems to be very different from the way this motif is used in other early Jewish or Christian literature.[85] The Johannine Jesus is the first who connects the manna to death and says that it is inferior to another kind of bread.[86] This underlines how bold and radical Jesus' claims in John are. It is clear that he is not just explicating the true meaning of a scriptural text and correcting likely misinterpretations of this text.[87]

---

[82] In *m. Sanh.* 10:3 there appears a discussion about whether the wilderness generation will share in the world to come or not. According to Richter (1977, 228) and Kotila (1988, 177), the words of the Johannine Jesus reflect this discussion.

[83] Thus Richter 1977, 229.

[84] Luz 1981, 127; Theobald 1997, 362.

[85] For manna traditions in the Palestinian targums, see Malina 1968, 42–93. For the manna motif in Philo, see Borgen 1965, 99–146. Early Christian references to the manna appear in 1 Cor 10:3 and in Rev 2:17.

[86] Thus Anderson 1996, 204 and 1997, 35.

[87] Pace Borgen 1965, 62–65. According to Borgen, John uses in 6:32 a midrashic pattern used also in Palestinian midrashim and by Philo. This pattern gives a philological correction of a scriptural text using the formula אל תקרי . . . אלא (do not read . . . but . . .). Using this pattern the Johannine Jesus gives a different reading of the Old Testament quotation, which becomes clear as the verbs are translated back into Hebrew. Instead of reading the perfect נָתַן (ἔδωκεν in v. 31/δέδωκεν in v. 32a) Jesus reads the participle נוֹתֵן which in the Greek may be rendered in the present tense (δίδωσιν in v. 32b) or in the future tense (δώσω in v. 52). Jesus also corrects the subject of the verb "give" and says that it is not Moses but "my Father" who gives the bread from heaven. Borgen is followed by Brown 262; Barrett 290.

Jesus' reply to the crowd is presented in the form of an authoritative statement ("Truly, truly I say to you") that is not subordinate to the cited text but is valid in itself. Jesus does not put a scriptural interpretation against another interpretation, but presents his own words as an authoritative alternative to the scriptural manna tradition.[88]

The above analysis has revealed that Jesus takes a critical stand on the manna given by Moses. It has not, however, become clear why Jesus dissociates himself so sharply from the manna. The answer has to with the symbolic overtones the manna had in many Jewish traditions.

The Manna as a Symbol for the Law

It is implied in many texts that the manna was taken as a symbol for the law God had given to Israel through Moses. The exact identification of the manna as the law appears in *Mek. Bešallaḥ* 1. Rabbinic literature also speaks of the bread of wisdom as the bread of the law (e.g. *Gen. Rab.* 43, 54, and 70). These views date back to pre-Rabbinic Judaism.[89]

Some passages in Philo suggest that there is a very close connection between the manna and the law.[90] Philo calls the manna the words that God gives out of heaven (*Alleg. Interp.* III 162). Philo also says that the manna is the heavenly wisdom (ἡ οὐράνιος σοφία) sent from above (*Names* 259–260) or the divine word and the ethereal wisdom (ἡ αἰθέριος σοφία) dropped by God from above (*Flight* 137–138). As the the divine word (λόγος θεῖος) the manna is a synonym for the rock (Deut 8:15) that is identified as the divine wisdom (*Worse* 118). C. H. Dodd rightly notes, that "the equation of manna with σοφία

Martyn (1979, 126–128) says that Borgen has shown that the evangelist is employing in 6:31 "a midrashic method recognizable as such." But Martyn also says that the change of the verb tense is "much more than a matter of midrash," because "John allows Jesus to employ a form of midrashic discussion in order to terminate all midrashic discussion." But it is doubtful whether this verse really follows the so called *Al-Tiqri* method at all. The exegetical terminology corresponding to the *Al-Tiqri* method is not used in John, as is noted by Richter (1977, 236) and Theobald (1996, 346 n. 76). In other passages the narrator of the gospel translates many basic Hebrew or Aramaic words (cf. 1:38, 41, 42; 9:7; 20:16), and it is unclear how the readers of the gospel could have appreciated subtle exegesis based on Hebrew.

[88] Theobald 1997, 346.

[89] See Sandelin 1986, 231–233.

[90] For these passages, see Borgen 1965, 111–115 and 136–141; Sandelin 1986, 96–97 and 108–109.

in Philo almost necessarily implies that in some circles it was taken to be a symbol of Torah."[91]

The same symbolism appears in wisdom literature. It is noteworthy that Jesus' words in 6:35 have a quite near parallel in Sir 24:21.[92] In this passage wisdom declares that those who eat of her will hunger for more, and those who drink of her will thirst for more (cf. also John 4:14). The connection between wisdom and the law is a very close one in the Book of Sirach, although it is a matter of debate whether wisdom is identified with the law or not (cf. Sir 15:1–3; 24:23).[93] Be that as it may, the allusion to Sir 24:21 in John 6:35 reinforces the possibility that the manna in John 6 stands for the law. So many scholars are on the right track when they see the manna in close connection to the Mosaic law here.[94]

Many features in Jesus' speech become clearer if the manna is taken as a symbol for the law. According to Jesus, only he himself as the bread of life is capable of giving life whereas those who ate the manna have died. Jesus assumes here the role given to the law in the scriptures and subsequent Jewish tradition where the law is said to bring life for those who keep it (for example, Lev 18:5; Deut 30:46–47; Ezek 20:11).[95] The way Jesus reformulates the scriptural citation of the crowd also suggests that he has the law in mind; the crowd repeats the words of the Psalm and speaks of the bread that Moses gave to the fathers, but Jesus answers that Moses has not given you the bread (οὐ Μωϋσῆς δέδωκεν ὑμῖν) from heaven. Both the change in the tense of the verb from the aorist to the perfect and the use of the second person plural indicate that Jesus is not just referring to a miracle experienced by a past generation but to something that is of on-going significance for his listeners. This matches perfectly with the law to which the opponents of Jesus appeal several times elsewhere in the gospel.

---

[91] Dodd 1953, 336.

[92] See Borgen 1965, 155; Brown 269; Schnackenburg II 59; Lindars 259; Sandelin 1986, 178; Kotila 1988, 171; Kügler 1988, 201.

[93] Many scholars have argued for the identification of the personified wisdom and the law of Moses in the Book of Sirach. For the discussion, see Sandelin 1986, 49–53. According to Sandelin, the personified wisdom and the law are not identical in Sirach, although there is a close tie between them. The law of God is an essential part of the teaching given by wisdom (p. 52).

[94] Thus Odeberg 256; Dodd 1953, 336–337; Borgen 1965, 148–154; Brown 262; Pancaro 1975, 468–471; Barrett 290; Sandelin 1986, 183; Kotila 1988, 170–173; Theobald 1997, 353; M. M. Thompson 1997, 227.

[95] For rabbinic examples, see Borgen 1965, 148–149.

Also, the fact that Moses is presented as the giver of the manna is understandable if Jesus has the law in mind here. In the original Psalm cited by the crowd and in the rest of the scriptures, God is presented as the one who gave the manna. There is no parallel in the scriptures or in contemporary literature for the identification of Moses with the giver of the manna (6:32). The belief that Moses was the author of the manna miracle appears in some later rabbinic traditions that can be dated at the earliest to the end of the third century c.e.[96] Despite the late dating of these traditions, some scholars see them to be in the background of John's passage. The connection between John and these late traditions is explained in different ways.

In some writings that are closer to John in time there appears a view that God gave the manna because of Moses' prayer or appeal (Philo *Migration* 121f.; Jos. *Ant.* 3.26–32; t. *Soṭah* 11.10; *L.A.B.* 20.8). This view is seen as a link between John and later traditions that say explicitly that Moses gave the manna.[97] But it is two different things to say that God gave the manna because of Moses and to say that Moses gave the manna. So some scholars argue that the conviction that Moses was the author of the manna miracle was alive at the end of the first century c.e., but was later supressed by rabbinic Judaism, only to emerge again in the 3rd–4th century c.e.[98] This conviction could be seen as a part of Moses-centered piety, in which there was a tendency to deify Moses and claim that his wonders showed that he had a share in God's power.[99] But John 6:31–32 does not support this view, because Jesus' reply is not directed against the view that regarded Moses as the author of the manna miracle. We do not need to assume special Moses piety in the background of John 6:31–32, because it is fully understandable that Moses is presented as the giver of the manna if the manna symbolizes the law here.[100] The Johannine Jesus says in John 7:19 that Moses has

---

[96] For these traditions, see Malina 1968, 87–88; Menken 1988a, 46–47.

[97] Richter 1977, 217–219; Theobald 1997, 345 n. 75.

[98] Malina 1968, 88; Menken 1988a, 47–48. Both Malina and Menken say that the reason for the supression of this tradition was a reaction against the Christian deification of their Messiah; Jesus was seen by the Christians as parallel to Moses. This argumentation goes back to Daube 1958/59, 177–178.

[99] Thus Menken 1988a, 53. Cf also Meeks 1967, 286–319. Meeks argues that the gospel as a whole contains polemic directed against Jewish groups that had high esteem for Moses.

[100] Thus Borgen 1965, 173; Sandelin 1986, 183.

given the law using almost exactly the same words as he uses in 6:32 when speaking of the manna (cf. also 1:17).

The contrast between the manna and the true bread from heaven appears in a new light if the manna is seen as a symbol for the law. Jesus as the bread of life is presented as the only source of life whereas the manna/the law is denied any life-producing capacity. Those who appeal to the fathers or to the law make a mistake because the traditions of the past have nothing in common with the salvation reserved for those who receive Jesus.[101] It is clear that Jesus' revelation is not presented as a natural continuation of the past but as a superior alternative to the past traditions. Jesus' opponents refer to scriptural traditions that see the manna as a part of Israel's glorious history. Jesus does not validate these traditions but rather presents himself as an exclusive source of life, which denies scriptural traditions their significance for salvation.[102] There is not a typological continuity between the manna and Jesus' revelation either: rather than being a preceding type of the true bread from heaven the manna of Moses is its anti-type, unable to bring life.[103]

Jesus' speech about the bread of life shows that the Johannine attitude to the traditions and the law of the Jews is ambivalent. According to Jesus' words in 5:39–47, there is a continuity between Jesus' revelation and what Moses has written: Moses and his scriptures bear witness to Jesus. In the bread of life discourse, however, it is not continuity but contrast that characterizes the relationship

---

[101] Cf. Theobald 1997, 355.

[102] Pace M. M. Thompson 1997, 236: "John 6 presupposes the story of Israel's Exodus and wanderings, the role of Moses and the gift of manna, for it presupposes the activity of the one God in nourishing and leading the people of God. This link implies that the revelation through Jesus builds upon, rather than supplants, what has preceded. The historical narrative, rather that being rejected, is validated, but it must be heard through the grid of the christological interpretation of the passage."

[103] Cf. Hahn 1967, 349: "Die Manna-Speisung unter Mose kann jetzt nur noch den Charakter einer zwar besonderen, aber gleichwohl irdischen Speisung gehabt haben. . . . Das bedeutet dann aber, daß die Typologie hier keineswegs die Analogie betont und allenfalls das Motiv der Steigerung impliziert; der Antitypos ist in einem radikal antithetischen Sinne dem alttestamentlichen Typos gegenübergestellt. Daraus folgt jedoch nicht, daß der Typos ohne Belang wäre, wohl aber ist hiermit zum Ausdruck gebracht, daß angesichts des offenbar gewordenen Antitypos der Typos selbst jede eigene Heilswirklicheit verloren hat." Thus also Kügler 1988, 198. The manna miracle is, however, seen as "a valuable type of the bread of life" by Barrett 290. Cf. also Borgen 1965, 175; Pancaro 1975, 471. This typological interpretation is rejected with good arguments by Theobald 1997, 335.

between the law of Moses and Jesus' revelation. This ambivalent
relationship between Jesus' revelation and Moses and his scriptures
is characteristic of the whole gospel.[104] The passages speaking of the
contrast between Jesus and Moses should not be harmonized with
passages that emphasize the continuity between them.[105] Both tendencies should be taken seriously as we try to create a general view
of John's relationship to Moses and the law.[106]

5.3. *Conclusion: Jesus, Moses and the Law in John*

Markku Kotila has tried to to explain the different roles Moses and
his scriptures play in the gospel in terms of the compositional history of the gospel.[107] According to Kotila, the earliest layers of the
gospel (the sign source) reflect the situation where the right use of
the law (orthopraxis) in the community was still discussed. The evan-

---

[104] Cf. Meeks 1967, 288; See also Kotila 1988, *passim*; Dietzelbringer 1996,
210–212; Theobald 1997, 361–366.

[105] In John 1:17 the narrator states that "the law indeed was given through Moses;
grace and truth came through Jesus Christ." Some scholars have interpreted the
verse so that it implies a salvific-historical relationship between the law and Jesus'
revelation. See Pancaro 1975, 540. Others emphasize that the verse implies a sharp
contrast between Jesus and the law. See Kotila 1988, 142–143; Hofius 1996, 24–32.
In this connection I cannot enter into the discussion about the meaning of this
verse. Different interpretations of this verse, however, illustrate that Jesus' relationship to the law is ambivalent in the gospel. Both ways of interpreting John 1:17
have support in some passages of the gospel.

[106] For a harmonizing picture of Jesus' relationship to the law in John, see Pancaro
1975, 470–471. Pancaro claims that John 6 "does not seem . . . to cast the least
doubt upon the divine origin of Moses' teaching." Pancaro admits that "if there is
an opposition, it is between the teaching Moses *gave* and the teaching the Father
(Jesus) *gives*" (p. 470). He further says that the central point of contrast between
these two revelations is the power of giving life, because "the bread from heaven
Moses gave is incapable of giving life." Still Pancaro devalues the crucial significance
of this contrast by saying that "the manna and the true bread from heaven do
not . . . stand opposed to each other in other respects" (p. 472). Because of this kind
of harmonizing interpretations, Pancaro is not able to give due emphasis to the
ambivalence that characterizes the role of the law in the gospel. Pancaro sees only
the prophetic or witnessing function the law or the scriptures have in John, but
ignores the passages that indicate a more critical stance on the law. So Pancaro
concludes: "Jn's view of the Law is basically positive. . . . The misunderstanding of
the Law by the Jews, whereby the Law is considered opposed to Christ (viz. Christ
to the Law), is viewed negatively by Jn, but not the Law as such" (p. 528).

[107] See Kotila 1988, 201–214 and 235–236. Dietzfelbinger (1996, 212–213) says
that there were two different ways to understand Jesus' relationship to Moses in
the Johannine community. The evangelist tried to address the adherents of these
both views, and thus incorporated both views in the gospel.

gelist, however, used the scriptures mainly as a testimony for his christological views (e.g. 5:39, 45–47). In the latest editorial stages the authority of the law was challenged and the sending-out-christology was seen to be in opposition to the law (e.g. 6:28–33).

It must be asked, however, whether it is necessary to ascribe the different views on the role of the law to different redactional stages and to different historical periods in the life of the Johannine community.[108] It is clear that in the present gospel these different views are not to be separated from each other. It is not just that different passages indicate different attitudes towards the law. Rather, there seems to a connection between these different views, but this connection is not clear if the passages containing different views are analyzed apart from each other. The conviction that sees Moses and his scriptures as witnesses for Jesus (5:39–47) seems to present Jesus' relationship to Moses in positive terms, but as soon as Jesus' relationship to the scriptures is elaborated in the connection of an individual scriptural text as in ch. 6, this relationship appears to be more ambivalent. Nils Alstrup Dahl, who emphasizes that "the continuity between Israel and the Church is . . . not dissolved" in John, still quite clearly sees the ambiguity of John's position on Moses and the law:

> The question may remain as to whether the OT is not, factually, deprived of a historical meaning of its own when Moses and the prophets are simply made supporters of John's own testimony to Christ.[109]

It seems inevitable that John's view of the scriptures as a witness for Jesus leads to the denial of the relevance of the scriptures in their original context as the sacred story of God's saving acts.[110] It is denied that the events that the scriptures themselves see as a part of God's salvational deeds for the people of Israel are of any relevance for salvation. In a sense, this denial is already built into the conviction that the only function of the scriptures is to testify for Jesus, but it

---

[108] Kotila (174–177) also notes that the attitude of the redactor towards the law was not exclusively negative but admitted positive applications of the law also. I think this ambivalence characterizes John as a whole.

[109] Dahl 1986 (1962), 137.

[110] Cf. Luz 1981, 128: "[Der Offenbarer] bestimmt und erließt den Sinn des Alten Testaments und des Gesetzes völlig neu, beruft sich zwar in einzigartiger Weise auf es, aber er vereinnahmt es so vollständig, daß es einen Bezug auf seine eigene Geschichte verliert und ganz von johanneischem Sinn erfüllt wird. *Er beruft sich aus das Alte Testament, aber dieses wird zum blossen Sprachmodus seines eigenes Wortes*" (italics original).

becomes evident only when there appears an individual example of
Jesus' way of dealing with scriptural traditions. The positive and the
negative functions of Moses are, therefore, two sides of the same coin.[111]

The belief that the scriptures bear witness to Jesus (besides John
5:37–47) becomes especially evident when the narrator tells of Jesus'
passion and resurrection; in the passion narrative, which has mainly
fallen outside the scope of this study, the scriptures are frequently
cited with the fulfillment formula (cf. 12:38; 13:18; 15:25; 17:12;
18:9, 32; 19:24, 36). It is noteworthy that in the first part of the
gospel, which focuses on Jesus' conflict with the Jews, the fulfillment
formula does not appear at all, even though Jesus states generally
to his Jewish opponents that Moses and the scriptures bear witness
to him. Johannes Beutler has noted that in the controversies between
Jesus and the Jews "the author seems to be more interested in the
fact of the witness of scripture to Jesus than in details of it."[112]
According to Beutler, this may reflect "the fact the evangelist writes
in a period already remote from the first decades of Christianity."
For John, "the individual proof text no longer counts, but rather,
the whole scripture is at stake." The question is whether the scriptures as a whole point to Jesus or not. As Beutler notes, this shows
how the Johannine use of the scripture is

> in a sense circular: The individual 'proof texts' lead to Jesus, but they
> can only be understood as a whole when the belief which they should
> lead is already presupposed.[113]

If Beutler is right, as I think, then the role of the scriptures as a
witness to Jesus in John 1–12 is primarily intended to reinforce the
self-identity of the Johannine believers, not to convince the outsiders
that Jesus is the Messiah promised in the scriptures. If we consider
how the role of Moses and his scriptures in John may reflect the
self-understanding of the Johannine Christians, then we may understand somehow the ambiguous references to Moses. The ambiguous
role Moses has in John's textual world may reflect a certain discrepancy
between the symbolic universe of the Johannine Christians and their
real world situation in relation to other Jews and the markers of
Jewish identity.

---

[111] Theobald 1997, 361–362.
[112] Beutler 1996, 147–158, esp. p. 158.
[113] Beutler 1996, 158.

The emphasis on the continuity between Moses and Jesus could be understood as an expression of the symbolic universe of the Johannine Christians, who try to keep up their connection to the heart of their former Jewish faith, even though in the real world they have become alienated from the company of other Jews and the Jewish way of life. I have shown in the previous chapter that the Johannine Christians had already abandoned basic individual markers of Jewish identity that were based on the Mosaic law and that in the real world drew a boundary between a Jew and a non-Jew.[114] But even though the separation from other Jews had probably taken place as a sociological fact, in their symbolic universe the Johannine believers held to their Jewish faith and emphasized the continuity with their past. The view that reduces Moses and his scriptures to the witnesses to Jesus already contains in itself a contrast between Jesus and Moses, because it is does not acknowledge any independent role for Moses. So even though the continuation between Moses and Jesus is emphasized in the symbolic universe of the Johannine Christians, this universe is also transparent to their actual alienation from basics of Jewish identity. This real world breaking away from the main body of the Jews and Jewish tradition comes to the fore in John 6, where the manna/law of Moses and Jesus' revelation are contrasted with each other. The ambiguous role of Moses could be understood thus as an effort to come to terms with the discontinuity between the actual situation of the Johannine Christians and the traditional Jewish way of life by asserting that Moses' witness leads directly to the faith in Jesus.

Considering the ambiguous role of Moses in John, it is interesting that in John 9:27–29 discipleship of Jesus is presented as incompatible with discipleship of Moses. The Pharisees seize the ironic suggestion of the once blind man, "Do you also want to become his disciples," and revile him by saying, "You are his disciple, but we are disciples of Moses." This discussion is often taken as an expression of the self-understanding of the Jewish religious leaders at the time the gospel was written. It is said that these leaders considered themselves the disciples of Moses and understood this to exclude the possibility that one can be a disciple of Jesus at the same time.[115]

---

[114] Many scholars agree that John reflects a detachment from the Mosaic law. See, for example, Luz 1981, 119–128; Zeller 1983, 176–177; Räisänen 1987, 217–218; Kügler 1984, 55–56; Freyne 1985, 125–126.

[115] Thus most recently de Boer 2001, 272–273; Menken 2001, 456–457.

However, there is not much evidence that Jewish identity was formulated by any Jewish group in terms of discipleship to Moses. Given
the crucial role of Moses and his law among different Jewish groups,
it is actually amazing that there is only one exact terminological parallel that scholars have been able to trace in the bulk of Jewish literature to the expression 'the disciples of Moses.'[116] But a *baraitah*
in *b. Yoma* 4a does not support the view that Jewish legal authorities used generally the self-expression 'the disciples of Moses' in the
first century C.E. The discussion connected with the Day of Atonement
explains the appearance of the term in this *baraitah*, but this discussion hardly reflects the first century practice.[117] The evidence in the
first century sources for the widespread use of the term 'the disciples of Moses' is also rare.[118] This lack of terminological parallels
may not be accidental, but may suggest that the passage in John
does not reflect the self-expression of the real world Jewish legal
experts at the time the gospel was written.

After all, μαθητής is a most common Christian term used for Jesus'

---

[116] Already Strack–Billerbeck (II 535) refers to *b. Yoma* 4a. De Boer (2001, 272)
admits that "there is scarcely (to my knowledge) any other attestation for the precise wording." In some other rabbinic passages—mostly from the Babylonian Talmud
(*b. Ber* 3b; b. *Soṭah* 12b)—appears the expression "Moses our teacher." Cf. Menken
2001, 457 n. 39.

[117] The *baraitah* in *b. Yoma* 4a discusses the practice according to which the high
priest should be removed from his duty for seven days before the Day of Atonement
(cf. Lev 9:1). This practice is explained with a reference to the example of Moses
and Aaron: "Aaron was removed for seven days and then officiated for one day,
and Moses handed over to him throughout the seven days to train him in this service. Also for the future the high priest is to be removed for seven days and to
officiate for one day, and two scholars of the disciples of Moses (that excludes the
Sadducees) transmitted to him throughout the seven days to train him in service."
Because the special task given to those who train the high priest is seen as an imi-
tation of what Moses did to Aaron, it is only natural that they are called "the disciples of Moses" here. This *baraitah* hardly reflects the actual practice during the
second temple period, because it does not sound credible that the high priest would
have submitted himself to the instructions of the Pharisees in the way described;
furthermore, it is not likely that the Sadducees would have been passed over completely as the *baraitah* implies.

[118] Menken (2001, 456–457) traces the idea "that Jews and especially Jewish legal
authorities considered themselves as disciples of their teacher Moses" to the first
century C.E. by referring to some passages in Philo (*Heir* 81, *Spec. Laws* 1.59, 345)
and a passage in Matthew (23:2). In the philonic passages the word that is translated in the Loeb edition by the word "disciple" is γνώριμος. But the use of this
word by Philo hardly speaks for the general use of the word "disciple" for the
Israelite people in general or the legal authorities in particular. Matt 23:2 refers
only to the seat of Moses, whose exact meaning is much debated.

early followers in the gospel traditions.[119] It has sometimes been used to describe the group of Jesus' opponents, although this usage is not without problems (Mark 2:18; Matt 22:16).[120] It is understandable, however, that even Jesus' opponents are sometimes presented as a kind of disciple circle. When it comes to John, it is interesting that the contrast between Jesus and Moses in John 9:27–29 resembles very much the contrast between Moses' manna and Jesus as the true bread from heaven in ch. 6. From the Johannine point of view, the faith that Moses and his gift could bring life is antithetic to the faith in Jesus who alone can give life to those who receive him. It is most probable that this contrast reflects the real life breaking away from the community of the Jews. But even though the Johannine Christians had broken away from the Jewish identity based on the observance of the Mosaic law, they also understood themselves in continuity with Jewish tradition by claiming that they have Moses on their side. One way to come to terms with this discrepancy is to externalize the choice between Jesus and Moses by attributing it to those who represent the hostile parent body of the believers in the gospel. From the Johannine point of view, it is not the believers themselves who have put Jesus and Moses in opposition to each other, but the leaders of the Jews, who have made them to make a choice between Jesus and Moses.[121] But in reality the way Jesus and Moses are contrasted in John 6 suggests that the choice between Jesus and Moses reflects the ambiguities of the Johannine Christians themselves in relation to their Jewish heritage.[122]

---

[119] The term appears in Matthew 72 times, Mark 46, Luke 37 and John 78.

[120] Both Mark 2:18 (with text critical variants) and Matt 22:16 speak of "the disciples of the Pharisees." This is a rare and problematic expression. Cf. Marcus 2000, 233: "[The disciples of the Pharisees] is an odd locution, because 'disciple' implies adhesion to a particular master such as John the Baptist, Jesus, Hillel, not membership in a group such as the Pharisaic party." The appearance of the term in these two instances in early Christian literature has to do probable with the widespread use of the term to describe Jesus' followers; it has occasionally been used also for the the Pharisees, whose group formation is seen to mirror that of early Christians.

[121] Cf. de Boer 2001, 276. I think, however, that de Boer too hastily takes this Johannine self-understanding as a reflection of the policy of the contemporary rabbinic leaders who "both initiate and arbitrate the matter of Jewish identity."

[122] This also seems to be the conclusion reached by Meeks 1967, 319. Meeks notes that the Johannine Jesus fulfills the functions elsewhere attributed to Moses, and "does this in a superior and exclusive way, so that Moses is now stripped of those functions and made merely a 'witness' to Jesus. Therefore one who had formerly accounted himself a 'disciple of Moses' would now have to decide whether

I cannot but see in the Johannine understanding of Moses and
the scriptures a point of departure for a later Christian belief that
saw the Hebrew Bible exclusively in the light of christology.[123] This
belief denies the Jews the legitimacy of their scriptural heritage and
also interprets the content of the Hebrew Bible very narrowly.[124] In
modern Jewish-Christian dialogue, the dangers of this exclusive view
should be made clear and confronted critically.[125]

---

he would become instead a 'disciple of Jesus.' If he did not, then from the viewpoint of this gospel he had in fact deserted the real Moses, for Moses only wrote
of Jesus and true belief in Moses led to belief in Jesus."

[123] Schnackenburg (II 176) is right in connecting the Johannine understanding of
the scriptures to that of Justin. They both see the scriptures exclusively in christological light.

[124] Pace Klappert (1990, 627) who wants to keep the Johannine understanding
of Moses and the scriptures distinct from the kind of theology represented by Justin
and other Church Fathers. According to Klappert, this latter theology has been
harmful for the dialogue between the Jews and the Christians, while the Johannine
understanding of the scriptures gives a more positive starting point to Jewish-Christian
dialogue (pp. 639–640).

[125] Thus also Luz 1981, 127; Obermann 1996, 429; Theobald 1997, 365–366.

CHAPTER SIX

THE BELIEVING JEWS, ABRAHAM AND
THE DEVIL (8:31–59)

In John 8 there is a long discussion in which the break between Jesus and the Jews is lifted to a new, cosmological level. The most interesting part of the discussion for the characterization of the Jews begins in 8:31 where Jesus' words prompt the Jews who are described as believers to claim that they are Abraham's seed. Jesus says that these believing Jews are from the devil, a charge that has often been characterized as one of the most anti-Jewish passages in the New Testament (8:44). In the following analysis I claim that these words should be read in light of both their narrative context in John and dualistic views that also appeared in other earlier or contemporary Jewish writings. The close reading of what the Johannine Jesus says of the believing Jews, Abraham and the devil reinforces the results of my earlier analyses and suggests that the Johannine writer tries to cement the break between the Johannine Christians and other Jews by presenting the Jews as the children of the devil. But the appearance of believing Jews here and also elsewhere in John may suggest that this break was not so complete as the Johannine writer might have wished.

Jesus' harsh words to the believing Jews call forth a difficult question concerning John's supposed anti-Judaism. I suggest that the reading of Jesus' words in 8:44 in light of other similar kinds of views shows what is specific in John's use of the dualistic currents of his day. Rather than mitigating John's anti-Jewish potential, this reading shows how John anticipates the emergence of some recurrent themes in the later development of Christian anti-Judaism.

The Context of the Dialogue

John 7 and 8 are connected closely.[1] The setting of the discussion is not mentioned in John 8:12, but it is probable that this discussion

---

[1] The story of the adulteress in John 7:53–8:11 is missing from the best manuscripts, and there is a universal consensus that it was not part of the original gospel. Therefore, John 8:12 had originally followed 7:52.

continues the series of discussions taking place during the feast of
Tabernacles (cf. 7:2, 14, 37). The themes in the discussion in John
8 also have many common points with earlier discussions. The most
significant theme for the characterization of the Jews that reappears
in John 8 is the mention that many believed in Jesus as he spoke
(8:30). In the next verse the narrator says that Jesus' following words
were addressed to the Jews who had believed him (8:31). This mention is quite surprising in light of the following discussion where Jesus
says that his interlocutors seek to kill him (8:37, 40).[2] But the mention
of the believing Jews in John 8:30–31 should be connected to what
the narrator relates about various responses to Jesus in John 7. The
narrator says that Jesus' words evoked bewilderment and debate
among his audience (7:12; 25–27), and that many of the people
believed in Jesus even though their faith is hardly full faith in the
Johannine sense (7:31). The narrator mentions also that some said
that Jesus is really the prophet, and others that he is the Christ,
while some others rejected these claims. This dispute remains unset-
tled, and the narrator notes only that there was a division among
the people over Jesus (7:40–44). The meeting between the chief
priests and the Pharisees, where Nicodemus speaks for Jesus, suggests that the division over Jesus was not restricted to the common
people (7:45–52).

It is noteworthy that neither the narrator nor Jesus comment on
these cautiously favourable responses to Jesus in any way. This raises
the question as to what will eventually happen to those who have
shown some signs of initial faith. This highlights the importance of
Jesus' programmatic saying in 8:12: "I am the light of the world.
Whoever follows me will never walk in darkness but will have the
light of life." Scholars have often been at pains to explain the function
of this saying in its present narrative context, because the theme of
light is not developed further until John 9, where Jesus heals the
blind man.[3] But Jesus' saying also has an important narrative function
in John 8. As a metaphor, light functions in two ways: it refers to

---

[2] This is the reason why some scholars regard John 8:31 as a later gloss. Cf.
Brown 354; Lindars 323.

[3] Cf. Bultmann (237–238) who placed John 8:12 after 9:1–41 and regarded it as
the beginning of the *Lichtrede* consisting of various fragments (12:44–50; 8:21–29;
12:34–36). It is more common, however, to regard John 8:12 as a piece of oral
tradition that the evangelist has incorporated into its present context. Thus, for
example, Becker 339.

revelation as well as to judgment.[4] Jesus as the light is the revealer of God that shines in the darkness of the world (1:5, 11), but the coming of light also means judgment because people love darkness more than light and their works are evil (3:19–20). So "within the present context of discussion, doubt, and *schisma*, Jesus indicates that the presence of the light is also a call to decision."[5]

The mention of believing Jews in John 8:30–31 reopens the question concerning the potential faith among Jesus' Jewish audience. The narrator uses here slightly different expressions in speaking of believers. In v. 30 he says that as Jesus spoke, "many believed in him" (πολλοὶ ἐπίστευσαν εἰς αὐτόν). In v. 31 the narrator notes that Jesus was speaking to the Jews "who had believed him" (ἔλεγεν . . . πρὸς τοὺς πεπιστευκότας αὐτῷ Ἰουδαίους). These different expressions are sometimes taken to mean that the narrator is speaking of two different groups here.[6] V. 30 would refer to those whose faith is deeper than the faith of those mentioned in v. 31. The text does not, however, warrant this reading.

The perfect participle πεπιστευκότες in v. 31 could be taken as a pluperfect meaning "those who had believed in him (but do so no longer)."[7] The use of the perfect participle, however, is hardly sensible in this connection unless there is some earlier indication of the group to which it refers.[8] It is thus natural to take it to refer back to the previous sentence. The use of οὖν-historicum in v. 31 suggests that this verse is closely connected to the previous verse. The use of the verb πιστεύω with the preposition εἰς in v. 30 and the use of the same verb with the dative in v. 31 does not indicate that the faith of many in v. 30 is more authentic than the faith of the believing Jews in v. 31.[9] Both these forms are used interchangeably for partial and authentic faith in the gospel.[10] There is thus no reason to think that the narrator is speaking in John 8:30–31 of two different groups.[11]

---

[4] Cf. Lindars 314.
[5] Moloney 1996, 94.
[6] Thus Swetnam 1980, 106–107; Moloney 1996, 103.
[7] Thus Swetnam 1980, 107–109.
[8] Thus Dodd 1968, 42.
[9] Thus, however, Moloney 1996, 103.
[10] See Painter 1993, 385–388. Cf. also Brown 1979, 76: "In 8:31 there begins a long dialogue between Jesus and 'the Jews who had believed in him.' One should take this designation literally and not argue that, because *pisteuein* is used with the dative rather than with *eis* ('in'), lesser faith is intented. The whole attempt . . . to diagnose Johannine theology on the exact use of prepositions is . . . untenable."
[11] Thus also Bultmann 332; Dodd 1968, 43.

The perfect participle in 8:31 suggests that the narrator is not just thinking of those who believed in Jesus at this point of the story. The believing Jews in John 8:30–31 can rather be taken as representatives of all Jews who have believed in the course of the narrative. So the appearance of this group here connects the following dialogue to the previous narrative characterized by the division over Jesus. Now the time has come for those who have been wavering between light and darkness to make their final decision concerning Jesus. Jesus' words in 8:31–32 show this: "If you continue in my word, you are truly my disciples, and you will know the truth, and the truth will make you free." The word "truly" (ἀληθῶς) suggests that Jesus' words are both a challenge to continue in his word and a promise of truth and freedom. So the following dialogue can be seen as a test that reveals whether the believing Jews want to become true disciples and to come to know the truth that makes them free.[12]

The Believing Jews and the Death of Jesus

The first words of the believing Jews already indicate that they will not pass the test to become true disciples; they claim that they are descendants of Abraham, and have never been slaves to anyone (v. 33). Their refusal to accept the freedom Jesus offers shows that belonging to Abraham matters to them more than becoming the disciple of Jesus.[13] The following dialogue makes this more evident by disclosing that the faith of the Jews is not real faith at all.[14]

Jesus repeatedly returns in the dialogue with the believing Jews to his original promise that emphasizes the importance of abiding in his word (v. 31). He says that the Jews he is debating with are seeking to kill him because his word finds no place in them (v. 37). Jesus further explains that the Jews cannot understand his speech because they cannot hear his word (v. 43). He also promises that anyone who "keeps my word will never see death" (v. 51). But this promise does not have to do with the Jews of the story anymore, because they

---

[12] See Bultmann 332; Neyrey 1987 and 1988, 43–51. Neyrey regards John 8:21–59 as a legal process that starts in 8:21–30 where Jesus judges the Jews. Neyrey finds in 8:31–59 five tests with the help of which the evangelist shows that the believing Jews are really pseudo-believers. But I think Neyrey traces too formal a process here, even though he is right in regarding the dialogue in 8:31–59 as a test for the believing Jews.
[13] Neyrey 1987, 520–521.
[14] Cf. Barrett 344; Becker 355.

try to stone Jesus at the end of the story (v. 59). This proves right Jesus' claim that also they seek his life.

The characterization of the devil as a liar is of significance for the characterization of the believing Jews (8:44). This description is well in line with the traditional role of the devil. Already in Gen 3 the serpent in Paradise is presented as the one who deceives Adam and Eve (Gen 3:13). The serpent was not originally seen as the devil, but the devil was later closely connected to the serpent, and the two were eventually equated.[15] According to some traditions, the devil seduced Eve in the form of an angel (*L.A.E.* 9:1; *Apoc. Mos.* 17:1), traditions presumably known also to Paul (2 Cor 11:14).[16] Deceitfulness was thus among the primary characteristics of the devil, and it was also known that the devil could hide himself in different guises (*T. Job* 6:4; 17:2; 23:1). It is thus not a great surprise that the Johannine Jesus describes the allegedly believing Jews as the children of the devil, the father of lies. Just like their father, these Jews hide their true nature and appear to believe in Jesus, although they in fact are seeking to kill him.[17]

It is not without significance that Jesus addresses his harshest words in the gospel to those Jews who are said to believe in him. Had Jesus spoken to those who are openly hostile to him right from the beginning, the effect of his words would not have been so shocking. Now Jesus' words destroy any illusion the reader may have concerning the capability of the Jews to believe. The alleged faith on the part of many Jews is used "to show that in reality Jews are anything but believers."[18] Jesus' condemnation of the seemingly believing Jews blurs any distinction among different Jewish groups and labels as murderers both the believing and the openly hostile Jews. Marinus de Jonge is right as he speaks of John's vagueness in the description of Jewish groups:

---

[15] See Foerster 1954, 577–578. It is not exactly clear when the serpent in Paradise was identified with the devil. Wis 2:24 already suggests a close relationship between the two. In pseudepigraphic literature the serpent is called the vehicle (σκεῦος) of the devil (*Apoc. Mos.* 16:5; cf. also 26:1) or the garment (ἔνδυμα) of the devil (3. *Bar.* 9:7). The full equation of the two is suggested by such passages as *L.A.E.* 16 and *Liv. Proph.* 12:13. Also some passages in the New Testament presuppose this equation (Rom 16:20; 2. Cor 11:3; Rev 12:9; 20:2).

[16] See Windisch 1924, 342–343; Martin 1986, 351–352.

[17] Cf. Neyrey 1987, 530–531 and 1988, 46.

[18] Haenchen 369–370.

> All these people are outsiders, they do not really understand Jesus,
> their faith is, therefore, imperfect and insufficient: they do not belong
> to the group of true believers. Seen from the standpoint of the Johannine
> group and its theology, there is no real difference between sympa-
> thizing Jews and Jewish Christians if the latter are still thinking along
> what the Fourth Gospel considers to be purely Jewish lines.[19]

The present passage confirms what other passages in the gospel also
suggest: from the Johannine point of view, it is not just a closed
group of Jewish leaders that is responsible for Jesus' death. It is true
that especially the authorities of the Jews, the Pharisees and the chief
priests, are presented as most openly hostile to Jesus. They are also
the ones who most clearly seek Jesus' life and finally decide to carry
out their plans (7:32, 45–53; 11:47–52). But the Johannine narrator
tells in 7:40–44 about a division caused by Jesus' words among the
crowd; as a result of this division "some of them wanted to arrest
him" (v. 44). A similar kind of division is seen in 11:45–46 when
some of the Jews who saw Jesus raising Lazarus believe in him, while
some go to the Pharisees and report what Jesus has done. There
appears in John 12:9–11 a great crowd of the Jews who believed in
Jesus on account of Lazarus, and in 12:12–15 the crowd receives
Jesus enthusiastically in Jerusalem. But although the narrator mentions believers among the crowd he does not seem to separate the
crowd from the Jews in his pessimistic conclusion to the book of the
signs (12:37–43). In their immediate narrative context these verses
seem to deal with the crowd with which Jesus has been debating
earlier (12:29, 34). But most scholars read these verses as the conclusion to the entire first major part of the gospel.[20] The narrator
explains here why Jesus met rejection and unbelief during his public life but does not seem to make any distinction between the crowd
and the Jews, whom he has last mentioned in 12:11.

It is not at all surprising that in John 18:35 Pilate says to Jesus,
"Your own nation and the chief priests have handed you over to me."
These words may appear on the lips of a Roman official, but they
still summarize aptly the Johannine view that unbelief and a hostile
attitude to Jesus are not a characteristic of only a clearly defined
Jewish group. This is most clearly seen in John 8 where Jesus reveals

---

[19] De Jonge 1977, 101–02:
[20] Cf. Dodd 1953b, 379ff.; Brown 484ff.; Lindars 436–439; Barrett 429ff.;
Schnackenburg II, 513 and IV, 143; Becker 105, 435 and 475.

that the believing Jews seek to kill him and even in this respect do not differ from the openly hostile Jews.[21] Jesus' words in John 8:44 also add a significant feature to the plot of the gospel because they show that to seek Jesus' life and to be the children of the devil are closely connected to. Because Jesus makes this charge against the believing Jews, it is not just the openly hostile Jewish authorities who are characterized as being of the devil here.[22]

Jesus' harsh words to the believing Jews make clear that this group does not differ in any significant way from those Jews who are characterized as openly hostile to Jesus in the rest of the narrative. It has often been suggested that John refers here to some Jewish Christians in his surroundings.[23] But it should be noted that the passage does not discuss any of those issues that seem to have been the very characteristics of Jewish Christians. According to the letter to the Galatians, circumcision and the continuing obligation of the Mosaic law were at the center of the disputes between Paul and Jewish Christians.[24] Scattered mentions of the church fathers make clear too that the observance of central Jewish practices was one of the main characteristics of later Jewish-Christian groups.[25] The appearance of Abraham both in John and in the disputes between Paul and 'Judaizers' (Gal 3) does not necessarily mean that John's passage deals with the specific beliefs of Jewish Christians. The way the believing Jews in John appeal to Abraham is not without parallels in the rest of the gospel; this scene is rather another variation of the Johannine theme of how different characters appeal to the founding fathers or to the basic institutions of Israel as opposing what Jesus

---

[21] Cf. De Jonge 2000, 225.

[22] Many scholars, however, want to tone down the anti-Jewish potential of John 8:44 by saying that Jesus' words of the devil concern only a particular group of Jewish authorities who killed Jesus or persecuted the Johannine Christians. See Reim 1984, 623; Schnelle 161; Barrett 2001, 406; De Boer 2001, 268–269.

[23] See Dodd 1968, 43–45; Schnackenburg II 259–260; Martyn 1977, 166–170; Brown 1979, 77; Dozeman 1980, 343; Bondi 1997, 490.

[24] Cf. Dodd 1968, 47–48. According to Dodd, the *Sitz im Leben* of John 8 was the same struggle that is reflected in Galatians and that was waged throughout the latter half of the first century. Still, Dodd sees quite clearly that the questions prominent in Paul are not mentioned in John, but the Johannine dialogue boils down to the question of whether Jewish Christians are or are not loyal to the teaching of Christ. Dodd speculates that "by the time, or in the circle, in which John wrote, these questions [circumcision, the obligation of the law] were no longer alive, or it may be that he [the evangelist] considered them merely consequential and not fundamental issues. In any case he does not here stand on Pauline ground."

[25] See Myllykoski & Luomanen 1999, 327–348.

has done or said (cf. 4:12; 5:39, 45; 6:31; 9:29–30).[26] Thus the believing Jews do not seem to have any particular beliefs here that would be characteristic of them only, but are lumped together with other Jews.

If these Jews represent some sort of Jewish Christians who do not want to break away from their traditional faith altogether, it should be explained why they are presented as the ones who seek Jesus' life.[27] It is remarkable that Jesus neither shows any sympathy nor tries to confirm these Jews in their faith in any way.[28] Rather, the sharpness of his words suggests that he is not really trying to lead Jewish Christians to the true faith here.[29] The interpretation that sees the believing Jews in John's narrative as representatives of some secret Christians who do not dare to confess their faith is dependent to a great extent on the very problematic view which sees the leaders of the emerging rabbinic movement as powerful and terrifying guardians of the Jewish community.[30] Because of the problems with this view, I suggest that the believing Jews in John may reflect John's social reality in a different way.

---

[26] For this theme, see Wead 1970, 63–64.

[27] See Martyn 1977, 168–169. According to Martyn, the believing Jews in John 8:30–31 are Christian Jews who tried secretly to maintain a dual allegiance, after the Jewish authorities had decided that one must be either a disciple of Moses or a disciple of Jesus. For the Johannine Christians "these former colleagues of theirs turned out to be horribly instrumental in the martyrdom of some of the Johannine evangelists, presumably by functioning as informers intent on preserving monotheism" (p. 169). This view very much presumes the persecution scenario that I have criticized in detail in the second chapter. Furthermore, there is nothing in Jesus' words here that would support the view that the Jews in question take part only indirectly in the killing of Jesus. These Jews seek to kill Jesus (v. 37); are children of the devil, a murderer (v. 44); and finally try to stone Jesus (v. 59). Thus they are chasing actively after Jesus and so are different from those Jews who act as informers later in the gospel when they tell the Pharisees how Jesus raised Lazarus (11:45).

[28] For a different view, see Schnackenburg II 260. According to Schnackenburg, the attempt to confirm the believing Jews is combined with the polemic against the Judaism of John's time in this section. Schnackenburg notes that the polemical aspect is more prominent in the subsequent discussion, because a rebuttal of the Jewish counter-arguments was necessary for the sake of uncertain Jewish Christians. But it is unclear to me how a discussion that portays the believing Jews as Jesus' possible murderers can confirm in any way uncertain Jewish-Christian believers.

[29] Thus also Becker 355. Dodd (1968, 45) admits that "the difficulty raised by the unsparing condemnation of these 'believers'" is not overcome completely if Jesus' interlocutors are seen to represent "'judaizing' Christians" rather than non-Christian Jews. Dodd refers to Paul's polemic against the 'Judaizers,' but he seems to read the Johannine passage in the light of Paul's writings, although he recognises that John is not dealing here with the same issues as Paul.

[30] See chapter 2.

The Johannine writer tends to see Jews in general as representatives of the hostile world. But some portions in the narrative may suggest that the situation in the real world was more complicated and the response of at least some Jews to these Christians was more or less positive. Adele Reinhartz has noted that neutral and even positive references to some Jews in the gospel—especially in John 11—show that the reading focusing on the expulsion passages tends to over-look "other models within the Gospel of the relationship between Jesus' followers and the synagogue."[31] In light of the diversity that still characterized Judaism long after 70 c.e., there was probably not just one way to respond to the challenge presented by early Christians.

A person showing sympathy to a religious group may sometimes be taken as some kind of secret devotee by the group in question. In this way a person who shows sympathy to the believers often becomes a mirror image of the believers themselves. Shaye J. D. Cohen has noted that "the Jews tended to regard gentile benefac-tors as motivated by some special affection for, or devotion to, Judaism," even though this view is hardly true historically.[32] Some Jewish storytellers even presented such gentile rulers as Alexander the Great as converts to Judaism. Could there be something similar in how John refers to those who believed in Jesus among the Jews and even among the Jewish leaders? Some kind of friendly or sym-pathetic attitude among the Jews in John's environment would have been hard to reconcile with the portrayal of the Jews as misunder-standing and hostile. A way to come to terms with this would have been to present these sympathetic Jews as *de facto* believers, whose faith was seen as a failure if compared to the faith of true disciples. At the same time, however, the faith of these Jews showed for the Johannine Christians that the best among the Jews had to recognize Jesus as the Messiah.

Because their own identity was at stake, the Johannine Christians may have played down the role of more sympathetic Jews in their symbolic universe. In a situation where they tried to define their identity in relation to Jewishness anew, contacts with other Jews may have created anxiety which resulted in presenting them mostly in an extremely bad light.[33] Claudia Setzer has discerned a similar tendency

---

[31] See Reinhartz 1998, 121–138, esp. p. 137.
[32] Cohen 1999c, 148.
[33] Cf. Reinhartz 1998, 136.

in other early Christian sources in which negative portrayals of Jews predominate, even though Jews are every now and then presented also as fair-minded and tolerant. Setzer asks whether the trend to depict Jews in more positive terms "is not underrepresented in ancient literature."[34] The mentions of favorable Jews would not have served early Christian communities because

> if Jews are sensible and fair-minded, their refusal of Christianity becomes more problematic than if they are hard-hearted, vicious, and ignorant of their own Scripture.[35]

The above interpretation could explain why the believing Jews are condemned so harshly in John. From the Johannine point of view, the believing Jews are an example that shows that it is impossible to continue to practice traditional Judaism and to be a believer at the same time. But this warning example could be directed more against those who belong to the Johannine group than to those who still are in the synagogue. After all, the gospel was written for the insiders who heard it read in their gatherings. In this context the strict boundary between the true believers and the Jews who are all exposed as unbelievers and even as murderers would have functioned as a warning against seeking contacts with any Jews who did not belong to the community. This may suggest that the most urgent problem from the point of view of the spiritual leaders in the Johannine community was some members *inside* the community, not secret believers in the synagogue. Maybe some members of the Johannine group were uncertain about cutting their ties with other Jews and found the practice of basic matters of Jewishness still attractive, even though the gospel as a whole presupposes the abandonment of these practices.[36]

The narrator relates that after Jesus' bread of life speech many of his disciples were offended by his bold words and thus "turned back and no longer went about with him" (John 6:66). This is often taken as an indication of a later schism inside the Johannine group, a schism not dissimilar from that referred to in the Johannine Epistles.[37] I argued in the previous chapter that the contrast between Moses' manna and Jesus' revelation characterizes the whole narrative dia-

---

[34] Setzer 1994, 167.
[35] Setzer 1994, 168.
[36] Cf. Kimelman 1981, 234–235; Reinhartz 1998, 136–137.
[37] For the discussion, see de Boer 1996a, 63–67 and 250.

logue in John 6:26–59. Thus it may be that these disciples were offended by the content of the entire speech, not just by its final section possibly dealing with the eucharist (6:52–59).[38] Still in his final words of the speech Jesus emphasizes the contrast between his bread and the manna eaten by the wilderness generation (6:58). The narrator says that some of Jesus' disciples murmured (γογγύζω) at his words (6:61) which connects these disciples to the Jews who have earlier murmured at Jesus (6:41) and to the wilderness generation who showed their unbelief by murmuring. The disciples who turn back may stand for those who did not see any contradiction between Moses and Jesus, and so did not follow the evangelist and his circle away from the Jewish community. The reason for their not joining the Johannine group may not have been fear at all, but the desire to hold to basic matters of Jewish identity abandoned by the Johannine believers. The Johannine writer maintained that there was no real difference between these Jews and those who had been responsible for Jesus' death and thus disqualified their position.

The dialogue between the believing Jews and Jesus concerning Abraham makes clear the discontinuity between the faith of the Johannine group and traditional Jewish beliefs. The close reading of this dialogue gives further support for the conclusion I have reached in the earlier chapters: the Johannine Christians view such basic figures of Jewish tradition as Abraham from the standpoint of outsiders.

Jesus, the Jews and Abraham

The believing Jews introduce Abraham into the discussion as they answer Jesus' words about the truth that could make them free: "We are descendants of Abraham and have never been slaves to anyone. What do you mean by saying, 'You will be made free'?" (8:33) The Jews refer here to their status as the legitimate heirs of the promise God gave to the seed of Abraham (e.g., Gen 15). Their claim is fully understandable in light of the important role Abraham enjoyed among different Jewish groups.[39] Even though the portrayal of Abraham is not uniform in ancient sources, he was regarded generally as a

---

[38] However, Brown (1979, 74) suggests that John 6:66 refers to "Jewish Christians who are no longer to be considered true believers because they do not share John's view of the eucharist."

[39] For the role of Abraham in Jewish literature, see Sandmel 1971, 30–95; Berger 1977, 372–380; Hansen 1989, 175–199.

great ancestor who was chosen by God and who was the first to
worship the true God; he was known for his obedience to God, and
it was also thought that his descendants are rewarded because of his
merits. Abraham's

> importance to the writers, and by inference to the readers, is such that
> they feel no need to go into details. Abraham has become intimately
> part of their assumptions and pre-dispositions.[40]

Already in some scriptural passages 'the seed of Abraham' is used as
a synonym for such expressions as 'Israel,' or 'the children of Jacob'
(2 Chr 20:7; Ps 105:6; Isa 41:8). In some subsequent writings 'the
seed of Abraham' becomes synonymous with the word Jew (e.g.,
3 Macc 6:3; 4 Macc 18:1; *Pss. Sol.* 9:9; 18:3,4).[41] In rabbinic writings, there appears a view that even the poorest Israelites are regarded
as gentle folk who have lost their fortunes, for they are the children
of Abraham, Isaac, and Jacob (*m. B. Qam.* 8:6, cf. also *m. B. Meṣiʿa.*
7:1). The appeal of the Jews in John is well in line with these views
according to which Abraham and his election were a continuous
source of honor and pride for those who regarded themselves as his
descendants.

Jesus' reply also has precedents in earlier Jewish and Christian
traditions. Some sources deny a common view that the merits of the
fathers devolve on their children (2 *Bar.* 85:12; 4 *Ezra* 7:102–115;
2 *Enoch* 53:1; *L.A.B.* 33:5).[42] It was claimed that the merits of the patriarchs benefit only those who act like the patriarchs did (Philo in
Virtues 207; *L.A.B.* 33:5; *T. Abr.* B 9:4). The contrast between an
appeal to the fathers, notably to Abraham, and good works is familiar also in early Christian tradition (Matt 3:7–9; Luke 3:7–9). Paul
makes a distinction between those who are Abraham's seed according to the flesh and those who believe in Christ and are thus regarded
as the true seed of Abraham (Rom 9:6–8; cf. also Gal 3–4). The
question of who has the right to call themselves the true seed of
Abraham is a recurrent theme also in rabbinic writings.[43] So the
Johannine Jesus follows a beaten track in opposing the claim of the
Jews to be free descendants of Abraham. But the close analysis of

---

[40] Sandmel 1971, 38.
[41] Thus Sandmel 1971, 37; Hansen 1989, 188.
[42] See Berger 1977, 377.
[43] See Sandmel 1971, 93–94.

what Jesus says and what he does not say is needed so that the Johannine passage is not read in the light of what is said in some other sources—particularly in Paul's letters.

Jesus answers the Jews' appeal to Abraham by saying that everyone who commits a sin is a slave of sin (v. 34). Jesus does not specify here what he means by sin, but his earlier words suggest that it means the refusal to accept him (8:21 and 24).[44] It is possible, however, that sin has a more specific meaning here. The Jews Jesus is confronting were characterized as believers in 8:30–31, and it has not yet become clear that they refuse to accept Jesus. It is thus likely that Jesus anticipates the more explicit charge he makes later (v. 37, 40). The sinfulness of these Jews is evident especially in their willingness to kill Jesus, which proves that they are not free descendants of Abraham but slaves to sin.[45] What the Jews of the story finally do shows that they appeal to Abraham in vain. This is a main theme in the following discussion where Jesus explicates what is the true relationship between Abraham and the Jews (8:37–40).

It is noteworthy that Jesus accepts the basic claim of his opponents that they are Abraham's descendants (v. 37). While Paul deals with such questions as who the heirs of the promise given to Abraham are (cf. Rom 4:13–14), or who the true descendants of Abraham are (Rom 9:6–8; Gal 3:7), the Johannine Jesus does not deny here that his opponents have the right to the heritage of Abraham. The point is rather that they are not behaving as they should as Abraham's descendants.[46] Jesus develops this idea further in 8:39–40, but the interpretation of these verses is difficult, because it is uncertain what the original text is.

The problem concerns Jesus' words in 8:39. These words read in the Nestle-Aland εἰ τέκνα τοῦ Ἀβραάμ ἐστε, τὰ ἔργα τοῦ Ἀβραὰμ ἐποιεῖτε.[47] Manuscripts are divided on what kind of conditional sentence we have here. Most manuscripts read here the forms ἦτε . . .

---

[44] According to Dozeman (1980, 355), the slavery to sin is the same as the slavery to the law in Paul's letters. Dozemann says that John is disputing with the law-observant Jewish Christians here. But Dozeman reads Paul's problems into John here, even though there is not a single reference to the law in the present passage.

[45] Thus Becker 357.

[46] The difference between John and Paul is emphasized by Brown 363; Dodd 1968, 49.

[47] For a detailed and balanced discussion of the problem, see Mees 1981, 119–130. Cf. also Brown 356–357; Barrett 347.

ἐποιεῖτε (ἄν) and take the sentence as a contrary-to-fact condition meaning, "If you were Abraham's children, you would do what Abraham did".[48] This reading, however, lacks the support of the oldest manuscripts; furthermore, it is a *lectio facilior* that improves the grammar of the text by reading a pure contrary-to-fact conditional sentence instead of a mixed conditional sentence. Two other readings that both have good support in the manuscripts are (1) a reading that has the forms ἐστε … ἐποιεῖτε (2) a reading that has the forms ἐστε … ποιεῖτε. The first reading produces a mixed condition the idea of which is that the Jews are really Abraham's children but deny it by their actions.[49] According to the second reading, the sentence is a real condition and the verb ποιεῖτε must understood as an imperative: "If you are Abraham' children, do what Abraham did".[50]

Readings (1) and (2) have equal support in the manuscripts, and it is difficult if not impossible to determine which one is the original reading.[51] It is not necessary, however, to make the final decision, because the two readings are not so far away from each other. The first reading admits that the Jews are really Abraham's children, but they are not doing his works. The second reading urges the Jews to do the works of Abraham, because they are his children. Jesus' following words show that the Jews act contrary to their status as Abraham's children (8:40). This is in accordance with what Jesus said earlier in 8:37 where he admitted that the Jews are Abraham's seed. It is not necessary to suppose that the Johannine Jesus makes here a fine distinction between the expressions 'the seed of Abraham' (σπέρμα Ἀβραάμ) and 'the children of Abraham' (τέκνα

---

[48] Some manuscripts read the form ἐποιεῖτε with the modal particle ἄν, while some lack it. A pure contrary-to-fact condition would require that ἄν is used in the apodosis, but it was no longer obligatory in Koine. Cf. Blass/Debrunner/Rehkopf 1984 § 360. It is clear that ἄν was not used in the original text.

[49] Thus Brown 357. This reading is supported by such manuscripts as 𝔓⁷⁵, ℵ*, B², D and T.

[50] This reading is supported by 𝔓⁶⁶, B*, ff and the Vulgate.

[51] Cf. Mees 1981, 130. Mees says that on the basis of textual criticism only it is impossible to decide the original reading. Mees adds that "aus Interpretationsgründen mag man mehr der gemischten Form zuneigen." It is often claimed that other readings are attempts to correct the original mixed condition (ἐστε … ἐποιεῖτε) by making the text grammatically more "correct." Thus Brown 357; Metzger 1994, 225. It is, however, difficult to assess which reading is the most "correct" one, because none of them is against the grammar. Cf. Martini (1978–79, 295) who regards the real condition (ἐστε … ποιεῖτε) as the original reading and says that other readings are "grammatical refinements."

τοῦ Ἀβραάμ) and concedes that the Jews are Abraham's physical descendants but denies that they are Abraham's spiritual children.[52] As C. H. Dodd notes, it is a plain but irrelevant fact for John that the Jews trace their origin back to Abraham; the question is rather whether "the descendants of Abraham reproduce the character and behaviour of their ancestor."[53] This becomes clearer if we compare what Jesus says a little later of the Jews and Abraham to what he says of the Jews and God.

The focus of the dialogue changes in 8:41. It is no longer the status of the Jews as Abraham's children that is under discussion but the status of the Jews as the children of God. There is a small but notable difference in how Jesus speaks of the Jews as God's children and how he earlier addressed the Jews as Abraham's children. Jesus says to the Jews: "If God were your (ἦν) father, you would love (ἠγαπᾶτε ἄν) me" (v. 42). This is a pure contrary-to-fact sentence making clear that God is not the father of the Jews, because they do not love Jesus. Jesus' words are "a blunt denial" of the claim that God is the father of the Jews, whereas he earlier admitted that the Jews are Abraham's children.[54]

The same difference between how Jesus refers to God and to Abraham is evident later in the dialogue. In 8:54 Jesus says: "It is my Father who glorifies me, he of whom you say, 'He is our God.'" The Jews may claim God their Father, but Jesus' choice of words makes it clear that this claim is wrong. Jesus later says to the Jews: "Your ancestor Abraham rejoiced that he would see my day" (v. 56). After all that has been said of Abraham, Jesus still speaks of Abraham as the father of the Jews. This supports the conclusion that the point of the earlier discussion was not to deprive the Jews of the privilege of being Abraham's children, but rather to show that they are not acting worthy of this privilege.[55]

---

[52] Dodd (1968, 50 n. 1) is right as he says that "an attempt to distinguish between σπέρμα (conceded) and τέκνα (denied) seems quite arbitrary." For different views, see Schnackenburg II 283; Siker 1991, 136–139; Moloney 1996, 107. Siker tries to show that σπέρμα is used in contrast to τέκνα throughout the gospel. But the two words are used so seldom in the gospel that Siker's attempt is not convincing. Besides the present passage σπέρμα appears only once (ἐκ τοῦ σπέρματος Δαυίδ ... ἔρχεται ὁ Χριστός in 7:42) and τέκνα only twice (τέκνα θεοῦ in 1:12 and 11:52).

[53] Dodd 1968, 49.

[54] Brown 364.

[55] Those who claim that Jesus wants to deny in 8:37–40 that the Jews are

There is probably a particular tradition about Abraham in the
background of Jesus' claim that the Jews are not acting as Abraham
did (8:40). This tradition is based on Gen 18 where Abraham welcomed at the oaks of Mamre three men who were sent by God and
who were presumably angels.[56] Later interpreters emphasized that
Abraham did not know the messengers but regarded them as strangers.
The story was held as a prime example of Abraham's great hospitality, even towards strangers, and hospitality was considered a major
characteristic of Abraham.[57] It is likely that we have here a reference to the works of hospitality from which Abraham was known.[58]
Jesus speaks of Abraham's works here, and, therefore, he does not
seem to have Abraham's faith in mind.[59] Jesus presents himself as
the messenger of God by saying to the Jews, "But now you are trying to kill me, a person (ἄνθρωπος)[60] who has told you the truth that
I heard from God." This is reminiscent of the messengers of God
that Abraham met at Mamre. The response of the Jews to Jesus is
presented here as exactly the opposite of Abraham's welcome of the
divine messengers at Mamre. The point is not so much to show that
those who have welcomed Jesus have replaced the Jews as Abraham's
true children, but to show that the Jews are not acting as Abraham
did. The way the relationship between Jesus and Abraham is developed in the rest of the dialogue shows that Abraham is only of limited significance for the narrator.

Abraham's children have problems with 8:56 where Jesus speaks of Abraham as
the father of the Jews. Siker (1991, 141) suggests that the words "your father
Abraham" in 8:56 can be understood to mean "Abraham, whom you *claim* to be
your father" (italics original). It can be expected, however, that the writer would
have selected his words more carefully, if he had meant this.

[56] For this tradition, see Ward 1968, 286–287 and 1976, 178; Sandmel 1971,
84–85; Neyrey 1987, 524.

[57] See Philo *Abraham* 107, 114–116, 132; Josephus *Ant.* 1.196; *T. Abr.* A 1:1–2;
2:2; 17:7; B 4:10; 13:5; Heb 13:2; *1 Clem* 10:7. For rabbinic traditions, see Ward
1968, 286–287; Sandmel 1971, 84–85.

[58] Thus Brown 357; Ward 1976, 178; Neyrey 1987, 524; Moloney 1996, 107.
Siker (1991, 141) says that the works of Abraham refer to Abraham's rejoicing at
seeing Jesus' day (v. 56). The connection between 8:39–40 and 8:56 is not clear,
however. The pluralistic expression, the works of Abraham, does not suit very well
what is described as a single act of Abraham, the seeing of Jesus' day (cf. the aorists
used in v. 56: Ἀβραὰμ ὁ πατὴρ ὑμῶν ἠγαλλιάσατο ἵνα ἴδῃ τὴν ἡμέραν τὴν ἐμήν, καὶ
εἶδεν καὶ ἐχάρη).

[59] Pace Bultmann 339 n. 4; Schnackenburg II 284.

[60] ἄνθρωπος is usually taken here in the sense of τις. Cf. Blass/Debrunner/Rehkopf
1984 § 301, 2.

After John 8:37–40 Abraham fades away from the discussion until 8:52 where the Jews make another appeal to him. But now the point of the discussion is different. Jesus' claim that "Whoever keeps my word will never see death" (v. 51), prompts a protest from the Jews: "Now we know that you have a demon. Abraham died, and so did the prophets; yet you say, 'Whoever keeps my word will never see death.' Are you greater than our father Abraham, who died? The prophets also died. Who do you claim to be?" (8:52–54). These words put Jesus and Abraham in comparison. The reader can anticipate the answer to the question raised by the Jews on the basis of the previous narrative. Jesus is indeed greater than Abraham in the same way as he is greater than Jacob (4:12–14), or greater than Moses whose manna was unable to give life (6:31–58).

In the following discussion Jesus presents Abraham as a witness who has seen his day and rejoiced (8:56). Traditions according to which Abraham was allowed to see the secrets of coming ages are probably behind Jesus' words.[61] Jesus' claim makes the Jews to wonder how it is possible that Jesus has seen Abraham. It is noteworthy that Jesus speaks of Abraham who has seen his day, whereas the Jews ask, "have you seen Abraham?"[62] The Jews of the story think that Abraham is superior to Jesus and, therefore, give priority to seeing him rather than to seeing Jesus.[63] This change in the point of view is significant, however, because it gives a final reason for Jesus to make clear that it is by no means impossible that he has seen Abraham. Jesus says, "Before Abraham was, I am," which refers not only to Jesus' superiority over Abraham but also to his preexistence (8:58).[64]

---

[61] For these traditions, see Moloney 1996, 112.

[62] According to some old manuscripts (e.g. $\mathfrak{P}^{75}$, $\aleph$*), the Jews ask Jesus, "has Abraham seen you?" whereas most manuscripts read, "have you seen Abraham." The latter reading is supported by $\mathfrak{P}^{66}$, $\aleph^c$, A, B^c (B* reads ἑώρακες), C, D, K, and many others, and it is most likely the original reading. The alternative reading is an adaption to Jesus' previous words that Abraham has seen Jesus' day. Cf. Brown 360; Barrett 352; Metzger 1994, 226–227.

[63] Cf. Brown 360; Metzger 1994, 226–227.

[64] Pace M. Davies (1992, 86) who argues that the verb γένεσθαι in John 8:58 may be "an addition occasioned by later christological developments." This verb gives Jesus' saying a temporal meaning ("before Abraham was . . ." or "before Abraham came into being . . ."), but the support in the manuscripts for the exclusion of this verb is minimal (D and old Latin versions). Davies takes Jesus' statement not as a literal reference to time, but as a metaphorical reference to Jesus' precedence over Abraham. This is a part of Davies's attempt to deny that John presents

It is not easy to reconcile what is said of Abraham and Jesus here to what was said earlier of Abraham and the Jews. It was said in 8:37–40 that the Jews are not doing what Abraham did and what they should also do as Abraham's children, while in 8:52–59 Jesus makes clear that he himself is the standard by which even Abraham should be measured. Abraham has a positive function in salvation history, but only in his relation to Jesus. The Jews' appeal to Abraham is rejected in two different ways: first, it is said that their relationship to Abraham is wrong, and then it is said that Abraham has only a subsidiary role to play in the divine drama as a witness of Jesus.[65]

What Jesus says of Abraham is close to what he has earlier said of Moses. Both Abraham and Moses are portayed as witnesses of Jesus, but the Johannine Jesus makes clear too that they both lack what he himself has. The contrast between Jesus and Moses (John 6) is presented in sharper terms than the one between Jesus and Abraham (John 8). But the same contrast between life and death that characterizes John 6 is evident also in John 8 where the dead Abraham is compared with Jesus who gives life to his followers.[66] From the Johannine point of view,

---

Jesus as a pre-existent figure; she claims that one can find pre-existent christology in John only if the gospel is interpreted mistakenly in the light of later dogmatic developments. Davies is right in saying that later christological confessions should not be read into John, but it is still impossible to remove pre-existential features from the Johannine portrait of Jesus.

[65] Cf. Bondi 1997, 492–493.

[66] For a different interpretation, see Boyarin 2001, 275–276. Boyarin interprets John 8:39–40 and 8:56–58 in the light of his reading of the prologue of the gospel (John 1:1–18). Boyarin takes all that is said in the prologue before 1:14 as a reference to the time before the incarnation. According to Boyarin, those "who received him" and "believed in his name" and "became children of God" (1:13) are such people as Abraham who received the Logos even before the incarnation. So in John 8:56–58 "the Logos clearly claims to have appeared to Abraham (presumably in the theophany at Mamre); Abraham, of course, rejoiced, received the Logos handsomely, and was saved." I have some doubts about Boyarin's reading of the prologue, but it is noteworthy also that Jesus never says in 8:56–58 that Abraham saw him; the words "your father Abraham rejoiced that he was to see my day; he saw and was glad," rather indicate that Abraham saw the coming eschatological fulfilment, which is suggested also by traditions connected to Abraham (cf. above n. 61). I also see a more pointed contrast here between Jesus as the giver of life and the dead Abraham than Boyarin. In a similar way I see the difference between Jesus and Moses in sharper terms than Boyarin who says that "for John . . . Jesus comes to fulfill the mission of Moses, not to displace it. The Torah simply needed a better exegete, the *Logos Ensarkos*, a fitting teacher for flesh and blood" (p. 280).

Abraham, for all his greatness, belongs to the sequence of events that mark time. There was a time when he belonged to a narrative. His story is finished; he has come and gone. 'The Jews' are only able to call upon the memory of his story.[67]

The difference between Jesus and Abraham is even clearer here if there is a particular tradition in the background of this scene. According to the *Testament of Abraham*, dying Abraham tried to ward off death but could not escape it in the end (*T. Abr.* A 7; 15; 16; 19–20).[68] The connection between this tradition and John remains uncertain, however, but even without this connection Jesus' superiority over Abraham is clear.

I noted earlier that Jesus' way of speaking of Abraham is not without precedents in earlier Jewish traditions. In accordance with many writings, the Johannine Jesus emphasizes that it does not help anyone to be Abraham's children unless one does the works Abraham did. But the Johannine view does not grant any independent role to Abraham and other patriarchs. John's basic conviction of Jesus as the sole source of revelation and as the pre-existent messenger of God clashes with any Jewish tradition for which Abraham and other patriarchs were representative figures of the antiquity and the wisdom of the Jews. In antiquity the old age of a religion was a source of pride for its believers and was praiseworthy even to outsiders. Many non-Jewish and Jewish writers frequently refer to Abraham and other patriarchs with admiration for their nobility and wisdom.[69] It is possible that the surprised questions of the Jews in John, "Are you greater than our father Abraham, who died?" or "You are not yet fifty years old, and have you seen Abraham?" echo these admiring views about the patriarchs. But from the Johannine point of view, "any Jewish tradition that might seek to build itself on their foundation is seriously misled and can make no claim to the truth."[70]

In light of Abraham' symbolic significance, it seems that "John's community had turned their back on a central aspect of Jewish tradition," which indicates "how socially isolated they had become from Judaism."[71] It is no longer being reckoned among Abraham's children

---

[67] Moloney 1996, 113.
[68] For this tradition, see Ward 1976, 178–179.
[69] The material is gathered by Feldman 1993, 177–219.
[70] Freyne 1986, 126.
[71] Esler 1994, 89. Esler takes this to support his view that the Johannine community is an 'introversionist sect' not unlike the Qumran community. But I think

that counts for the Johannine narrator and his readers—all that matters in the last analysis is whether one believes in Jesus or not. This is not just an adjustment of wrong and exclusive views that the Johannine Jews may have had of Abraham and election, but John's passage implies a complete rethinking of a basic part of Jewish identity.[72] For the Johannine writer, Abraham is a part of the heritage of the Jews who fail to follow his example and receive Jesus. But in all other respects, Abraham's role is considered from the point of view of an outsider and he remains "your father."

My analysis of what the Johannine Jesus says of Abraham has pointed in the same direction as the earlier chapters of this work: for the Johannine narrator and his readers faith in Jesus represents the fulfilment of earlier Jewish tradition, but, at the same time, they interpret this tradition so exclusively in the light of this faith that basic matters of Jewishness cease to be integral parts of their identity. From the Johannine point of view, Jesus not only continues earlier Jewish tradition but also supersedes it, which explains why it is that Jesus is at times put in contrast with such key figures of Jewish tradition as Jacob, Moses and Abraham. This contrast probably reflects a break that had occurred between the Johannine Christians and Jews who continued to observe basic matters of Jewish identity. The appearance of believing Jews in the narrative may suggest that this break was not so complete as the Johannine writer would have

---

that the break from Jewish tradition evident here and also elsewhere in John is so thorough that it is doubtful whether we should speak of the Johannine community as a Jewish sect at all. For the development of this idea, see the next, concluding chapter of this work.

[72] Pace Pedersen (1999, 188) who takes the sin of the believing Jews to be "that belonging to Abraham's seed (σπέρμα Ἀβραάμ) is seen as an expression of an exclusive salvation history within the Creation." Consequently, "the liberation spoken of for the Christian Jews is . . . a liberation from the enslaving untruth, which does not have the Creator's life within it, that to be children of Abraham is tantamount to enjoying a special status in the history of salvation, and a liberation into the Son's 'truth' that we are God's children altogether by virtue of the Creation (1.11–12)." Pedersen does not notice that what he regards as "sin" or as "the enslaving untruth" comes very close to how the role of Israel was understood in different forms of Judaism. An important aspect of Jewish identity was a sense of the privileged position that was based on God's election, and so "exclusivism was part and parcel of Judaism" (E. P. Sanders 1992, 266). John's view of τέκνα θεοῦ hardly means that "we [who we?] are God's children altogether by virtue of the Creation." It is clear that only those who receive Jesus are regarded as God's children in John (1:12; 11:52). Pedersen traces profound creation theology in John but fails to attach due weight to the dualistic thinking that characterizes all John says about creation.

wished, and so he tried to deepen the gulf between the Johannine
believers and other Jews by doing away with the difference between
overtly hostile and believing Jews. As a part of his attempt to make
a clear distinction between the true believers and Jews, John connects the Jews with the devil by saying "you are from your father,
the devil." In the following I analyse this charge in the light of its
narrative context and dualistic views that increasingly appeared in
Jewish writings of the time.

The Children of a Murderer: John 8:44 and Apocalyptic Polemic

Jesus' harsh words about the Jews as the children of the devil (8:44)
are an essential part of the argumentation that is developed in John
8. In the course of the dialogue Jesus uses dualistic expressions that
highlight the difference between himself and his discussion partners.
At the beginning of the dialogue, Jesus refers to the difference between
light and darkness (8:12). During the following dialogue he says: "I
know where I come from and where I am going, but you do not
know" (v. 14); "you judge by human standards" (v. 15); "you know
neither me nor my Father" (v. 19); "you are from below, I am from
above; you are of this world, I am not of this world" (8:23). These
dualistic contrasts prepare the way for Jesus' claim that the ultimate
distinction between him and the Jews is that he has God as his
father, while the Jews are of their father, the devil (v. 44).[73]

Jesus' claim in 8:44 is also closely connected to the theme of father-
hood that has an important role in the previous discussion. The
Pharisees ask Jesus in 8:19, "Where is your Father?" and Jesus answers,
"You know neither me nor my Father; if you knew me, you would

---

[73] Pace von Wahlde 2001, 421. Von Wahlde recognizes in John 8:12–37 "a number of elements which exhibit a kind of dualism." But he takes these features as
"contrasts" that do not "represent a true dualism for they are not the result of opposed
principles but rather reflect the presence or absence of a given trait." This gnostic
"true dualism" is found in 1QS and in a modified form also in John 8:38–47, but
this dualism is not the same as earlier "contrasts" in 8:12–37 (p. 421 n. 8, 442
n. 37). Von Wahlde is at pains to show that John's dualism is "an ethical, or modified,
dualism" that "is distinguished from the absolute dualism of gnosticism" (p. 424).
But when depicting the absolute gnostic dualism as "true dualism" von Wahlde
gives a very narrow definition of dualism. It is clear that all dualisms in early Jewish
and Christian sources are "modified" and that dualistic views may be expressed
using different categories that emphasize different dimensions of dualistic worldview
(see below). It is not at all clear whether even writings often described as gnostic
represent that kind of "true" or "absolute" dualism from which von Wahlde tries to
distinguish the Johannine dualism. Cf. M. A. Williams 1996, 96–115, esp. p. 100.

know my Father also." Later the narrator notes that the Jews did
not understand that Jesus "was speaking to them of the Father"
(8:27). These sayings anticipate Jesus' affirmation that he and the
Jews have a different father: "I declare what I have seen in the
Father's presence; as for you, you do (NRSV: should do) what you
have heard from the father" (8:38). It is likely that there is a veiled
allusion to the devil as the father of the Jews already at this point of
the discussion.[74] Jesus later repeats this charge but still refuses to reveal
exactly who the father of the Jews is, as he states: "You are indeed
doing what your father does" (8:41). The Jews protest these words
and say, "We are not illegitimate children." Only after this does
Jesus finally proceed to reveal that the devil is their true father (8:44).
This harsh claim is the culmination of the discussion in which the
question of fatherhood grows little by little into the main theme.
This theme of fatherhood is closely connected to the dualistic distinction between God and the devil and it is imperative to ask how
John and his readers understood this distinction.

In earlier scholarship, the background of John's dualism was found
in gnosticism. Especially Rudolf Bultmann claimed that John changed
gnostic cosmological dualism to a dualism of decision, according to
which different responses to Jesus, not their predetermined substances,
divide people into the sons of light or darkness.[75] Since the discovery of the Dead Sea scrolls, however, most scholars have found parallels to the Johannine dualism in them.[76] The most striking parallel

---

[74] Thus Bultmann 338; Barrett 346–347; Schnackenburg II 282–283. According
to this interpretation, the first part of the sentence refers to God, the father of Jesus,
while the latter part refers to the devil, the father of the Jews. Many manuscripts
make this explicit by adding the possessives (μου and ὑμῶν) to the text. Jesus' words
could also be taken as a command if the verb ποιεῖτε is read as an imperative. In
this case, Jesus would be telling the Jews to do the works of their father, Abraham.
Thus Brown (356) who says the appearance the devil as the father of the Jews here
would make the development of thought in 8:41–44 senseless. It is, however, fully
understandable that Jesus makes here a covert allusion to a theme that is later
developed in detail.

[75] Bultmann 1984 (1948), 373. This view is developed further by Schottroff 1970,
228–245 and 289–296. According to Schottroff, the cosmological dualism was already
interpreted existentially in gnostic writings, and, therefore, John's dualism does not
break away from the gnostic way of thinking (p. 241). For Schottroff John is the
first known system of gnosis that has adopted Christian traditions (p. 293). Most
recently Barrett (2001, 402–405) has interpreted dualistic views in John 8 in light
the of John's "affinity with gnosticism."

[76] See Brown 1957 (1955), 184–195; Becker 1964, 217–237; Böcher 1965; Braun
1966, 119–132; Charlesworth 1991 (1968–69), 76–106; Ashton 1991, 205–237;
Painter 1993, 36–47.

appears in a section of the Community Rule (1QS). This section contains the doctrine of the two spirits, the spirits of truth and deceit, that struggle to dominate the people of the world (1QS 3:13–4:26). This doctrine shares with John not only general dualistic distinction between light and darkness but also some common terminology which suggests that there is some connection between views appearing in 1QS 3:13–4:26 and John's dualism.[77] In both writings, dualism is expressed in terms of two cosmic spirits that explain the presence of evil in the world: the doctrine speaks of the spirit of deceit or of the Angel of Darkness who is in total dominion over the sons of deceit (1QS 3:19–21), while John speaks of the ruler of this world (12:31; 14:30; 16:11); both writings speak of the spirit of truth (1QS 3:18–19; 4:21–23; John 14:17; 15:26; 16:13); the doctrine refers to the "spirit of holiness," and John to the "Holy Spirit" (1QS 4:21; John 14:26; 20:22); both writings mention the sons of light (1QS 3:13, 24–25; John 12:36), the light of life (1QS 3:7; John 8:12) and those who "walk in the darkness" (1QS 3:21; 4:11; John 8:12; 12:35). This clearly raises a question as to the connection between 1QS 3:13–4:26 and John.

Recent studies on 1QS have emphasized that there are many parallel copies of 1QS among the scrolls. Some copies probably representing a more original text than 1QS do not contain the doctrine of the two spirits at all. There are also parallels to the doctrine, and these parallels suggest that the doctrine itself has gone through a process of redaction.[78] As a matter of fact, the views appearing in 1QS 3:13–4:26 are quite unique among the Qumran texts and, therefore, the doctrine of the two spirits should not be taken as a representative of the sect's theology.[79] The doctrine in all likelihood has a pre-Essene origin, possibly in some sapiental traditions, and is only secondarily connected to its present context in the Community Rule.[80] Significant parallels to the doctrine of the two spirits appear, for example, in the *Testaments of the Twelve Patriarchs* (*T. Judah* 20:1; *T. Asher* 1:3–9).[81]

---

[77] For these parallels, see Charlesworth 1991, 101–102 and 1996, 81–82.
[78] H. Stegemann 1988, 96–100; Lange 1995, 126–128; Metso 1997, 113–114 and 135–140; Frey 1997, 289–290.
[79] H. Stegemann 1988, 125–130; Metso 1997, 138; Frey 1997, 290.
[80] Lange 1995, 128–130; Metso 1997, 138 n. 99; Frey 1997, 295–300.
[81] For a recent comparison of dualisms in John, 1QS and the *Testaments*, see von Wahlde 2001, 418–444.

So we may discard all speculations that take 1QS 3:13–4:26 as a
distinctive summary of the theology of the Qumran community and
that argue that some members in the Johannine community had personal links with Qumran.[82] The obvious similarities suggest rather
that dualistic views were not distinctive only to 1QS 3:13–4:26 and
John, but were fairly widespread in certain Jewish circles at the
beginning of the Common Era; this common background is enough
to explain the affinities between these two writings.[83] It is also important
to note that the dualism found in 1QS 3:13–4:26 is not the only
pattern of dualistic thinking in the Qumran writings, but that dualistic ideas may appear in different forms.[84] So when we ask for characteristics of John's dualism, we must ask how John develops different
dimensions of the dualism found in 1QS and some other writings.

Scholars often distinguish in dualistic views different dimensions
that may appear in different combinations.[85] Jörg Frey has described
the dualism in the doctrine of the two spirits as

---

[82] According to Charlesworth (1991, 104), John "probably borrowed some of his
dualistic terminology and mythology from 1QS 3:13–4:26." Charlesworth has later
said that he has never claimed that the evangelist had direct access to a Qumran
scroll (1996, 87–90). But it is still possible for Charlesworth that there were some
former Essenes in the Johannine community who had memorized portions of the
scrolls (at least 1QS 3:13–4:14). One of these former Essenes was perhaps the author
of the Odes of Solomon. Ashton (1991, 236–237) takes a significant step further;
according to him, the similarities between 1QS 3:13–4:26 and John cannot be
explained unless it is supposed that the evangelist once was an Essene himself. John
"retained the pattern of thinking with which he was probably familiar with from
an early age, maybe from childhood."

[83] Thus already Brown 1957, 205–206; Price 1991, 10–11; Painter 1993, 35–36.
[84] Frey 1997, 278.
[85] See Charlesworth 1991, 76 n. 1; Frey 1997, 280–285. Both Charlesworth and
Frey distinguish ten types or dimensions of dualism, even though they name these
types differently. For the analysis of Biblical and related literature the following distinctions are most relevant: *cosmic* dualism divides the universe into two opposing
forces, although it is self-evident that in Jewish tradition God is always above this
division; *spatial dualism* makes a distinction between heaven and earth, above and
below; *eschatological dualism* divides time into the present and future eras; *ethical dualism* divides people into the righteous and the wicked according to their virtues and
vices; *soteriological dualism* divides people into two groups on the basis of their response
to a saviour or to a certain salvific act; *physical dualism* signifies the division between
matter and spirit; *anthropological dualism* signifies the opposition between body and
soul; *psychological dualism* sees the contrast between good and evil taking place in the
heart of a person in which opposite principles or inclinations are struggling.

creation-founded and eschatologically confined cosmic dualism with a subordinate ethical dualism, that comes to effect not only in the respective deeds, but even in a psychological division within every single person as well.[86]

These dimensions of dualism are present also in John, with the exception that John's dualism is hardly psychological because there is no interest in the fight of the two opposite forces, God and the devil, in the heart of a person.[87] The dividing line is rather between those who accept Jesus and those who reject him (1:11–12), while in 1QS 4:23–24 the two spirits keep struggling in the heart of a person till the day of God's judgment.[88] But ethical, eschatological and cosmic dualisms appear in John, even though these have all been interpreted in light of John's basic conviction that Jesus is the final revealer of God. This feature is characteristic of John and distinguishes the Johannine dualism from other dualistic views of the time.[89]

According to ethical dualism, the deeds of people show their true origin. 1QS 4:2–11 names different virtues and vices that distinguish the sons of light from the sons of darkness, and *Testaments of the Twelve Patriarchs* also repeatedly describe actions characteristic of those who follow either the Lord or Beliar (e.g. *T. Asher* 1:3–5:4).[90] John shares with these views the conviction that the works of people show whether they belong to light or darkness (3:19–21). The origin of people does not depend on some predetermined decree according to which people are divided into two spheres by their substance, but their actions determine their origin.[91] But while the teaching of the two spirits and related literature often contains lists of virtues and vices that reveal the division of humankind into two spheres, there is only one 'work' in John that is relevant in this respect: the response to Jesus. So perhaps it would be better call John's dualism soteriolocal

---

[86] Frey 1997, 294 (italics original). Charlesworth (1991, 77–89) finds in 1QS 3:13–4:26 dimensions of cosmic, ethical and eschatological dualism, but denies that it contains psychological dualism (p. 85).

[87] Thus Böcher 1965, 74.

[88] A cryptic astrological text explains that the lot of a person in the 'house of light' and the 'house of darkness' may vary according to the signs of the zodiac (4Q186). For the relationship between this text and the doctrine of the two spirits, see Frey 1997, 293–294; Lange 1997, 389–390.

[89] Thus Brown 1957, 194–195; Becker 1964, 222.

[90] For ethical dualism in the *Testaments*, see von Wahlde 2001, 430–434.

[91] Cf. Becker 1964, 231; Von Wahlde 2001, 425 n. 14.

rather than ethical, although John shares same basic lines of thinking with ethical dualism.[92]

Both the doctrine of the two spirits and *Testaments* represent eschatological dualism because the ultimate triumph of the spirit of truth
over the spirit of wickedness is already anticipated (1QS 3:18; 4:18–23;
T. Dan 6:3; *T. Levi* 18:12; *T. Judah* 25:3). John's dualism is also ori-
ented eschatologically because Jesus' coming into the world marks
the beginning of a new era. But while 1QS 3:13–4:26 and other
writings containing apocalyptic elements anticipate the coming of the
new era in the future, one of the basic teachings of the gospel is
that the hour of salvation has already come (4:23; 5:25).[93] This
difference also characterizes the elaboration of cosmic dualism in
John which is the most disputed part of the Johannine dualism. While
the 'Prince of Light' and the 'Angel of Darkness' are in a fight with
each other in 1QS 3:20–21, some scholars deny that the devil is
presented as a cosmic spirit struggling against Jesus in John. They
demythologize the references to 'the devil' (6:70; 8:44; 13:2), 'Satan'
(13:27) or 'the ruler of this world' (12:31; 14:30; 16:11) and say that
John does not represent cosmic dualism.[94] This view, however, sounds
too sophisticated and modern in light of the development that is
reflected in many writings of the Second Temple Period.[95] As a result
of this development, dualistic views became more and more common in Jewish writings. John shares in this development which suggests that the devil was not just a figure of speech for the Johannine
narrator and his readers but an essential part of their view of the world.

The idea of a cosmic battle between God and the forces of evil
was especially developed in some apocalyptic writings. The book of
Daniel gave an impetus to this development by presenting the events
at the time of Antiochus Epiphanes as a cosmic struggle between
different angelic forces.[96] In subsequent apocalyptic tradition, the battle imagery was applied to different contexts.[97] But the use of this

---

[92] Charlesworth (1991, 96) says that "the Johannine 'dualism' is essentially soteriological and ethical."

[93] Cf. Charlesworth 1991, 93.

[94] Bultmann 1984 (1948), 369; Charlesworth 1991, 93; Ashton 1991, 207; Bondi
1997, 496.

[95] Thus Painter 1993, 41; Kovacs 1995, 227–247; Piper 2000, 271–276.

[96] See J. J. Collins 1998, 85–115.

[97] For examples, see Kovacs 1995, 236–237. The most important Christian adaptation of cosmic battle appears in the book of Revelation.

imagery was not confined to apocalyptic writings only. One of the first works that developed the conflict of angelic figures towards a dualistic presentation of the history of Israel was the book of *Jubilees* where appears a single leader of all evil spirits, Mastema, who is the main opponent of God and his angels.[98] The *Testaments of the Twelve Patriarchs* combined dualistic battle imagery and ethical exhortation and focused evil spirits into a single figure of Beliar who controls those who are inclined to evil. Both the Lord and Beliar have their own laws and kingdoms that are characterized by the distinction between light and darkness (e.g. *T. Levi* 19:1; *T. Dan* 6:1–4; *T. Naph.* 2:6; *T. Jos.* 20:2).[99] A dualism appears in 1QS 3:13–4:26 that may have originated from some sapiental traditions while other Qumran scrolls contain examples of a sheer cosmic dualism.[100] The most famous example is the War Rule that presents a cosmic battle between the 'sons of light' led by the angel Michael and the 'sons of darkness' whose prince is Belial.[101] The Qumran library also quite likely contains some pre-Essene writings that show that this kind of cosmic dualism was not the invention of the sect.[102]

John is not alone in presenting the events of early Christian history in the language of a cosmic battle; the devil appears as the opponent of Christ and his followers in all forms of early Christian literature.[103] The Johannine literature notwithstanding, the clearest example of cosmic dualism appears in 2 Cor 6:14–7:1 where Beliar is Christ's opponent; the passage contains several un-Pauline features, and it has been discussed whether it reflects a tradition known to Paul or whether it is a later addition to 2 Corinthians.[104] Be that as it may, the passage nevertheless shows how dualistic imagery attracted some circles among early Christians. Also, some passages in the synoptics imply that Jesus' life was seen as a battle against the devil and his

---

[98] J. J. Collins 1997, 271.

[99] Cf. Böcher 1965, 28–30; Russell 1977, 209–211; J. J. Collins 1997, 397–399 and 1998, 139–140.

[100] Cf. Frey 1997, 307.

[101] Cf. Frey 1997, 310–316; J. J. Collins 1998, 167–171.

[102] See Frey 1997, 316–326. Pagels (1995, 84) says that "within the ancient world, so far as I know, it is only Essenes and Christians who actually escalate conflict with their opponents to the level of cosmic war." This is not quite true because a sheer cosmic dualism also seems to be a pre-Essene phenomenon.

[103] For the devil in the New Testament, see Russell 1977, 221–249; Baumbach 1992, 23–42.

[104] For this discussion, see Hulmi 1999, 27–28.

forces, even though these views are not fully developed.[105] The fourth
gospel shares in this development, but its dualism is also more intense
than in any other writing of the New Testament.

The conflict between the forces of light and darkness is always
combined with the belief in one God who has created the world in
Jewish and early Christian tradition. The power of the devil over
the world is always restricted, and the eschatological defeat of the
forces of evil is anticipated.[106] In John, "the belief in one supreme
and good God is held in tension with acknowledgement of a dualistic
conflict in which the forces of good and evil are locked."[107] This tension may sometimes be resolved with myths that explain the origin
of evil but this is not always the case.[108] The lack of cosmological
mythology dealing with the nature and the origin of the devil does
not necessarily suggest that the references to the devil are void of
any cosmic relevance.[109] Hence it is not surprising that John does
not explain "how the world has been subdued by the the power of
evil."[110] The mentions of the devil are rather a part of the implicit
view of the world that John shares with some other writings and
that is taken more or less for granted by the readers of the gospel.
According to this worldview, the world is God's creation, but it is
currently under the dominion of the devil, the ruler of this world;
it is Jesus' task as the Son of God to destroy the devil.[111] So John
does not tell only a historical tale of Jesus or an ecclesiological tale
of the Johannine community but also a cosmological tale that opens
a framework for interpreting the whole narrative in the light of Jesus'
battle against the devil.[112] The closest terminological parallel to John's

---

[105] See Pagels 1994, 17–40 and 1995, 3–34 and 63–111.
[106] It is still an open question how dualistic views developed in Jewish tradition,
which was formerly strictly monistic. If some Persian views were influential, these
views were adapted to the Jewish context so that God remained above the dualism between good and evil. See J. J. Collins 1997, 294 and 1998, 153–155, 169–170.
Cf. also Frey 1997, 282.
[107] Painter 1993, 43.
[108] For these myths, see J. J. Collins 1997, 287–299.
[109] Thus Price 1991, 21. Price refers to *Hôdāyôt* (1QH) that does not offer a cosmological explanation for the origin of evil but still contains passages representing
cosmic dualism.
[110] Marjanen 1998, 133. Marjanen shows that John's view of the world comes
very close to that of the *Gospel of Thomas*.
[111] Becker 1964, 224.
[112] Cf. Reinhartz 1992, 16–28.

'ruler of this world' is found in the *Martyrdom of Isaiah* where Beliar is called 'the angel of iniquity who rules this world' (2:4).[113]

John shares features of cosmic dualism with many writings, but it also develops these features in a particular way. In apocalyptic tradition, the definitive fight between God and the devil lies in the future; the ultimate destruction of the devil and his kingdom was expected at the end of time at the last judgment.[114] But from the Johannine point of view, Jesus has already overcome the devil. This view becomes evident especially in three passages speaking of the ruler of this world.[115] Jesus refers to his coming death in John 12:31 and says: "Now is the judgment of this world; now the ruler of this world will be driven out." In his farewell speech to the disciples Jesus says: "I will no longer talk much with you, for the ruler of this world is coming. He has no power over me" (14:30). Later Jesus describes the future activity of the Paraclete and says: "The ruler of this world has been condemned" (16:11). These references indicate that John interprets Jesus' death on the cross and his exaltation in the light of cosmic battle imagery; for John Jesus' death is the decisive victory over the devil (cf. also 1 John 3:8).[116] John may not be the first to make the connection between Jesus' death and the battle against the devil in early Christian tradition, but this connection is developed most consistently in John, and the role of the devil and the role of those who belong to him is defined there in a significant way.[117] A

---

[113] Charlesworth 1991, 97.

[114] *Jub.* 23:29; 1 *Enoch* 55:3–56:4; *T. Dan* 6:3; *T. Levi* 18:12; *T. Judah* 25:3; *T. Mos.* 10:1; 1QM 18:1, 11–12; 4Q174 1:7–9; Rom 16:20; Rev 20. See Kovacs 1995, 238–240.

[115] Theissen (1999, 51 and 203) takes the Johannine references to the devil and to the ruler of this world as an example of the demonization of the Romans and their emperor; so "the Satan is a symbolic concentration of this power of the Romans which makes people dependent." I think that neither John nor references to the devil in other Jewish and early Christian sources support this conclusion.

[116] See Brown 1957, 189 and his commentary pp. 364, 477 and 655–656; Lindars 433; Becker 458; Price 1991, 21–22; Kovacs 1995, 227–247; Pagels 1995, 101; Marjanen 1998, 132–133. It is not quite clear in what sense the devil has been defeated by the death of Jesus in the Johannine thought. For this question, see Piper 2000, 271–276.

[117] It is disputed whether "the rulers of this age" who crucified Jesus according to 1 Cor 2:6–8 are supernatural powers or not. Kovacs (1989, 217–236) says that Paul is here influenced by apocalyptic battle imagery. Luke connects the devil to Jesus' death much more clearly than Mark and Matthew. Luke ends his version of the story of Jesus' temptations by saying that the devil "departed from him until an opportune time" (Luke 4:12). This opportune time seems to be the time of Jesus'

glance at different roles of the devil in contemporary literature reveals what is characteristic of John's view about the devil and his allies.

The devil has many different roles in Jewish and early Christian sources; he is referred to by different names and connected to all that different writers see as evil.[118] A recurrent characteristic of the devil is his will to destroy human beings. According to Wis 2:24, death entered the world through the devil's envy.[119] A more detailed elaboration of this theme is found in the *Life of Adam and Eve* where the devil envies and hates Adam and Eve and tries to destroy them (*L.A.E.* 9–17). The devil furiously persecutes those who escape his dominion in *Joseph and Aseneth* (12:9–10) and in the *Testament of Job* (4:4). The will to destroy humanity is also a characteristic of the forces of evil in some myths explaining the origin of evil in the world (*Jub.* 10:5). In the *Testaments of the Twelve Patriarchs* the devil, called Beliar, causes such vices as sexual promiscuity (*T. Reuben* 4:7–11; 6:3; *T. Sim.* 5:3; *T. Dan* 5:6), anger (*T. Dan* 1:7–8; 4:7–5:1; *T. Gad* 4:7), two-facedness (*T. Asher* 3:2) and falsehood (*T. Dan* 3:6; 4:7). In the Damascus Document, the three nets of Belial are fornication, wealth and the defilement of the temple (CD 4:17). According to *Mart. Isa.* 2:4–6, the devil is the source of apostasy, magic, divination, fornication, adultery, and the persecution of the righteous. *T. Sol.* 6:1–4 says that the devil causes wars, tyranny, demon worship, jealousy and murders.

Just as the actitivities of the devil may vary, those groups who are demonized also vary. *Jub.* 15:33 says that "all the sons of Beliar will leave their sons without circumcising just as they were born." In *T. Dan* 5:6 Satan is called the prince of those sons of Dan who will abandon the Lord in the last days; they are described as "committing the revolting acts of the gentiles and chasing after wives of lawless men." The sons of Belial are mentioned as the opponents of the sons of light in some writings of the Qumran community that speak of the eschatological battle (1QM passim); according to 4Q174 1:8, these sons of Belial are those who make the sons of light to fall. Paul calls those he sees as false apostles the servants of Satan (2 Cor 11:13–15). According to 1 John 3:8–10, everyone who commits a

---

death, because the devil reappears on the stage as he enters Judas Iscariot, who begins to seek an opportunity to betray Jesus (22:3–6). See Pagels 1995, 90.

[118] See Riley 1999, 246–249.

[119] Cf. Lindars 329; Barrett 349. This text is often connected also to Paul's words in Rom 5:12.

sin is of the devil; it is probable that the writer has especially in mind those who are called antichrists and who have left the community of the writer (2:18–19).[120] In Revelation, the Jewish opponents of the writer are called a synagogue of Satan (Rev 2:9; 3:9).

It is remarkable that in John the activity of the devil concentrates solely on the death of Jesus. In addition to the passages mentioning the ruler of this world (12:31; 14:30; 16:11), the devil is mentioned in connection with Judas Iscariot who assists in bringing Jesus to death by betraying him (6:70; 13:2, 27) and the Jews who seek Jesus' life (8:44). John has focused all dualistic cosmology on Jesus' death, which explains why he also presents the devil pointedly as a murderer, a depiction stemming from conventional imagery where the will to destroy was often attached to the devil.[121] But the Johannine view also means a significant intensification of the role of the devil as the murderer who in a cosmic drama defends his dominion over the world and thus tries to destroy Jesus. It seems that John has connected both Judas and the Jews to the devil in particular because they have played a crucial role in the events leading to Jesus' death. The believing Jews are described as being of the devil in John 8:44 because Jesus charges that also they take part in the battle against God's envoy by fulfilling the murderous intentions of their father.[122]

---

[120] Cf. von Wahlde 2001, 439.

[121] There is no need to think that the words "a murderer from the beginning" would describe Cain, the first murderer in Gen 4, rather than the devil. For this possibility, see Wellhausen 43; Dahl 1964, 76–79; Reim 1984, 619–624. They suggest that the text originally referred to Cain, because the words "you are of the father, the devil" (ὑμεῖς ἐκ τοῦ πατρὸς τοῦ διαβόλου ἐστέ) are grammatically problematic. It is often claimed that the text as it now stands should be read "you are of the father of the devil," an interpretation put forward by some gnostic interpreters (for these interpretations, see Dahl 1964, 76; Pagels 1973, 100–102). Instead of reading the text in this way, Dahl and Reim correct the text and propose that the original reading was "you are of Cain's father, the devil." But it is not clear whether the words ἐκ τοῦ πατρὸς τοῦ διαβόλου are as problematic as a standard grammar claims. Cf. Blass/Debrunner/Rehkopf 1984 § 268.5; Bultmann 241. τοῦ διαβόλου is best explained as an apposition to τοῦ πατρός, and appositions may be used quite freely in Greek: the article is sometimes used and sometimes not, and the apposition may precede or follow its main word (Mayser 1934, 103). The repetition of articles in connection with appositions is sometimes taken as a characteristic of John's style (Radermacher 1925, 107–108, 111). Such passages as John 6:1, 27, 7:2; 18:1, 17 show that the text may well be translated "you are of the father, the devil."

[122] Cf. Reinhartz (1992, 71–98) who has noted that the roles of the Jews and the devil intermingle in John 10:1–5; in the cosmological tale the devil is "the thief" of the parable who "kills and destroys," while the Jews do his work at the level of the historical tale.

The above discussion has shown how deeply Jesus' words "your are of the father, the devil" are embedded in an apocalyptic view of the world. As Urban C. von Wahlde has suggested, references to the devil and his allies are often made in apocalyptic polemic on a quite general level; polemic is not necessarily levelled at any specific group of opponents but its purpose is a general exhortation of an author's followers.[123] I concur with von Wahlde that in John a more specific group is intended. But I part company with von Wahlde when he claims that this group is those "who rejected Jesus during his ministry and who oppose the beliefs of the Johannine community." For von Wahlde, John 8:44

> simply restates the basic conviction that, because his opponents do not accept what he has to say, they are wrong. . . . The reader would certainly understand that the writer recognized the other group as an opponent and was accusing them of doing evil. They would also recognize that the argument had no more hostility to it than any other case in apocalyptic polemic.[124]

But the Jews are not just presented as opponents on a general level and connected to the devil in an unspecified way in John 8:44. Rather, they are presented as being of the devil, because they seek to kill Jesus. John here joins a well known tendency evident also in other early Christian sources, most notably in passion narratives, according to which Jesus' Jewish opponents rather than Roman officials are charged with Jesus' death. John connects this charge to his apocalyptic view of the world, in light of which he focused the cosmic battle between Jesus and the devil on Jesus' death. From John's narrative point of view, the reason why the Jews are on an equal footing with the devil has to do with the crucial moment of salvation history that now belongs to the past of the storytime. Just as Jesus' victory over the ruler of this world is a unique event for John and his readers, so also is the role of those who sided with the devil in the fight against Jesus. As the children of the devil, the Jews are not just symbolic representatives of the unbelief of the world.[125]

It is possible to interpret John's reference to the devil and the Jews not only as an expression of an underlying apocalyptic worldview, but also as a reflection of the social situation of the Johannine

---

[123] Von Wahlde 2001, 439.
[124] Von Wahlde 2001, 442.
[125] Pace Bultmann 240; Gräßer 1973a, 66; 1973b, 79–80.

Christians. It is not an accident that the increasing role of the devil in writings stemming from the Second Temple Period coincides with the emergence of different sectarian groups among Judaism.[126] The members of these groups made a distinction between ethnic and moral identity, and regarded only themselves as the true and obedient Israel. Their fellow Jews not sharing their convictions were associated with the devil; so it is not surprising that most references to the devil's companions deal with Jews who did not match the ideals of various writers.[127] As von Wahlde has noted, the purpose of this kind of polemic is "to exhort and to strengthen the author's followers rather than to convert others."[128] This means that the references to the devil serve the need of sectarian groups to define themselves in relation to the outside world. This need is most probably in the background of John's dualistic views as well.

In the earlier chapters I have tried to show that John's references to some basic matters of Jewish identity probably reflect a break that had occurred between the Johannine group and other Jews. Earlier in this chapter I suggested that the appearance of the believing Jews in John's narrative may echo, despite this break, that the Johannine Christians still related to the Jews in their surroundings in a variety of ways, not just negatively. In this kind of context, dualistic imagery serves the strivings of the Johannine community to clearer self-understanding and separation from Jews who did not share their views on Jesus. This imagery intensifies their alienation from other Jews by lifting their conflict with them to a cosmological level. The Jews, hostile and believing alike, are presented as fulfilling the desires of their father, a murderer from the beginning, which strongly supports the withdrawal from their company.

The Johannine dualism can be taken as an expression of a symbolic universe that clearly defines the border between the believers and the outside world. I still want to emphasize that this symbolic universe should not be taken as a direct reflection of John's social reality in a sense that there were no longer contacts between the

---

[126] For this development, see Pagels 1991, 105–28, esp. p. 108; 1995, 35–62.

[127] An exception is found in *Joseph and Aseneth*, where the devil is presented as the father of the Egyptian gods (12:9).

[128] Von Wahlde 2001, 441. Von Wahlde here argues convincingly against Motyer (1997, 197–199) who says that the polemic in John 8 is intended to convert the Jews and save them.

Jews and the Johannine group. I do not even think that the sharp
dualism in John indicates that John would deny a possibility of salvation to those whom he labels as the children of the devil.[129] There
are passages in the gospel that speak for a genuine hope that all,
including the Jews who are presented as the unbelievers *par excellence*
in the story, will finally know Jesus and will be driven to him (8:28;
12:32). But in the gospel as whole, these hopeful views remain in
the shadow of a dualistic distinction between the believers and the
Jews. I take this distinction to suggest that by the time of the writing
of the gospel the author no longer had in sight a situation where those
who remained in the synagogue would join the Johannine believers.
Rather, the sharp dualism in John may reflect bitter disappointment
caused by a growing realization of how a great majority of the Jews
in Johannine surroundings refused to accept Jesus as the fulfilment
of Jewish tradition. Dualistic polemic in John is not written with the
outsiders in mind but tries to confirm the insiders who are faced
with the world's rejection; this polemic aims at justifying the decision to turn their backs on central aspects of Jewish traditions. Social
contacts of the Johannine Christians with other Jews perhaps never
ceased, but the borders were drawn in the minds of people. The
Johannine group was already emerging as an identifiable group of
its own, separated from other Jews by its exclusive views on Jesus
that caused them to cease the observance of basic matters of Jewish
identity. The evangelist contributed to this development by putting
his story of Jesus in a context of a cosmic battle and thus created
an imaginary universe where the sons of light and the sons of darkness are much more clearly distinct from each others than they ever
were in real life.

John 8:44 and Christian anti-Judaism

The discussion above has suggested that John's dualism stems from
contemporary apocalyptic views of the world, but I also have shown
how John has developed these dualistic ideas in the light of faith in
Jesus. I think this development shows that we can no longer speak

---

[129] Pace Becker 354: "Während im allgemeinen der Gesandte des Vaters nach
E für alle Menchen die prinzipielle Ermöglichung zum Glauben und damit zur
Rettung bringt (Joh 3; 6), wird das Judentum, von dieser Allgemeinheit nach Joh
8 ausgeschlossen; es ist vielmehr vorab und nicht revidierbar dem Teufel zugeordnet."

of totally intra-Jewish polemic in the case of John. Many passages in John reflect a detachment from basics of Jewishness, and this is apparent also in John's use of dualistic imagery. In apocalyptic polemic not only are some more general moral vices frequently seen as caused by the devil, but the alliance with the devil is also quite often connected to what writers see as erroneous views on central aspects of Jewishness. Hence laxity in the observation of circumcision (*Jub.* 15:33), the defilement of the temple (CD 4:17), apostasy (*Mart. Isa.* 2:4), demon worship and the wickedness of priests (*T. Sol.* 6:4) and the lifestyle of the gentiles (*T. Dan.* 5:6) are among the characteristic of those led by the devil. This is quite in line with the emergence of sectarian groups that were distinguished from other Jews in the society by strict views on a number of central aspects of Jewish identity.[130]

John assesses all aspects of Jewishness exclusively in the light of his faith in Jesus, and this faith also defines John's dualism so that it is solely the response to Jesus that marks the dividing line between good and evil. Rosemary Radford Ruether has claimed that the difference between prophetic self-criticism and anti-Judaism

> lies in the relation of the critic to the covenant and the Torah of Israel. . . . At the point where the Church regarded the covenant with Abraham as superseded by a New Covenant in Jesus, requiring modes of faithfulness that no longer required adherence to the Torah as the 'way' to the future promise, the Church became anti-Judaic.[131]

I believe some seeds for later development of Christian anti-Judaism are sown in John 8:31–59 where John connects his conviction that Jesus supersedes Abraham to a dualistic framework according to which people are divided to God's and the devil's children. Jesus' polemical statement in 8:44 is levelled in its immediate narrative context at the believing Jews, which has the effect of obliterating the distinctive characteristics of different Jewish groups and putting them all on the same level with the devil.

Attempts to interpret John 8:44 as just another variation of prophetic criticism in the Hebrew Bible or in the light of standard conventions of ancient polemic cannot totally do away the shocking potential of John's polemic against the Jews. Craig A. Evans compares some passages in the New Testament (e.g. John 8:42–47) to prophetic

---

[130] For a more complete development of this theme, see the following chapter.
[131] Ruether 1979, 235–236.

criticism found in the Hebrew Bible and concludes: "There are no statements in the New Testament that approximate these angry expressions."[132] In a similar vein, Luke T. Johnson says:

> By the measure of Hellenistic conventions, and certainly by the measure of contemporary Jewish polemic, the NT's slander against fellow Jews is remarkably mild.[133]

Although these comparisons are helpful in putting the NT's polemic in a larger literary context, they do this primarily on the level of rhetorics, which may conceal some obvious differences in worldviews between writings containing similar kinds of polemical expressions. Apocalyptic polemic represented by 1QS, the *Testaments of the Twelve Patriarchs* and John sees the world divided in dualistic realms, which quite evidently makes this polemic different from anything said in the Hebrew Bible—or anything said by Josephus and Philo who do not see the world in dualistic terms and do not engage in demonizing their opponents although they otherwise repeatedly launch virulent verbal attacks against them. There may be a significant difference also between the apocalyptic polemic found in John and the polemics of Hellenistic philosophical schools. Johnson does not treat in detail with John 8:44 but he seems to have especially this passage in mind as he writes:

> If Socrates was suspect because of his 'demon' and sophists are 'evil-spirited' and the brothers of Joseph are driven by evil-spirits, and all dwellers on earth have evil spirits and the sons of the pit are children of Belial, should we be surprised to find that Samaritans have demons, or that Jesus has a demon, or that his opponents have the devil as their father, or that when he betrays Jesus, Judas is said to have Satan enter his heart?[134]

---

[132] Evans 1993, 6. Evans sees the shift from the in-house criticism represented by the prophets to "bludgeoning" of outsiders to have taken place only after the New Testament writings were written. Thoma (1978, 240) also takes John 8:44 as a piece of inner-Jewish polemic. He ridicules the claim that some portions of the NT are anti-Jewish by saying that in that case the Hebrew Bible is even more anti-Jewish. Thoma is followed by Pedersen 1999, 191 n. 68.

[133] Johnson 1989, 441. Cf. also Dunn 2001, 58: "The 'diabolizing' of 'the Jews' in John 8 . . . was evidently a standard topos in the ancient Jewish/Christian rhetoric of vilification."

[134] Johnson 1989, 440–441. For criticism of Johnson, see Pagels 1995, 84: "But philosophers did not engage, as Matthew does here, in *demonic* vilification of their opponents" (italics original)." I think that Pagels' word apply much better to John, because John demonizes his opponents much more clearly than Matthew.

But Albert I. Baumgarten has recently suggested that Jewish sectarian groups and such Greco-Roman voluntary associations as philosophical schools should not be put on the same level as sociological phenomena. Baumgarten speaks of "the greater intensity of Jewish sectarian life" and says that "none of the real Graeco-Roman groups (as opposed to utopias) were marked by such exclusivity" as Jewish sects.[135] A part of this difference may be a dualistic worldview that many—but not all—Jewish sects had. Dualism may well be another side of social exclusivism, and so in exclusive circles that were attracted by dualism the same polemical expressions, which may be taken as more or less individual rhetorical slanders in some other contexts, have a great potential in demarcating boundaries between the group in question and outside society. John 8:44 functions in this way by emphasizing the difference between the Johannine Christians and Jews who did not share their faith.

It cannot be assessed whether some polemical statements are "milder" or "angrier" than some others merely on the basis of how rhetorically skillful and richly colored these statements are. A significant part of the damaging potential of John's view of the devil is the plainness of this view.[136] John concentrates the activities of the devil upon Jesus' death, and the same concentration characterizes the Jews as the children of the devil; in this sense John contributed to the development that concentrated evil in Christian writings more and more on the Jews who rejected Jesus.[137] As Stephen G. Wilson notes, the fact that John lifts the conflict between Jesus and the Jews to a cosmological level does not mitigate John's view of the Jews but "compounds the anti-Judaism and pushes it in a disastrous direction."[138]

---

[135] Baumgarten 1998, 93–111, esp. pp. 102 and 105.

[136] Cf. Limbeck 1974, 367: "Die Bedeutung der johanneischen Schriften für den christlichen Teufelsglauben ergibt sich weniger aus der Vielfalt als aus der Eindeutigkeit ihrer satanologischen Aussagen."

[137] Cf. Baumbach 1992, 40: "Somit stellt das Joh innerhalb des Neuen Testaments den Höhepunkt einer Entwicklung dar, die mit dem ältesten Paulusbrief (vgl. 1 Thess 2,15f) begann und bei den Synoptikern von Markus bis hin zu Lukas zunahm, so daß die größten Berührungen an diesem Punkt zwischen dem lukanischen und dem johanneischen Schrifttum zu beobachten sind. Auf diese Weise erfolgte zunehmend eine Konzentration des Bösen auf die christliche Heilsbotschaft mehrheitliche ablehnende jüdische Volk, das zum Typus des Unglaubens und des Feindes des Evangeliums wurde and darum mit den Satan als 'dem Feind' und 'dem Bösen' in direkte Beziehung gesetzt wurde."

[138] Wilson 1995, 334 n. 165; Cf. also Becker 354: "So wird aus der bitteren Erfahrung mit dem Judentum und aus tendenziell antijüdischer Haltung ein positioneller Antijudaismus."

John 8:44 joins the charge that the Jews are of the devil to the charge that they murdered Jesus. This has given a strong impetus to the growth of anti-Jewish Christian tradition where these two charges had a prominent role. John cannot be kept completely apart from this sad and far-reaching development, even though the evangelist and his community could in no way anticipate the coming horrors of history.

CHAPTER SEVEN

SYNTHESIS:
THE JOHANNINE CHRISTIANS, THE
JEWS AND JEWISHNESS

I have already drawn together the main conclusions of each chapter and I do not repeat these results in detail here. In this synthesis I do not only summarize my earlier findings but develop them
further in order to find a proper way to assess John's relationship
to Jews and Jewishness. First, I describe what I see as a common
thread in the passages that deal with basics of Jewish identity: Jesus'
ambivalent attitude to these matters. I think it is probable that this
ambivalence reflects the ambivalence of the Johannine group itself.
Thus, the question emerges concerning how we should understand
the relationship of this group to different Jewish groups of the time.
I suggest that a comparison of John with the Dead Sea Scrolls clearly
shows how differently the Johannine community and the Qumran
community understood some basics of Jewishness. I also propose that
the sweeping use of the term οἱ Ἰουδαῖοι in John is a main sign of
this difference; this term is closely related to John's ambivalent attitude to Jewishness. In the conclusion of this book, I offer some
remarks about anti-Judaism and John, although I am fully aware
that I do not have any final answers as to how we should deal with
this dark side of our Christian heritage to the growth of which John's
views of the Jews have contributed.

7.1. John's Ambivalent Relationship to Jewishness

In the second chapter of this book I have claimed that what John
says of the Jews and Jewishness is not a response to hostile actions
of a Jewish establishment in John's surroundings. This view still pre-
vails today, but it is based to a great extent on an outdated view of
the power and influence of the early rabbinic movement. It is claimed
that rabbis emerged as new leaders of Jewish communities in the
turbulent years following the destruction of the Jerusalem temple in

70 C.E. According to this often repeated consensus, the rabbis defined what it meant to be a Jew in a new way. They no longer tolerated such groups as the Johannine Christians and so they began to harass these groups which finally led to the expulsion of these groups from the synagogue. This interpretation says that the hostile policy of the rabbis explains why the Johannine Christians became alienated from other Jews. The parting of the ways between the Johannine group and the Jews is understood as the result of an identity crisis that the Jewish groups were faced with. In my detailed criticism of this view, I have shown how little evidence there is for this view both in rabbinic and early Christian sources. Therefore, I suggest that we should not look for some external reasons that could explain John's presentation of Jewishness. While some scholars may admit that John, at times, reflects an outsider's perspective on basic Jewish beliefs and practices, they often rationalize this perspective by referring to the persecution of the Johannine Christians at the hands of their Jewish opponents. I suggest, however, that the Johannine Christians themselves interpreted their faith in Jesus in such a way that it led them on a collision course with basic matters of Jewishness. The passages dealing with central matters of Jewish identity show how ambivalent is John's relationship to these matters.

The portrayal of the Johannine Jesus is a prime example of the ambivalence of John's presentation of Jewishness. Jesus is pointedly presented as a Jew in the gospel, he is even the Messiah of the Jews. As a Jew, Jesus shows the superiority of the Jews over the Samaritans by stating, "we know what we worship, for salvation is from the Jews" (4:22). The Johannine Jesus stands in the best Jewish traditions when he furiously attacks the ongoing defilement of the temple (John 2). He also appeals to such representative figures of Jewish tradition as Moses and Abraham when arguing against his opponents. He says that Moses has written of him and Abraham has seen his day and so presents himself as the fulfilment of past promises.

I have tried to show in my analyses that John's references to these central aspects of Jewishness not only show continuity but a significant amount of discontinuity as well. In John 2, Jesus' strivings for the purity of the cult soon fade away from the picture and his body is presented as the replacement of the material temple. From John's point of view, the defilement of the material temple at the hands of Jesus' contemporaries justifies this replacement. In John 4, Jesus' words to the Samaritan woman suggest that he does not aim to solve the age-long controversy concerning the right place of worship. His words rather suggest that he is speaking from the point of view of a new group distinct from both the Samaritans and the Jews, a group whose 'true worship' supersedes earlier forms of worship. In this context, Jesus' words "salvation is from the Jews" add irony to the story, showing how the salvation Jesus offers is received by non-Jews while the Jews reject the Messiah who comes from their midst.

Jesus the Jew also violates Jewish Sabbath regulations and does this on purpose to show that he is equal to God, who does not rest on the Sabbath. The whole story in John 5:1–18 is told in such a way that it is no surprise to the readers that Jesus broke the Sabbath. Jesus' liberal attitude to the Sabbath is taken for granted and developed into a christological argument which shows that the writer is not interested in details connected to literal observance of the Sabbath. Thus when the Johannine Jesus later returns to his healing on the Sabbath in John 7:19–24, he does not attempt to show that what he did on the Sabbath was not against the law; the reference to circumcision on the Sabbath rather indicates, for him, that even the Jews do not keep the law in all instances. Jesus sees here a discrepancy between two central obligations of the law, circumcision on the eighth day and the Sabbath, and uses this discrepancy to undermine his opponents' appeal to the law. I think this implies that these two basic aspects of Jewish identity are viewed from the standpoint of an outsider.

It is not only continuity but also contrast that characterizes Jesus' relationship with Moses and Abraham. In John 5:37, the Johannine Jesus makes an implicit allusion to the revelation Moses received at Sinai which was quite commonly seen as a foundation of Jewish identity; Jesus makes it clear, however, that the revelation at Sinai is of no significance unless his opponents believe in him. In John 6, Jesus as the true bread of life is contrasted with the manna given by Moses. It is likely that the manna has a close relationship with the law here which makes this contrast all the more significant. The manna is presented as unable to give life, which highlights the great difference between it and Jesus as the giver of life. From the Johannine point of view, Abraham is dead, while Jesus' followers will never die (John 8). While Moses and Abraham have positive functions in John as Jesus' witnesses, Jesus' superiority over these figures is also made clear.

I have suggested in earlier chapters that we should not tone down some obvious tensions in John's presentation of Jewishness. These tensions are significant because they may be suggestive of a discrepancy between the symbolic universe of the Johannine Christians and their situation in the real world. In this sense, Jesus' ambivalent attitude to such integral matters of Jewishness as the temple, the Sabbath, circumcision, the revelation at Sinai, Moses, the law and Abraham may well reflect the ambivalent stance of the Johannine Christians on these matters. The Johannine Christians assessed various aspects of Jewishness exclusively in light of their faith in Jesus which had the effect of obliterating the relevance of these matters as fundamentals of Jewish identity. These matters no longer defined the identity of the Johannine Christians, but they created their identity at least partly in confrontation with the matters that were self-evident parts of Jewishness, both for many Jews and outsiders as well.

There is enough evidence to suggest that the Johannine Christians no longer regarded such central Jewish practices as Sabbath observance or circumcision as integral to their identity. This makes it likely that the break between the Johannine Jesus and basic matters of Jewish identity reflects a break that had taken place between the Johannine community and Jews who based their identity on these matters. My reading of John 8, where Jesus denounces Jews who believe in him and portrays them as the children of the devil, suggests that this break may not have been as complete as the Johannine writer would have hoped for. As a result of this, the evangelist did away with a clear distinction between different Jewish groups, which no doubt intensified the separation of those who acknowledged his authority from other Jewish groups. Therefore, John's sharp dualism may be taken as both a result of the growing alienation of the Johannine group from its surrounding society and as an attempt to intensify this alienation.

It is important to recognize the interplay between features showing both continuity and discontinuity in John's portrayal of Jewishness. These conflicting features may give us an opportunity to get a glimpse of some Christians who had their roots deep in Jewish traditions, but who interpreted their faith in Jesus in such a way that they eventually became alienated from these roots. Conflicting views on basic matters of Jewishness may be taken as an expression of a complex symbolic universe of people who lived in a situation where their former identity, based on these matters, was changing. Jesus' character can be seen as a self-expression of a community which was willing to see itself as the culmination of Jewish tradition although it had turned away from central aspects of this tradition. In the symbolic universe of the Johannine Christians, Jesus the Jew and the Messiah formed a bridge between their Jewish heritage and their actual alienation from Jewish identity.

I think continuity and discontinuity with the past also characterizes how different Jewish traditions are developed in John. That John largely draws from diverse Jewish traditions and develops them further is nothing new in light of the studies done during recent decades. The analyses in this book have confirmed that many Johannine ideas are based on the Hebrew Bible and the traditions nurtured by it; but the gospel also shows familiarity with ideas that do not directly stem from the scriptures but are derived from traditions and interpretations current among different Jewish groups.[1] There is no precedent for the Johannine dualism in the Hebrew Bible, for example, but John draws on dualistic views which developed among some Jewish groups in the last two centuries B.C.E. The Johannine view of Moses and the manna is based on the previous and contemporary elaboration of scriptural traditions rather than on the exposition of the scriptures. John also picks up a tradition which denied that God rests on the Sabbath, and uses this tradition when arguing that Jesus' Sabbath breakings show that he is equal to God. John knows a practice of performing circumcision even on the Sabbath, a practice that has no scriptural foundation but that was common in the first century C.E. This kind of knowledge and reinterpretation of Jewish tradition reinforces the view that the fourth gospel originates from a Jewish world, although it simultaneously portrays a breach with that world. Therefore, even though I support the admissions of tensions in John's view of Jewishness, I think there is no return to the view that prevailed in the first decades of the 20th century when John was mainly regarded as a product of the non-Jewish, Hellenistic world.

Faith in Jesus is the sole revelation of God in John. This means that many Jewish traditions have gone through such a thorough

---

[1] See, however, M. Davies 1992, 312: "Of the Jewish practices referred to in the Gospel, most could have been known from a reading of Scripture or the synoptics, but one suggests independent knowledge: circumcision taking precedence over the Sabbath." Davies speaks here of Jewish practices only, but if we take into account various Jewish traditions used in the gospel, it is clear that the gospel contains independent information about contemporary Jewish beliefs that is not derived only from the Scriptures or the synoptics.

reinterpretation that they have been deprived of the significance they once had in their original context. Wayne A. Meeks has suggested that, while John applies to Jesus a common Jewish view that described Moses as the agent of God, he also forces this notion

> to the breaking point of Jewish consciousness—at least of the Jews *he* had in mind. His use of Jewish tradition is a kind of *reductio ad absurdum*; the result in Jewish ears was blasphemy.[2]

This also describes well John's use of other motifs derived from diverse Jewish traditions so that "originally Jewish elements . . . have received a later, non-Jewish form through interpretation."[3] The knowledge and use of various Jewish traditions in John in no way excludes the conclusion that these traditions are, more often than not, used to underscore the faith in Jesus as a superior alternative to Jewish beliefs and practices. This shows how originally Jewish elements may well have contributed to the emergence of an identity that was not based on central matters of Jewishness but was, at least at some points, created in conscious opposition to them.

Occasionally John betrays poor knowledge of current Jewish practices and realities in first century Palestine. For example, John's description of the conditions in the temple is unrealistic. This description shows that the narrator and the readers were informed enough that they knew how disgraceful it would have been if someone had brought quadrupeds into the temple; but they seem to know the temple cult only as a thing from past which is in line with how they presuppose its cessation after the destruction of the temple. The Johannine Jesus also shares the stereotyped Jewish attitude that the Samaritans were syncretists, a view that does not do justice to the nature of first century Samaritanism. The view that Jesus' opponents were seeking his life because of his Sabbath healing is also based on a stereotype John shares with some other early Christian writings, since more lenient punishments were quite commonly allowed for these transgressions. These kinds of stereotypes are fully understandable as a reflection of a situation where the Johannine Christians formulated anew their relationship to basic matters of Jewishness; stereotyped descriptions of Jewish beliefs and practices contributed to their self-understanding which was no longer based on these beliefs and practices.

---

[2] Meeks 1975, 173.
[3] Barrett 1975, 61.

My readings of John's passages dealing with central aspects of Jewishness make it possible to work out in what sense John is a Jewish text and in what sense it is not. John's symbolic universe is Jewish in so far as it is based on the rendering of diverse Jewish traditions, and so John clearly originates from the multiform Judaism of the first century. But John's symbolic universe is, at the same time, non-Jewish in the sense that matters that were essential parts of Jewish identity are no longer relevant to the Johannine Christians' formulations of their faith in Jesus in relation to these matters. The gospel is a witness to the development that was taking place among the Johannine Christians; these Christians interpreted their faith in Jesus so exclusively that "Jesus finally became a black hole into which all their Judaism disappeared"—to use Lloyd Gaston's words.[4]

7.2. *John as a Sectarian Jewish Writing?*

The way I have reconstructed the Johannine symbolic universe calls forth a question concerning the relation of this symbolic universe to the symbolic universes of other contemporary Jewish groups. Is there anything unique in the way the Johannine group reinterpreted the Jewish traditions it inherited? Did not similar reinterpretations take place among other Jewish groups as well? The Johannine community has repeatedly been understood in recent decades as another Jewish group among many flourishing in the first century. Many scholars have described the Johannine community as a Jewish sect not dissimilar from the Qumran sect.[5] In the following, I refer to some examples that are enough to suggest that there is a significant difference between the symbolic universe of the Qumran sect and the Johannine group.[6] My results are in line with two recent comparisons of the Qumran writings to some New Testament writings.[7]

---

[4] Gaston 1993, 122.

[5] A classic article that contributed to the understanding of the Johannine community as a sect is Meeks 1972. Esler (1994, 70–91) has described both the Johannine community and the Qumran group as 'introversionist sects.' For a discussion of applicability of the concept of 'sect' to describe emerging early Christian groups, see Luomanen 2002, 107–130.

[6] I speak in the following of the Qumran sect, but not in a strictly defined, sociological sense. The Qumran group has often been understood as a Jewish sect, but there are problems in the use of this term if it is not clearly defined. For full discussion, see Jokiranta 2001, 223–239.

[7] Destro & Pesce (2001, 201–227) compare the religious systems in John and in

The interpretation of temple traditions in the Qumran scrolls shows both similarity with and dissimilarity from the way Jesus' relationship to the temple is presented in John. It should be noted immediately that we do not have only one attitude to the temple in the scrolls, but several.[8] It is debated how severe a breach with the Jerusalem temple the Damascus Document presupposes. The key passage is CD 6:11–14 which could be interpreted as forbidding the members of the sect to enter the defiled temple.[9] According to an alternative interpretation, the passage attacks the current defilement of the temple but suggests that "those who possess the (true) law need not abandon it."[10] This interpretation would be in accordance with how the laws discussed elsewhere in the document seem to presuppose participation in the cult in Jerusalem (e.g., 6:17–18; 11:17–12:2).[11]

Be that as it may, in the case of CD, a clearer break from the temple is evident in the Community Rule where the community is seen as a substitute for the Jerusalem temple.[12] It would be appealing to take this view as a close parallel to the Johannine view of Jesus as the replacement for the Jerusalem temple, but there are marked differences between these views. In 1 QS, the view that the community is the substitute for the material temple does not lead to the abandonment of temple traditions, but, on the contrary, to their application to the community. The laws concerning ritual purity, which were earlier connected to the temple, are now connected to the life of the community in an even stricter form.[13]

Temple traditions continued to attract the members of the sect also in other ways. Many writings show that the functions connected with the priests had an important role in the community.[14] Some scrolls show that hopes for the restoration of the cult and the com-

---

1QS, and my conclusions support their views. In the same volume, Räisänen (2001, 173–200) compares Paul's and Qumran's Judaisms, and concludes that "there is an enormous difference between Qumran and Paul on the practical level" (p. 199).

[8] This is emphasized especially by P. R. Davies 2000, 40–43.

[9] Thus Schiffman 1999, 271.

[10] Thus P. R. Davies 2000, 35. For detailed arguments, see P. R. Davies 1996, 52ff.

[11] P. R. Davies 2000, 34.

[12] Schiffman 1999, 272–274; P. R. Davies 2000, 39. The material found in the Qumran cave 4 suggests that CD and 1QS may relate to each other at some pre-redactional level. It is not self-evident that the different rules in these two documents point to different social groups behind them. Cf. Metso 2000, 85–93.

[13] E. P. Sanders 1992, 352–360; P. R. Davies 2000, 39.

[14] García Martínez 1999, 303–319.

ing of the new temple were alive among the members of the sect
(1QM; 11QT). Even though it is not likely that the sect developed
a sacrificial cult of its own, some scrolls suggest that sacrificial laws
were studied, at least by some segments of the community.[15] Part of
the discussions of extreme purity laws and the description of the
future temple may contain unrealistic features, but they nevertheless
exemplify how great a symbolic role the temple had in the minds
of the Qumran group even in a situation where its connection to
Jerusalem was endangered or even broken. In this way, the scrolls
anticipated the emergence of different forms of post-70 Judaism that
continued to lean on temple traditions, as rabbinic literature and
archaeological remains in the Diaspora indicate.

The role of the temple is quite different in John. The Johannine
writer portrays the conditions in the temple in an exaggerated way
to present Jesus as a reformer of the corrupted cult. But while the
Qumran people build upon concrete cultic laws, the Johannine Jesus
is not interested in restoring the cult in Jerusalem. In John, Jesus'
body as the new temple replaces the material temple, and this replacement makes earlier traditions connected to the temple irrelevant. As
Adriana Destro and Mauro Pesce note, "in John there is no further
need for members' purity; nor for any priestly functions. The Temple
does not exist even in a metaphorical sense."[16] For the Qumran
group, the fact that they became separated from the temple and its
rituals in the real world did not mean a decrease in its value in
their symbolic universe. On the contrary, it can be argued that the
loss of the connection to the Jerusalem temple increased its symbolic
significance for them while the destruction of the temple opened a
way for the Johannine Christians to form a symbolic universe where
these kinds of symbols are only marginal.

A similar difference is discernible in how the Qumran sect and
the Johannine group relate to Moses and the law. Again, there are
some points in common. Both the Qumran community and the
Johannine group—and other early Christian groups as well—were
faced with a dilemma as to how to explain the connection between
Mosaic law and a later revelation that both of these groups thought
only they have.[17] Both groups emphasized the continuity with the

---

[15] Schiffman 1999, 274–276.
[16] Destro & Pesce 2001, 220.
[17] Cf. E. P. Sanders 1992, 378: "[The people at Qumran] do not explicitly explain

past. The Qumran people understood joining community as a "return"
to the covenant of Moses (1QS 5:8; CD 15:5–16:6). Furthermore, it
is probable that the community saw no distinction between its own
rules and the regulations of the Torah. The redactional process of
the Community Rule shows that scriptural quotations were inserted
into the document to show that the rules of the community have
scriptural authority.[18]

Continuity with the past is also emphasized in John where Moses
is presented as a witness for Jesus. But I have shown that the role
of Moses is much more complicated than this. Moses, his covenant,
and the law are stripped of any significance apart from this witnessing function which makes it understandable that Jesus' revelation clashes with that of Moses as the scriptural traditions are developed
further in John 6. There is no sign in the Qumran scrolls that the
members of the sect saw their relationship to the Mosaic inheritance
in antithetic terms. The role of the particular commandments in the
practical life of the communities shows most clearly the difference
between the two groups. I have demonstrated that John's references
to the Sabbath and circumcision indicate that the Johannine Christians
had ceased their literal observance. In the Qumran community such
basics of Jewishness as circumcision continued to be an important
part of the everyday life of the community (e.g., CD 16:6). The
Damascus Document speaks for a stricter observance of the Sabbath
than was usual among other Jews. Thus, social withdrawal from their
fellow Jews did not lead the members of the sect towards laxity in
regard to the common symbols of Jewish identity, but to their more
intensified observance. In this sense, the Qumran group is an example of how the Jewish sects of the time did not create completely
new symbolic worlds but held on in an extreme fashion to convictions common to all Jews.[19] Albert. I. Baumgarten has defined different Jewish sects at the end of the Second Temple Period as "variations

---

this: how the law could have been given to Moses and yet contain secrets that were
later revealed to the Zadokite priests. But, in their view, Israelites who did not seek
for and discover the secret revelations broke the law, and people who joined 'returned'
to it." See also Räisänen 2001, 199. Referring to Sanders, Räisänen says that the
Qumranites "were caught in a salvation-historical dilemma reminiscent of Paul's."

[18] See Metso 2000, 92–93.

[19] Thus Baumgarten 1997, 34. Cf. also E. P. Sanders 1992, 378–379: "Everything
about the sectarians requires the use of superlatives: the most pious, the most rigorous and legalistic, the most conscious of human failing, the most reliant on the
grace of God, the most radical, the most exclusive."

of the same theme;" despite differences between these sects there is also "fundamental similarity of different groups" in that they present "competing answers to the same sets of questions raised by the circumstances of their era."[20] The answers may vary greatly, which explains the antagonistic relations among different groups, but still the common denominator is the discussion around basics of Jewish identity. The Qumran group had particular views on the calendar, the temple, ritual purity, and the Sabbath legislation, and these views led to their separation from the body of other Jews, who had different views on *these* matters. In case of the Qumran sect, the social alienation from other Jews led to the more intense holding on to the principal pillars of common Jewish identity, but the Johannine Christians eclectically took some elements from their former Jewish identity, and created a new identity no longer based on these elements.

Despite the affinities between the Qumran community and the Johannine group, the symbolic universes of these two groups are strikingly different. After a complete comparison between John and 1QS, Adriana Destro and Mauro Pesce aptly describe the difference between these two writings:

> 1QS is a Jewish religious system because it maintains it is the true Israel that is preparing the future people of Israel on the purified land of Israel and because it preserves and reformulates all the main Jewish symbols and rituals. John, on the contrary, reflects a religious system that is not Jewish because it is autonomous from the point of view of the social group (it defines the identity of the members independently of the land of Israel and the concept of Israel), from the point of view of religious practices (it has a cult that leaves out of account the Temple and has its own autonomous system of expiation), and from the point of view of the vision of the world (it believes it possesses direct revelation of God that does not reveal the secrets of the law of Moses, but is simply a new and complete revelation).[21]

7.3. *Who Are the Johannine Jews?*

A significant way in which the Johannine symbolic universe differs from Jewish sectarian writings is the way the term οἱ Ἰουδαῖοι is used to describe Jesus' enemies. Even though Jewish writings are not

---

[20] Baumgarten 1997, 55–58.
[21] Destro & Pesce 2001, 227.

short of polemical attacks against outsiders, we do not have any
example of this kind of generalized use of language in other writings. Graham Harvey has concluded that the term יהודה, "Judah"
is used in the Dead Sea Scrolls as a self-designation of the Community
that sees itself as "the house of Judah" or as the Judaeans *par-excel-
lence*. But the term may also refer, in some instances, to the opponents of the community who are seen as "Princes of Judah."[22] This
double usage suggests that this term did not have a great role in
how the community marked itself off from the surrounding world.[23]
In John, however, the use of the term οἱ Ἰουδαῖοι serves to a great
extent this end, and its use is one of the main indicators that show
that the Johannine Christians were adopting a non-Jewish identity.

I already noted in the introduction to this study that attempts at
defining the meaning of the term οἱ Ἰουδαῖοι as referring only to
some particular Jewish group are not convincing. I concluded that
it is better not to define too rigidly the meaning of the word before
the passages dealing with the Jews and the matters of Jewish identity
in the gospel are analyzed. The analyses in my work suggest that οἱ
Ἰουδαῖοι in John are not just a specific group of Jewish authorities.

It is clear in many passages that the term οἱ Ἰουδαῖοι refers to
those among the Jews who are in an authoritative position and have
power. This is the case with such passages as John 9:1–41 where it
is used interchangeably with the word Pharisees, or the passion narrative where it is used for the chief priests. However, a closer scrutiny
of some passages where the term is connected to those who seem
to be the leaders of the Jews shows that the distinction between these
leaders and other Jews is not quite clear. In John 5:1–18, those who
are offended because of Jesus' Sabbath action and finally begin to
seek his life are presented as an authoritative group called simply
the Jews. But in John 7:19–24, Jesus returns to this previous incident

---

[22] Harvey 1996, 21–42, esp. p. 41.
[23] For this reason, I do not find appealing the suggestion made by Van Henten
2001, 117–118. Van Henten compares the anti-Judaism in early Christian writings
(especially in Revelation) to the polemics against outsiders in the Qumran scrolls
and concludes that the scrolls are anti-Jewish. But the scrolls, while sharing a similar kind of polemical language with early Christian literature, do not exhibit a
detachment from Jewish identity and do not use sweeping language to express this
detachment. Thus, I think that the scrolls are not anti-Jewish in the same sense
that some early Christian writings are. I fully share, however, van Henten's point
that writings stemming from a Jewish world can contain also anti-Jewish features.
Cf. my remarks on anti-Judaism below on pp. 238–242.

on the Sabbath, and his interlocutors are called the crowd (v. 20). Jesus' argumentation here makes sense only if those with whom he speaks are those who made the allegation in the first place, i.e., the Jews of the story in 5:1–18. The crowd in 7:20 is not to be strictly separated from these Jews, and not, additionally, from the Jews mentioned in 7:15.

It is noteworthy that Jesus argues in 7:20 about the Sabbath and circumcision with the crowd. This suggests that, from John's point of view, Jesus' controversy over the Sabbath does not concern a group of Jewish pietists alone, but more generally all those in whose religion the Sabbath and circumcision has a crucial role. This is why the Johannine Jesus accuses his opponents by saying, "No one of you keeps the law," and refers to the alleged inconsistency in the Jewish observance of the law. Jesus also elsewhere debates about the law with the crowd (John 6:25–40; 7:27, 40; 12:23–36), not only with the Jews or the Pharisees. These passages undo the claim of the Johannine Pharisees that the crowd do not know the law (7:49) and show that the controversy over the law is not restricted only to some group of religious experts among the Jews. This speaks against attempts to define οἱ Ἰουδαῖοι solely as experts on Mosaic law, distinct from the common people.[24]

The above conclusion is in line with the fact that convictions related to the essentials of Jewish identity are not the property of a single group in John. In John 5:31–47, Jesus' references to those who search the scriptures and who set their hope on Moses in vain are addressed to those Jews who were offended by his action on the Sabbath (5:16, 18). In John 6, it is the crowd in Galilee that brings up Moses' manna miracle; in 7:19–24, Jesus says to the crowd in Jerusalem that they have received the law and circumcision from Moses although they fail to keep the law; in John 9, the Pharisees define themselves as the disciples of Moses. These passages are not isolated from each other; for example, the way Moses and Jesus are contrasted is similar in John 6 and in John 9:27–29.

In some other passages, other groups hold to common Jewish convictions. In John 4, the Samaritan woman calls Jacob the father of the Samaritans, not Joseph who was a symbolic figure for Samaritan self-understanding. The appeal to Jacob suggests that this passage is

---

[24] Thus, however, most recently de Boer 2001, 277.

closely connected to John 8:31–59 where the believing Jews appeal
to Abraham, and where Jesus shows that he is greater than Abraham.
Both these passages are close to John 6:31 where the crowd mentions Moses' manna, which gives Jesus the opening to contrast his
revelation with the revelation of Moses. It is hardly convincing to
regard the appeals to Jacob, Moses or Abraham as characteristic of
each of these groups only. Rather, we have here different variations
of one and the same Johannine theme according to which Jesus is
greater than the founding fathers of Jewish religion. This shows that
these different groups are bunched together in a way that they lose
their distinctive characteristics.

Jesus' clash with his opponents in John is not over some esoteric
or marginal beliefs of a particular kind of Judaism, but over matters shared among many Jewish groups. Therefore, it is no surprise
that the narrator refers even to common Jewish festivals and customs as an outsider by emphasizing their Jewishness. This is another
token of John's alienation from Jewishness. John Ashton, with many
others, regards Jesus' conflict with the Jews in John as another Jewish
family row, but even he admits that "the Gospel's heavy-sounding
insistence on the Jewishness of Jewish feasts and customs" indicates

> the (increasing) disaffection of the Johannine group from the official reli-
> gion of the central Jewish party. . . . Even Greek converts, surely, would
> hardly need reminding that the Passover was a 'feast of the Jews.'[25]

But such festivals as the Passover or the feast of Tabernacles were
an established and self-evident part of Jewishness both in the land
of Israel and in the Diaspora, not an expression of "the official religion of the central Jewish party."[26] Rather than family disagreements,
we have here an expression of an identity that was not created on
the foundation of things shared by many Jews. As Alan Segal notes,
the use of the term οἱ Ἰουδαῖοι suggests that "the Johannine community has passed over the boundary between being Jewish and
Christian, which was not yet passed for the synoptics."[27]

Jack T. Sanders has utilized sociological conflict theory to explain
why Christianity tended to see the Jews as "the essential enemy" as

---

[25] Cf. Ashton 1991, 159.
[26] For these festivals in Judaism, see E. P. Sanders 1992, 119–145.
[27] Segal 1987, 31.

the conflict between Christianity and Judaism "became more rou-
tine." Sanders notes that conflicts often produce "an interest in unity
of the enemy." Thus John—and later parts of Acts as well—reflect
a situation where the Jews had become the essential opponents of
Christianity that "could hardly define itself without reference to this
enemy."[28] This "interest in unity of the enemy" very much explains
why the Johannine writer presents Jews in general as Jesus' opponents.
He tends to lump different Jewish groups together, for example, in
John 12:37–43 where he explains the reasons for unbelief without
making a distinction between the crowd and the Jews. The clearest
example of this generalizing tendency is John 8:31–59 where even
the believing Jews are counted among those who try to kill Jesus,
which shows that the line between distinctive Jewish groups is rather
fluid in John. This generalizing tendency may be most disturbing
from the point of view of our modern sensitivities, but we should
not try to conceal this feature of the gospel narrative. Whether we
like it or not, John is a significant step toward blurring fine distinctions between different Jewish groups and presenting the Jews in
general as Jesus' opponents and persecutors—though this generalizing tendency had already started before John.[29]

This kind of indiscriminate use of language is, of course, quite
illogical and unhistorical in a narrative whose characters are all Jews.[30]
But even though John is quite insensitive to these kinds of inconsis-
tencies, he is quite consistent in not calling any of those figures who
are models of Jesus' true followers—the blind man in John 9, Mary

---

[28] J. T. Sanders 1993, 127–128.

[29] Cf. Brown 1979, 41. Brown speaks of how the term οἱ Ἰουδαῖοι is used interchangeably with other terms in the gospel and says that "this interchangeability is
not to be interpreted benevolently as it is by those who wish to remove the term
'the Jews' from the Fourth Gospel by substituting 'Jewish authorities.'" Brown adds
in a note referring to 1 Thess 2:14–16: "This makes John guilty of offensive and
dangerous generalizing, but he was not the one who began the process." Brown
also resists all the attempts to tone down these features in the gospel: "It would be
incredible for a twentieth-century Christian to share or to justify the Johannine contention that 'the Jews' are the children of the devil, an affirmation which is placed
on the lips of Jesus (8:44); but I cannot see how it helps contemporary Jewish-
Christian relationships to disguise the fact that such an attitude once existed."

[30] This has recently been understood as one of the main reasons why the term
Ἰουδαῖοι should not be translated with the English word 'Jews' in modern Bible
translations. Cf. different articles in Kee & Borowsky 1998. But we would not only
have to retranslate but rewrite large parts of the New Testament, if we try to elim-
inate all that is historically untrue. Cf. Räisänen 2000, 16–17.

and Martha, Mary Magdalene and the disciples—a Jew.[31] This use
of language is anachronistic in the framework of Jesus' story in the
Palestine of the 30's, but it probably reflects quite well the symbolic
universe of the Johannine Christians who made a sharp distinction
between the true believers and the Jews.

There is nothing surprising in the prominent role of the Pharisees
and the chief priests in John. John only continues here a tendency
evident in the synoptic tradition, where the Pharisees emerge more
and more as Jesus' main opponents; both Matthew and Luke tend
to insert the Pharisees into more narrative settings than Mark.[32] The
chief priests and, to some extent, the Pharisees (Mark 3:6 and *par.*;
Mark. 12:13 and *par.*) play a crucial role in the events leading to
Jesus' death. The Synoptics also show some signs of a generalizing
tendency which pays little attention to distinctions among different
Jewish groups.[33] John continues to portray Jesus' life as a series of
struggles with prominent Jewish groups, but the fact that he, unlike
the synoptic writers, often chooses to use the term οἱ Ἰουδαῖοι when
speaking of these groups does not mean that the meaning of the
term would be confined to these groups alone. By using the term
οἱ Ἰουδαῖοι in the way he does, John generalizes the Jewish opposition to Jesus.[34]

It is only natural in a narrative focusing on Jesus' conflict with
the Jewish hierarchy residing in Judaea that the term οἱ Ἰουδαῖοι in
many cases seems to refer to those who, besides being authorities,
are also Judaeans.[35] It is, after all, one of the most obvious differences

[31] I think Dunn (2001, 57) fails to notice this when writes: "There are the Jews,
including those like Nicodemus and the blind man of chapter 9, who had to be persuaded to come and take their stand fully within the light of the revelation of Jesus."

[32] Cf. Saldarini 1992, 295–297.

[33] Cf. Schams 1998, p. 269 n. 813.

[34] Cf. Schams 1998, 268–269. Schams discusses why the Johannine author is
silent with regard to the scribes that figure prominently in the synoptics. She regards
as "conceivable that the author generalized the Jewish opposition to Jesus, because
it seemed of no importance to him to preserve distinctions between various groups.
Designations such as rulers (ἄρχοντες) and chief priests . . . are general terms and
do not indicate that the author was interested in, or knowledgeable about, differences
between groups within the Jewish leadership." To be sure, Schams also offers an
alternative explanation for the lack of references to the scribes in John, pp. 269–270.

[35] Cf. Schram 1974, 190: "The fact that IOUDAIOS is often used to refer to
Jews who live in Judea, since much of the action of the narrative takes place there,
does not mean that there is a clearly defined usage such that IOUDAIOS has the
sense 'Jews-who-live-in-Judea-in-contrast-to-those-who-live-elsewhere.' . . . There is a

between the synoptics and John that the latter tells of Jesus' several visits to Jerusalem thus locating much of Jesus' public life in a Judaean context. While the synoptics present many conflict stories taking place in Galilee, the only passage in John where Jesus comes into conflict with the Galileans is John 6—and, remarkably enough, in this Galilean setting his opponents are also called οἱ Ἰουδαῖοι.

The above discussion has shown that R. Alan Culpepper is right in noting that "the gospel does not attempt to distinguish and separate these groups; all are called Ἰουδαῖοι. They are one group in John."[36] This indiscriminate use of language shows that even in those instances where οἱ Ἰουδαῖοι could be understood as a specific group of Jewish leaders or Judaeans, the conflict between these groups and Jesus is raised to a new and more general level.[37] As Adele Reinhartz says, the various ways of using the term οἱ Ἰουδαῖοι in John tend

> to blur the fine distinctions and nuances and to generalize the meaning to its broadest possible referent, that is, the Jews as a nation defined by a set of religious beliefs, cultic and liturgical practices, and a sense of peoplehood.[38]

Or, in Stephen Wilson's words, "the term has shifted decisively from a local to a universal plane of meaning. *Hoi Ioudaioi* have become the Jews in general."[39] The general use of the term οἱ Ἰουδαῖοι suggests that the Johannine writer was well aware of his drift away from Jewishness no matter how greatly he tried to keep a connection to his Jewish past in his symbolical universe. John and his community no longer understood themselves in terms of Jewish identity and, consequently, chose to refer to Jews using the term covering the widest possible referent; they thus acknowledged that those things that were common to different Jewish groups were no longer theirs.

---

natural restriction of the national reference to people who live in the area where the action occurs or people who have a specific national function."

[36] Culpepper 1983, 126.

[37] Cf. Culpepper 1996, 114: "Even if the Greek term *hoi Ioudaioi* once denoted Judeans or the Jewish authorities, the Gospel of John generalized and stereotyped those who rejected Jesus by its use of this term and elevated the bitterness and hostility of the polemic to a new level."

[38] Reinhartz 2001, 348.

[39] Wilson 1995, 76. Cf. also Harvey 1996, 97: "By Ἰουδαῖοι John meant not only 'the inhabitants of Judea' but also 'all Jews everywhere, at any time'. This is an important part of his Gospel, his message and his Christology."

7.4. John and the Development of an Autonomous Christian Religion

It may be misleading to describe both the Qumran and the Johannine group as Jewish sects. Leaning on the distinction made by R. Stark and W. S. Bainbridge, Petri Luomanen has recently made a suggestion that early Christian groups—particularly Matthew's community—should not be regarded as sects but rather as new cults.[40] In their theory of religion, Stark and Bainbridge describe the emergence of new religious movements by making a distinction between a sect and a cult; a sect is "a deviant religious organization with traditional beliefs and practices," while a cult is "a deviant religious organization with novel beliefs and practices."[41] What is common to a sect and a cult is that they are both in tension with their surrounding society and culture.[42] But this tension is expressed in different terms. Sects may give a particular emphasis to some parts of the religious tradition they share with their parent body, but despite these differences, they still share much of the common culture.[43] This seems to be true in case of Jewish sects in the Second Temple Period, because "in spite of their mutual hostility, . . . there was not that much difference in world outlook or fundamental ideology between the groups."[44] Cults, however, are based on the innovation of new religious ideas that gain social acceptance, and thus a group devoted to these ideas is created.[45] This does not mean that new ideas are formulated out of thin air. Beliefs and practices of a cult may be more or less similar to those of its parent body which means that the decree of innovation is different in different cults.[46] Therefore, sects and cults are not totally opposite religious phenomena, but "there is also a continuous spectrum of degrees of novelty between sect movements and cult movements."[47]

Given the diversity in Judaism at the beginning of the Common Era, it may not always be so easy to say what religious ideas were

---

[40] Luomanen 2002, 126–130. Cf. also Räisänen 2001, 199–200. Räisänen draws on an earlier draft of Luomanen's article and applies the distinction between a sect and a cult to the Qumran community and Pauline communities.

[41] Stark & Bainbridge 1987, 124.

[42] Stark & Bainbridge 1987, 125.

[43] Stark & Bainbridge 1987, 127.

[44] Baumgarten 1997, 55–56.

[45] Stark & Bainbridge 1987, 156.

[46] Stark & Bainbridge 1987, 170–178.

[47] Luomanen 2002, 128.

traditional and what represented an innovation.[48] Nevertheless, the above sketch suggests that we should place the Qumran group and the Johannine community at different ends of a continuum that has traditional sects at one end and new cult movements at the other. Faith in Jesus is expressed in John in such a way that it makes basic matters of Jewishness all but extraneous. This faith contributes to the emergence of a new independent religious movement, a cult, which shares many things with the religious culture from which it emerges, but still splits away from that culture on many crucial points.

The reasons for the Johannine group abandoning common aspects of Jewishness should not be located in the Johannine christology alone.[49] It may well be that John is dependent to a great extent on former Jewish traditions even in his christological views. For example, Daniel Boyarin has recently suggested that John's logos christology may be taken as a development of various Jewish motifs; this leads Boyarin to conclude that such early Christian groups as the Johannine Christians did not

> distinguish themselves from non-Christian Jews theologically, but only in their association of various Jewish theologoumena and mythologoumena with this particular Jew, Jesus of Nazareth. The characteristic move that constructs what will become orthodox Christianity is, I think, the combination of obviously Jewish Messianic soteriology with equally Jewish Logos theology in the figure of Jesus.[50]

---

[48] Cf. Chilton 2001, 236. Chilton criticizes Räisänen's description of the Qumran community as a sect and the Pauline communities as a cult; Chilton says that it is problematic to decide "what is 'traditional' and what is 'novel'" because "both systems manifest a fascinating blend of traditional and innovative elements." While Chilton considers it problematic to make a distinction between the Qumran sect and the Pauline cult, he nevertheless thinks that this distinction is valid if we compare the Qumran sect to the Johannine community (cf. below n. 56).

[49] See, however, Casey 1991, 23–40. Casey's conclusions concerning John's presentation of Jewishness come close to my views in many ways, but I part company with Casey in the interpetation of the Johannine christology. Casey sees christology as the main indicator of how the Johannine Christians had drifted away from Jewishness and adapted "Gentile self-identity." For Casey, this gentile self-identification is "a necessary cause of belief in the deity of Jesus, a belief which could not be held as long as the Christian community was primarily Jewish" (p. 38). But basic features of the Johannine christology are derived from diverse Jewish traditions, and the development of these features does not indicate *as such* a break with Judaism. For criticism of Casey, see McGrath 2001, 9–17. I also have some problems with Casey's way of using the word "Gentile self-identity" in connection with the Johannine group. The distinction between Jews and gentiles, or between Christians and gentiles, is very much an expression of Jewish or Christian self-understanding, but who would have defined themselves as gentiles?

[50] Boyarin 2001, 281.

But this view seems to ignore the fact that many Christian groups, in my view including John's group, distinguished themselves from other Jews on the level of religious practice, if not on the level of theology. In the second chapter of this book I referred to some early Christian groups, most notably the Hellenists in the Jerusalem early church, who became alienated from other Jews not only because of their faith in Jesus, but because they made some modifications on the basis of this faith regarding the observance of major Jewish practices. I suggest that the same could have happened in case of the Johannine group, even though John's obsession with 'high christology' has the effect of concealing any signs of possible discussions dealing with these practices. Some passing references in such passages as John 10:16, "I have other sheep that do not belong to this fold," or John 11:51–52, "Jesus was about to die for the nation, and not for the nation only, but to gather into one the dispersed children of God," may suggest that the Johannine writer was not unaware of discussions connected to the presence of gentiles in early Christian communities. It may even be that these passages suggest that the Johannine community consisted of both those who were of Jewish origin and of the gentiles, although John otherwise presupposes a predominantly Jewish setting.[51] This would at least partly explain why the narrator emphasizes the Jewishness of the customs and festivals of the Jews. In this kind of context, the construction of a new Christian non-Jewish identity could never take place on the level of theological ideas alone, but must also take place on the level of religious practices. John's references to central aspects of Jewishness suggest that this was also the case among the Johannine Christians.

---

[51] Pace Martyn (1996, 124–143) who denies the common view that these passages refer to a mission to the gentiles. For Martyn, these passages show that the evangelist saw his own community "to be a sort of mother church to other Jewish-Christian churches." Thus John here "informs his community that there are other Jewish-Christian communities," who share with the Johannine Christians "an essentially common history of persecution by Jewish authorities." But this interpretation escalates the geographical scope of the conflict between the Johannine community and the early rabbis and exaggerates the influence of formative Judaism in a way that is untenable today. Martyn does not discuss here at all John 6:45 which seems to suggest the inclusion of gentiles in the Christian community. John here refers to Isa 54:13 but says "they all shall be taught by God" while Isa 54:13 speaks of "all your sons" meaning the sons of Israel. The omission of the words "your sons" is quite usually taken to suggest that, for John, salvation exceeds the borders of Israel. Cf. Schlatter 176; Freed 1965, 19–20; Lindars 264; Schnackenburg II 77; Wilckens 105. Cf. also the scholars listed by Menken 1988b, 170 n. 35.

It is noteworthy that the fourth gospel had no impact among those Jewish-Christian groups that continued to flourish well into the fourth and even fifth century and that combined faith in Jesus with the observance of Jewish identity markers. The information concerning these groups is sparse, but some remarks by the Church Fathers suggest that they used either a gospel somehow akin to the gospel of Matthew or a gospel harmony based on the synoptics—but not on John.[52] This is another token that John does not belong together with discussions connected to Jewish identity, but it rather marks the beginning of new kinds of discussions focusing mainly on christology. The christological controversies in the Johannine Epistles may well be the first evidence of the discussions that the gospel evoked around Jesus' person.[53] What is missing in the Epistles is any discussion connected to the basics of Jewishness. I believe William Wrede already was on the right track when he said that the themes in the fourth gospel are hardly "questions of Jewish horizon."[54] His contemporary colleague, Julius Wellhausen, expressed the same by saying that the battle with Judaism in the first part of the gospel is not fight on common ground; this fight is, in reality, "a protest against Judaism because it is not Christianity."[55]

The need for a new self-definition led the Johannine writer and his group to create an autonomous symbolic universe that was no longer Jewish in the sense that basic matters of Jewish identity had but a peripheral role. It may be a matter of choice whether we use the word 'Christian' to describe this symbolic universe or not, the

---

[52] For Jewish-Christian gospels, see Klijn 1992, 27–43. The so-called gospel according to the Ebionites shows a harmonizing tendency similar to Tatian's Diatessaron. But where Tatian made an extensive use of John in his gospel harmony, these Jewish Christians composed their gospel harmony with the help of the three synoptic gospels alone (p. 38). The gospel of the Nazoraens, however, is usually seen to be somehow connected to the gospel of Matthew (p. 42). This is another reason why I think that Martin de Boer is wrong when he tries to combine these later traditions of Jewish Christians to the Johannine Christianity. Cf. de Boer 1998, 243.

[53] Cf. Brown 1982, 69–115.

[54] Wrede 1933 (1903), 25.

[55] Wellhausen 111: "Der Kampf mit dem Judentum . . . wird nicht auf einem gemeinsamen Boden geführt und ist in Wahrheit ein Protest gegen das Judentum, weil es nicht Christentum ist." It is actually striking that seventy years later E. P. Sanders described with almost the same words Paul's relationship to Judaism. See E. P. Sanders 1977, 552. Sanders summarized Paul's view of Judaism in a famous and controversial saying: "In short, this is what Paul finds wrong in Judaism: it is not Christianity." Sanders nowhere refers to Wellhausen's commentary on John in his book, and he seems to have reached his conclusion independently of Wellhausen.

point being that it points away from what most Jewish groups—and
outsiders as well—regarded as essential for Jewish identity.[56] It is self-
evident that the Johannine symbolic universe was not the first attempt
at defining the faith of those who regarded Jesus as the Messiah in
relation to Jewishness. No matter what John's exact tradition-histor-
ical relationship to other currents in early Christianity is, John shares
many common convictions with other early Christians, develops them
further in a particular way, and thus continues a process that was
already in progress. In his description of what he calls "primitive
Christianity," Gerd Theissen has described John as the culmination
of a process that meant "the grounding of new Christian religion by
its own basic narrative and the demarcation from its mother religion."[57]
According to Theissen, John's significance for the development of
early Christian religion is that "here this new religion not only actually organizes itself around its christological centre but becomes aware
of this."[58] Theissen speaks of "the internal autonomy of the primitive
Christian sign world" that founds its expression in John; this is well
in line with my conclusions about the independent Johannine symbolic universe. But I still want to correct a possible misunderstanding that may arise on the basis of the previous discussion.

    Even though the way some early Christian convictions are for-
mulated in John had a crucial role in the development of early
Christianity as a religion of its own, I do not return to the thinking that we may find *the* point in history—in John or in elsewhere—
when Christianity finally parted ways with Judaism. Many recent
studies have emphasized that early Christian groups related to the
Jewish heritage they all shared in many different ways.[59] We have
evidence—however sparse it may be—of Jewish Christians and gen-

---

[56] Cf. Chilton (2001, 236–337) who says that Adriana Destro and Mauro Pesce
(cf. above) have shown "that, by 100 C.E., Christianity indeed emerged within its
own terms of reference as a religious system autonomous of Israel, because the category of 'Israel' itself was no longer deployed to describe its way of life, view of
the social order, or worldview. Then it was indeed a 'cult,' both in Räisänen's sociological sense and in the suspicious regard of the Greco-Roman world." This seems
to be at odds with how Chilton and Jacob Neusner has earlier described early
Christianity. Cf. Chilton & Neusner 1995, 5. When describing all New Testament
Christianity as a Judaism, they note that John, in spite of his fierce condemnation
of the Jews, "valued Israel and certainly adhered to the Torah as he read it."
[57] Theissen 1999, 185–206, esp. p. 186.
[58] Theissen 1999, 205.
[59] Cf. the conclusions reached by Wilson 1995, 285–301.

tile Judaizers long after John was written.[60] The relationship between
the emerging early Christianity and Judaism was not defined once
and for all—not by Paul, not by John, not by anyone else.

Daniel Boyarin has even suggested that we should not think of
Christianity and Judaism in late antiquity as different religions at all
but as "points on a continuum" so that

> on one end were the Marcionites . . . and on the other the many Jews
> for whom Jesus meant nothing. In the middle, however, were many
> gradations that provided social and cultural mobility from one end of
> this spectrum to the other.[61]

I have some doubts concerning this view, but if we were to follow
Boyarin, I think John belongs nearer to the Marcionite end of the
continuum, because it was one of those forces that pulled Jews and
Christians apart from rather than bound them together. Boyarin says
that only the emergence of authoritative and orthodox leadership,
both on the Jewish and on the Christian side, produced two different
religions.[62] It is significant that John was used especially by those on
the Christian side, Origen, John Chrysostom and others, who wanted
to secure the border between a Jew and a Christian. This is not an
accident, because later promoters of Christian orthodoxy could lean
on those features in John that already suggest a break from Jewishness.
It may sound paradoxical that such a writing originating so deeply
in diverse Jewish traditions contributed in this way to the development of a non-Jewish Christian identity; I think this paradox is
already there in John's ambivalent portrayal of Jewishness.

I have approached John's narrative world as an expression of self-
understanding of a particular early Christian group, but identity
matters are never easily defined but are always fluctuating. This is
the reason why it is impossible to tell exactly when the identity of

---

[60] For these groups, see Wilson 1995, 169–194.
[61] Boyarin 1999, 8.
[62] Boyarin (1999, 15) even claims that, "without the power of the orthodox Church
and the rabbis to declare people heretics and outside the system, it remained impossible to declare phenomenologically who was a Jew and who was a Christian." This
statement may be true in case of some Jewish-Christians groups, but if it is meant
as a general description of the relationship between Jews and Christians, I think it
is an overstatement. I have referred in my introduction to the history of the Christian
community in the city of Rome, which suggests that even the outsiders, the Roman
officials, were to some extent capable of distinguishing Christians from Jews already
in the 60's.

a person or a group ceases to be Jewish and begins to be something else. But I have referred to the heuristic distinction between a sect and a cult in order to show that the Johannine symbolic universe indicates that a change of identity was taking place among *these people* to whose faith the gospel is a witness. In John, a new Christian identity is contrasted in such a sweeping way with diverse Jewish traditions that the gospel could also be meaningful in other contexts where early Christians were moving away from their common Jewish foundation and creating their autonomous religious identity. The dark side of this process is that the formation of a new identity took place to a great extent in an opposition to basics matters of Jewishness and those people who continued to retain these matters.

In their struggle to define their identity in relation to basics of Jewishness, the Johannine Christians were not alone. Rather, the Johannine group shares in more general developments that were going on at the end of the first century. When the gospel was written, the Johannine group still had its own distinctive characteristics which marked it off from other early Christian communities. The members of this community had abandoned some basics of Jewish identity and reformulated many traditions they shared with various Jewish groups. In a situation where they were growing apart from Jews and the Jewish way of life, they defined themselves anew, partly in fierce opposition to their Jewish past but still seeing themselves as having some continuity with that past too. However paradoxical this may be, this is the way these Christians were able to claim a new identity for themselves. Eventually we lose their traces and they disappear among other early Christian communities. But the Johannine writer left us a gospel, a mark of a struggle for self-understanding. Through this writing, this group of early Christians made a lasting contribution to the future development of Christian identity—"for better or for worse."

7.5. *Concluding Remarks*

It has become clear that I cannot help but think that the long tradition of Christian anti-Judaism that has pervaded so much of our common heritage from antiquity to this day somehow has its point of departure in parts of the New Testament. Of course, John is not the only writer who contributed to this future development. Matthew also shows some signs of anti-Judaism, as is shown in a careful reading by Amy-Jill Levine.[63] Moreover, even Paul, who no doubt understood himself as a Jew, may have contributed to this development.[64] But by his indiscriminate use of language and by his choice to place the Jews alongside the devil in the battle against Jesus, John has given a strong impetus to anti-Jewish bias in Christian tradition. We should, of course, remember that John, no more than any other New Testament writer, can be blamed for developments in later times. The reasons why Jews have been oppressed over the course of history even before the rise of modern anti-Semitism have varied and so has the intensity of this oppression. Religious motives have been only one factor in this development among different social, economic, political, or national factors. It has also become customary to make a distinction between Christian anti-Judaism and modern anti-Semitism dating back to the 19th century. But even though we should not overstate the meaning of 'mystical anti-Semitism' evident in Christian tradition, I think it is right to say that John—and some other New Testament writings—were used to justify persecution of Jews in societies dominated by Christians.[65]

It would be fair to admit that the above conclusion is not necessarily based on a superficial reading.[66] On the contrary, I think that a careful reading of the gospel frustrates our attempts to find fine nuances and adjustments in its portrayal of Jewishness. When I claim that there are already some seeds of anti-Judaism in John, I have in mind how R. Kendal Soulen has defined theological anti-Judaism; Soulen says that theological anti-Judaism concentrates on superses-

---

[63] A.-J. Levine 1999.

[64] See E. P. Sanders 1999b, 276. Sanders says that, while the term "anti-Jewish" seems to be "essentially misleading" in case of Paul, "those who wish to be sensitive to the question of whether or not Paul broke with Judaism, as well as to the painful subject of subsequent Christian anti-Judaism, should see the anti-Jewish possibilities in Paul's letters."

[65] For mystical anti-Semitism, see W. D. Davies 1999, 248–296.

[66] Dunn (2001) repeatedly implies that his position defending John against the charges of being anti-Jewish is more nuanced than these superficial charges: "We are reminded that the issue of 'anti-Judaism' within John's gospel needs to be much more carefully nuanced than a simple reference to Joh 8:31–59 would suggest" (p. 57); "The character of John's 'anti-Judaism' needs careful analysis and statement before it is straightforwardly described and denounced as 'anti-Judaism." (p. 59); "John's account of the insults and hurtful exchanges . . . when taken out of context is easily heard as anti-Jewish in a later sense" (p. 66).

sionism, a thinking according to which "the church supersedes or replaces the Jewish people as God's covenant community." Such notions constitute "the heart of doctrinal anti-Judaism."[67] It may not be appropriate to speak of full-blown supersessionism in the case of John, but the beginnings of many ideas that were influential on the later development of Christian theology are already there in John.[68] It has never been strange to Christian anti-Jewish tradition based on supersessionism to hold to Jewish scriptures, or to maintain that Jesus was really a Jew, things that were totally unacceptable for later anti-Semitic propagandists in Nazi Germany.[69] But we go astray, if we take these later formulations as a standard of anti-Judaism and exclude the New Testament writings from it because these writings appeal to common Jewish heritage. It is also misleading to isolate New Testament writings from later developments by making Marcion a standard to measure anti-Judaism.[70] In light of some recent suggestions, the whole question concerning Marcion's alleged anti-Judaism in relation to the anti-Judaism of those Church Fathers who opposed him should perhaps be re-evaluated. When subjecting the Hebrew Bible to severe criticism and finally rejecting it, Marcion "attacked the symbols but left the people alone," while his opponents "took over the symbols and attacked the people. Judaism was the loser in either case."[71] It is not difficult to see that Marcion's opponents could find support for their case in John.

I cannot see how the emphasis on John's Jewishness helps to rescue the gospel from having an anti-Jewish stamp. As Judith Lieu notes,

---

[67] Soulen 1998, 149.

[68] Cf. Rensberger 1999, 145: "It is not hard to see in such declarations the roots of Christian supersessionism, the claim that Christianity and the church have superseded Judaism and the Jews as the religion and the people of God." But Rensberger excuses this supersessionism by referring to the alleged hostile policy of John's opponents: "In its own context and not in that of later centuries, John's gathering up of Jewish values into Jesus served more a defensive that an offensive purpose. The Jews in the Johannine community were themselves suffering dispossession from their heritage."

[69] For these German Christians, see Bergen 1996, 154–164.

[70] Cf. Townsend 1979, 81: "The evangelist was no Marcion. He valued much that is Jewish, including Hebrew Scriptures, and he affirmed the Jewishness of Jesus, whom he depicted as the Jewish Messiah." Wilken 1999, 179: "A more serious objection to the term 'anti-Judaism' is that it has Marcionite overtones. Indeed, one might say that in calling early Christianity anti-Jewish, we make Christianity into the very thing that it struggled valiantly to overcome. Anti-Judaism, like Marcionism, collapses the dialectic that is built into Christianity's relation to Judaism."

[71] Wilson 1995, 221. For a full discussion see also Räisänen 1997, 64–80.

a simplistic assertion that the evidence of 'Jewishness' disproves any 'anti-Jewishness' is both naive and pre-empts the exercise of definition and of investigation.[72]

We do not need to return to views that prevailed in the first half of 20th century and regard John as a product of Hellenistic culture and alien to Judaism if we take it as an expression of Christian anti-Judaism. The emphasis on Jewishness and anti-Jewish tendencies are both there in John, very much in the same way they have been together in later Christian tradition. Therefore, I am skeptical whether we can really deconstruct John's anti-Jewish bias by appealing to some other features in the gospel, for example to John 4:22.[73] We need to go beyond what John says of the matter on our way towards some kind of solution.

Fernando F. Segovia has urged that New Testament scholars should not stop short of exposing anti-Jewish biases in the New Testament but provide "a reading strategy for the theologian or interpreter to address the problem."[74] I am not able to meet this enormous challenge but can only offer some modest personal thoughts. I fully concur with James Dunn who doubts that some kind of solution could be reached by translating the Johannine Ἰουδαῖοι with some other term, be it the Judaeans or the Jewish leaders.[75] But while I agree with Dunn on this matter, I think that Dunn's appeal to historical criticism as a solution can be only part of the answer.[76] I have argued that the anti-Judaism in John cannot be seen as a response to the hostile policy of John's opponents. What is needed is a search for new ways to define Christian identity in relation to Judaism. Instead of traditional supersessionist theology, some other kinds of models are needed, and I am fully aware of some promising suggestions that have been made.[77] Maybe these quests for new models might also go beyond the borders of our canon. Stephen Wilson has suggested that the evidence concerning some Jewish-Christian groups is important because it

---

[72] Lieu 2001, 127. In a similar vein A.-J. Levine 1999, 24: "The suggestion that to be Jewish precludes an attitude of anti-Judaism is naive if not racist."

[73] This procedure is suggested by Culpepper 2001, 76–91.

[74] Segovia 1996, 247.

[75] Dunn 2001, 60–62.

[76] Dunn 2001, 62–64.

[77] For example, see Culbertson 1991, 145–173.

demonstrates that the views that Christians took of Judaism were far more diverse than the monochrome, negative portrait that was later to dominate the Christian tradition.[78]

Gerd Theissen asks whether the church lost by rejecting the Jewish-Christian gospels "the voices of a very impressive Christianity which was not less valuable than the Christianity close to Judaism in the Letter of James or in Matthew."[79]

I believe that we should not take what John says of Jewishness and the Jews as a foundation for building Christian identities in relation to the Jews and Judaism in today's world.[80] Instead of taking the lead from what John says of Jewishness, we could perhaps follow the example of the Johannine Christians in that we who are Christians are also ready to search for new ways to define ourselves in relation to our tradition.[81] Whatever those exact experiences were that put in motion the process of self-definition for the Johannine Christians, they were ready to interpret all of their earlier tradition in a new light. This new self-definition led to formulations that are unacceptable in our eyes, but it still contributed to the formation of a Christian identity that all Christians share in some way or another. A new self-definition led the Johannine Christians to hold some self-contradictory and ambiguous convictions, and it may be impossible for Christians in our days to combine in any logical way the basis of Christian identity, faith in Jesus, with a pluralistic view that admits the legitimacy of other independent religious identities. But just as the Johannine writer combined contradictory tendencies in his narrative, perhaps we can also blend these conflicting tendencies together, not as dogma, but as different aspects of identity. In John's insistence on Jewish traditions, when he actually was breaking away from these traditions, or in his strivings for continuity when there was mostly discontinuity, I recognize something similar to my own stance in a pluralistic society where I try to define my identity in relation to my Christian faith. As always, in John's days and in our days, identity matters are fluctuating and ambiguous, but yet impossible to let go. Especially as these matters, disturbing and deeply rooted as they are, remind us that identity matters.

---

[78] Cf. Wilson 1995, 141.

[79] Theissen 1999, 284.

[80] I understand I am moving in the opposite direction from Stephen Motyer who ends his book on these matters by saying that "John offers a model for Christians today." See Motyer 1997, 220.

[81] I am inspired by Räisänen's discussion on Paul here, Räisänen 1997, 31–32.

BIBLIOGRAPHY

The author-date form of citation is used in the footnotes, with the exception of the commentaries on the fourth gospel which are cited by the name of the author alone. The abbreviations follow the style recommended in *The SBL Handbook of Style: For Ancient Near Eastern, Biblical, and Early Christian Studies*, (eds.) P. H. Alexander, J. K. Kutsko, J. D. Ernest, S. A. Decker-Lucke and for the Society of Biblical Literature D. L. Petersen. Peabody, Mass.: Hendrickson, 1999.

Sources, Translations and Reference Works

Bachmann, H. & Slaby W. A. (eds.)
    1987³   *Concordance to the Novum Testementum Graece*. Berlin/New York: Walter de Gruyter.

Bauer, Walter & Aland, Kurt & Aland, Barbara
    1988⁶   *Griechisch-deutsches Wörterbuch zu den Schriften des Neuen Testaments und der frühchristlichen Literatur*. Berlin/New York: Walter de Gruyter.

Berkowitz, L. & Squitier, K. A.
    1990³   *Thesaurus Linguae Graecae: Canon of Greek Authors and Works*. Oxford: University Press.

Blass F. & Debrunner, A. & Rehkopf, F.
    1984¹⁶   *Grammatik des neutestamentlichen Griechisch*. Göttingen: Vandenhoeck & Ruprecht.

Braude, William G. (Gershov Zev) and Kapstein, Israel J.
    1975   *Pĕsiḳta dĕ-Raḇ Kahăna. R. Kahana's Compilation of Discourses for Sabbaths and Festal Days*. The Littman Library of Jewish Civilization. London: Routledge & Kegan Paul.
    1981   *Tanna Dĕbe Eliyyahu: The Lore of the School of Elijah*. Philadelphia: The Jewish Publication Society of America.

Charlesworth, James H. (ed.)
    1983, 1985 *The Old Testament Pseudepigrapha*. Two Volumes. London: Darton, Longman & Todd.

Danby, Herbert (ed.)
    1933   *The Mishnah*. Translated from the Hebrew with Introduction and Brief Explanatory Notes. Oxford: University Press.

Elliger, K. & Rudolph W. (eds.)
    1990⁴   *Biblia Hebraica Stuttgartensia. Editio funditus renovata*. Stuttgart: Deutsche Bibelgesellschaft.

Epstein, I. (gen. ed.)
    1961   *The Babylonian Talmud*. Reprinted in 18 vols. London: Soncino Press.

Feldman, Louis H. & Reinhold, Meyer (eds.)
    1996   *Jewish Life and Thought among Greeks and Romans: Primary Readings*. Edinburgh: T. & T. Clark.

Freedman, H. & Simon, M. (gen. eds.)
    1939–1951 *Midrash Rabbah: Complete in Ten Volumes*. London: Soncino Press.

García Martínez, Florentino & Tigchelaar, Eibert J. C. (eds.)
    1997–98   *The Dead Sea Scrolls: Study Edition*. Two volumes. Leiden: Brill.

Josephus
              Josephus in Nine Volumes. LCL. Ed. and trans. H. StJ. Thackeray (vols
              1–5), Ralph Marcus (vols 5–8) and Louis Feldman (vols 9–10).
              London: William Heinemann/Cambridge, Massachusetts: Harvard
              University Press. 1926–1965.
Justin Martyr
              Writings of Saint Justin Martyr. Translated by Thomas B. Falls. The
              Fathers of the Church 6. Washington, D. C.: The Catholic University
              of America Press.
Klein, Michael L.
    1980   *The Fragment-Targums of the Pentateuch*. Two volumes. AnBib 76. Rome:
              Biblical Institute Press.
Liddell, H. G. & Scott, R.
    1968⁹   *A Greek-English Lexicon. With a Supplement*. Oxford: Clarendon Press.
Maher, Michael
    1992   *Targum Pseudo-Jonathan: Genesis*. The Aramaic Bible 1B. Edinburgh:
              T. & T. Clark.
Mayser, Edwin
    1934   *Grammatik der griechischen Papyri aus der Ptolemäerzeit. Mit Einschluss der
              gleichzeitigen Ostraka und der in Ägypten verfassten Inschriften. Vol. II, 2.
              Satzlehre*. Berlin/Leipzig: Walter de Gruyter.
McNamara, Martin
    1992   *Targum Neofiti 1: Genesis*. The Aramaic Bible 1A. Edinburgh: T. & T. Clark.
Moulton, J. M.
    1908³   *A Grammar of New Testament Greek. Vol I, Prolegomena*. Edinburgh:
              T. & T. Clark.
Moulton, J. M. & Turner, N.
    1963   *A Grammar of New Testament Greek. Vol III, Syntax*. Edinburgh: T. &
              T. Clark.
Nestle, Erwin & Aland, Kurt (eds.)
    1993²⁷   *Novum Testamentum Graece*. Stuttgart: Deutsche Bibelgesellschaft.
Neusner, Jacob (ed.)
    1977–1986 *The Tosefta*. Translated from Hebrew. Six volumes. Hoboken, New
              Jersey: KTAV Publishing House.
    1982–1993 *The Talmud of the Land of Israel*. A Preliminary translation and expla-
              nation. Chicago Studies in the History of Judaism. 42 Vols. Chicago:
              Chicago University Press.
    1985   *Genesis Rabbah: The Judaic Commentary to the Book of Genesis*. A New
              American Translation. Three Volumes. BJS 104–106. Atlanta, Georgia:
              Scholars Press.
    1987a   *Pesiqta deRab Kahana*. An Analytical Translation. Two Volumes. BJS
              122 and 123. Atlanta, Georgia: Scholars Press.
    1988a   *The Mishnah*. A New Translation. New Haven and London: Yale
              University Press.
    1988b   *The Mekhilta according to Rabbi Ishmael*. An Analytical Translation. Two
              Volumes. BJS 148 & 154. Atlanta, Georgia: Scholars Press.
Philo
              Philo in Ten Volumes (and two Supplementary Volumes). LCL. Ed. and
              trans. F. H. Colson (vols 1–10) and G. H. Whitaker (vols 1–5).
              London: William Heinemann/Cambridge, Massachusetts: Harvard
              University Press. 1929–1953.
Radermacher, Ludwig
    1925²   *Neutestamentliche Grammatik: Das Griechisch des Neuen Testaments im
              Zusammenhang mit der Volkssprache*. HNT 1. Tübingen: Mohr-Siebeck.

Rahlfs, Alfred (ed.)
   1979 (1935)   *Septuaginta. Id est Vetus Testamentun graece iuxta LXX interpretes.* Stuttgart: Deutsche Bibelgesellschaft.
Robertson, A. T.
   1934   *A Grammar of the Greek New Testament in the Light of Historical Research.* Nashville, Tennessee: Broadman Press.
Robinson, James M. (ed.)
   1988³   *The Nag Hammadi Library in English.* San Francisco: Harper San Francisco.
Stern, Menahem
   1974–1984   *Greek and Latin Authors on Jews and Judaism.* Three volumes. Jerusalem: The Israel Academy of Sciences and Humanities.
Smyth, Herbert Weir
   1984 (1920)   *Greek Grammar.* Revised by Gordon M. Messing. Harvard: University Press.

Commentaries on the Fourth Gospel

Barrett, Charles Kingsley
   1978²   *The Gospel According to St. John. An Introduction with Commentary and Notes on the Greek Text.* London: SPCK.
Bauer, Walter
   1925²   *Das Johannesevangelium.* HNT 6. Tübingen: Mohr-Siebeck.
Beasley-Murray, George R.
   1987   *John.* WBC 36. Waco, Texas: Word Books.
Becker, Jürgen
   1991³   *Das Evangelium nach Johannes. I–II.* ÖTK 4. Gütersloh and Würzburg: Gütersloher Verlagshaus Gerd Mohn and Echter-Verlag.
Bernard, J. H.
   1928   *A Critical and Exegetical Commentary on the Gospel according to St. John.* Two Volumes. ICC. Edinburgh: T. & T. Clark.
Brown, Raymond E.
   1966, 1970   *The Gospel According to John.* Two Volumes. AB 29. Garden City, New York: Doubleday & Company Inc.
Büchsel, Friedrich
   1937   *Das Evangelium nach Johannes.* NTD. Ersten Bandes 2. Halbband, 3. Auflage. Göttingen: Vandenhoeck & Ruprecht.
Bultmann, Rudolf
   1986²¹ (1941) *Das Evangelium des Johannes.* KEK 2. Göttingen: Vandenhoeck & Ruprecht.
Carson, D. A.
   1991   *The Gospel according to John.* Grand Rapids:Eerdmans/Leicester: Inter-Varsity Press.
Haenchen, Ernst
   1980   *Das Johannesevangelium. Ein Kommentar aus den nachgelassenen Manuskripten herausgegeben von Ulrich Busse.* Tübingen: Mohr-Siebeck.
Hoskyns, Edwyn Clement
   1947²   *The Fourth Gospel.* Edited by F. N. Davey. London: Faber and Faber.
Lindars, Barnabas
   1972   *The Gospel of John.* NCB. Grand Rapids: Eerdmans/London: Marshall, Morgan & Scott.
Malina, Bruce J. & Rohrbaugh, Richard L.
   1998   *Social-Science Commentary on the Gospel of John.* Minneapolis: Fortress Press.

Odeberg, Hugo
    1968² (1929)   *The Fourth Gospel: Interpreted in Its Relation to Contemporaneous Religious Currents in Palestine and the Hellenistic-Oriental World.* Amsterdam: B. R. Grüner.
Sanders, J. N. & Mastin, B. A.
    1968   *A Commentary on the Gospel According to St. John.* BNTC. London: Adam & Charles Black.
Schlatter, A.
    1930   *Der Evangelist Johannes. Wie er spricht, denkt and glaubt. Ein Kommentar zum vierten Evangelium.* Stuttgart: Calwer Vereinsbuchhandlung.
Schnackenburg, Rudolf
    1967² 1971,   *Das Johannesevangelium.* Four Vols. HThK 4.
    1976² 1984   Freiburg/Basel/Wien: Herder.
Schnelle, Udo
    1998   *Das Evangelium nach Johannes.* HKNT 4. Leipzig: Evangelische Verlagsanstalt.
Schulz, Siegfried
    1983   *Das Evangelium nach Johannes.* NTD 4, 15. Auflage, 4. Aufl. dieser Fassung. Göttingen: Vandenhoeck & Ruprecht.
Strathmann, Hermann
    1954   *Das Evangelium nach Johannes.* NTD 4, 7. Auflage, 2. verbesserte Auflage der neuen Bearbeitung. Göttingen: Vandenhoeck & Ruprecht.
Wellhausen, Julius
    1908   *Das Evangelium Joannis.* Berlin: Georg Reimer.
Wengst, Klaus
    2000–2001   *Das Johannesevangelium.* Two Volumes. Theologischer Kommentar zum Neuen Testament 4. Stuttgart: W. Kohlhammer.
Wilckens, Ulrich
    1998   *Das Evangelium nach Johannes.* NTD 4, 17. Auflage. Göttingen: Vandenhoeck & Ruprecht.

Other Studies

Ådna, Jostein
    1993   *Jesu Kritik am Tempel: Eine Untersuchung zum Verlauf und Sinn der soge-nannten Tempelreinigung Jesu, Markus 11,15–17 und Parallelen.* Dissertation. Tübingen/Stavanger.
Alexander, Philip S.
    1983   "Rabbinic Judaism and the New Testament," *ZNW* 74, 237–246.
    1992   " 'The Parting of the Ways' from the Perspective of Rabbinic Judaism," *Jews and Christians: The Partings of the Ways A.D. 70 to 135,* ed. J. D. G. Dunn. WUNT 66. Tübingen: Mohr-Siebeck. 1–25.
Alon, Gedalyahu
    1977   "The Origin of the Samaritans in the Rabbinic Tradition," G. Alon, *Jews, Judaism and the Classical World: Studies in Jewish History in the Times of the Second Temple and Talmud.* Translated from the Hebrew by Israel Abrahams. Jerusalem: The Magnes Press, the Hebrew University. 354–373.
Anderson, Paul N.
    1996   *The Christology of the Fourth Gospel: Its Unity and Disunity in the light of John 6.* WUNT, 2. Reihe 78. Tübingen: Mohr-Siebeck.
    1997   "The Sitz im Leben of the Johannine Bread of Life Discourse and Its Evolving Context," in Culpepper 1997, 1–59.
Ashton, John
    1991   *Understanding the Fourth Gospel.* Oxford: Clarendon Press.

Asiedu-Peprah, Martin
  2001 *Johannine Sabbath Conflicts as Juridical Controversy*. WUNT, 2. Reihe 132.
        Tübingen: Mohr-Siebeck.
Attridge, Harold W.
  1980 "Thematic Development and Source Elaboration in John 7:1–36," *CBQ*
        42, 160–170.
Augenstein, Jörg
  1997 " 'Euer Gesetz'—Ein Pronomen und die johanneische Haltung zum Gesetz,"
        ZNW 88, 311–313.
Bacchiocchi, Samuele
  1981 "John 5:17: Negation or Clarification of the Sabbath?" *Andrews University
        Seminary Studies* 19, 3–19.
Back, Sven-Olav
  1995 *Jesus of Nazareth and the Sabbath Commandment*. Åbo: Åbo Akademi University
        Press.
Bammel, Ernst
  1970 "EX ILLA ITAQUE DIE CONSILIUM FECERUNT . . .," *The Trial of
        Jesus. Cambridge Studies in honour of C. F. D. Moule*, ed. Ernst Bammel. SBT
        2nd Series 13. London: SCM Press.11–40.
Barclay, John M. G.
  1996 *Jews in the Mediterranean Diaspora from Alexander to Trajan (323 BCE—117
        CE)*. Edinburgh: T. & T. Clark.
  1998 "Who was considered an Apostate in the Jewish Diaspora?" *Tolerance and
        Intolerance in Early Judaism and Christianity*, eds. G. N. Stanton and G. G.
        Stroumsa. Cambridge: Cambridge University Press. 80–98.
Barrett, C. K.
  1975 *The Gospel of John and Judaism*. Translated from the German Original *Das
        Johannesevangelium und das Judentum* (1970) by D. M. Smith. Philadelphia:
        Fortress Press.
  2001 "John and Judaism," In Bieringer et al. 2001a, 401–417.
Bassler, Jouette M.
  1981 "The Galileans: A Neglected Factor in Johannine Community Research,"
        CBQ 43, 243–257.
Bauckham, Richard
  1999 "For What Offence Was James Put to Death," *James the Just and Christian
        Origins*, eds. B. Chilton and C. G. Evans. NovTSup 98. Leiden: Brill.
        199–232.
Baumbach, Günther
  1992 "Die Funktion des Bösen in neutestamentlichen Schriften," *EvT* 52, 23–42.
Baumgarten, Albert, I.
  1983 "The Name of the Pharisees," *JBL* 102, 411–428.
  1997 *The Flourishing of Jewish Sects in the Maccabean Era: An Interpretation*. JSJSup
        55. Leiden: Brill.
  1998 "Graeco-Roman Voluntary Associations and Ancient Jewish Sects," *Jews
        in a Graeco-Roman World*, ed. M. Goodman. Oxford: Clarendon Press.
        93–111.
Beall, Todd S.
  2001 "History and Eschatology at Qumran: Messiah," *Judaism in Late Antiquity,
        Part Five, The Judaism of Qumran: A Systematic Reading of the Dead Sea Scrolls,
        Volume Two: World View, Comparing Judaisms*, eds. A. J. Avery-Peck, J. Neusner
        and B. D. Chilton. HO, Section One vol. 57. Leiden: Brill. 125–146.
Becker, Jürgen
  1964 *Das Heil Gottes: Heils- und Sündenbegriffe in den Qumrantexten und im Neuen
        Testament*. SUNT 3. Göttingen: Vandenhoeck & Ruprecht.

1997   "Endzeitliche Völkermission und antiochenische Christologie," *Eschatologie und Schöpfung. FS E. Gräßer*, eds. M. Evang, H. Merklein and M. Wolter. BZNW 89. Berlin/New York: Walter de Gruyter. 1–21.

van Belle, Gilbert
2001   " 'Salvation is from the Jews': The Parenthesis in John 4:22b," in Bieringer et al. 2001a, 270–400.

Belser, J.
1902   "Der Ausdruck οἱ Ἰουδαῖοι im Johannesevangelium," *TQ* 48, 168–222.

Bergen, D. L.
1996   *Twisted Cross: The German Christian Movement in the Third Reich*. Chapel Hill and London: The University of North Carolina Press.

Berger, Klaus
1977   "Abraham im Frühjudentum und Neuen Testament," *TRE* 1, 372–382.

Berger, Peter L. & Luckmann, Thomas
1967   *The Social Construction of Reality*. Garden City, NY: Doubleday.

Betz, Otto
1987   "To Worship in Spirit and in Truth: Reflections on John 4, 20–26," O. Betz, *Jesus, der Messias Israels: Aufsätze zur biblischen Theologie*. WUNT, 2. Reihe 42. Tübingen: Mohr-Siebeck. 420–438. (Originally appeared in *Standing before God: Studies in Prayer in Scriptures and in Tradition. Essays in Honor of John M. Oesterreicher*. New York: Ktav, 1981. 53–71.)

Beutler, Johannes
1972   *Martyria: Traditionsgeschichtliche Untersuchungen zum Zeugnisthema bei Johannes*. Frankfurter Theologische Studien 10. Frankfurt am Main: Josef Knecht.
1986   "Das Hauptgebot im Johannesevangelium," *Das Gesetz im Neuen Testament*, ed. Karl Kertelge. QD 108. Freiburg/Basel/Wien: Herder. 222–236.
1996   "The Use of 'Scripture' in the Gospel of John," in Culpepper and Black 1996, 147–162.
2001   "The Identity of the 'Jews' for the Readers of John," in Bieringer et al. 2001a, 229–238.

Bieringer, R., Pollefeyt, D. and Vandecasteele-Vanneuville, F. (eds.)
2001a   *Anti-Judaism and the Fourth Gospel: Papers of the Leuven Colloquium, 2000*. Jewish and Christian Heritage Series 1. Assen: Royal van Gorcum.
2001b   "Wrestling with Johannine Anti-Judaism: A Hermeneutical Framework for the Analysis of the Current Debate," in Bieringer et al. 2001a, 3–44.

Blank, Josef
1964   *Krisis: Untersuchungen zur johanneischen Christologie und Eschatologie*. Freiburg im Breisgau: Lambertus-Verlag.

Bloedhorn, Hanswulf & Hüttenmeister, Gil
1999   "The Synagogue," *The Cambridge History of Judaism, Volume Three: The Early Roman Period*, eds. W. Horbury, W. D. Davies & J. Sturdy. Cambridge: Cambridge University Press. 267–297.

Böcher, Otto
1965   *Der johanneische Dualismus im Zusammenhang des nachbiblischen Judemtums*. Gütersloh: Gerd Mohn.

de Boer, Martinus C.
1996a   *Johannine Perspectives on the Death of Jesus*. Kampen: Pharos.
1996b   "L'évangile de Jean et le Christianisme juif (nazoréen)," *Le déchirement: Juifs et chrétiens au premier siècle*, ed. D. Marguerat. Le monde de la Bible 32. Genève: Labor et Fides. 179–202.
1998   "The Nazoreans: Living at the Boundary of Judaism and Christianity," *Tolerance and Intolerance in Early Judaism and Christianity*, eds. G. N. Stanton and G. G. Stroumsa. Cambridge: Cambridge University Press. 239–262.
2001   "The Depiction of the 'Jews' in John's Gospel: Matters of Behavior and Identity," In Bieringer et al. 2001a, 260–280.

Bondi, Richard A.
1997   "John 8:39–47: Children of Abraham or of the Devil?" *JES* 34, 473–498.

Borgen, Peder
1965   *Bread from Heaven: An Exegetical Study of the Concept of Manna in the Gospel of John and the Writings of Philo*. NovTSup 10. Leiden: Brill.
1997   "John 6: Tradition, Interpretation and Composition," in Culpepper 1997, 95–114. (Originally appeared in *From Jesus to John: Essays on Jesus and New Testament Christology in Honour of Marinus de Jonge*, ed. Martinus C. de Boer. JSNTS 84. Sheffield: Sheffield Academic Press, 1993. 268–291.)

Botha, J. Eugene
1991   *Jesus and the Samaritan Woman: a Speech Act Reading of John 4:1–42*. NovTSup 65. Leiden: Brill.

Boyarin, Daniel
1999   *Dying for God: Martyrdom and the Making of Christianity and Judaism*. Stanford, California: Stanford University Press.
2001   "The Gospel of the *Memra*: Jewish Binitarianism and the Prologue to John," *HTR* 94, 243–284.

Brändle, Rudolf & Stegemann, Ekkehard W.
1998   "The Formation of the First 'Christian Congregations' in Rome in the Context of the Jewish Congregations," *Judaism and Christianity in First-Century Rome*, eds. K. P. Donfried & P. Richardsson. Grand Rapids, Michigan: Eerdmans. 117–127.

Braun, Herbert
1966   *Qumran und das Neue Testament, Band II*. Tübingen: Mohr-Siebeck.

Brooke, George J.
1988   "Christ and the Law in John 7–10," *Law and Religion: Essays on the Place of the Law in Israel and Early Christianity*, ed. B. Lindars. Cambridge: James Clark & Co. 102–112.

Brown, Raymond E.
1957 (1955) "The Qumran Scrolls and the Johannine Gospel and Epistles," *The Scrolls and the New Testament*, ed. K. Stendahl. New York: Harper & Brothers. 183–207. (Originally appeared in *CBQ* 17 [1955], 559–574.)
1979   *The Community of the Beloved Disciple: The Life, Loves, and Hates of an Individual Church in New Testament Times*. London: Geoffrey Chapman.
1982   *The Epistles of John*. AB. New York: Doubleday.
1994   *The Death of the Messiah: From Gethsemane to the Grave*. Two Volumes. The Anchor Bible Reference Library. New York, NY: Doubleday.

Bultmann, Rudolf
1984[9] (1948) *Theologie des Neuen Testaments*. Tübingen: Mohr-Siebeck.
1967   *Exegetica: Aufsätze zur Erforschung des Neuen Testaments*, ed. E. Dinkler. Tübingen: Mohr-Siebeck.

Carson, D. A.
1982   "Jesus and the Sabbath in the Four Gospels," *From Sabbath to Lord's Day: A Biblical, Historical and Theological Investigation*, ed. D. A. Carson. Grand Rapids, Michigan: Zondervan. 57–97.

Casey, P. M.
1991   *From Jewish Prophet to Gentile God: The Origins and Development of New Testament Christology*. Cambridge, England: James Clarke/Louisville, Kentucky: Westminster/John Knox Press.
1999   "Some Anti-Semitic Assumptions in the *Theological Dictionary of the New Testament*," *NovT* 41, 280–291.

Charlesworth, James H.
  1990 "Exploring Opportunities for Rethinking Relations among Jews and
        Christians," *Jews and Christians: Exploring the Past, Present, and Future*, ed. J. H.
        Charlesworth. New York: Crossroad. 35–59.
  1991 "A Critical Comparison of the Dualism in 1QS 3:13–4:26 and the 'Dualism'
        Contained in the Gospel of John," *John and the Dead Sea Scrolls*, ed. J. H.
        Charlesworth, Enlarged Edition. New York: Crossroad. 76–106. [Originally
        appeared in *NTS* 15 (1968–69), 389–418.]
  1996 "The Dead Sea Scrolls and the Gospel according to John," in Culpepper
        and Black 1996, 65–97.
Chilton, Bruce
  1992 *The Temple of Jesus: His Sacrificial Program Within a Cultural History of Sacrifice.*
        University Park, Pennsylvania: The Pennsylvania State University Press.
  1997 "The Whip of Ropes ([ΩΣ] ΦΡΑΓΕΛΛΙΟΝ ΕΚ ΣΧΟΙΝΙΩΝ) in John 2:15,"
        Bruce Chilton and Craig A. Evans, *Jesus in Context: Temple, Purity, and
        Restoration.* AGJU 39; Leiden: Brill, 441–454. (First appeared in *Templum
        Amicitiae: Essays on the Second Temple presented to Ernst Bammel*, ed. W. Horbury.
        JSNTSup 48; Sheffield: JSOT Press, 1991, 330–344.)
  2001 "Reading the Scrolls Systemically," *Judaism in Late Antiquity, Part Five, The
        Judaism of Qumran: A Systematic Reading of the Dead Sea Scrolls, Volume Two:
        World View, Comparing Judaisms*, eds. A. J. Avery-Peck, J. Neusner and B. D.
        Chilton. HO, Section One vol. 57. Leiden: Brill. 234–246.
Chilton, Bruce & Neusner, Jacob
  1995 *Judaism in the New Testament: Practices and Beliefs.* London and New York:
        Routledge.
Chilton, Bruce & Neusner, Jacob & Avery-Peck, Alan J.
  2001 "Preface," *Judaism in Late Antiquity, Part Five, The Judaism of Qumran: A System-
        atic Reading of the Dead Sea Scrolls, Volume Two: World View, Comparing Judaisms*,
        eds. A. J. Avery-Peck, J. Neusner and B. D. Chilton. HO, Section One
        vol. 57. Leiden: Brill. vii–xii.
Cogan, Mordechai
  1988 "For We, like You, Worship your God: Three Biblical Portrayals of Samaritan
        Origins," *VT* 38, 286–292.
Coggins, R. J.
  1975 *Samaritans and Jews: the Origins of Samaritanism Reconsidered.* Oxford: Basil
        Blackwell.
  1987 "The Samaritans in Josephus," in *Josephus, Judaism, and Christianity*, eds.
        Louis H. Feldman and Gohei Hata. Leiden: Brill. 257–273.
Cohen, Shaye J. D.
  1980 "A Virgin Defiled: Some Rabbinic and Christian Views on the Origins of
        Heresy," *USQR* 36, 1–11.
  1981 "Epigraphical Rabbis," *JQR* 72, 1–17.
  1984 "The Significance of Yavneh: Pharisees, Rabbis, and the End of Jewish
        Sectarianism," *HUCA* 55, 27–53.
  1987 *From the Maccabees to the Mishnah.* Library of Early Christianity. Philadelphia:
        The Westminster Press.
  1990 "The Modern Study of Ancient Judaism," *The State of Jewish Studies*, eds.
        S. J. D. Cohen & E. L. Greenstein. Detroit: Wayne State University.
        55–73.
  1992 "The Place of the Rabbi in Jewish Society of the Second Century," *The
        Galilee in Late Antiquity*, ed. L. I. Levine. New York and Jerusalem: The
        Jewish Theological Seminary of America. 157–173.
  1997 "Were Pharisees and Rabbis the Leaders of Communal Prayer and Torah
        Study in Antiquity: The Evidence of the New Testament, Josephus, and
        the Church Fathers," *The Echoes of Many Texts: Reflections on Jewish and*

> *Christian Traditions. Essays in Honor of Lou H. Silberman*, eds. W. G. Dever & J. E. Wright. BJS 313. Atlanta, Georgia: Scholars Press. 99–114.

1999a   "The Rabbi in Second Century Jewish Society," *The Cambridge History of Judaism, Volume Three: The Early Roman Period*, eds. W. Horbury, W. D. Davies & J. Sturdy. Cambridge: Cambridge University Press. 922–990.

1999b   "The Temple and the Synagogue," *The Cambridge History of Judaism, Volume Three: The Early Roman Period*, eds. W. Horbury, W. D. Davies & J. Sturdy. Cambridge: Cambridge University Press. 298–325.

1999c   *The Beginnings of Jewishness: Boundaries, Varieties, Uncertainties*. Berkeley/Los Angeles/London: University of California Press.

Cohn, Dorrit

1990   "Signposts of Fictionality: A Narratological Perspective," *Poetics Today 11*, 775–804.

Collins, John J.

1985   "A Symbol Of Otherness: Circumcision and Salvation in the First Century, *"To see Ourselves as Others See Us": Christians, Jews, "Others" in Late Antiquity*, eds. J. Neusner and E. S. Frerichs. Studies in the Humanities 9. Chico, California: Scholars Press.163–186.

1997   *Seers, Sibyls & Sages in Hellenistic-Roman Judaism*. JSJSup 54. Leiden: Brill.

1998²   *The Apocalyptic Imagination: An Introduction to Jewish Apocalyptic Literature*. Grand Rapids, Michigan: Eerdmans.

1999²   *Between Athens and Jerusalem: Jewish Identity in the Hellenistic Diaspora*. Grand Rapids, Michigan: Eerdmans & Livonia, Michigan: Dove Booksellers.

Collins, Raymond F.

2001   "Speaking of the Jews: 'Jews' in the Discourse Material of the Fourth Gospel," In Bieringer et al. 2001a, 281–300.

Conway, Colleen M.

2002   "The Production of the Johannine Community: A New Historist Perspective," *JBL* 121, 479–495.

Cotton, Hannah

1998   "The Rabbis and the Documents," *Jews in a Graeco-Roman World*, ed. M. Goodman. Oxford: Clarendon Press. 167–179.

1999   "The Impact of the Documentary Papyri from the Judaean Desert on the Study of Jewish History from 70 to 135 CE," *Jüdische Geschichte in hellenistisch-römischer Zeit. Wege der Forschung: Vom alten zum neuen Schürer*, ed. A. Oppenheimer. Schriften des Historischen Kollegs: Kolloquien 44. München: R. Oldenbourg Verlag. 221–236.

2000   "Recht und Wirtschaft: Zur Stellung der jüdischen Frau nach den Papyri aus der judäischen Wuste," *Zeitschrift für Neues Testament* 6, 23–30.

Culbertson, Philip L.

1991   "The Seventy Faces of the One God: The Theology of Religious Pluralism," *Jewish-Christian Relations*, eds. M. Shermis & A. E. Zannonini. Mahwah: New Jersey. 145–173.

Cullmann, Oscar

1966   "Sabbat und Sonntag nach dem Johannesevangelium. ΕΩΣ ᾽ΑΡΤΙ (Joh 5,17)," *Vorträge und Aufsätze 1925–1962*, ed. Karlfried Fröhlich. Tübingen: Mohr-Siebeck/Zürich: Zwingli Verlag. 187–191. (Originally appeared in *In memoriam Ernst Lohmeyer*, ed. W. Schmauch. Stuttgart: Evangelisches Verlagswerk, 1951. 127–131.)

1975   "Von Jesus zum Stephanuskreis und zum Johannesevagelium," *Jesus und Paulus. FS W. G. Kümmel*, eds. E. E. Ellis and E. Gräßer. Göttingen: Vandenhoeck & Ruprecht. 44–56.

Culpepper, R. Alan

1983   *Anatomy of the Fourth Gospel: A Study in Literary Design*. Philadelphia: Fortress Press.

1993   "John 5.1–18: A Sample of Narrative Critical Commentary," *The Gospel of John as Literature: An Anthology of Twentieth-Century Perspectives*, ed. M. W. G. Stibbe. New Testament Stools and Studies, 17. 193–207. Leiden: Brill. (Originally appeared in *La communauté johannique et son histoire*, eds. J.-D. Kaestli, J. M. Poffet & J. Zumstein. Geneva: Labor et fides, 1990. 131–151. Translated from the French by J.-D. Kaestli.)

1996   "The Gospel of John as a Document of Faith in a Pluralistic Culture," *"What is John?": Readers and Readings of the Fourth Gospel*, ed. F. F. Segovia, SBLSymS 3. Atlanta, Georgia: Scholars Press. 107–127.

1997 (ed.)   *Critical Readings of John 6*. Biblical Interpretation Series 22. Leiden: Brill.

2001   "Anti-Judaism in the Fourth Gospel as a Theological Problem for Christian Interpreters," in Bieringer et al. 2001a, 68–91.

Culpepper, R. Alan & Black, C. Clifton
1996   *Exploring the Gospel of John: In Honor of D. Moody Smith*. Louisville, Kentucky: Westminster John Knox Press.

Dahl, Nils Alstrup
1964   "Der Erstgeborene Satans und der Vater des Teufels (Polyk. 7:1 und Joh 8:44)," *Apophoreta, Festschrift für Ernst Haenchen*, eds. W. Eltester and F. H. Kettler. BZNW 30. Berlin: Alfred Töpelmann. 70–84.

1986 (1962) "The Johannine Church and History," *The Interpretation of John*, ed. John Ashton. IRT 9. Philadelphia: Fortress Press/London: SPCK. 122–140. (Originally appeared in *Current Issues in New Testament Interpretation*, eds. W. Klassen and G. F. Snyder. New York: Harper & Row/London: SCM Press, 1962, 124–142.)

Daube, David
1956   *The New Testament and Rabbinic Judaism*. London: The Athlone Press.
1958/59   "The Earliest Structure of the Gospels," *NTS* 5, 174–187.

Davies, Margaret
1992   *Rhetoric and Reference in the Fourth Gospel*. JSNTS, 69. Sheffield: JSOT Press.

Davies, Philip R.
1996   *Sects and Scrolls: Essays on Qumran and Related Topics*. South Florida Studies in the History of Judaism 134. Atlanta, Ga.: Scholars Press.

2000   "The Judaism(s) of the Damascus Document," *The Damascus Document: A Centennial of Discovery. Proceedings of the Third International Symposium of the Orion Center for the Study of the Dead Sea Scrolls and Associated Literature, 4–8 February, 1998*, eds. J. M. Baumgarten, E. G. Chazon & A. Pinnick. STDJ 34. Leiden: Brill. 27–43.

Davies, W. D.
1999   *Christian Engagements with Judaism*. Harrisburg, Pennsylvania: Trinity Press.

Deines, Roland
1993   *Jüdische Steingefäße und pharisäische Frömmigkeit: Ein archäologisch-historischer Beitrag zum Verständnis von Joh 2,6 und der jüdischen Reinheitshalacha zur zeit Jesu*. WUNT, 2. Reihe 52. Tübingen: Mohr-Siebeck.

1997   *Die Pharisäer: Ihr Verständnis im Spiegel der christlichen und jüdischen Forschung seit Wellhausen und Graetz*. WUNT 2. Reihe, 101. Tübingen: Mohr-Siebeck.

Delling, Gerhard
1984   "The 'One Who Sees God' in Philo," *Nourished with Peace: Studies in Hellenistic Judaism in Memory of Samuel Sandmel*, eds. Frederick E.

Greenspahn, Earle Hilgert and Burton L. Mack. Chico, California: Scholars Press. 27–41.

Denniston, J. D.
1954² *The Greek Particles*. Oxford: Clarendon Press.

Derrett, J. Duncan M.
1977 "The Zeal of the House and the Cleansing of the Temple," *The Downside Review* 95, 79–94.
1991 "Circumcision and Perfection: A Johannine Equation (John 7:22–23)," *EvQ* 63, 221–224.

Destro, Adriana & Pesce, Mauro
2001 "The Gospel of John and the Community Rule of Qumran: A Comparison of Systems," *Judaism in Late Antiquity, Part Five, The Judaism of Qumran: A Systematic Reading of the Dead Sea Scrolls, Volume Two: World View, Comparing Judaisms*, eds. A. J. Avery-Peck, J. Neusner and B. D. Chilton. HO, Section One vol. 57. Leiden: Brill. 201–229.

Dexinger, Ferdinand
1981 "Limits of Tolerance in Judaism: The Samaritan Example," *Jewish and Christian Self-Definition, Vol. 2: Aspects of Judaism in the Graeco-Roman Period*, eds. E. P. Sanders, A. I. Baumgarten and Alan Mendelson. Philadelphia: Fortress Press. 88–114.
1985 "Der 'Prophet wie Mose' in Qumran und bei den Samaritanern," in *Mélanges bibliques et orientaux en l'honneur de M. Mathias Delcor*, eds. A. Caquot, S. Légasse & M. Tardieu. AOAT 215. Kevelaer: Butzon und Bercker; Neukirchen-Vluyn: Neukirchener Verlag. 97–111.

Dietzfelbinger, Christian
1996 "Aspekte des Alten Testaments im Johannesevangelium," *Geschichte—Tradition—Reflexion. Festschrift für Martin Hengel zum 70. Geburtstag, 3. vls*, eds. H. Cancik, H. Lichtenberger and P. Schäfer. Tübingen: Mohr-Siebeck. Vol. 3, 203–218.

Dodd, Charles H.
1953 *The Interpretation of the Fourth Gospel*. Cambridge: Cambridge University Press.
1963 *Historical Tradition in the Fourth Gospel*. Cambridge: Cambridge University Press.
1968 "Behind a Johannine Dialogue," C. H. Dodd, *More New Testament Studies*. Manchester: Manchester University Press. 41–57. (The french original "A l'arrière-plan d'un dialogue Johannique [Joh 8:33–58]" appeared in *RHPR* 37 [1957], 5–17.)

Douglas, Mary
1973 *Natural Symbols: Explorations in Cosmology*. London: Barrie & Jenkins.

Dozeman, Thomas B.
1980 "*Sperma Abraam* in John 8 and Related Literature: Cosmology and Judgment," *CBQ* 42, 342–358.

Dube, Musa W.
1996 "Reading for Decolonization," *Semeia* 75, 37–59.

Duke, Paul D.
1985 *Irony in the Fourth Gospel*. Atlanta: John Knox Press.

Dunderberg, Ismo
1994 *Johannes und die Synoptiker: Studien zu Joh 1–9*. AASF Diss. 69. Suomalainen tiedeakatemia: Helsinki.
1998 "Thomas' I-sayings and the Gospel of John," *Thomas at the Crossroads: Essays on the Gospel of Thomas*, ed. Risto Uro. Studies of the New Testament and Its World. Edinburgh: T. & T. Clark. 33–64.

Dunn, James D. G.
1991 *The Partings of the Ways Between Christianity and Judaism and Their Significance*

for the Character of Christianity. London & Philadelphia: SCM Press & Trinity Press.

1992   "The Question of Anti-semitism in the New Testament Writings of the Period," *Jews and Christians: The Partings of the Ways A.D. 70 to 135*, ed. J. D. G. Dunn. WUNT 66. Tübingen: Mohr-Siebeck. 177–211.

2001   "The Embarrassment of History: Reflections on the Problem of 'Anti-Judaism' in the Fourth Gospel." In Bieringer et al. 2001a, 47–67.

Efron, Joshua
1987   *Studies on the Hasmonean Period*. SJLA 39. Leiden: Brill.

Eppstein, Victor
1964   "The Historicity of the Gospel Account of the Cleansing of the Temple," *ZNW* 55, 42–58.

Esler, Philip F.
1994   *The First Christians in their Social Worlds: Social-Scientific Approaches to New Testament Interpretation*. London and New York: Routledge.

Evans, Craig A.
1993   "Introduction. Faith and Polemic: The New Testament and First-century Judaism," *Anti-Semitism and Early Christianity: Issues of Polemic and Faith*, eds. C. A. Evans and D. A. Hagner. Minneapolis: Fortress Press. 1–17.

1997   "Jesus' Action in the Temple: Cleansing or Portent of Destruction," in Bruce Chilton and Craig A. Evans, *Jesus in Context: Temple, Purity, and Restoration*. AGJU 39; Leiden: Brill, 395–439. [An earlier version appeared in *CBQ* 51 (1989), 237–270.]

Feldman, Louis H.
1993   *Jew and Gentile in the Ancient World: Attitudes and Interactions from Alexander to Justinian*. Princeton, New Jersey: Princeton University Press.

Fine, Steven
1997   *This Holy Place: On the Sanctity of the Synagogue during the Greco-Roman Period*. Christianity and Judaism in Antiquity 11. Notre Dame, Indiana: University of Notre Dame Press.

Finkel, Asher
1981   "Yavneh's Liturgy and Early Christianity," *JES* 18, 231–250.

Flesher, Paul V. M.
2001   "Prolegomenon to a Theory of Early Synagogue Development," *Judaism in Late Antiquity, Part Three, Where We Stand: Issues and Debates in Ancient Judaism, Volume Four: The Special Problem of the Synagogue*, eds. A. J. Avery-Peck and J. Neusner. HO, Section One vol. 55. Leiden: Brill. 121–153.

Foerster, Werner
1954   "ὄφις," TWNT V, 566–582.

Forkman, Göran
1972   *The Limits of the Religious Community: Expulsion from the Religious Community within the Qumran Sect, within Rabbinic Judaism, and within Primitive Christianity*. ConBNT 5. Lund: CWK Gleerup.

Fortna, Robert Tomsom
1970   *The Gospel of Signs. A Reconstruction of the Narrative Source Underlying the Fourth Gospel*. SNTSMS 11. Cambridge: Cambridge University Press.

1988   *The Fourth Gospel and Its Predecessor: From Narrative Source to Present Gospel*. Edinburgh: T. & T. Clark.

Freed, Edwin D.
1965   *Old Testament Quotations in the Gospel of John*. NovTSup 11. Leiden: Brill.

1969   "The Manner of Worship in John 4:23f," *Search the Scriptures: New Testament Studies in Honor of Raymond T. Stamm*, eds. J. M. Myers, O. Reimherr, and H. N. Bream. Gettysburg Theological Studies 3. Leiden: Brill. 33–48.

1970   "Did John Write his Gospel Partly to Win Samaritan Converts?" *NovT* 12, 241–256.
Frey, Jörg
    1997   "Different Patterns of Dualistic Thought in the Qumran Library: Reflections on their Background and History," *Legal Texts and Legal Issues: Proceedings of the Second Meeting of the International Organization for Qumran Studies, Cambridge 1995. In Honour of Joseph M. Baumgarten*, eds. M. Bernstein, F. García Martínez and J. Kampen. STDJ 23. Leiden: Brill. 275–335.
Freyne, Sean
    1985   "Vilifying the Other and Defining the Self: Matthew's and John's Anti-Jewish Polemic in Focus, *"To see Ourselves as Others See Us": Christians, Jews, "Others" in Late Antiquity*, eds. J. Neusner and E. S. Frerichs. Studies in the Humanities 9. Chico, California: Scholars Press. 117–143.
    2000   *Galilee and Gospel: Collected Essays.* WUNT, 2. Reihe 125. Tübingen: Mohr-Siebeck.
García Martínez, Florentino
    1998   "The History of the Qumran Community in the Light of Recently Available Texts," *Qumran between the Old and New Testaments*, eds. F. H. Cryer and T. L. Thompson. JSOTSup 290. Sheffield: Sheffield Academic Press. 194–216.
    1999   "Priestly Functions in a Community without Temple," *Gemeinde ohne Tempel, Community without Temple: Zur Substituierung und Transformation des Jerusalemer Tempels und seines Kults im Alten Testament, antiken Judentum und frühen Christentum*, eds. B. Ego, A. Lange & P. Pilhofer. WUNT 118. Tübingen: Mohr-Siebeck. 303–319.
Gaston, Lloyd
    1993   "Lobsters in the Fourth Gospel," *Approaches to Ancient Judaism, New Series 4: Religious and Theological Studies*, ed. J. Neusner. South Florida Studies in the History of Judaism 81. Atlanta, Ga.: Scholars Press. 115–123.
Geiger, Georg
    1984   "Aufruf an Rückkehrende: Zum Sinn des Zitats von Ps 78,24b in Joh 6,31," *Bib* 65, 449–464.
Genette, Gérard
    1990   "Fictional Narrative, Factual Narrative," *Poetics Today 11*, 755–774.
Goldenberg, David
    1982   "Once More: Jesus in the Talmud," *JQR* 73, 78–86.
Goldstein, Jonathan A.
    1976   *I Maccabees.* AB 41. Garden City, New York: Doubleday.
    1983   *II Maccabees.* AB 41a. Garden City, New York: Doubleday.
Goodblatt, David
    1989   "The Place of the Pharisee in First Century Judaism: The State of the Debate," *JSJ* 20, 12–30.
    1994   *The Monarchic Principle: Studies in Jewish Self-Government in Antiquity.* TSAJ 38. Tübingen: Mohr-Siebeck.
Goodman, Martin
    1983   *State and Society in Roman Galilee, A.D. 132–212.* Totowa, New Jersey: Rowman & Allanheld.
    1991   "Babatha's Story," *JRS* 81, 169–175.
    1996   "The Function of Minim in Early Rabbinic Judaism," *Geschichte-Tradition-Reflexion: Festschrift für Martin Hengel zum 70. Geburtstag. Band I: Judentum*, eds. H. Cancik, H. Lichtenberger & P. Schäfer. Tübingen: Mohr-Siebeck. 501–510.
Grabbe, Lester L.
    1977   "Orthodoxy in First Century Judaism: What are the Issues," *JSJ* 8, 149–153.

1995   "Synagogues in pre-70 Palestine: A Re-Assessment," *Ancient Synagogues:
        Historical Analysis and Archaeological Discovery*, eds. D. Urman & P. V. M.
        Flesher. SPB 47, 1. Leiden: Brill. 17–26.
1999   "Sadducees and Pharisees," *Judaism in Late Antiquity, Part Three, Where we
        Stand: Issues and Debates in Ancient Judaism, Volume One*, eds. J. Neusner and
        A. J. Avery-Peck. HO, Section one, vol 40. Leiden: Brill. 35–62.
2000   "The Pharisees: A Response to Steve Mason," *Judaism in Late Antiquity,
        Part Three, Where we Stand: Issues and Debates in Ancient Judaism, Volume Three*,
        eds. J. Neusner and A. J. Avery-Peck. HO, Section One, vol. 53. Leiden:
        Brill. 35–47.

Gräßer, Erich
1973   *Text und Situation: Gesammelte Aufsätze zum Neuen Testament*. Gütersloh:
        Gütersloher Verlagshaus Gerd Mohn.

Green, William Scott
2000a   "Rabbi in Classical Judaism," *The Encyclopaedia of Judaism Vol III*, eds.
        J. Neusner, A. J. Avery-Peck & W. S. Green. Leiden: Brill. 1124–1132.
2000b   "Heresy, Apostasy in Judaism," *The Encyclopaedia of Judaism Vol I*, eds.
        J. Neusner, A. J. Avery-Peck & W. S. Green. Leiden: Brill. 366–380.

Günther, Walther
1971   "ἀδικία," *Theologisches Begriffslexikon zum Neuen Testament, Band II,2*, eds.
        Lothar Coenen, Erich Beyreuther and Hans Bietenhard. Wuppertal: Rolf
        Brockhaus. 1192–1195.

Hachlili, Rachel
1997   "The Origin of the Synagogue: A Re-Assesment," *JSJ* 28, 34–47.
1998   *Ancient Jewish Art and Archaeology in the Diaspora*. HO, Section one, vol 35.
        Leiden: Brill.

Hahn, Ferdinand
1967   "Die alttestamentlichen Motive in der urchristlichen Abendmahls-
        überlieferung," *EvT* 27, 337–374.
1970   "Der Prozeß Jesu nach dem Johannesevangelium: Eine redaktions-
        geschichtliche Untersuchung," *EKKNT, Vorarbeiten Heft 2*. Einsiedeln:
        Neukirchener Verlag. 23–96.
1996   "'Das Heil kommt von den Juden': Erwägungen zu Joh 4.22b," F. Hahn
        *Die Verwurzelung des Christentums im Judentum: Exegetische Beiträge zum christlich-
        jüdischen Gespräch*. Neukirchen-Vluyn: Neukirchener Verlag. 99–118.
        (Originally appeared in *Wort und Wirklichkeit: Studien zur Afrikanistik und
        Orientalistik Eugen Ludwig Rapp zum 70. Geburtstag*, eds. B. Bezing, O. Böcher
        and G. Mayer. Meisenheim: Hain, 1976. 67–84)

Hall, Bruce W.
1987   *Samaritan Religion from John Hyrcanus to Baba Rabba: A Critical Examination
        of the Relevant Material in Contemporary Christian Literature, the Writings of
        Josephus, and the Mishnah*. Studies in Judaica 3. Sydney: Mandelbaum
        Trust, University of Sydney.

Hansen, G. Walter
1989   *Abraham in Galatians: Epistolary and Rhetorical Contexts*. JSNTS 29. Sheffield:
        JSOT Press.

Hare, Douglas R. A.
1967   *The Theme of Jewish Persecution of Christians in the Gospel According to Matthew*.
        SNTSMS 6. Cambridge: Cambridge University Press.

Hartman, Lars
1989   "'He spoke of the Temple of his Body' (Jn 2:13–22)," *Svensk Exegetisk
        Årsbok* 54, 70–79.

Harvey, Graham
1996   *The True Israel: Uses of the Names Jew, Hebrew and Israel in Ancient Jewish
        and Early Christian Literature*. AGJU 35. Leiden: Brill.

Hasel, Gerhard F.
  1992   "Sabbath." *ABD* V, 849–856.
Hayes, Christine E.
  1998   "Displaced Self-Perceptions: The Deployment of *Mînîm* and Romans in
          B. Sanhedrin 90b–91a," *Religious and Ethnic Communities in Later Roman
          Palestine*, ed. Hayim Lapin. Studies and Texts in Jewish History and Culture
          5. Bethesda, Md: University Press of Maryland. 249–289.
Hengel, Martin
  1971   "Proseuche und Synagoge. Jüdische Gemeinde, Gotteshaus und Gottesdienst
          in der Diaspora and in Palästina," *Tradition und Glaube: Das Frühe Christentum
          in seiner Umwelt. Festschrift für Karl Georg Kuhn*, eds. G. Jeremias, H.-W. Kuhn
          & H. Stegemann. Göttingen: Vandenhoeck & Ruprecht. 157–184.
  1974   *Judaism and Hellenism: Studies in Their Encounter in Palestine during the Early
          Hellenistic Period.* Two Volumes. Translated from the German original
          *Judentum und Hellenismus: Studien zu ihrer Begegnung unter besonderer Berücksichtigung
          Palästinas bis zur Mitte des 2. Jh. v. Chr* (1969) by John Bowden. London:
          SCM Press.
  1989   *The Zealots: Investigations into the Jewish Freedom Movement in the Period from
          Herod I until 70 A.D.* Translated from the German Original *Die Zeloten:
          Untersuchungen zur Jüdischen Freiheitsbewegung in der Zeit von Herodes I bis 70 n.
          Chr.* (1961; 1976²) by D. Smith. Edinburgh: T. & T. Clark.
  1993   *Die johanneische Frage: Ein Lösungsversuch.* WUNT 67. Tübingen: Mohr-Siebeck.
Hengel, Martin & Deines, Roland
  1995   "E. P. Sanders' 'Common Judaism', Jesus, and the Pharisees," *JTS* 46, 1–70.
van Henten, Jan Willem
  2001   "Anti-Judaism in Revelation? A Response to Peter Tomson," In Bieringer
          et al. 2001a, 111–125.
Herford, R. Travers
  1930   *Christianity in Talmud and Midrash.* London: Williams & Norgate.
Hezser, Catherine
  1997   *The Social Structure of the Rabbinic Movement in Roman Palestine.* TSAJ 66.
          Tübingen: Mohr-Siebeck.
Hofius, Otfried
  1996   "'Der in des Vaters Schoß ist' Joh 1,18," O. Hofius and H.-C. Kammler,
          Johannesstudien: Untersuchungen zur Theologie des vierten Evangeliums. WUNT 88.
          Tübingen: Mohr-Siebeck. 24–32. (Originally appeared in *ZNW* 80 [1989],
          163–171.)
Holtz, Traugott
  1986   *Der erste Brief an die Thessalonicher.* EKKNT 13. Zürich/Neukirchen-Vluyn:
          Benziger Verlag/Neukirchener Verlag.
Horbury, William
  1998   *Jews and Christians in Contact and Controversy.* Edinburgh: T. & T. Clark.
van der Horst, Pieter W.
  1994   "The Birkat ha-minim in Recent Research," *ExpTim* 105, 363–368.
Hulmi, Sini
  1999   *Paulus und Mose: Argumentation und Polemik in 2 Kor 3.* Schriften der Finnischen
          Exegetischen Gesellschaft 77. Helsinki/Göttingen: Finnische Exegetische
          Gesellschaft/Vandenhoeck & Ruprecht.
Hunzinger, Claus-Hunno
  1980   "Bann. II: Frühjudentum und Neues Testament," *TRE* V, 161–167.
Jacobs, Louis
  1961   *Studies in Talmudic Logic and Methodology.* London: Vallentine, Mitchell.
Jacobs, Martin
  1995   *Die Institution des jüdischen Patriarchen: Eine quellen- und traditionskritische Studie
          zur Geschichte der Juden in der Spätantike.* TSAJ 52. Tübingen: Mohr-Siebeck.

Japhet, Sara
  1989 (1973) *The Ideology of the Book of Chronicles and Its Place in Biblical Thought.*
               Beiträge zur Erforschung des Alten Testaments und des antiken
               Judentums 9. Translated by Anna Barber. Bern: Peter Lang.
Jeanrond, Werner
  1991   *Theological Hermeneutics: Development and Significance.* London: SCM
               Press.
Jeremias, Joachim
  1958²   *Jerusalem zur Zeit Jesu: Kulturgeschichtliche Untersuchung zur neutestamentlichen
               Zeitgeschichte.* Göttingen: Vandenhoeck & Ruprecht.
Johnson, Luke T.
  1989   "The New Testament's Anti-Jewish Slander and the Conventions
               of Ancient Polemic," *JBL* 108, 419–441.
Jokiranta, Jutta M.
  2001   "'Sectarianism' of the Qumran 'Sect': Sociological Notes," *RevQ*
               78, 223–239.
de Jonge, Marinus
  1977   *Jesus: Stranger from Heaven and Son of God: Jesus Christ and Christians in
               Johannine Perspective.* Edited and translated by John E. Steely. SBLSBS
               11. Missoula, Montana: Scholars Press.
  2000   "Christology, Controversy and Community in the Gospel of John,"
               *Christology, Controversy and Community: New Testament Essays in Honour
               of David. R. Catchpole*, eds. D. G. Horrell and C. M. Tuckett.
               NovTSup 99. Leiden; Brill. 209–229.
Kalmin, Richard
  1994   "Christians and Heretics in Rabbinic Literature of Late Antiquity,"
               HTR 87, 155–169.
  1999   *The Sage in Jewish Society of Late Antiquity.* London and New York:
               Routledge.
Katz, Steven T.
  1984   "Issues in the Separation of Judaism and Christianity after 70 C.E.:
               A Reconsideration," *JBL* 103, 43–76.
Kee, Howard Clark & Borowsky, Irvin J. (eds.)
  1998   *Removing the Anti-Judaism from the New Testament.* Philadelphia,
               Pennsylvania: American Interfaith Institute/World Alliance.
Kiilunen, Jarmo
  1985   *Die Vollmacht im Widerstreit. Untersuchungen zum Werdegang von Mk
               2,1–3,6.* AASF Diss. 40. Suomalainen tiedeakatemia: Helsinki.
Kimelman, Reuven
  1981   "*Birkat Ha-Minim* and the Lack of Evidence for an Anti-Christian
               Jewish Prayer in Late Antiquity," *Jewish and Christian Self-Definition.
               Vol II: Aspects of Judaism in the Greco-Roman Period*, eds. E. P. Sanders,
               A. I. Baumgarten and A. Mendelson. Philadelphia: Fortress Press.
               226–244.
  1997   "The Literary Structure of the Amidah and the Rhetoric of
               Redemption, *The Echoes of Many Texts: Reflections on Jewish and Christian
               Traditions. Essays in Honor of Lou H. Silberman*, eds. W. G. Dever &
               J. E. Wright. BJS 313. Atlanta, Georgia: Scholars Press. 171–218.
  1999   "Identifying Jews and Christians in Roman Syria-Palestine," *Galilee
               through the Centuries: Confluence of Cultures*, ed. Eric M. Meyers. Duke
               Judaic Studies Series 1. Winona Lake, Indiana: Eisenbrauns.
               301–333.
Kippenberg, Hans Gerhard
  1971   *Garizim und Synagoge: Traditionsgeschichtliche Untersuchungen zur samari-
               tanischen Religion der aramäischen Periode.* Religionsgeschichtliche Versuche
               und Vorarbeiten 30. Berlin, New York: Walter de Gruyter.

Klappert, Bertold
1990   " 'Moses hat von mir geschrieben.' Leitlinien einer Christologie im Kontext des Judentums Joh 5,39–47," *Die Hebräische Bibel und ihre zweifache Nachgeschichte. Festschrift für Rolf Rendtorff zum 65. Geburtstag*, eds. E. Blum, C. Macholz and E. W. Stegemann. Neukirchen-Vluyn: Neukirchener Verlag. 619–640.
Klijn, A. F. J.
1992   *Jewish-Christian Gospel Tradition*. VCSup 17. Leiden: Brill.
Koester, Craig R.
1990   " 'The Savior of the World' (John 4:42)," *JBL* 109, 665–680.
Kotila, Markku
1988   *Umstrittener Zeuge. Studien zur Stellung des Gesetzes in der johanneischen Theologiegeschichte*. AASF Diss. 48. Suomalainen tiedeakatemia: Helsinki.
Kovacs, Judith L.
1989   "The Archons, the Spirit and the Death of Christ: Do We Need the Hypothesis of Gnostic Opponents to Explain 1 Cor. 2.6–16?," *Apocalyptic and the New Testament: Essays in Honor of J. Louis Martyn*, eds. J. Marcus and M. L. Soards. JSNTS 24. Sheffield: Sheffield Academic Press. 217–236.
1995   " 'Now Shall the Ruler of This World Be Driven Out': Jesus' Death as Cosmic Battle in John 12:20–36," *JBL* 114, 227–247.
Kraabel, Alf Thomas
1979   "The Diaspora Synagogue: Archaeological and Epigraphic Evidence since Sukenik," *ANRW* II. 19.1, 477–510.
1981   "Social Systems of Six Diaspora Synagogues," *Ancient Synagogues: The State of Research*, ed. J. Gutmann. BJS 22. Ann Arbor, Michigan: Scholars Press. 79–91.
Kügler, Joachim
1984   "Das Johannesevangelium und seine Gemeinde—kein Thema für Science Fiction," *BN* 23, 48–62.
1988   *Der Jünger den Jesus liebte. Literarische, theologische und historische Untersuchungen zu einer Schlüsselgestalt johanneischer Theologie und Geschichte. Mit einem Exkurs über die Brotrede in Joh 6.* SBB 16. Stuttgart: Verlag Katholisches Bibelwerk.
Kuhn, Karl George
1938   " Ἰσραήλ, Ἰουδαῖος, Ἑβραῖος" in der nach-at.lichen jüdischen Literatur, *TWNT* III, 360–370.
Kümmel, Werner Georg
1972   *The New Testament: The History of the Investigation of Its Problems*. Translated from the German original *Das Neue Testament: Geschichte der Erforschung seiner Probleme* (1970) by S. M. Gilmour and H. C. Kee. Nashville & New York: Abingdon.
Kuula, Kari
1999   *The Law, the Covenant and God's Plan, vol. 1: Paul's Polemical Treatment of the Law in Galatians*. Publications of the Finnish Exegetical Society 72. Helsinki & Göttingen: The Finnish Exegetical Society/Vandenhoeck & Ruprecht.
Kysar, Robert
1993   "Anti-Semitism and the Gospel of John," *Anti-Semitism and Early Christianity: Issues of Polemic and Faith*, eds. C. A. Evans and D. A. Hagner. Minneapolis: Fortress Press. 113–127.
1997   "The Dismantling of Decisional Faith: A Reading of John 6:25–71," in Culpepper 1997, 161–181.
Labahn, Michael
1999   *Jesus als Lebensspender: Untersuchungen zu einer Geschichte der johanneischen Tradition anhand ihrer Wundergeschichten*. BZNW 98. Berlin/New York: Walter de Gruyter.
Lane, William L.
1998   "Social Perspectives on Roman Christianity during the Formative Years from Nero to Nerva: Romans, Hebrews, 1. Clement," *Judaism and Christianity in First-Century Rome*, eds. K. P. Donfried & P. Richardson. Grand Rapids, Michigan: Eerdmans. 196–244.

Lange, Armin
  1995   *Weisheit und Prädestination: Weisheitliche Urordnung und Prädestination in den
          Textfunden von Qumran.* STDJ 18. Leiden: Brill.
  1997   "The Essene Position on Magic and Divination," *Legal Texts and Legal
          Issues: Proceedings of the Second Meeting of the International Organization for Qumran
          Studies, Cambridge 1995. In Honour of Joseph M. Baumgarten,* eds. M. Bernstein,
          F. García Martínez and J. Kampen. STDJ 23. Leiden: Brill. 377–435.
Lapin, Hayim
  1995   *Early Rabbinic Civil Law and the Social History of Roman Galilee: A Study of
          Mishnah Tractate Baba' Meṣi'a'.* BJS 307. Atlanta, Georgia: Scholars Press.
  1998   "Introduction: Locating Ethnicity and Religious Community in Later
          Roman Palestine," *Religious and Ethnic Communities in Later Roman Palestine,*
          ed. Hayim Lapin. Studies and Texts in Jewish History and Culture 5.
          Bethesda, Md: University Press of Maryland. 1–28.
Lee, Dorothy A.
  1994   *The Symbolic Narratives of the Fourth Gospel: The Interplay of Form and Meaning.*
          JSNTS 95. Sheffield: JSOT Press.
Leidig, Edeltraud
  1981²   *Jesu Gespräch mit der Samaritanerin und weitere Gespräche im Johannesevangelium.*
          Theologische Dissertationen, Band XV. Basel: Friedrich Reinhardt.
Leistner, Reinhold
  1974   *Antijudaismus im Johannesevangelium: Darstellung des Problems in der neueren
          Auslegungsgeschichte und Untersuchung der Leidensgeschichte.* Theologie und
          Wirklichkeit 13. Bern: Peter Lang.
Léon-Dufour, Xavier
  1981   "Towards a Symbolic Reading of the Fourth Gospel," *NTS* 27, 439–456.
Levine, Amy-Jill
  1999   "Anti-Judaism and the Gospel of Matthew," *Anti-Judaism and the Gospels,*
          ed. William R. Farmer. Harrisburg, Pennsylvania: Trinity Press. 9–36.
Levine, Lee I.
  1987   "The Second Temple Synagogue: The Formative Years," *The Synagogue
          in Late Antiquity,* ed. L. I. Levine. Philadelphia, Pennsylvania: The American
          Schools of Oriental Research. 7–31.
  1997   "The Nature and Origin of the Palestinian Synagogue Reconsidered,"
          JBL 115, 425–448.
  1999a   "The Development of Synagogue Liturgy in Late Antiquity," *Galilee through
          the Centuries: Confluence of Cultures,* ed. Eric M. Meyers. Duke Judaic Studies
          Series 1. Winona Lake, Indiana: Eisenbrauns. 123–144.
  1999b   "The Patriarchate and the Ancient Synagogue," *Jews, Christians, and
          Polytheists in the Ancient Synagogue: Cultural Interaction during the Greco-Roman
          Period,* ed. S. Fine. London & New York: Routledge. 87–100.
  2000   *The Ancient Synagogue: The First Thousand Years.* New Haven & London:
          Yale University Press.
Levy, B. Barry
  1986   *Targum Neophyti 1: A Textual Study. Introduction, Genesis, Exodus, vol. 1.* Studies
          in Judaism. Lanham, New York, London: University Press of America.
Lieu, J. M.
  1996   *Image and Reality: The Jews in the World of the Christians in the Second Century.*
          T. & T. Clark: Edinburgh.
  1998   "Accusations of Jewish persecution in early Christian sources, with par-
          ticular reference to Justin Martyr and the Martyrdom of Polycarp,"
          Tolerance and Intolerance in Early Judaism and Christianity, eds. G. N. Stanton
          and G. G. Stroumsa. Cambridge: Cambridge University Press. 279–295.
  1999   "Temple and Synagogue in John," *NTS* 45, 51–69.

2001 "Anti-Judaism in the Fourth Gospel: Explanation and Hermeneutics," in Bieringer et al. 2001a, 126–143.

Limbeck, Meinrad
1974 "Satan und das Böse im Neuen Testament," H. Haag, *Teufelsglaube*. Mit Beiträgen von K. Elliger, B. Lang und M. Limbeck. Tübingen: Katzmann Verlag. 271–388.

Lindars, Barnabas
1992 "The persecution of Christians in John 15:18–16:4a," B. Lindars, *Essays on John*, ed. C. M. Tuckett. Studiorum Novi Testamenti Auxilia 17. Leuven: University Press. 131–152. (Originally appeared in *Suffering and Martyrdom in the New Testament. Studies presented to G. M. Styler*, eds. W. Horbury and B. McNeil. Cambridge: Cambridge University Press, 1981. 48–69)

Lohse, Eduard
1971 "σάββατον," *TDNT* VII, 1–35.

Lowe, Malcolm
1976 "Who were the IOUDAIOI?," *NovT* 18, 101–130

Luomanen, Petri
1998 *Entering the Kingdom of Heaven. A Study on the Structure of Matthew's View of Salvation*. WUNT, 2. Reihe 101. Tübingen: Mohr-Siebeck.
2002 "The 'Sociology of Sectarianism' in Matthew: Modeling the Genesis of Early Jewish and Christian Communities," *Fair Play: Diversity and Conflicts in Early Christianity. Essays in Honour of Heikki Räisänen*, eds. I. Dunderberg, C. Tuckett & K. Syreeni. NovTSup 103. Leiden: Brill. 107–130.

Luz, Ulrich
1978 "Die Erfüllung des Gesetzes bei Matthäus," *ZTK* 75, 398–435.
1981 "Das Neue Testament," Rudolf Smend and Ulrich Luz, *Gesetz*. Biblische Konfrontationen 1015. Stuttgart: W. Kohlhammer. 58–139, 149–156.
1989² *Das Evangelium nach Matthäus*. 1. Teilband Mt 1–7. EKKNT, I/1. Zürich/Braunschweig: Benziger Verlag. Neukirchen-Vluyn: Neukirchener Verlag.
1990 *Das Evangelium nach Matthäus*. 2. Teilband Mt 8–17. EKKNT, I/2. Zürich/Braunschweig: Benziger Verlag. Neukirchen-Vluyn: Neukirchener Verlag.
1999 "Das 'Auseinandergehen der Wege:' Über die Trennung des Christentums vom Judentum," *Antijudaismus—christliche Erblast*, eds. W. Dietrich, M. George and U. Luz. Stuttgart: Kohlhammer.

MacDonald, John
1964 *The Theology of the Samaritans*. London: SCM Press.

Maier, Johann
1978 *Jesus von Nazareth in der talmudischen Überlieferung*. Erträge der Forschung 82. Darmstadt: Wissenschaftliche Buchgesellschaft.
1982 *Jüdische Auseinandersetzung mit dem Christentum in der Antike*. Erträge der Forschung 177. Darmstadt: Wissenschaftliche Buchgesellschaft.

Malina, Bruce J.
1968 *The Palestinian Manna Tradition: The Manna Tradition in the Palestinian Targums and Its Relationship to the New Testament Writings*. AGJU 7. Leiden: Brill.

Manns, Frédéric
1988 *John and Jamnia: How the Break Occurred Between Jews and Christians c. 80–100 A.D.* Jerusalem: Franciscan Printing Press.

Marcus, Joel
2000 *Mark 1–8. A New Translation with Introduction and Commentary*. AB 27. New York: Doubleday.

Marjanen, Antti
1998 "Is *Thomas* a Gnostic Gospel?" *Thomas at the Crossroads: Essays on the Gospel of Thomas*, ed. Risto Uro. Studies of the New Testament and Its World. Edinburgh: T. & T. Clark. 107–139.

Martin, Ralph P.
    1986   *2 Corinthians*. WBC 40. Waco, Texas: Word Books.
Martini, Carlo M.
    1977–78   "Is There a Late Alexandrian Text of the Gospels?," *NTS* 24,
                    285–296.
Martyn, J. Louis
    1977   "Glimpses into the History of the Johannine community: From Its
                    Origin through the Period of Its Life in Which the Fourth Gospel
                    Was Composed," *L'Évangile de Jean: Sources, rédaction, théologie*, ed.
                    M. de Jonge. BETL 44. Leuven: University Press. 149–175.
    1979² (1968)   *History and Theology in the Fourth Gospel*. Nashville: Abingdon Press.
    1986   "Source Criticism and Religionsgeschichte in the Fourth Gospel,"
                    The Interpretation of John, ed. John Ashton. IRT 9. Philadelphia/London:
                    Fortress Press/SPCK. 99–121. [Originally appeared in *Jesus and
                    Man's Hope, vol. I*, ed. D. G. Buttrick. Pittsburgh 1970, 247–273.]
    1996   "Gentile Mission That Replaced an Earlier Jewish Mission," in
                    Culpepper and Black 1996, 124–144.
Mason, Steve
    1999   "Revisiting Josephus's Pharisees," *Judaism in Late Antiquity, Part Three,
                    Where we Stand: Issues and Debates in Ancient Judaism, Volume Two*, eds.
                    J. Neusner and A. J. Avery-Peck. HO, Section One, vol. 41. Leiden:
                    Brill. 23–56.
McCready, Wayne O.
    1990   "Johannine Self-Understanding and the Synagogue Episode of John
                    9," *Self-Definition and Self-Discovery in Early Christianity: A Study in
                    Changing Horizons. Essays in Appreciation of Ben F. Meyer from Former
                    Students*, eds. D. J. Hawkin & T. Robinson. Studies in the Bible
                    and Early Christianity 26. Lewinston/Queenston/Lampeter: The
                    Edwin Mellen Press.
McGrath, James F.
    2001   *John's Apologetic Christology: Legitimation and Development in Johannine
                    Christology*. SNTSMS 111. Cambridge: Cambridge University Press.
McKelvey, R. J.
    1969   *The New Temple: The Church in the New Testament*. Oxford Theological
                    Monographs. Oxford: University Press.
Meeks, Wayne A.
    1967   *The Prophet-King: Moses Traditions and the Johannine Christology*. NovTSup
                    14. Leiden: Brill.
    1972   "The Man from Heaven in Johannine Sectarianism," *JBL* 91, 44–72.
    1975   "'Am I a Jew?'—Johannine Christianity and Judaism," *Christianity,
                    Judaism and Greco-Roman Cults. Studies for Morton Smith at Sixty. Part
                    One*, ed. J. Neusner. SJLA 12. Leiden: Brill. 163–186.
    1976   "The Divine Agent and His Counterfeit in Philo and the Fourth
                    Gospel," *Aspects of Religious Propaganda in Judaism and Early Christianity*,
                    ed. Elisabeth Schüssler Fiorenza. Notre Dame: University of Notre
                    Dame Press.
    1985   "Breaking Away: Three New Testament Pictures of Christianity's
                    Separation from the Jewish Communities," *"To see Ourselves as Others
                    See Us": Christians, Jews, "Others" in Late Antiquity*, eds. J. Neusner
                    and E. S. Frerichs. Studies in the Humanities 9. Chico, California:
                    Scholars Press. 94–115.
    1990   "Equal to God," *The Conversation Continues: Studies in Paul & John in
                    Honor of J. Louis Martyn*, eds. R. T. Fortna and B. R. Graventa.
                    Nashville: Abingdon Press. 309–321.

Mees, Michael
 1981 "Realer oder irrealer Kondizionalsatz in Joh 8:39?," *New Testament Textual Criticism: Its Significance for Exegesis. Essays in Honour of Bruce M. Metzger*, eds. Eldon Jay Epp and Gordon D. Fee. Oxford: Clarendon Press. 119–130.
Mendner, Siegfried
 1956 "Die Tempelreinigung," *ZNW* 47, 93–112.
Menken, M. J. J.
 1988a "The Provenance and Meaning of the Old Testament Quatation in John 6:31," *NovT* 30, 39–56.
 1988b "The Old Testament Quotation in John 6,45: Source and Redaction," *ETL* 64, 164–172.
 1997 "John 6:51c–58: Eucharist or Christology," in Culpepper 1997, 183–204.
 2001 "Scriptural Dispute between Jews and Christians in John: Literary Fiction or Historical Reality? John 9:13–17, 24–34 as a Test Case," in Bieringer et al. 2001a, 445–460.
Merenlahti, Petri
 2002 *Poetics for the Gospels: Rethinking Narrative Criticism*. Studies of the New Testament and Its World. London & New York: T. & T. Clark.
Merenlahti, Petri & Hakola, Raimo
 1999 "Reconceiving Narrative Criticism," *Characterization in the Gospels: Reconceiving Narrative Criticism*, eds. D. Rhoads and K. Syreeni. JSNTS 184. Sheffield: Sheffield Academic Press. 13–48.
Metso, Sarianna
 1997 *The Textual Development of the Qumran Community Rule*. STDJ 21. Leiden: Brill.
 1998 "Constitutional Rules at Qumran," *The Dead Sea Scrolls After Fifty Years: A Comprehensive Assessment, Vol I*, eds. P. W. Flint and J. C. VanderKam. Leiden: Brill. 186–210.
 2000 "The Relationship between the Damascus Document and the Community Rule," *The Damascus Document: A Centennial of Discovery. Proceedings of the Third International Symposium of the Orion Center for the Study of the Dead Sea Scrolls and Associated Literature, 4–8 February, 1998*, eds. J. M. Baumgarten, E. G. Chazon & A. Pinnick. STDJ 34. Leiden: Brill. 85–93.
Metzger, Bruce M.
 1994² *A Textual Commentary on the Greek New Testament*. Stuttgart: Deutsche Bibelgesellschaft/United Bible Societies.
Meyers, Eric M.
 1999 "Recent Archaeology in Palestine: Achievements and Future Goals, *The Cambridge History of Judaism, Volume Three: The Early Roman Period*, eds. W. Horbury, W. D. Davies & J. Sturdy. Cambridge: Cambridge University Press. 59–74.
Meyers, Eric M. & Kraabel, A. Thomas
 1986 "Archaeology, Iconography, and Nonliterary Written Remains," *Early Judaism and Its Modern Interpreters*, eds. R. A. Kraft & G. W. E. Nickelsburg. SBLBMI 2. Philadelphia, Pennsylvania and Atlanta, Georgia: Fortress Press and Scholars Press. 175–210.
Miller, Stuart S.
 1993 "The *Minim* of Sepphoris Reconsidered," *HTR* 86, 377–402.
 1999 "New Perspectives on the History of Sepphoris," *Galilee through the Centuries: Confluence of Cultures*, ed. Eric M. Meyers. Duke Judaic Studies Series 1. Winona Lake, Indiana: Eisenbrauns. 145–159.
Modrzejewski, Joseph Mélèze
 1995 *The Jews of Egypt from Rameses II to Emperor Hadrian*. Translated from the French Original *Les Juifs d'Egypte, de Ramses II à Hadrien* (1992) by R. Cornman. Edinburgh: T. & T. Clark.

Moloney, Francis J.
    1993   *Belief in the Word. Reading John 1–4*. Minneapolis: Fortress Press.
    1996   *Signs and Shadows: Reading John 5–12*. Minneapolis: Fortress Press.
    1997   "The Function of Prolepsis in the Interpretation of John 6," in
                    Culpepper 1997, 129–148.
    1998   *Glory not Dishonor: Reading John 13–21*. Minneapolis: Fortress Press.
Montgomery, James Alan
    1968 (1907)   *The Samaritans: The Earliest Jewish Sect. Their History, Theology and Liter-
                    ature*. New York: KTAV Publishing House.
Motyer, Stephen
    1997   *Your Father the Devil? A New Approach to John and 'the Jews.'* Carlisle:
                    Paternoster Press.
Mussner, Franz
    1979   *Traktat über die Juden*. Munich: Kösel Verlag.
Myllykoski, Matti
    1991   *Die letzten Tage Jesu: Markus und Johannes, ihre Traditionen und die his-
                    torische Frage. Band I*. AASF ser. B 256. Suomalainen tiedeakatemia:
                    Helsinki.
Myllykoski, Matti & Luomanen, Petri
    1999   "Varhaisen juutalaiskristillisyyden jäljillä [On the Trail of Early
                    Judaeo-Christianity (With an English Abstract)]," *Teologinen Aikakanskirja*,
                    104, 327–348.
Neusner, Jacob
    1962   *A Life of Rabban Yohanan ben Zakkai. Ca. 1–80 C.E.* SPD 6. Leiden:
                    Brill.
    1971   *The Rabbinic Traditions about the Pharisees before 70: Part III Conclusions*.
                    Leiden: Brill.
    1973a   *Eliezer ben Hyrcanus: The Tradition and the Man. Part One: The Tradition*.
                    SJLA 3. Leiden: Brill.
    1973b   *Eliezer ben Hyrcanus: The Tradition and the Man. Part Two: Analysis of
                    the Tradition*. SJLA 4. Leiden: Brill.
    1975   *Early Rabbinic Judaism: Historical Studies in Religion, Literature and Art*.
                    SJLA 13. Leiden: Brill.
    1981   *A History of the Mishnaic Law of Appointed Times*. Part One: Shabbat.
                    Translation and Explanation. SJLA 34. Leiden: Brill.
    1983a   *Formative Judaism: Religious, Historical and Literary Studies. Third Series:
                    Torah, Pharisees, and Rabbis*. BJS 46. Chico, California: Scholars Press.
    1983b   *Judaism in Society: The Evidence of the Yerusalmi*. Chicago & London:
                    The University of Chicago Press.
    1987b   *Judaism and Christianity in the Age of Constantine: History, Messiah, Israel,
                    and the Initial Confrontation*. CSJH. Chicago & London: The University
                    of Chicago Press.
    1988c   *Judaism: The Evidence of the Mishnah*. Second Edition, Augmented.
                    BJS 129. Atlanta: Georgia: Scholars Press.
    1989   "The Absoluteness of Christianity and the Uniqueness of Judaism,"
                    Interpretation 43, 18–31.
    1999   *The Mishnah: Social Perspectives*. HO, Section One vol. 46. Leiden:
                    Brill.
Neyrey, Jerome H.
    1979   "Jacob Traditions and the Interpretation of John 4:10–26," *CBQ* 41,
                    419–437.
    1987   "Jesus the Judge: Forensic Process in John 8, 21–59," *Bib* 68, 509–541.
    1988   *An Ideology of Revolt: John's Christology in Social-Science Perspective*.
                    Philadelphia: Fortress Press.

1996   "The Trials (Forensic) and Tribulations (Honor Challenges) of Jesus: John 7 in Social Science Perspective," *BTB* 26, 107–124.

Obermann, Andreas
1996   *Die christologische Erfüllung der Schrift im Johannesevangelium: Eine Untersuchung zur johanneischen Hermeneutik anhand der Schriftzitate.* WUNT, 2. Reihe 83. Tübingen: Mohr-Siebeck.

O'Day, Gail
1986   *Revelation in the Fourth Gospel: Narrative Mode and Theological Claim.* Philadelphia: Fortress Press.

Okure, Teresa
1988   *The Johannine Approach to Mission: A Contextual Study of John 4:1–42.* WUNT 31. Tübingen: Mohr-Siebeck.

Olsson, Birger
1974   *Structure and Meaning in the Fourth Gospel. A Text-Linguistic Analysis of John 2:1–11 and 4:1–42.* Translated by Jean Gray. ConBNT 6. Lund: CWK Kleerup.

Pagels, Elaine
1973   *The Johannine Gospel in Gnostic Exegesis: Heracleon's Commentary on John.* SBLMS 17. Nashville & New York: Abingdon Press.
1991   "The Social History of Satan, the 'Intimate Enemy': A Preliminary Sketch," *HTR* 84, 105–28.
1994   "The Social History of Satan, Part II: Satan in the New Testament Gospels," *JAAR* 62, 17–58.
1995   *The Origin of Satan.* London: Penguin Books.

Painter, John
1979   "The Church and Israel in the Gospel of John: A Response," *NTS 25*, 103–112
1993²   *The Quest for the Messiah: The History, Literature and Theology of the Johannine Community.* Nashville: Abingdon.
1997   "Jesus and the Quest for Eternal Life," in Culpepper 1997, 61–94.

Pamment, Margaret
1982   "Is There Convincing Evidence of Samaritan Influence on the Fourth Gospel," *ZNW* 73, 221–230.

Pancaro, Severino
1969–70   "'People of God' in St. John's Gospel," *NTS 16*, 114–129.
1974–75   "The Relationship of the Church to Israel in the Gospel of John." *NTS* 21, 396–405.
1975   *The Law in the Fourth Gospel: The Torah and the Gospel, Moses and Jesus, Judaism and Christianity according to John.* NovTSup 42. Leiden: Brill.

Parkes, James
1961 (1934)   *The Conflict of the Church and the Synagogue: A Study in the Origins of Antisemitism.* Cleveland and New York: The World Publishing Company/Philadelphia: The Jewish Publication Society of America.

Patte, Daniel
1975   *Early Jewish Hermeneutic in Palestine.* SBLDS 22. Missoula: Scholars Press.

Pazdan, Mary Margaret
1987   "Nicodemus and the Samaritan Woman: Contrasting Models of Discipleship," *BTB 27*, 145–148.

Pedersen, Sigfred
1999   "Anti-Judaism in John's Gospel: John 8," *New Readings in John: Literary and Theological Perspectives. Essays from the Scandinavian Conference on the Fourth Gospel in Århus 1997,* eds. J. Nissen and S. Pedersen. JSNTS 182. Sheffield: Sheffield Academic Press. 172–193.

Piper, Ronald A.
    2000   "Satan, Demons and the Absence of Exorcisms in the Fourth Gospel,"
            *Christology, Controversy and Community: New Testament Essays in Honour of David
            R. Catchpole*, eds. D. G. Horrell and C. M. Tuckett. NovTSup 99. Leiden:
            Brill. 253–278.
Porter, Stanley E.
    1989   *Verbal Aspect in the Greek of the New Testament, with Reference to Tense and
            Mood*. Studies in Biblical Greek 1. New York: Peter Lang.
Potterie, I. de la
    1983   " 'Nous adorons, nous, ce que nous connaissons, car le salut vient des
            Juifs.' Histoire de l'exégèse et interprétation de Jn 4, 22," *Bib* 64, 74–115.
Powell, Mark Allan
    1993   *What is Narrative Criticism? A New Approach to the Bible*. London: SPCK.
            [First published in the USA by Augsburg Fortress, Minneapolis. 1990.]
    2001   *Chasing the Eastern Star: Adventures in Biblical Reader Response Criticism*. Louisville,
            Kentucky: Westminster John Knox Press.
Price, James L.
    1991   "Light from Qumran upon Some Aspects of Johannine Theology," *John
            and the Dead Sea Scrolls*, ed. J. H. Charlesworth, Enlarged Edition. New
            York: Crossroad. 9–37.
Pritz, Ray A.
    1988   *Nazarene Jewish Christianity: From the End of the New Testament Period Until Its
            Disappearance in the Fourth Century*. SPB 37. Jerusalem/Leiden: The Magnes
            Press, The Hebrew University/Brill.
Purvis, James D.
    1975   "The Fourth Gospel and the Samaritans," *NovT* 17, 161–198.
Räisänen, Heikki
    1987²   *Paul and the Law*. WUNT 29. Tübingen: Mohr-Siebeck.
    1992   *Jesus, Paul and Torah: Collected Essays*. Translations from the German by
            D. E. Orton. JSNTSup 43. Sheffield: Sheffield Academic Press.
    1997   *Marcion, Muhammad and the Mahatma: Exegetical Perspectives on the Encounter of
            Cultures and Faiths*. London: SCM Press.
    2000   "Biblical Critics in the Global Village," *Reading the Bible in the Global Village:
            Helsinki*, H. Räisänen, E. Schüssler Fiorenza, R. S. Sugirtharajah,
            K. Stendahl and J. Barr. Atlanta: Society of Biblical Literature.
    2001   "Paul's and Qumran Judaism," *Judaism in Late Antiquity, Part Five, The
            Judaism of Qumran: A Systematic Reading of the Dead Sea Scrolls, Volume Two:
            World View, Comparing Judaisms*, eds. A. J. Avery-Peck, J. Neusner and
            B. D. Chilton. HO, Section One vol. 57. Leiden: Brill. 173–200.
Rajak, Tessa
    2001   *The Jewish Dialogue with Greece and Rome: Studies in Cultural and Social Interaction*.
            AGJU 48. Leiden: Brill.
Reed, Jonathan
    1999a   "Stone Vessels in Second Temple Judaism: Religious and Socio-economic
            Aspects," A Paper presented in the 1999 AAR/SBL Annual Meeting in
            Boston.
    1999b   "Galileans, 'Israelite Village Communities,' and the Sayings Gospel Q,
            Galilee through the Centuries: Confluence of Cultures, ed. Eric M. Meyers. Duke
            Judaic Studies Series 1. Winona Lake, Indiana: Eisenbrauns. 87–108.
Reif, Stefan C.
    1999   "The Early Liturgy of the Synagogue," *The Cambridge History of Judaism,
            Volume Three: The Early Roman Period*, eds. W. Horbury, W. D. Davies &
            J. Sturdy. Cambridge: Cambridge University Press. 326–357.

Reim, Günter
  1984   "Joh. 8.44—Gotteskinder/Teufelskinder: Wie antijudaistisch ist 'die wohl antijudaistischste Äusserung des NT?,'" *NTS* 30, 619–624.
Reinhartz, Adele
  1989   "Rabbinic Perceptions of Simeon Bar Kosiba," *JSJ* 20, 171–194.
  1992   *The Word in the World: The Cosmological Tale in the Fourth Gospel.* SBLMS 45. Atlanta, Georgia: Scholars Press.
  1997   "A Nice Jewish Girl Reads the Gospel of John," *Semeia* 77, 177–193.
  1998   "The Johannine Community and its Jewish Neighbors: A Reappraisal," *"What is John?" Vol. II: Literary and Social Readings of the Fourth Gospel*, ed. F. F. Segovia. SBLSymS 7. Atlanta, Georgia: Scholars Press. 111–138.
  2001a   *Befriending the Beloved Disciple: A Jewish Reading of the Gospel of John.* New York: Continuum.
  2001b   "'Jews' and Jews in the Fourth Gospel," in Bieringer et al. 2001a, 341–356.
Rensberger, David
  1989   *Overcoming the World: Politics and Community in the Gospel of John.* London: SPCK. (Originally published in the USA by the Westminster Press in 1988 as *Johannine Faith and Liberating Community*.)
  1997   *1 John, 2 John, 3 John.* Abingdon New Testament commentaries. Nashville: Abingdon Press.
  1999   "Anti-Judaism and the Gospel of John," *Anti-Judaism and the Gospels*, ed. William R. Farmer. Harrisburg, Pennsylvania: Trinity Press. 120–157.
Richter, Georg
  1977   *Studien zum Johannesevangelium*, ed. Josef Hainz. Biblische Untersuchungen 13. Regensburg: Friedrich Pustet.
Ricoeur, Paul
  1981   *Hermeneutics and the Human Sciences: Essays on Language, Action and Interpretation.* Edited, translated and introduced by J. B. Thompson. Cambridge: University Press.
Riley, G. J.
  1999[2] "Devil—Διάβολος", *Dictionary of Deities and Demons in the Bible*, eds. K. van der Toorn, B. Becking & P. van der Horst. Leiden & Grand Rapids, Michigan: Brill & Eerdmans. 244–249.
Robinson, John A. T.
  1985   *The Priority of John.* London: SCM Press.
Rochais, Gérard
  1993   "Jean 7: une construction littéraire dramatique, à la manière d'un scénario," *NTS* 39, 355–378.
Rowland, C.
  1982   "A Summary of Sabbath Observance in Judaism at the Beginning of the Christian Era," *From Sabbath to Lord's Day: A Biblical, Historical and Theological Investigation*, ed. Carson, D. A. 43–55. Grand Rapids, Michigan: Zondervan.
Ruether, Rosemary Radford
  1979   "The *Faith and Fratricide* Discussion: Old Problems and New Dimensions, *Antisemitism and the Foundations of Christianity*, ed. A. T. Davies. New York: Paulist Press. 230–256.
Runesson, Anders
  2001   *The Origins of the Synagogue: A Socio-Historical Study.* ConBNT 37. Stockholm: Almqvist & Wiksell.
Russell, Jeffrey Burton
  1977   *The Devil: Perceptions of Evil from Antiquity to Primitive Christianity.* Ithaca and London: Cornell University Press.

Rutgers, Leonard Victor
    1998   "Roman Policy toward the Jews: Expulsions from the City of Rome dur-
            ing the First Century C.E.," *Judaism and Christianity in First-Century Rome*,
            eds. K. P. Donfried and P. Richardson. Grand Rapids, Michigan:
            Eerdmans. 93–116.
Saldarini, Anthony J.
    1986   "Reconstructions of Rabbinic Judaism," *Early Judaism and Its Modern
            Interpreters*, eds. R. A. Kraft & G. W. E. Nickelsburg. SBLBMI 2.
            Philadelphia, Pennsylvania and Atlanta, Georgia: Fortress Press and
            Scholars Press. 437–477.
    1989   *Pharisees, Scribes and Sadducees in Palestinian Society.* Edinburgh: T. & T. Clark.
    1992   "Pharisees," *ABD* 5, 289–303.
    1998   "The Social World of Christian Jews and Jewish Christians," *Religious
            and Ethnic Communities in Later Roman Palestine*, ed. Hayim Lapin. Studies
            and Texts in Jewish History and Culture 5. Bethesda, Md: University
            Press of Maryland. 115–154.
Sandelin, Karl-Gustav
    1986   *Wisdom as Nourisher: A Study of an Old Testament Theme, Its Development within
            Early Judaism and Its Impact on Early Christianity.* Acta Academiae Aboensis,
            Humaniora 64, 3. Åbo: Åbo Akademi.
Sanders, E. P.
    1977   *Paul and Palestinian Judaism: A Comparison of Patterns of Religion.* London:
            SCM Press.
    1985   *Jesus and Judaism.* London: SCM Press.
    1990   *Jewish Law from Jesus to the Mishnah: Five Studies.* London/Philadelphia:
            SCM Press/Trinity Press.
    1992   *Judaism: Practise and Belief 63 BCE–66 CE.* London/Philadelphia: SCM
            Press/Trinity Press.
    1993   *The Historical Figure of Jesus.* London: Penguin Books.
    1999a   "Common Judaism and the Synagogue in the First Century," *Jews,
            Christians, and Polytheists in the Ancient Synagogue: Cultural Interaction during the
            Greco-Roman Period*, ed. S. Fine. London & New York: Routledge. 1–17.
    1999b   "Reflections on Anti-Judaism in the New Testament and in Christianity,"
            Anti-Judaism and the Gospels, ed. William R. Farmer. Harrisburg, Pennsylvania:
            Trinity Press. 265–286.
Sanders, Jack T.
    1987   *The Jews in Luke-Acts.* London: SCM Press.
    1993   *Schismatics, Sectarians, Dissidents, Deviants: The First One Hundred Years of
            Jewish-Christian Relations.* Valley Forge, Pennsylvania: Trinity Press.
Sanders, James A.
    1998   "The Hermeneutics of Translation," *Removing the Anti-Judaism from the New
            Testament*, eds. H. C. Kee & I. Borowsky. Philadelphia, Pennsylvania:
            American Interfaith Institute/World Alliance. 43–62.
Sandmel, Samuel
    1971   *Philo's Place in Judaism: A Study of Conceptions of Abraham in Jewish Literature.*
            New York: KTAV Publishing House. (Originally appeared in *HUCA* 25
            [1954], 209–237; *HUCA* 26 [1955], 151–332.)
    1978   *Judaism and Christian Beginnings.* New York: Oxford University Press.
Satlow, Michael
    1993   "Reconsidering the Rabbinic *ketubah* Payment," *The Jewish Family in
            Antiquity*, ed. S. J. D. Cohen. BJS 289. Atlanta, Georgia: Scholars Press.
            133–151.

Schäfer, Peter
    1975   "Die sogenannte Synode von Jabne: Zur Trennung von Juden und Christen im ersten/zweiten Jh. n. Chr.," *Judaica* 31, 54–64, 116–124.
    1979   "Die Flucht Johanan b. Zakkais aus Jerusalem und die Gründung des 'Lehrhauses' in Jabne," *ANRW* II.19.2, 43–101.
Schams, Christine
    1998   *Jewish Scribes in the Second-Temple Period.* JSOTSup 291. Sheffield: Academic Press.
Schenke, Ludger
    1990   "Joh 7–10: Eine dramatische Szene," *ZNW* 80, 172–192.
Schiffman, L. H.
    1985a   "The Samaritans in Tannaitic Halakhah," *JQR* 75, 323–350.
    1985b   *Who Was a Jew? Rabbinic and Halakhic Perspectives on the Jewish Christian Schism.* Hoboken, New Jersey: KTAV Publishing Company.
    1999   "Community Without Temple: The Qumran Community's Withdrawal from the Jerusalem Temple," *Gemeinde ohne Tempel, Community without Temple: Zur Substituierung und Transformation des Jerusalemer Tempels und seines Kults im Alten Testament, antiken Judentum und frühen Christentum,* eds. B. Ego, A. Lange and P. Pilhofer. WUNT 118. Tübingen: Mohr-Siebeck. 267–284.
Schneider, Johannes
    1954   "Zur Komposition von Joh 7," *ZNW* 45, 108–119.
Schneiders, Sandra M.
    1999²   *The Revelatory Text: Interpreting the New Testament as Sacred Scripture.* Collegeville, Minnesota: The Liturgical Press.
Schnelle, Udo
    1996   "Die Tempelreinigung und die Christologie des Johannesevangeliums," *NTS* 42, 359–373.
Scholtissek, Klaus
    1998   "Ironie und Rollenwechsel im Johannesevangelium," *ZNW* 89, 235–255.
Schottroff, Luise
    1970   *Der Glaubende und die feindliche Welt: Beobachtungen zum gnostischen Dualismus und seiner Bedeutung für Paulus and das Johannesevangelium.* WMANT 37. Neukirchen-Vluyn. Neukirchener Verlag.
Schrage, Wolfgang
    1964   "συναγωγή," *TWNT* VII, 798–850.
Schram, Terry Leonard
    1974   *The Use of IOUDAIOS in the Fourth Gospel: An Application of some Linguistic Insights to a New Testament Problem.* Dissertation. Utrecht: University of Utrecht.
Schrenk, Gottlob
    1933   "ἄδικος, ἀδικία, ἀδικέω, ἀδίκημα," *TWNT* I, 150–163.
Schuchard, Bruce G.
    1992   *Scripture within Scripture: The Interrelationship of Form and Function in the Explicit Old Testament Citations in the Gospel of John.* SBLDS 133. Atlanta, Georgia: Scholars Press.
Schürer, Emil
    1979   *The History of the Jewish People in the Age of Jesus Christ (175 B.C.–A.D. 135).* Vol. II. A New Revised English Version, eds. G. Vermes, F. Millar and M. Black. Edinburgh: T. & T. Clark.
Schwartz, E.
    1907–08 "Aporien im vierten Evangelium, I–IV," *Nachrichten der Göttinger Gesellschaft der Wissenschaften, Phil.-hist. Klasse* (1907), 342–372, (1908) 125–148, 149–188 and 497–560.

Schwartz, Seth
    1999   "The Patriarchs and the Diaspora," *JJS* 50, 208–222.
Seeley, David
    1993   "Jesus' Temple Act," *CBQ* 55, 263–283.
Segal, Alan F.
    1977   *Two Powers in Heaven: Early Rabbinic Reports about Christianity and Gnosticism.*
                SJLA 25. Leiden: Brill.
    1981   "Ruler of This World. Attitudes about Mediator Figures: The Importance
                of Sociology for Self-Definition," *Jewish and Christian Self-Definition. Vol
                II: Aspects of Judaism in the Greco-Roman Period*, eds. E. P. Sanders, A. I.
                Baumgarten and A. Mendelson. Philadelphia: Fortress Press. 245–268.
    1986   "Judaism, Christianity, and Gnosticism," *Anti-Judaism in Early Christianity,
                Vol. 2: Separation and Polemic*, ed. S. G. Wilson. Studies in Christianity
                and Judaism 2. Waterloo: Wilfrid Laurier University Press. 133–161.
    1987   *The Other Judaisms of Late Antiquity.* Atlanta, Georgia: Scholars Press.
Segovia, Fernando
    1996   "Reading Readers of the Fourth Gospel and their Readings: An Exercise
                in Intercultural Criticism, *"What is John?": Readers and Readings of the
                Fourth Gospel*, ed. F. F. Segovia, SBLSymS 3. Atlanta, Georgia: Scholars
                Press. 211–277.
Setzer, Claudia
    1994   *Jewish Responses to Early Christians: History and Polemics, 30–150 C.E.*
                Minneapolis: Fortress Press.
Siker, Jeffrey S.
    1991   *Disinheriting the Jews: Abraham in Early Christian Controversy.* Louisville,
                Kentucky: Westminster/John Knox Press.
Smith, D. Moody
    1965   *The Composition and Order of the Fourth Gospel: Bultmann's Literary Theory.*
                New Haven and London: Yale University Press.
    1984   *Johannine Christianity: Essays on Its Setting, Sources, and Theology.* Columbia,
                South Carolina: University of South Carolina Press.
    1990a   "The Contribution of J. Louis Martyn to the Understanding of the
                Gospel of John," *The Conversation Continues: Studies in Paul and John in
                honor of J. Louis Martyn*, eds. R. T. Fortna and B. R. Gaventa. Nashville:
                Abingdon. 275–294.
    1990b   "Judaism and the Gospel of John," *Jews and Christians: Exploring the Past,
                Present, and Future*, ed. J. H. Charlesworth. New York: Crossroad. 76–96.
Smith, Morton
    1956   "Palestinian Judaism in the First Century," *Israel: Its Role in Civilization*,
                ed. M. Davis. New York. 67–81.
Söding, Thomas
    1992   "Die Tempelaktion Jesu," *TTZ* 101, 36–64.
    2000   "'Was kann aus Nazareth schon Gutes kommen?' (Joh 1.46): Die
                Bedeutung des Judeseins Jesu im Johannesevangelium," *NTS* 46, 21–41.
Solin, Heikki
    1983   "Juden und Syrer im westlichen Teil der römischen Welt. Eine eth-
                nisch-demographische Studie mit besonderer Berücksichtigung der
                sprachlichen Zustände," *ANRW* II.29.2, 587–789.
Soulen, R. K.
    1998   "Removing Anti-Judaism," *Removing the Anti-Judaism from the New Testament*,
                eds. H. C. Kee and I. J. Borowsky. Philadelphia, Pennsylvania: American
                Interfaith Institute/World Alliance, 1998. 149–156.
Staley, Jeffrey Lloyd
    1991   "Stumbling in the Dark, Reaching for the Light: Reading Character
                in John 5 and 9," *Semeia* 53, 55–80.

Starfelt, Eric
  1959   *Studier i rabbinsk och nytestamentlig skrifttolkning*. Studia theologica lun-
              densia 17. Lund: Håkan Ohlssons Boktyckeri.
Stark, Rodney & Bainbridge, William Sims
  1987   *A Theory of Religion*. Toronto Studies in Religion 2. New York: Peter
              Lang.
Stegemann, Ekkehard W.
  1990   "Zur Tempelreinigung im Johannesevangelium," *Die Hebräische Bibel
              und ihre zweifache Nachgeschichte. Festschrift für Rolf Rendtorff zum 65.
              Geburtstag*, eds. Erhard Blum, Christian Macholz and Ekkehard W.
              Stegemann. Neukirchen-Vluyn: Neukirchener Verlag. 503–516.
Stegemann, Hartmut
  1988   "Zu Textbestand und Grundgedanken von 1 QS III, 13–IV, 26,
              RevQ 13, 95–130.
Stemberger, Günther
  1977   "Die sogenannte 'Synode von Jabne' und das frühe Christentum,"
              Kairos 19, 14–21.
  1999   "Die Umformung des palästinischen Judentums nach 70: Der Aufstieg
              der Rabbinen," *Jüdische Geschichte in hellenistisch-römischer Zeit. Wege der
              Forschung: Vom alten zum neuen Schürer*, ed. A. Oppenheimer. Schriften
              des Historischen Kollegs: Kolloquien 44. München: R. Oldenbourg
              Verlag. 85–99.
Stern, Sacha
  1984   *Jewish Identity in Early Rabbinic Writings*. AGJU 23. Leiden: Brill.
Strack, Hermann L. & Billerbeck, Paul
  1921–1961   *Kommentar zum Neuen Testament aus Talmud und Midrash I–VI*. Munich:
              C. H. Beck.
Strack, Hermann L. & Stemberger, Günter
  1982⁷   *Einleitung in Talmud und Midrash*. Munich: C. H. Beck.
Suleiman, Susan Rubin
  1976   "Ideological Dissent from Works of Fiction: Toward a Rhetoric of
              the *roman à thèse*," *Neophilologus 60*, 162–177.
  1993²   *Authoritarian Fictions: The Ideological Novel As a Literary Genre*. Princeton,
              New Jersey: Princeton University Press.
Swetnam, James
  1980   "The meaning of πεπιστευκότας in John 8,31," *Bib* 61, 106–109.
Syreeni, Kari
  1990   "Matthew, Luke, and the Law: A Study in Hermeneutical Exegesis,"
              The Law in the Bible and in Its Environment, ed. T. Veijola. Publications
              of the Finnish Exegetical Society 51. Helsinki and Göttingen: The
              Finnish Exegetical Society and Vandenhoeck & Ruprecht.
  1994   "Separation and Identity: Aspects of the Symbolic World of Matt
              6:1–18," *NTS* 40, 522–541.
  1995   "Metaphorical Appropriation: (Post-)Modern Biblical Hermeneutic
              and the Theory of Metaphor," *Literature and Theology* 9, 321–338.
  1999   "Peter as Character and Symbol in the Gospel of Matthew,
              Characterization in the Gospels: Reconceiving Narrative Criticism, eds. D.
              Rhoads and K. Syreeni. JSNTS 184. Sheffield: Sheffield Academic
              Press. 106–152.
Syreeni, Kari & Myllykoski, Matti
              "Three Worlds in Biblical Interpretation." *ANRW*. Forthcoming.
Theissen, Gerd
  1999   *A Theory of Primitive Christian Religion*. Translated from the German
              original *Theorie der urchristlichen Religion* (1999) by John Bowden. London:
              SCM Press.

Theobald, Michael
    1997   "Schriftzitate im 'Lebensbrot'-dialog Jesu (Joh 6). Ein Paradigma fur den
            Schriftgebrauch des vierten Evangelisten," *The Scriptures in the Gospels*, ed.
            C. M. Tuckett. BETL 131. Leuven: University Press. 325–366.
Thoma, Clemens
    1978   *Christliche Theologie des Judentums*. Aschaffenburg: Paul Pattloch Verlag.
Thomas, John Christopher
    1991   "The Fourth Gospel and Rabbinic Judaism," *ZNW*, 159–182.
Thompson, Leonard L.
    1990   *The Book of Revelation: Apocalypse and Empire*. New York: Oxford University
            Press.
Thompson, Marianne Meye
    1997   "Thinking about God: Wisdom and Theology in John 6," in Culpepper
            1997, 221–246.
Thornton, T. C. G.
    1987   "Christian Understandings of the *Birkath ha-Minim* in the Eastern Roman
            Empire," *JTS* 38, 419–431.
Thyen, Hartwig
    1980   " 'Das Heil kommt von den Juden,' " *Kirche. Festschrift für Günther Bornkamm
            zum 75. Geburtsdag*, eds. D. Lührmann and G. Strecker. Tübingen: Mohr-
            Siebeck. 163–184.
Tomson, Peter J.
    2001   " 'Jews' in the Gospel of John as Compared with the Palestinian Talmud,
            the Synoptics and Some New Testament Apocraypha," in Bieringer et al.
            2001a, 301–340.
Townsend, John T.
    1979   "The Gospel of John and the Jews: The Story of a Religious Divorce,"
            Antisemitism and the Foundations of Christianity, ed. A. T. Davies. New York:
            Paulist Press. 72–97.
Tuckett, Christopher M.
    1996   *Q and the History of Early Christianity: Studies on Q*. Edinburgh: T. & T. Clark.
Turner, M. Max B.
    1982   "The Sabbath, Sunday, and the Law in Luke/Acts," *From Sabbath to Lord's
            Day: A Biblical, Historical and Theological Investigation*, ed. D. A. Carson. Grand
            Rapids, Michigan: Zondervan. 99–157.
Urbach, Ephraim E.
    1981   "Self-Isolation of Self-Affirmation in Judaism in the First Three Centuries:
            Theory and Practice," *Jewish and Christian Self-Definition. Vol II: Aspects of
            Judaism in the Greco-Roman Period*, eds. E. P. Sanders, A. I. Baumgarten and
            A. Mendelson. Philadelphia: Fortress Press. 269–298.
Urman, Dan
    1995   "The House of Assembly and the House of Study: Are They One and
            the Same," *Ancient Synagogues: Historical Analysis and Archaeological Discovery*,
            eds. D. Urman & P. V. M. Flesher. SPB 47, 1. Leiden: Brill. 232–255.
Urman, Dan & Flesher, Paul V.M.
    1995   "Ancient Synagogues—A Reader's Guide," *Ancient Synagogues: Historical
            Analysis and Archaeological Discovery*, eds. D. Urman & P. V. M. Flesher. SPB
            47, 1. Leiden: Brill. xvii–xxxvii.
Visotzky, Burton L.
    2000   "A Review W. Horbury's *Jews and Christians in Contact and Controversy*," *JBL*
            119, 780–782.
von Wahlde, Urban C.
    1980   "Faith and Works in Jn VI 28–29," *NovT* 22, 304–315.
    1981   "The Witnesses to Jesus in John 5:31–40 and Belief in the Fourth Gospel,"
            CBQ 43, 385–404.

1982   "The Johannine 'Jews': A Critical Survey," *NTS* 28, 33–60.

1984   "Literary Structure and Theological Argument in Three Discourses with the Jews in the Fourth Gospel," *JBL* 103, 575–584.

2000   " 'The Jews' in the Gospel of John: Fifteen Years of Research (1983–1998)", *ETL* 76, 30–55.

2001   " 'You Are of Your Father the Devil' in its Context: Stereotyped Apocalyptic Polemic in John 8:38–47," in Bieringer et al. 2001a, 418–444.

Walters, James C.

1998   "Romans, Jews, and Christians: The Impact of the Romans on Jewish/Christian Relations in First-Century Rome," *Judaism and Christianity in First-Century Rome*, eds. K. P. Donfried & P. Richardson. Grand Rapids, Michigan: Eerdmans. 175–195.

Ward, Roy Bowen

1968   "The Works of Abraham: James 2:14–26," *HTR* 61, 283–290.

1976   "Abraham Traditions in Early Christianity," *Studies on the Testament of Abraham*, ed. George W. E. Nickelsburg, Jr. SBLSCS 6. Missoula, Montana: Scholars Press. 173–184.

Wead, David W.

1970   *The Literary Devices in John's Gospel.* Theologische Dissertationen, Band IV. Basel: Friedrich Reinhardt Kommissionsverlag.

Weinfeld, Moshe

1991   *Deuteronomy 1–11.* AB 5. New York: Doubleday.

Weiss, Herold

1991   "The Sabbath in the Fourth Gospel," *JBL* 110, 311–321.

Welck, Christian

1994   *Erzählte Zeichen: Die Wundergeschichten des Johannesevangeliums literarisch untersucht. Mit einem Ausblick auf Joh 21.* WUNT, 2. Reihe 69. Tübingen: Mohr-Siebeck.

Wengst, Klaus

1992⁴   *Bedrängte Gemeinde und verherrlichter Christus: ein Versuch über das Johannesevangelium.* Munich: Chr. Kaiser Verlag.

Westbrook, Raymond

1992   "Punishments and Crimes," *ABD* 5, 546–556.

Whitacre, Rodney A.

1982   *Johannine Polemic: The Role of Tradition and Theology.* SBLDS 67. Chico, California: Scholars Press.

White, L. Michael

1990   *Building God's House in the Roman World: Architectural Adaptation among Pagans, Jews, and Christians.* Baltimore & London: The Johns Hopkins University Press.

Wilckens, Ulrich

1980   *Der Brief an die Römer.* 2. Teilband Röm 6–11. EKK VI/2. Zürich/Einsiedeln/Köln: Benziger Verlag. Neukirchen-Vluyn: Neukirchener Verlag.

Wilken, Robert Louis

1999   "Something Greater than the Temple," *Anti-Judaism and the Gospels*, ed. William R. Farmer. Harrisburg, Pennsylvania: Trinity Press. 176–202.

Williams, Margaret

1999   "The Contribution of Jewish Inscriptions to the Study of Judaism," *The Cambridge History of Judaism, Volume Three: The Early Roman Period*, eds. W. Horbury, W. D. Davies & J. Sturdy. Cambridge: Cambridge University Press. 75–93.

Williams, Michael Allen

1996   *Rethinking "Gnosticism:" An Argument for Dismantling a Dubious Category.* Princeton: Princeton University Press.

Williamson, H. G. M.

1977   *Israel in the Books of Chronicles.* Cambridge: Cambridge University Press.

Wilson, Stephen G.
  1995   *Related Strangers: Jews and Christians 70–170 C.E.* Minneapolis:
                Fortress Press.
Windisch, Hans
  1924   *Der zweite Korintherbrief.* KEK, 6. Abteilung—9. Auflage. Göttingen:
                Vandenhoeck & Ruprecht.
Witkamp, L. Th.
  1985   "The Use of Traditions in John 5.1–18," *JSNT* 25, 19–47.
Wrede, W.
  1933² [1903] *Charakter und Tendenz des Johannesevangeliums.* Sammlung Gemeinde-
                verständlicher Vorträge und Schriften aus dem Gebiet der
                Theologie und Religionsgeschichte, 37. Tübingen: Mohr-Siebeck.
Zalcman, Lawrence
  1991   "Christians, *Noserim*, and Nebuchadnezzar's Daughter," *JQR* 81,
                411–426.
Zangenberg, Jürgen
  1998   *Frühes Christentum in Samarien: Topographische und traditionsgeschichtliche
                Studien zu den Samarientexten im Johannesevangelium.* Texte und
                Arbeiten zum neutestementlichen Zeitalter 27. Tübingen &
                Basel: A. Francke Verlag.
Zeitlin, S.
  1963   "Hillel and Hermeneutical Rules," *JQR* 54, 161–173.
Zeller, Dieter
  1983   "Paulus und Johannes: Methodischer Vergleich im Interesse
                einer neutestamentlichen Theologie," *BZ* 27, 167–182.
Zumstein, Jean
  2001   "The Farewell Discourse (John 13:31–16:33) and the Problem
                of Anti-Judaism," In Bieringer et al. 2001a, 461–478.

INDEX OF MODERN AUTHORS

Aberle, M. von 16, 45
Ådna, Jostein 91
Aland, Barbara 122
Aland, Kurt 122
Alexander, Philip S. 45, 48, 50, 72, 139
Alon, Gedalyahu 98–99
Anderson, Paul N. 160, 162–63, 165
Ashton, John 4,–8, 12, 16, 18,
 42–43, 45, 67, 120–21, 125, 142,
 161, 198, 200, 202, 228
Asiedu-Peprah, Martin 114–15,
 120–21, 123, 125, 128, 146, 148,
 150–51, 157
Attridge, Harold W. 131
Augenstein, Jörg 139
Avery-Peck, Alan J. 27

Bacchiocchi, Samuele 117, 130
Back, Sven-Olav 116, 121, 134
Bainbridge, William S. 232
Bammel, Ernst 89, 95
Barclay, John M. G. 27–8
Barrett, Charles K. 42–43, 49, 70,
 88, 94–95, 105, 107, 121, 131,
 135–36, 139–41, 147–49,
 153–54, 160, 162, 164–65, 167,
 169, 180, 182–83, 189, 193, 198,
 206, 220
Bassler, Jouette M. 11
Bauckham, Richard 68–9
Bauer, Walter 89, 94, 121–22, 141,
 148, 150, 154, 160
Baum, Gregory 16
Baumbach, Günther 203, 213
Baumgarten, Albert I. 26, 68, 213,
 224–5
Baur, Ferdinand C. 5
Beall, Todd S. 83
Beasley-Murray, George 114, 131,
 136, 150–151, 153
Becker, Jürgen 42, 44, 77, 89, 94–95,
 101, 103–104, 108, 114, 119–122,
 127, 132, 135–37, 143, 148, 150,
 154, 158–19, 162, 164, 178, 180,
 182, 184, 189, 198, 201, 204–205,
 210, 213

Belle, Gilbert van 96, 111, 157
Belser, Johannes 12
Bergen, Doris L. 240
Berger, Klaus 187–188
Berger, Peter L. 35
Bernard, J. H. 102, 121, 136, 147,
 149, 153
Betz, Otto 101, 103–105, 108
Beutler, Johannes 14, 146, 150–51,
 153–54, 172
Bieringer, Reimund 18, 39, 111–12
Billerbeck, Paul 54, 70, 153, 174
Blank, Josef 149, 150, 153
Blass, Friedrich 94, 190, 192, 207
Bloedhorn, Hanswulf 63
Böcher, Otto 198, 201, 203
Boer, Martin de 1, 9, 32, 42, 44,
 46–7, 53, 78, 173–75, 183, 186,
 227, 235
Bondi, Richard A. 183, 194, 202
Borgen, Peder 151–52, 158–59,
 161–63, 165–68
Borowsky, Irvin J. 229
Botha, J. Eugene 100–101, 104
Boyarin, Daniel 25, 194, 232, 237
Brändle, Rudolf 24
Braun, Herbert 198
Bretschneider, Karl G. 5
Brooke, George J. 135–36
Brown, Raymond E. 42, 70, 79, 88,
 90, 94–95, 102, 107–108, 114,
 132–36, 139–40, 143, 146–49,
 151, 156, 159–60, 162, 165, 167,
 178–79, 182–83, 187, 189–93,
 198, 200–201, 205, 229, 235
Büchsel, Friedrich 92
Bultmann, Rudolf 6–8, 16, 36, 89,
 93–95, 101, 119, 121, 125, 131, 133,
 135–39, 141, 150–51, 153–54, 156,
 160, 178–80, 192, 198, 202, 207–208

Carroll, Kenneth L. 16
Carson, D. A. 118, 131, 135
Casey, Maurice 13, 31, 42, 233
Charlesworth, James H. 4, 23,
 198–202, 205

Chilton, Bruce   26–7, 30, 89–91, 95, 233, 236
Cogan, Mordechai   98
Coggins, Richard J.   98–99, 104, 106,
Cohen, Shaye J. D.   10–11, 14, 28, 30, 32, 48, 52, 54, 56–64, 71–72, 81, 111, 185
Cohn, Dorrit   34
Collins, John J.   28, 202–204
Collins, Raymond F.   15, 89, 103
Conway, Colleen M.   39
Cotton, Hannah   65–66
Culbertson, Philip L.   241
Cullmann, Oscar   88, 130, 143
Culpepper, R. Alan   18, 93–94, 113–15, 123, 159, 231, 241

Dahl, Nils Alstrup   150–51, 156, 171, 207
Daube, David   9, 168
Davies, Margaret   19–20, 91–92, 116, 121, 141, 193–94, 219
Davies, William D.   4, 6, 9, 22, 29, 82–83, 239
Davies, Philip R.   222
Debrunner, Albert   94, 190, 192, 207
Deines, Roland   56–57, 61–62
Delling, Gerhard   153
Denniston, John Dewar   90
Derrett, J. Duncan M.   88, 91, 136, 139, 140–41
Destro, Adriana   221–22, 223, 225, 236
Dexinger, Ferdinand   29–30, 102, 106
Dietzfelbringer, Christian   164, 170
Dodd, Charles H.   6–7, 9, 88, 94–95, 101, 114, 119, 131, 139, 149, 154, 164, 166–67, 179, 182–84, 189, 191
Douglas, Mary   21
Dozeman, Thomas B.   183, 189
Dube, Musa W.   38
Duke, Paul D.   94, 100, 102, 132, 159
Dunderberg, Ismo   110, 115, 120, 123, 133, 139, 141, 144
Dunn, James D. G.   12–13, 25, 42, 73, 111, 212, 230, 239, 241

Efron, Joshua   59
Eppstein, Victor   90
Esler, Philip F.   195–94, 221
Evans, Craig A.   85, 90, 211–12

Falls, Thomas B.   141
Feldman, Louis H.   129, 195
Fine, Steven   63

Finkel, Asher   46–47, 52
Flesher, Paul V. M.   52, 61
Foerster, Werner   181
Forkman, Göran   53
Fortna, Robert T.   87–88, 114, 119, 121, 124
Freed, Edwin D.   102, 108–109, 234
Frey, Jörg   199–201, 203–204
Freyne, Sean   11, 106, 120, 173, 195

García Martínez, Fernando   29, 222
Gaston, Lloyd   143, 221
Geiger, Georg   163
Genette, Gérard   34
Goldenberg, David   49
Goldstein, Jonathan A.   106
Goodblatt, David   56, 59,
Goodman, Martin   48, 52, 58–60, 65–66, 71–73
Goppelt, Leonhard   16
Grabbe, Lester   56–7, 61–62, 85
Graetz, Heinrich   41
Gräßer, Erich   7–8, 16, 36, 208
Green, William Scott   21, 55–6, 61, 71
Günther, Walther   133

Hachlili, Rachel   61, 63
Haenchen, Ernst   89–90, 101, 108, 110, 114, 118–19, 121–22, 133, 135, 140–41, 181
Hahn, Ferdinand   105–107, 121, 169
Hakola, Raimo   33–34, 37
Hall, Bruce W.   99, 102, 106
Hansen, G. Walter   187–88
Hare, Douglas R. A.   53–54, 68–69, 72, 75
Hartman, Lars   95
Harvey, Graham   52, 152, 226, 231
Hasel, Gerhard F.   116
Hayes, Christine E.   47–48
Hengel, Martin   56–57, 62, 67, 69, 78
Henten, Jan Willem van   226
Herford, R. Travers   47
Hezser, Catherine   41, 54–56, 58–61, 64–65, 69, 71, 79
Hofius, Otfried   170
Holtz, Traugott   82
Horbury, William   43, 45, 49, 53–54, 72, 76–77
Horst, Pieter W. van der   46
Hoskyns, Edwyn C.   88, 101–102, 103, 121, 133, 136, 150, 154
Hulmi, Sini   203

Hunzinger, Claus-Hunno 53–54
Hüttenmeister, Gil 63

Jacobs, Louis 139
Jacobs, Martin 59–60
Japhet, Sara 98
Jeanrond, Werner 38
Jeremias, Joachim 90
Johnson, Luke T. 105, 155, 212
Jokiranta, Jutta 26, 29, 221
Jonge, Marinus de 18, 182–83
Josz, J. 16

Kalmin, Richard 47, 71
Katz, Steven T. 46–47, 49–50, 54, 71
Kee, Howard C. 229
Kiilunen, Jarmo 144
Kimelman, Reuven 45–47, 49–50, 53, 65, 84–85, 186
Kippenberg, Hans G. 99, 101–102, 104
Klappert, Bertold 147, 176
Klijn, A. F. J. 235
Koester, Craig R. 97, 100, 106
Kotila, Markku 39, 115, 119–20, 131, 135–37, 140–41, 144, 149–50, 155–56, 164–65, 167, 170–71
Kovacs, Judith L. 202, 205,
Kraabel, Alf Thomas 63, 111
Kügler, Joachim 19, 167, 169, 173
Kuhn, Karl Georg 13
Kümmel, Werner Georg 5
Kuula, Kari 23
Kysar, Robert 42, 53, 89, 161

Labahn, Michael 120, 136, 141
Lane, William L. 24
Lange, Armin 199, 201
Lapin, Hayim 59, 61
Lee, Dorothy A. 123, 129, 147, 160, 164
Leidig, Edeltraud 103, 105–107
Leistner, Reinhold 4–5, 161
Léon-Dufour, Xavier 94
Levine, Amy-Jill 239, 241
Levine, Lee I. 52–53, 61–65, 72
Levy, B. Barry 100
Lieu, Judith M. 32, 77, 92, 94–95, 241
Limbeck, Meinrad 213
Lindars, Barnabas 42–44, 53, 55, 70, 76, 88–90, 93, 101, 103, 105, 108, 114, 119, 131, 134–137, 150, 153–55, 158, 160, 162, 167, 178–79, 182, 205–206, 234
Lohse, Eduard 117, 122

Lowe, Malcolm 10
Luckmann, Thomas 35
Luomanen, Petri 26, 30, 33, 85, 183, 221, 232
Luthardt, Christoph E. 10
Luz, Ulrich 85, 122, 137, 165, 171–72, 176

MacDonald, John 98, 102,
Maier, Johann 46–47, 49, 51–52
Malina, Bruce J. 134, 159, 162, 165, 168
Manns, Fréderic 42
Marcus, Joel 175
Marjanen, Antti 204–205
Martin, Ralph P. 181
Martini, Carlo M. 190
Martyn, John Louis 5, 16–20, 32, 36, 41–45, 54, 76, 80, 125, 144, 159, 166, 183–84, 234
Mason, Steve 56
Mastin, B. A. 121
Mayser, Edwin 207
McCready, Wayne 21
McGrath, James F. 42, 128, 233
McKelvey, R. J. 92, 94
Meeks, Wayne 4, 9, 11, 35, 53, 67, 72, 97, 99, 102–103, 121, 123, 127, 150–53, 156, 159, 162, 168, 170, 175–76, 220–21
Mees, Michael 189–90
Mendner, Siegfried 91, 93
Menken, Maarten J. J. 151, 159, 163, 168, 173, 174, 234
Merenlahti, Petri 33–37
Metso, Sarianna 27, 199, 222, 224
Metzger, Bruce M. 147, 160, 190, 193
Meyers, Eric M. 63, 111
Miller, Stuart S. 47–48
Modrzejevski, J. M. 52
Mollat D. 154
Moloney, Francis J. 42–43, 89–90, 93, 99–101, 105–106, 111, 131, 142, 162, 179, 191–93, 195
Montgomery, James A. 102, 105
Motyer, Stephen 209, 242
Mussner, Franz 97, 111
Myllykoski, Matti 26, 33–6, 94, 183

Neusner, Jacob 26–7, 30, 41, 47, 50, 56–8, 64, 69, 79, 92, 109, 116, 137, 140, 236
Neyrey, Jerome H. 99–100, 107, 119, 131, 133–34, 136–37, 180–81, 192

Obermann, Andreas   162–63, 176
O'Day, Gail   97, 100–102, 105
Odeberg, Hugo   6, 101–102, 105,
    108, 167
Okure, Teresa   101–106
Olsson, Birger   98–102, 105
Overbeck, Franz   5

Pagels, Elaine   203–207, 209, 212
Painter, John   42–44, 149, 154, 161–63,
    179, 198, 200, 202, 204
Pamment, Margaret   103, 105
Pancaro, Severino   39, 42, 94, 122,
    129–30, 134–36, 138, 140–41,
    148–51, 153, 155–56, 164, 167,
    169–70
Parkes, James   76
Patte, Daniel   140
Pedersen, Sigfred   196, 212
Pesce, Mauro   221–23, 225, 236
Piper, Ronald A.   202, 205
Pollefeyt, Didier   39, 111–12
Porter, Stanley E.   94
Potterie, Ignatius de la   97, 103, 105–107
Powell, Mark Allan   37
Price, James L.   200, 204–205
Pritz, Ray A.   46
Purvis, James D.   101–102

Radermacher, Ludwig   207
Räisänen, Heikki   29, 38, 74, 79–82,
    85, 134–35, 139, 173, 222, 224,
    229, 232–33, 240, 242
Rajak, Tessa   65, 77
Reed, Jonathan   39, 57
Rehkopf, Friedrich   94, 190, 192, 207
Reif, Stefan C.   52–53
Reim, Günter   183, 207
Reinhartz, Adele   3, 11, 18, 20–21,
    38, 156–57, 185–86, 204, 207, 231
Reinhold, Meyer   129
Rensberger, David   18, 21, 42–44, 53,
    55, 73, 78, 240
Richter, Georg   151, 153, 162–66, 168
Ricoeur, Paul   38
Riley, Gregory J.   206
Robbins, Vernon   33
Robinson, John A. T.   161
Rochais, Gérard   131
Rohrbaugh, Richard L.   135, 159
Rowland, Christopher   116, 125
Ruether, Rosemary Radford   211
Runesson, Anders   52, 61
Russell, Jeffrey B.   203
Rutgers, Leonard V.   24

Saldarini, Anthony J.   57, 62, 65–66,
    230
Sandelin, Karl-Gustav   164, 166–68
Sanders, E. P.   27–28, 30, 56–57, 59,
    62–64, 68–69, 75, 79–80, 82, 85,
    88, 91–92, 116–17, 124–25,
    129–30, 154, 196, 222–24, 228,
    235, 239
Sanders, J. N.   121
Sanders, Jack T.   42, 44, 68, 76–77,
    81, 228
Sanders, James A.   9
Sandmel, Samuel   133, 137, 187–88,
    192
Satlow, Michael   66
Schäfer, Peter   41, 45–46, 49, 56, 80
Schams, Christine   230
Schechter, Solomon   45
Schenke, Ludger   131
Schiffman, Lawrence H.   83, 222–23
Schlatter, Adolf   6, 99–100, 151, 153,
    234
Schnackenburg, Rudolf   42, 70, 87,
    88–90, 94–95, 101–102, 107–108,
    114, 119, 121–22, 131, 135, 150,
    153–54, 156, 162, 167, 176, 182,
    184, 191–92, 198, 234
Schneider, Johannes   131, 137
Schneiders, Sandra   38
Schnelle, Udo   88, 94–95, 148, 150,
    153–154, 183
Scholtissek, Klaus   134, 147
Schottroff, Luise   198
Schrage, Wolfgang   16, 54
Schram, Terry L.   4–5, 10, 12, 132,
    162, 230
Schrenk, Gottlob   133
Schuchard, Bruce G.   163
Schulz, Siegfried   140
Schürer, Emil   90
Schwartz, Eduard   159
Schwartz, Seth   58–59, 66
Schweitzer, Albert   6
Seeley, David   92
Segal, Alan   8, 71, 77, 127, 228
Segovia, Fernando   241
Setzer, Claudia   46, 50–51, 53, 55,
    68, 71–72, 74–75, 77, 186
Siker, Jeffrey S.   191–92
Smith, D. Moody   17, 19, 42–43, 53,
    55, 89, 121, 132
Smith, Morton   56
Söding, Thomas   88, 92, 111
Solin, Heikki   11
Soulen, R. Kendall   240

Staley, Jeffrey L. 115, 119
Starfelt, Eric 139
Stark, Rodney 232
Stegemann, Ekkehard W. 24, 90–91, 94
Stegemann, Hartmut 199
Stemberger, Günther 46, 49, 56, 59, 61, 66, 70, 85, 139
Stern, Sacha 47, 61, 69–71
Strack, Hermann 61, 70, 139, 153, 174
Strathmann, Hermann 118, 121, 146, 150, 159
Suleiman, Susan R. 37
Swetnam, James 179
Syreeni, Kari 33–7

Theissen, Gerd 205, 236, 242
Theobald, Michael 159, 162–63, 164–170, 172, 176
Thoma, Clemens 212
Thomas, John C. 138
Thompson, Leonard L. 79
Thompson, Marianne M. 161, 167, 169
Thornton, T. C. G. 48
Thyen, Hartwig 105, 107, 111
Tomson, Peter J. 13
Townsend, John D. 42, 240
Tuckett, Christopher M. 76
Turner, M. Max B. 47

Urbach, Ephraim 46
Urman, Dan 61, 65,

Vandecasteele-Vanneuville, Frederique 39, 111–12
Visotzky, Burton L. 54

Wahlde, Urban C. von 2–4, 12–15, 38, 131, 148, 150, 152–53, 158–60, 162, 197, 199, 201, 207–209
Walters, James 24
Ward, Roy Bowen 192, 195
Wead, David W. 94, 100, 184
Weinfeld, Moshe 151
Weiss, Herold 119, 123, 130, 141
Weiss, Johannes 6
Welck, Christian 115, 121
Wellhausen, Julius 89, 207, 235
Wengst, Klaus 19, 41–44, 67, 70, 84
Westbrook, Raymond 124
Whitacre, Rodney A. 147
White, L. Michael 63
Wikenhauser, Alfred 154
Wilckens, Ulrich 131, 147, 159, 234
Wilken, Robert Louis 240
Williams, Margaret 63–64
Williams, Michael Allen 197
Williamson, H. G. M. 98
Wilson, Stephen G. 23, 46, 49–52, 54–55, 76, 81, 83–84, 213, 231, 236–37, 240–42
Windisch, Hans 181
Witkamp, L. Th. 114–15, 119, 121, 125
Wrede, William 235

Zalcman, Lawrence 46
Zangenberg Jürgen 97, 99–102, 108–10
Zeitlin, S. 139
Zeller, Dieter 173
Zumstein, Jean 2–3, 44

INDEX OF PASSAGES

The Hebrew Bible

Genesis
3:5   126
3:13   181
3:22   126
4   207
15   187
17:12   137
18   192
35:4   106
44:8   139

Exodus
6:12   139
7:1   127
15:11   126
15:24   161
16   117, 159, 163
16:2   163
16:2–12   161
16:4   162, 163
16:15   163
19:21–22   151
20:8–11   117
20:11   126
20:13   135
20:22   151
23:12   117
24:9–11   151
31:12–17   117
31:14–15   124
33:20   151
34:21   117
35:2–3   117

Leviticus
9:1   174
12:3   137
18:5   153, 167
23:3   117

Numbers
11:4–6   163
14:2   161
14:20–24   165

14:26–36   161
16:28–35   165
15:32–36   124
16:11   161
16:41   161
17:5   161
17:10   161
25   70
25:13   70
26:63–65   165
28:11   91
28:11–29:38   91
28:19   91
28:27   91
29:2   91
29:8   91
29:12–38   91
32:11   165

Deuteronomy
1:35   165
3:24   126
4:12   151
4:15   151
4:32–35   151
4:36   151
5:12–15   117
6:4–5   154
6:6–7   152
8:15   166
11:18–19   152
30:11–14   152–53
30:46–47   167
31:19   156
31:21   156
31:25–27   156
31:27   139
32:46–47   152

Joshua
16–17   98

1 Samuel
15:22–23   108

1 Kings
8:23   126
8:27   108

2 Kings
17:24ff.   101
17:24–41   98, 105–6
17:29   98
17:32   105
17:32–33   98
17:34   105
17:41   98, 105

1 Chronicles
17:20   126

2 Chronicles
6:14   126
20:7   188
26:6–9   95

Ezra
10:8   53

Nehemiah
9:15   163
9:16–19   163
10:33–34   91
13:15–22   117, 124

Psalms
35:10   126
40:6   126
69:10   92
71:19   126
78:11   161
78:17–19   161
78:17–22   163
78:24   163
78:26   163
78:32–43   163
78:40–43   161
78:56–57   161

86:8   126
89:7   126
105:6   188
106:13–14   161
106:24–25   161

Isaiah
1:10–20   95, 108
9:7   82
14:14   126
40:25   126
41:8   188
44:7   126
46:5   126
54:13   234
66:1   108

Jeremiah
7:1–15   95
10:6   126
17:19–27   117–8, 123
23:5–6   82, 98
31:17–20   98

Ezekiel
5:1–11   95
8–11   95
20:11   167
28:2   126

Hosea
6:6   108

Micah
6:6–8   108

Zechariah
9:13   98
10:6f.   98

Malachi
1:6–2:9   95
3:1–3   95

New Testament

Matthew
3:7–9   188
5:17   85
5:19   122
5:21–22   135
9:5–6   123

10:17   75
12:14   123
16:21   93
21:12–17   90
22:16   175
23:2   62, 174

23:3	62	1:38	166
23:5–7	155	1:41	103, 166
23:6	62	1:42	166
23:13	62	1:44	97
23:23	135	1:46	97
23:28	62	1:47	149
24:2	94	2:1–11	87, 113
26:61	93	2:3	114
27:40	93	2:4	114
		2:5	114
Mark		2:6	11, 32, 88
2:1–3:6	123	2:7	114
2:9–11	123	2:10	114
2:18	175	2:11	87, 114
3:1–6	116, 144	2:13	88
3:6	68, 123, 230	2:13–22	2, 31, 87, 94,
3:22	161		108–10, 121
6:6	136	2:14	89–90
7:1	161	2:14–16	87
7:1–23	142	2:16	91, 95
8:31	93	2:18	88, 92
11:15–18	88, 90	2:19	92, 93, 94, 110
12:13	230	2:19–21	87, 90
12:38–39	62	2:19–22	88
13:2	94	2:21–22	93, 94
13:9	75	2:22	93
14:58	93	2:23	148
15:29	93	3:1–21	96
		3:2	148
Luke		3:7	136
3:7–9	188	3:11	105
4:12	205	3:19–20	178
5:24–25	123	3:19–21	201
6:11	123	3:25	32
11:43	62	4:1–42	38
19:42–43	94	4:5–6	97
19:45–48	90	4:9	89, 96, 101
20:46	62	4:12	97, 184
21:6	94	4:12–14	193
22:3–6	206	4:14	167
		4:16–19	100–1
John		4:19	101–2
1:1–18	194	4:20–24	2, 31, 96, 100,
1:5	179		109, 110
1:9	164	4:21	100, 104, 108
1:9–11	8	4:22	96–7, 101, 103,
1:11	97, 124, 179		105–7, 110,
1:11–12	196, 201		111, 216, 241
1:12	191, 196	4:23	100, 107, 164,
1:13	194		202
1:14	194	4:25	102
1:17	169, 170	4:26	103
1:17–18	100	4:27	136
1:31	136, 149	4:29	103

4:42 96
4:46–54 113
4:47 114
4:48 114
4:49–50 114
4:51–53 114
4:53 114
5 114
5:1 16, 31
5:1–9 89
5:1–15 115
5:1–16 119
5:1–18 120
2, 31, 113, 123, 129, 130, 142–44, 157, 217, 226, 227
5:3 114
5:4 114
5:6 114
5:7 114
5:9 115, 144
5:9–16 120
5:10 117, 119, 120, 144
5:10–18 132
5:11 119
5:13 119
5:14 119
5:15 117, 119
5:16 113, 118–21, 136, 144, 227
5:17 118–9, 123, 126–7, 129, 134
5:17–18 120
5:18 113, 120–3, 125, 127, 136, 144, 146, 227
146
5:19 120
5:19–30 136
5:20 202
5:25 136
5:28 146
5:30 147
5:31 146
5:31ff. 157
5:31–37 150, 227
5:31–47 148, 150
5:32 148
5:33–35 148–49
5:34 148, 150
5:36 106, 153
5:36–47 148–52, 217
5:37 96, 105, 150
5:37–38

5:37–39 150
5:37–47 2, 31, 146–47, 156–58, 172
5:38 100, 152–53
5:39 148, 150, 153, 171, 184
5:39–47 150, 169, 171
5:41–47 154
5:42 154
5:43 154
5:44 147, 154
5:45 148, 155, 184
5:45–47 147, 171
5:46 153
6 11, 170, 171, 173, 175, 194, 217, 224, 227, 231
207
6:1 158
6:1–15 161
6:1–40 160
6:2 89
6:4 160
6:5 159, 160
6:14–15 158
6:16–21 160
6:22 160
6:24 162
6:25–27 227
6:25–40 160
6:26 2, 31, 158, 187
6:26–59 164, 207
6:27 171
6:28–33 159, 161
6:30 158–60
6:30–31 158, 161–65, 184, 228
6:31 168
6:31–32 162, 193
6:31–58 100, 164–65, 168–69
6:32 162
6:32–48 160, 163, 167
6:35 160–61
6:36 161
6:36–40 160
6:40 161
6:40–71 15, 158, 160, 161, 163, 187
6:41 234
6:45 161
6:49 165
6:49–51 162
6:49–58

6:51	163
6:52	15, 158, 160, 165
6:52–59	187
6:58	161, 165, 187
6:61	187
6:65	136
6:66	186–87
6:70	202, 207
7:1	124, 131
7:2	89, 178, 207
7:12	178
7:12–13	132
7:13	131, 132
7:14	178
7:14–18	134
7:15	131–2, 134, 136, 161, 227
7:15–24	131
7:18	133
7:18–20	133
7:19	124, 131, 134, 135, 168
7:19–24	2, 31, 130–31, 133–4, 142–4, 217, 226, 227
7:20	131–2, 161, 227
7:21	119, 132, 133
7:21–24	132
7:22	97, 136
7:22–23	136, 139
7:23	119, 122, 132, 138, 141
7:24	134, 138
7:25	123, 131, 132
7:25–27	178
7:25–31	15
7:27	227
7:28–29	96, 105
7:30	131
7:31	148, 178
7:32	15, 182
7:33–36	15
7:35	15, 132
7:37	178
7:37–44	15
7:40	227
7:40–44	178, 182
7:41	97, 103
7:42	161, 191
7:44	131, 132, 182
7:45	15
7:45–52	15, 178, 182
7:49	227
7:52	97, 177

7:53–8:11	177
8	131, 194, 217, 218
8:12	177–78, 197, 199
8:12–37	197
8:14	197
8:15	197
8:17	139
8:19	197
8:21	189
8:21–29	178
8:21–30	180
8:21–59	180
8:23	197
8:24	189
8:25	159
8:27	198
8:28	210
8:30–31	178–80, 184, 189
8:31–32	180
8:31–59	2, 31, 177, 180, 211, 228, 229, 239
8:33	180, 187
8:34	189
8:37	131, 178, 180, 184, 189, 190
8:37–40	189, 191, 193, 194
8:37–59	106
8:38	198
8:38–47	197
8:39	189
8:39–40	189, 192, 194
8:39–44	157
8:39–47	38
8:40	131, 178, 189, 190, 192
8:41	191, 198
8:41–44	198
8:42	191
8:42–47	211
8:43	180
8:44	38, 133, 177, 181, 183–4, 197–8, 202, 207–8, 210–14, 229
8:45–46	133
8:47	136
8:48	132
8:51	180, 193
8:52	132, 193
8:52–54	193
8:52–59	194

8:53	100	12:34–36	178
8:54	191	12:35	199
8:55	96, 105	12:36	199
8:56	139, 154, 191–3	12:37–43	148, 182, 229
8:56–58	194	12:38	172
8:58	193	12:39	136
8:58–59	127	12:41	154
8:59	124, 131, 181, 184	12:42	17, 73
		12:43	155
9	16–7, 20, 21, 31, 142, 144, 178, 227, 229	12:44–50	178
		13:2	202, 207
	178, 226	13:11	136
9:1–41	118	13:18	172
9:4	166	13:27	202, 207
9:7	144	14:17	199
9:14	103	14:26	199
9:17	44	14:30	199, 202, 205, 207
9:18–23	17, 43		164
9:22	136	15:1	77
9:23	173, 175, 227	15:18	8
9:27–29	184	15:18–25	136
9:29–30	207	15:19	149
10:1–5	234	15:24	139, 172
10:16	136	15:25	199
10:17	132	15:26	17, 44, 70, 77, 79
10:20	159	16:2	199, 202, 205, 207
10:24	160	16:11	
10:25	124	16:13	199
10:31	127	16:15	136
10:33	139	17:3	147
10:34	122	17:12	172
10:35	20, 185	18:1	207
11	97	18:9	172
11:1	124	18:17	207
11:8	1	18:20	89
11:19	1	18:32	172
11:31	148, 184	18:35	182
11:45	182	18:39	89
11:45–46	182	19:3	89
11:47–52	94	19:11	136
11:48	234	19:24	172
11:51–52	191, 196	19:36	172
11:52	89	19:40	89
11:55	182	19:42	144
12:9–11	182	20:16	166
12:11	182	20:22	199
12:12–15	136		
12:18	227	*Acts*	
12:23–36	182	4:1	68
12:29	199, 202, 205, 207	5:17–33	68
12:31	210	5:34–40	68
12:32	161, 182	6–7	74
12:34		6:8–12	74

6:14	93	*Galatians*	
7:1	68	1:13–14	81
7:53	135	1:14	81
8:1	81	2:1–10	82
8:1–3	80	2:11–14	142
9:1	68	2:14	81
9:14	68	3 183	
9:21	68	3:7	189
10–11	142	3–4	188
12:1–3	74	4:8	23
15:1–21	142	5:11	81
23:1–11	68	6:12	81
Romans		*1 Thessalonians*	
2:17–29	135	2:3–6	155
2:28–29	155	2:14–16	82, 229
4:13–14	189	2:15f.	213
5:12	206		
9:6–8	188, 189	*Hebrews*	
9:24–29	24	13:2	192
11:25ff.	82		
16:20	181, 205	*1 John*	
		2:18–19	207
1 Corinthians		3:8	205
2:6–8	205	3:8–10	206
9:20–21	23	3:15	79
10:13	165	5:9–10	149
15:4	93		
		Revelation	
2 Corinthians		2:9	207
6:14–7:1	203	2:17	159, 165
11:3	181	3:9	207
11:13–15	206	12:9	181
11:14	181	17:7	136
11:23	75	20	205
11:24	75	20:2	181

Apocrypha and Pseudepigapha

Apocalypse of Moses		*1 Enoch*	
16:5	181	55:3–56:4	205
17:1	181		
26:1	181	*2 Enoch*	
		53:1	188
Baruch			
4:1	153	*4 Ezra*	
		7:102–115	188
2 Baruch			
29:8	159	*Joseph and Aseneth*	
85:12	188	12:9	209
		12:9–10	206
3 Baruch			
9:7	181		

Jubilees
2:25–33   129
2:30   117
10:5   206
15:33   206, 211
23:29   205
50:1–13   129
50:8   117
50:13   124

Letter of Aristeas
210   126

Liber antiquitatum biblicarum (Pseudo-Philo)
20:8   168
33:5   188

Life of Adam and Eve
9–17   206
9:1   181
16   181

Lives of the Prophets
12:13   181

1 Maccabees
2:41   116

2 Maccabees
6:2   106
9:12   126–7

3 Maccabees
2:33   54
6:3   188

4 Maccabees
18:1   188

Martyrdom of Isaiah
2:4   205, 211
2:4–6   206

Psalms of Solomon
4:1–12   155
9:9   188
14:1   153
17   82
18:3   188
18:4   188

Sibylline Oracles
7:148–149   159
fragm. 3:46–49   159

Sirach
15:1–3   167
17:13   152
17:17   152
24:21   167
24:23   167
50:26   106

Testament of the Twelve Patriarchs
Testament of Asher
1:3–9   199
1:3–5:4   201
3:2   206

Testament of Dan
1:7–8   206
3:6   206
4:7   206
4:7–5:1   206
5:6   206, 211
6:1–4   203
6:3   202, 205

Testament of Gad
4:7   206

Testament of Joseph
20:2   203

Testament of Judah
20:1   199
25:3   202, 205

Testament of Levi
7:2   106
18:12   202, 205
19:1   203

Testament of Naphtali
2:6   203

Testament of Reuben
4:7–11   206
6:3   206

Testament of Simeon
5:3   206

Testament of Abraham
1:1–2 (A)   192
2:2 (A)   192
4:10 (B)   192
9:4 (B)   188
13:5 (B)   192

15–16 (A)	195	*Testament of Moses*	
17:7 (A)	195	10:1	205
19–20 (A)	195		
		Testament of Solomon	
Testament of Job		6:1–4	206
4:4	206	6:4	211
6:4	181		
17:2	181	*Wisdom of Solomon*	
23:1	181	2:24	181, 206

Dead Sea Scrolls and Related Literature

Community Rule (1QS)		6:17–18	222
3:7	199	9:21	54
3:13	199	9:23	54
3:13–4:14	200	10:14–11:18	129
3:13–4:26	199–203	11:7–8	117
3:18	202	11:17–12:2	222
3:18–19	199	12:3–6	124
3:19–21	199	12:4–6	54
3:20–21	202	14:20–21	54
3:21	199	15:5–16:6	224
3:24–25	199	16:6	224
4:2–11	201	20:1–8	54
4:18–23	202		
4:21	199	*Florilegium (4Q174)*	
4:21–23	199	1:7–9	205
4:23–24	201	1:8	206
5:8	224		
6:24–7:25	54	*Horoscope*	
8:16–9:2	54	*(4Q186)*	201
9:9–11	82		
		War Scroll (1QM)	
Damascus Document (CD)		18:1	205
4:17	206, 211	18:11–12	205
6:11–14	222		

Philo

On the Life of Abraham (Abraham)		*On the Cherubim (Cherubim)*	
107	192	77	127
114–116	192	88	126
Allegorical Interpretation (Alleg. Interp.)		*On the Embassy to Gaius (Embassy)*	
I		75	127
5–6	126		
49	127	*On the Eternity of the World (Eternity)*	
II		43	126
3	127		
III		*On Flight and Finding (Flight)*	
162	166	137–138	166
205	148		

Who is the Heir? (Heir)
81   174

On the Migration of Abraham (Migration)
89–93   29
91   117, 122, 129
121f.   168

On the Change of Names (Names)
259–260   166

Questions and Answers on Genesis (QG)
II
28   162

On the Sacrifices of Cain and Abel
   (Sacrifices)
92   127

On the Special Laws (Spec. Laws)
I
59   174
345   174

On the Virtues (Virtues)
207   188

That the Worse Attacks the Better (Worse)
118   166

Josephus

Jewish Antiquities (Ant.)
1.196   192
3.26–32   168
9.288–291   98
9.291   98
11.340   54
11.341   98
11.346f.   54
12.10   104
12.256   104
12.257–264   106
13.12–13   116

13.74–79   104
13.294   69
18.12–15   62
18.15   57
18.17   57
18.318–324   116
20.199–203   68, 74

Jewish War (J.W.)
1.146   116
2.162   62
2.166   62

Mishnah, Talmud, and Related Literature

Mishnah
'Abot
4:5   155
4:21   155

Baba Meṣi'a
7:1   188

Baba Qamma
8:6   188

Berakot
9:5   47

'Erubin
6:2   117

Ketubbot
2:7   148

Makkot
1:10   69

Nedarim
3:11   137

Sanhedrin
7:8   124
9:6   70
10:3   165

Šabbat
7:1   124
7:2   129
7:3–9:7   117
10:5   117
14:2–3   116
14:3–4   116
18:3   137

19:1–3   137   *Berakot*
22:6   116   5:3   45, 51

Ta'anit   *Megillah*
4:3   47   3:4   64

Yoma   *Sanhedrin*
8:6   116   9:7   70

Tosefta   *Šabbat*
Hullin   1:4   78–9
1:1   47
2:20–21   43, 71–2, 76 Babylonian Talmud
2:20–24   44   *'Abodah Zarah*
2:24   43, 47   6a   47

Šabbat   *Berakot*
12:8–14   116   3b   174
15:16   140   28b-29   45, 50–1

Sotah   *Qiddušin*
11:10   168   32b   155

Palestinian Talmud   *Sanhedrin*
(Passages are cited according to *The*   90b   47
Talmud of the Land of Israel: A Preliminary 90b–91a   48
Translation and Explanation, ed.
J. Neusner)   *Ta'anit*
                                    27b   47

'Abodah Zarah   *Yoma*
3:2   99   4a174
5:4   106   38a   155
                                    85b   140

                    Targumic Texts

Frg. Tg.   *Tg. Ps.-J.*
Gen. 28:10   99   Gen. 28:10   99
                                    Gen. 29:10   99
Tg. Neof.
Gen. 28:10   99

                 Other Rabbinic Works

Mekilta   *Bahodeš*
Bešallah   3   152
1   166   9   152

Širata   *Neziqin*
3   152   1   140

Šabbeta
1   116, 140

92   139
94   99

Midrash Rabbah
Ecclesiastes Rabbah
1.9   159

Numeri Rabbah
21.3f.   70
21.4   70

Exodus Rabbah
30   126

Pesiqta de Rab Kahana
10   99

Genesis Rabbah
11   126
32   104
43   166
54   166
70   99, 166
81   104, 106

Seder Eliyahu Rabbah
14   155
25   152

Sipre Deuteronomy
38   155

Apostolic Fathers

1 Cleemens
10:7   192

Nag Hammadi Codices

Gospel of Thomas
71   93, 110

On the Origin of the World
105.24–25   152

Classical and Ancient Christian Writings

Epiphanius
Panarion
29.9.2.   48

27.4   135
27.5   141
38.1   43
137   48

Jerome
Comm. Isa.
5.18   48
49.7   48
52.5   48
Epistulae
112.13   48

Origen
Commentarii in evangelium Joannis
2.25   152

Seneca
Epistulae morales
95.47   129

Justin Martyr
Dialogue with Trypho
12.2   135
20.4   135

Suetonius
Divus Claudius
25.4   24